T0291198

ROUTLEDGE LIBRARY EDITIONS:
THE GERMAN ECONOMY

Volume 9

GERMAN INDUSTRY AND GERMAN INDUSTRIALISATION

GERMAN INDUSTRY AND GERMAN INDUSTRIALISATION

Essays in German Economic and Business History in the Nineteenth and Twentieth Centuries

Edited by
W. R. LEE

LONDON AND NEW YORK

First published in 1991 by Routledge

This edition first published in 2018
by Routledge
2 Park Square, Milton Park, Abingdon, Oxon OX14 4RN

and by Routledge
711 Third Avenue, New York, NY 10017

Routledge is an imprint of the Taylor & Francis Group, an informa business

British Library Cataloguing in Publication Data
A catalogue record for this book is available from the British Library

ISBN: 978-1-138-29360-1 (Set)
ISBN: 978-1-315-18656-6 (Set) (ebk)
ISBN: 978-0-415-78862-5 (Volume 9) (hbk)
ISBN: 978-1-315-22326-1 (Volume 9) (ebk)

German Industry and German Industrialisation

Essays in German Economic and Business History in the Nineteenth and Twentieth Centuries

Edited by

W. R. Lee

London and New York

First published in 1991
by Routledge
11 New Fetter Lane, London EC4P 4EE

Simultaneously published in the USA and Canada
by Routledge
a division of Routledge, Chapman and Hall, Inc.
29 West 35th Street, New York, NY 10001

Printed in Great Britain by T.J. Press (Padstow) Ltd, Padstow, Cornwall

British Library Cataloguing in Publication Data

German industry and German industrialisation : essays in German economic and business history in the nineteenth and twentieth centuries.
1. Germany. Economic development, history
I. Title
330.943

Library of Congress Cataloging in Publication Data

German industry and German industrialisation : essays in German economic and business history in the nineteenth and twentieth centuries / edited by W.R. Lee.
p. cm.
Includes bibliographical references and index.
1. Germany – Economic conditions – History – 19th century.
2. Germany – Economic conditions – History – 20th century. 3. Germany – Industries – History – 19th century. 4. Germany – Industries – History – 20th century. I. Lee, W. Robert.
HC285.G28 1991
338.0943—dc20 90–24704

ISBN 0 415 02155 3

CONTENTS

List of Tables and Figures
Preface

1 THE PARADIGM OF GERMAN INDUSTRIALISATION : SOME RECENT ISSUES AND DEBATES IN THE MODERN HISTORIOGRAPHY OF GERMAN INDUSTRIAL DEVELOPMENT . . 1
Robert Lee

2 FOREIGN COMPETITION AND TECHNOLOGICAL CHANGE : BRITISH EXPORTS AND THE MODERNISATION OF THE GERMAN IRON INDUSTRY FROM THE 1820s TO THE 1860s . 47
Rainer Fremdling

3 TARIFFS AND MARKET STRUCTURE : THE GERMAN ZOLLVEREIN AS A MODEL FOR ECONOMIC INTEGRATION . . 77
R.H.Dumke

4 BANKING AND ECONOMIC GROWTH : BANKS AND INDUSTRY IN GERMANY IN THE NINETEENTH-CENTURY AND THEIR CHANGING RELATIONSHIP DURING INDUSTRIALISATION . 116
Wilfried Feldenkirchen

5 CYCLICAL TRENDS AND THE MARKET RESPONSE : LONG SWINGS IN URBAN DEVELOPMENT IN GERMANY, 1850-1914 148
Richard Tilly

6 SECTORAL PERFORMANCE AND ECONOMIC DEVELOPMENT : THE BACKWARD LINKAGES OF THE GERMAN PIG-IRON INDUSTRY, 1871-1913, AS A FACTOR IN MACRO-ECONOMIC GROWTH . 185
Jochen Krengel

7 'NEW INDUSTRIES' AND THE ROLE OF THE STATE : THE DEVELOPMENT OF ELECTRICAL POWER IN SOUTH GERMANY FROM c.1880 TO THE 1920s 200
Hermann Schaefer

8 THE POLITICAL FRAMEWORK OF STRUCTURAL MODERNISATION : THE I.G. FARBENINDUSTRIE AG, 1904-1945 220
Gottfried Plumpe

9 GERMANY AND THE INTERNATIONAL ECONOMY : THE ROLE OF THE GERMAN INFLATION IN OVERCOMING THE 1920/1 UNITED STATES AND WORLD DEPRESSION 265
Carl L.Holtfrerich

10 OCCUPATION POLICY AND POST-WAR RECONSTRUCTION : BRITISH MANPOWER POLICY IN THE RUHR COAL-MINES, 1945-1947, AND WEST GERMAN ECONOMIC RECOVERY . . .286
Mark Roseman

List of Contributors 306

Index 309

TABLES AND FIGURES

Tables

2.1 Ratio of British bar-iron exports (including rails) to pig-iron exports, 1821-1870 61

2.2 Iron production in Prussia, 1836-1865, in 1000 metric tons and per cent (produced from charcoal and mineral fuel) 62

2.3 Railway-derived demand for iron (in pig-iron equivalents) in Germany, 1840-1859 63

2.4 National suppliers of the stock of rails on Prussian Railways, 1843-1863 (in per cent) 63

2.5 Belgian pig-iron exports to Germany, 1841-1856, (in tons and per cent) 64

2.A1 British pig-iron exports to major countries, 1821-1870, in per cent and metric tons 67

2.A2 British bar-iron exports to major countries, 1821-1870, in per cent and metric tons 68

2.A3 British exports of railway iron to Germany, Holland, France and the USA, 1856-1870, in per cent and metric tons 69

2.A4 British pig-iron and bar-iron exports to different countries, 1821-1835, annual averages in per cent . 70

2.A5 British pig-iron exports to different countries, 1836-1870, annual averages in per cent 72

2.A6 British bar-iron exports (until 1855 including rails) to different countries, 1836-1870, annual averages in per cent 74

2.A7 British exports of railway iron to different countries, 1856-1870, annual averages in

per cent 76
3.1 Investment, output and employment in German cotton mills, 1830-1842 111
3.2 Costs of tariff collection in German customs areas 112
3.3 The Structure of Central Government revenues in several Zollverein member states, 1820-1850 (per cent of total net revenues) 114
4.1 Average annual growth rates of balance sheet totals of enterprises in selected industrial sectors (in per cent), 1879-1913 144
4.2 Representation of the 'Big Banks' on the supervisory boards of German joint-stock companies, by sector (chairmen/vice-chairmen) . . 145
4.3 Share of bank balances in current assets, 1894/95-1913/14, in per cent 147
5.1 Annual average rates of growth of population in Prussian cities with 20,000 or more inhabitants, 1819-1910 179
5.2 Population growth and natural increase in Prussian cities, 1865-1905, (per 1000 inhabitants per year) 180
5.3 Zero-order correlations, housing stock and selected variables (rates of growth), Hamburg, 1874-1913 182
5.4 Indicators linking German urban growth and emigration, 1819-1910, (annual average rates of change in per cent) 183
6.1 The absolute and relative contributions of the German pig-iron industry to net national product and total employment, 1871-73,1908-11 195
6.2 The demand of the pig-iron industry as a share of the output of selected industrial sectors, 1871-73,1908-11 195
6.3 Total employment in selected industrial sectors and in the German economy (in 1,000), 1871-73, 1908-11 196
6.4 Induced employment (in 1,000) created by the demand of the pig-iron industry, 1871-73,1908-11 . 196
6.5 The direct and indirect contributions of the pig-iron industry to employment, in absolute terms (in 1,000), and as a proportion of total employment, 1871-73,1908-11 197
6.6 Induced employment generated by the pig-iron industry rearranged in absolute terms (in 1,000), and in relation to total sectoral employment, 1871-73,1908-11 197
6.7 Total value added in selected industrial branches and net national product in million Marks and in

	constant 1913 prices, 1871-73,1908-11	198
6.8	Induced value added generated by the pig-iron industry in mining and transportation, in million Marks and in constant 1913 prices, 1871-73, 1908-11	198
6.9	The direct and indirect contributions of the pig-iron industry to net national product, in absolute terms, in million Marks and in constant 1913 prices, and in per cent, 1871-73,1908-11 . .	199
8.1	I.G.sales, the proportional share of products, 1913-1943, in per cent	256
8.2	The regional distribution of I.G. export sales, 1913-1941, in per cent	257
8.3	The proportional composition of I.G. exports, 1913-1937, in per cent	257
8.4	Companies (with capital of more than 1 million R.M.) in which I.G. was involved, 1931	258
8.5	The twelve largest German chemical companies c.1929	261
8.6	Investment and staff in I.G., 1927-1942	262
8.7	I.G. sales during the depression (average rate of change, 1929-1933, in per cent)	263
8.8	I.G. investment priorities, 1933-1944, ranked by value	264
8.9	Output of selected products from 1933 until 1943 (in tons)	264
9.1	German foreign trade (special trade calculated in 1913 unit values), in million Goldmarks	276
9.2	The share of individual commodities in total German imports in 1921 (special trade calculated in 1913 unit values), and the proportion of products of US origin	277
9.3	The share of US exports to total US production for individual commodities (c.1920-3)	278
9.4	German imports of individual foodstuffs and raw materials (total, and from the US) in 1,000 tons .	279
9.5	US exports of goods of indigenous and foreign origin (1919-1923) in million dollars (total, to Europe, U.K. and to Germany)	280
9.6	US exports of indigenous cotton in million lbs and dollars, 1919-1923 (total, to U.K. and to Germany)	282
9.7	US export prices of indigenous goods in dollars (monthly average), 1919-1923	284

Figures

4.1 Number of stock companies founded between 1871 and 1913 and their respective average share capital in million Marks 124
4.2 Share capital of newly-founded joint-stock companies in million Marks, 1871-1913, and issue of stocks in industry in million Marks 1883-1913 . . 125
4.3 Placement of securities in Germany 1883-1913 in million Marks 130
5.1 Index of annual urban housing investment in Germany, 1867-1913 151
5.2 Annual rate of growth of housing stock and urban population in Prussia, 1816-1913 152
5.3 Annual rate of growth of stock of dwellings and population in three cities, 1815-1913 153
5.4 Annual growth rates of dwelling stock and net migration in Berlin, 1841-1909 (3-year moving averages) 154
5.5 Annual rate of growth of stock of dwellings, population and net migration, Hamburg, 1871-1913 (3-year moving averages) 155
5.6 Annual rate of growth of stock of dwellings in Hamburg, 1867-1912 156
5.7 Auto correlation, annual rate of growth of stock of dwellings in Hamburg, 1867-1912 157
5.8 Indices of housing investment, building costs and rents, Germany 1870-1913 (annual data, trend removed) 165
8.1 I.G. Farben industrie : AG Organisation Plan (1931) 226

PREFACE

This collection of papers grew out of two earlier symposia held by the North West Forum on German Economic and Social History at the University of Liverpool, to which other contributors have been added. In most cases, these also represent papers held at meetings organised either by the Economic History department, or by the Centre for Interdisciplinary German Studies at the University of Liverpool, but they have been specifically selected, or newly commissioned, in order to provide coverage of key areas in German economic and business history. Although english-speaking readers have been comparatively well served by a series of publications providing an insight into recent research in Germany in a number of interrelated fields of social and labour history,(1)and the German Society for Business History provides an annual selection of generally useful articles in translation,(2)the core area of economic history has been strangely neglected.

The contributions to this volume are designed to redress this imbalance. Collectively they reflect a broad spectrum of issues and research interests in German economic and business history in the nineteenth-and twentieth-centuries. Without wishing to claim any ideal comprehensiveness, the individual papers do provide an important insight into the direction and extent of recent research within the general field of modern German economic history. They should hopefully be of interest, not only to economic and business historians, but also perhaps to a wider audience concerned with comparative models of industrial development and economic performance in historical perspective. The overall dynamic of European industrialisation can only be understood within a broad comparative framework. However it is equally important that contemporary research should still seek to elucidate the historically unique conditions of industrialisation at the level of the nation state, federal authority or individual economic region. In this sense, many of the individual contributions to the present volume provide an overdue corrective to the traditional paradigm of German industrialisation and economic growth, based on earlier typologies which no longer retain sufficient explanatory power, even if they still indirectly inform many of the writings of political historians concerned with explaining the peculiar and tragic patterns of German historical development. The essays provide a re-appraisal of some of the dominant themes in German economic and business history, and they might also, in the long term, thereby assist in the broader, but infinitely more complicated, process of developing new typologies for European economic growth and industrialisation as a whole.

I am particularly indebted to the Economic and Social Research Council (formerly SSRC), and to the Deutsche Forschungsgemeinschaft, for providing funding for the two symposia, which form the basis of this collection of essays, as well as to the individual contributors and Richard Stoneman of Croom Helm for their infinite patience during what proved to be a protracted production process. In this case, the dominant new technology failed to reveal any comparative advantage in relation to more traditional processes of publishing. However I am immensely grateful for the meticulous attention to detail shown by June Summers, without whose constant commitment this book would never have appeared in print, and also to Pat Brooksbank.

Robert Lee
University of Liverpool
Department of Economic History.

NOTES

1. See, for example, R.J.Evans and W.R.Lee (eds.), The German Family: Essays on the Social History of the Family in Nineteenth-and Twentieth-Century Germany, (London, 1981); R.J.Evans (ed.). The German Working Class 1888-1933 : The Politics of Everyday Life, (London, 1982); R.J.Evans and W.R.Lee (eds.). The German Peasantry, Conflict and Community in Rural Society from the Eighteenth to the Twentieth-Centuries, (London, 1986); W.R.Lee and E.Rosenhaft (eds.). The State and Social Change in Germany, 1880-1960, (Leamington Spa, 1988); P.Stachura (ed.). Unemployment and the Great Depression in Weimar Germany. (London, 1986); R.J.Evans and D.Geary (eds.), The German Unemployed, (London, 1987).

2. W.Engels and H.Pohl (eds.). German Yearbook on Business History, (Berlin, Heidelberg, New York, 1981), and subsequent volumes.

Chapter One

THE PARADIGM OF GERMAN INDUSTRIALISATION: SOME RECENT ISSUES AND DEBATES IN THE MODERN HISTORIOGRAPHY OF GERMAN INDUSTRIAL DEVELOPMENT

W.R.Lee.

In seeking to explain the aberrant pattern of recent German history, the various protagonists in the debate on the Sonderweg have inevitably focused attention on the economic framework of political change. Germany's failure to develop politically along the lines of a western-style liberal democracy is increasingly seen as a result of 'a fateful discrepancy between economic development on the one hand, and social values and political forms on the other'.(1) However a rigorous assessment of this hypothesis is hampered by the fact that a leading actor on the stage of German historiography is apparently not fully prepared for its role. German economic history, it is argued, has been 'relatively neglected', primarily because of structural and administrative factors implicit in the organisation of the West German educational system.(2) Not only was Richard Tilly entirely justified in bemoaning the absence of a theoretical analytical framework in his earlier critical survey of German economic history, but, according to Krohn, despite a relative growth in productivity in the 1960s and 1970s, this critical branch of historical research is still characterised by 'a certain backlog'.(3) It is not surprising, therefore, that Blackbourn and Eley consistently refer to the general accounts of German economic development provided by Boehme and Kitchen, despite their limitations, and even view Clapham's pioneering work of 1921 as a volume which 'retains high value among the works in English'.(4) The study of German economic history has been distorted by a 'national consensus', based upon the continuing subordination of economic history to political developments and the process of national unification, despite Sheehan's claim that, like German culture, the German nineteenth-century economy remains a heuristic abstraction 'which encourages us to focus our attention on one sort of historical experience at the expense of others'.(5)

It is within this context that the present book has been devised. It brings together nine essays, none of which has previously appeared in English, on German economic and business history in the nineteenth and twentieth centuries.(6) In terms of the overall process of German industrialisation the individual contributions focus on a number of key sectors of the economy: the iron industry, both in the period from the late 1820s to the 1840s and between 1871 and 1913; the banking and house construction sectors; the electricity and chemical industries, which played an increasing role within the German economy from the late nineteenth-century onwards, and the coal industry, within the context of economic reconstruction after 1945. At the same time this collection of essays addresses a number of central issues relating to the nature of German industrialisation: the role of foreign competition in fostering technological change; the importance of market integration for economic development, within the framework of the customs union (Zollverein), the response by German banks to industrialisation; the effectiveness of the market in responding to the unprecedented need for urban housing in the second half of the nineteenth-century; and the political framework for structural change and economic growth both in relation to the development of the electricity and chemical industries, and within the context of the problems of reconstruction in the Ruhr coal mine industry. Broader questions, such as the role of putative leading sectors in European economic development, as in the case of the German pig-iron industry in the latter decades of the nineteenth-century, as well as the validity of Gerschenkron's general propositions concerning the dependence of Europe's relative latecomers in the development of modern industry, such as Germany, on the banking infrastructure and the state for investible capital and entrepreneurial assistance are also critically assessed. The international framework of Germany's economic development during the nineteenth-and early twentieth-century is evident in the analysis of the impact of British exports on the modernisation of the German iron industry at the beginning of this period, in the important re-appraisal of the role of German inflation in 1920 and 1921 in facilitating international economic recovery, and in the critical assessment of the wider foreign policy considerations behind British man-power policy in the Ruhr mines between 1945 and 1947. No collection of essays can ever be entirely comprehensive, but the present volume focuses on a wide range of issues of central relevance to our understanding of the process of German economic development during this period. They provide collectively a clear illustration of the extent of recent developments within the sphere of German economic history, particularly in relation to conceptual, methodological and theoretical issues, and help to provide an important corrective to the traditional paradigm of German industrialisation in the nineteenth-and twentieth-centuries, which still informs many of the writings of political historians concerned with such broader issues as the German *Sonderweg*.

A number of the present contributors are concerned either directly or indirectly with the role of the state in the process of German industrialisation, whether in the context of tariff policy (Rainer Fremdling) and market structure (Rolf Dumke), or the political framework affecting the development of 'new industries', such as electrical power and chemicals in the second phase of industrialisation from the late nineteenth-century onwards (Hermann Schaefer and Gottfried Plumpe respectively). Richard Tilly's innovative analysis of long swings in German urban development, also touches upon the increasing pressure for the state, both nationally and at the local authority level, to resolve the urban 'housing problem', although urban housing remained essentially a market product in the pre-1914 period. Finally, within this context, Mark Roseman's essay on the problems of post-war reconstruction in the Ruhr mining industry provides an important insight into a different facet of the role of the state, embodied in this instance by the occupation policy of the British authorities; a transitional and externally imposed state form, not necessarily sympathetic to narrowly defined German interests.

Many commentators view the role of the state as having been a critical factor in promoting or facilitating economic growth and industrialisation in Germany. The state apparently had a crucial role to play in clearing away many of the obstacles in the way of economic development, and economic advance has been portrayed as at least a by-product of 'real politik'.(7) German industrialisation, within the framework of this paradigm, was achieved with the support of the state, and, at a regional level, the state frequently provided the pre-conditions for long-term industrial development.(8) Indeed in the absence of enterprising state authorities it has been argued that the bourgeoisie, as a social class, was not able to fulfil its required function within the developing capitalist system, which, in turn, acted as a contraint on economic growth.(9)

In a broader sense the overall political environment is a key determinant of the dynamic of economic development. The legislative, administrative and entrepreneurial function of the state inevitably involves a continuing process of interaction with the economy, and the role of the state as a consumer and investor has immediate implications in the economic sphere.(10) A particularly positive role is ascribed to the impact of state intervention in Germany in the educational sphere, which Kocka has viewed as the 'single most important contribution' to the development of an industrial system.(11) However state intervention could also assume a more direct form, within the context of tariff and patent policy, or exercise an indirect function by providing the appropriate legal and administrative framework for stimulating innovation within the economy.(12) The nature and scale of state intervention in the German economy varied substantially over time. There has been an increasing concern, therefore, with the temporal scale of state involvement in economic affairs, and whether clearly delineated stages can be detected in the development of state-industry relations, culminating in the so-called 'command economy' of the Third Reich.(13) It is difficult, however, to quantify with any accuracy the absolute extent of state intervention in the economy, particularly during different phases of economic development and political ideology. Despite a visible neo-mercantilist legacy, the separate economic functions of the state in the early nineteenth-century were seldom coordinated, and in terms of influencing regional specialization, product cost, and rates of technological innovation, state intervention was frequently only passive.(14) Moreover the temporal evolution of state-industry relations seldom followed narrowly prescribed paths. Even during the period of increasing liberalisation in the second half of the nineteenth-century, entrepreneurs and state administrators remained closely interrelated, particularly at the lower and middle levels. Despite the shifting influence and effectiveness of business representation, state intervention in many economic spheres remained durably persistent.(15) Equally it is frequently assumed that the Nazi state after 1933 was invariably willing and able to enforce its policies against the particular interests of individual companies.(16) Although Nazi economic policy undoubtedly benefitted big concerns by reinforcing the existing tendency to monopolisation, by 1936-37 entrepreneurial autonomy had been significantly curtailed. The debate on the exact definition of the German economy between 1933 and the out-break of the Second World War will undoubtedly continue, but it is important to note that it may well have fallen short of functioning as a 'command economy'.(17) The direction of state economic policy was often confused and inconsistent, reflecting an intense rivalry between the state and party bureaucracies as well as internal divisions within the party hierarchy.(18)

Within the context of this debate Gottfried Plumpe's analysis of I.G.Farben provides the basis for an important critique of existing interpretations of state-industry relations during the Third Reich, which also has wider implications for understanding the long-term pattern of state intervention in the German economy. I.G.Farben is justifiably viewed as one of the most important German industrial enterprises during the entire inter-war period, with the chemical sector as a whole regarded as a special feature of

German industrialisation from the 1870s onwards. Nazi economic policy, it has been argued, effectively integrated entrepreneurs within a state controlled system of contracts and marketing, and within the framework of the drive for autarchy German industry achieved a position of leadership in the field of technological research.(19) However it is important to break away from a discussion of state-industry relations during this period from traditional interpretations which examine the interplay between the Nazi state and 'big business' within the framework of competing paradigms of either the 'primacy of politics' or the 'primacy of economics'.(20)

The precise nature and shifting balance of state-industry relations can only be effectively analysed on a micro-level basis by concentrating on the individual firm. Certainly in relation to I.G.Farben there can be little doubt as to its ability to successfully represent its own interests, to preserve its autonomy and to influence state economic policy.(21) German business in general from the 1880s onwards had sought a more effective presentation of collective interests and sectoral attitudes in its dealings with the state and its administrative agencies.(22) However in seeking to maximise the potential of interest representation and to exploit the increasing willingness of the state to provide price and sales guarantees German industry was by no means exceptional. Government support for the development of the hydrogenation process by the Imperial Chemicals Industry (I.C.I.) in Britain was of fundamental importance and reflected very much the firm's claim that investment in this field would provide immediate relief to the depressed coal industry and contribute significantly to the defence both of the Realm and of the Empire. Close government-industry links also existed in both cases at the personnel level. If former employees of I.G.Farben, such as Karl Krauch, played a central role in the implementation of the Four Year Plan, I.C.I. was not without significant 'public service' connections.(23) Equally from an organisational point of view, the management structures of I.G.Farben were not in essence dissimilar from those of its major international rivals.(24) To some extent, therefore, the institutional evolution of a firm such as I.G.Farben reflected broader economic forces operating in this sector of industry internationally. New production processes were often high risk undertakings, which could only be implemented initially with state support.(25) The increase in international competition during the inter-war period as a whole reinforced the perceived necessity for tariff protection, both pre- and post- 1933. Undoubtedly 'big business' in general and I.G.Farben in particular benefitted substantially from Nazi re-armament objectives (26), which also served to reinforce, in turn, the existing trend towards a more technocratic management form. However the specific context of state - industry relations, even in the Nazi era, did not fundamentally affect the general dynamic of the firm's institutional development which was primarily a response to technological change and international competition within industry as a whole. Indeed the prioritisation of autarchy also had negative consequences, as it implied a withdrawal from a traditional export-orientation, a loss of important Third World markets and a reduction in research development.

Clearly one cannot ignore the role of the state in German industrialisation, even if it is difficult to quantify precisely at a sectoral level. Throughout the nineteenth-and twentieth-centuries the private domain of the entrepreneur was frequently influenced by public policy. If the concept of economic liberalism did enter into German law, there was no radical break with the corporative past and state policy in relation to the formation and operation of cartels appears to have been based on the assumption that the public good was best served by restraints on effective competition. The Trade Regulation Law of 1869, despite its general declaration in favour of freedom of trade, was not followed by any effective prohibition of anti-competitive combines.(27) Public bureaucratic traditions were readily assimilated by industrial concerns, as a means of resolving problems of managerial control and organisation.(28) In specific sectors, such as the railways, where the direct role of the state had expanded considerably by the end of the nineteenth-century, the 'mixed system' of dual ownership provided a further basis for the development of an intimate and informal relationship between business and government.(29) Even when the role of entrepreneurs was essentially reactive, as in the case of the introduction of government insurance and welfare programmes, industrialists quickly appreciated the direct benefits which might accrue in principle from such legislation.(30)

Particularly in relation to the 'new industries' of the late nineteenth-and early twentieth-centuries, such as the chemical and electricity industries, relative German predominance is often explicitly linked with the direct role of the state. In the case of the electrical industry state involvement may have provided an important stimulus to development, with German capitalists accepting more rapidly than elsewhere in Europe the fact that the state could be a useful ally in their attempt to accommodate technological change. The purchasing demand of the state critically affected supply side developments and the spatial diffusion of production.(31) In Saxony, which was well advanced in the trend towards the provision of electric power by the late nineteenth-century, the predominance of local authority investment in major urban centres restricted the role of private capital to the construction of overland power-stations.(32) In Baden, although the initial developmental phase was dominated by private enterprise, the state gradually began to assume the role of entrepreneur and actively created an electric supply system.(33)

However in terms of the public environment for innovation and industrial growth, the interconnections between industrialists and individual sectors of production, on the one hand, and state agencies on the other, could often be extremely complex. Indeed it is important to remember that a multiplicity of state forms continued to exist in nineteenth-century Germany; a reality which must inform any discussion of the specific role of the state in German economic development.(34) In the case of South Germany, Hermann Schaefer's contribution to the present volume points to the existence of three significantly different state attitudes to the development of electricity supply. In contrast to the Duchy of Baden, where the state increasingly assumed an active and supportive role in the promotion of this sector, state policy in Bavaria towards the electrical industry was characterised by hesitancy and uncertainty, which, in turn, only served to delay the push towards regional take-off. In Wuerttemberg, on the other hand, municipal authorities continued to exercise a dominant role in the overall development of electricity supply, and the state had only a marginal influence even in the sphere of policy formulation.(35) The network of contacts and relationships developed by individual firms in the electricity industry, such as Siemens, was often directed at influencing specific elements of the state bureaucracy, and only at a later stage was it utilised in an attempt to structure the legislative process affecting this sector as a whole.(36) The strongest influence was brought to bear at the local authority level, particularly in relation to electricity supply and the provision of electric trams. Schaefer's contribution emphasises the extent to which any comparative analysis of national responses to industrial innovation needs to be supplemented by a more rigorous assessment of the specific role of local and regional authorities. The different attitudes of the three South German states to energy policy had implications for the nature and timing of regional economic development, as well as for the nature of local state-industry relations. Indeed German entrepreneurs, particularly when operating in industrial sectors, such as the electricity industry, dominated by a small number of leading firms, may well have benefitted from the continuing regional fragmentation of state authority, which allowed them to pursue selectively different models of industrial development and to evolve variegated strategies of state-industry relations.

However as the differentiated state response to the possibility of developing electric power supply in southern

Germany indicates, the nature of government-business relations seldom conformed to a single stereotype. Indeed the sense of interdependence between state and industry was itself subject to a wide degree of regional variation, and the effective articulation of entrepreneurial interest was frequently affected by different regional rivalries.(37) Although the state certainly played a supportive role in industrialising regions, the net financial contribution may well have had only a marginal effect and regional economic growth in the nineteenth-century, was more a function of macro-economic forces, including the impact of contemporary developments in England, Belgium and France, rather than of state-led initiatives.(38) Even if the legal framework apparently encouraged the emergence of large-scale monopoly concerns, its specific function in determining processes of integration and diversification in key sectors of German industry is not unequivocal.(39) Structural change in the organisation of firms was primarily a response to technological innovation and shifting market conditions, and despite a high degree of integration in specific sectors prior to 1914 the medium-sized company was still the main prop of the German economy.(40) To this extent, as the contributions to the present volume on the electrical and chemical industries indicate, the case of Germany does not necessarily confirm the Gerschenkronian hypothesis that state support for industrialisation was predetermined by existing market imperfections and relative economic backwardness. Indeed the nature of state-industry relations was inevitably more complex and its development over time less linear than earlier analysts have supposed.

Tariff policy was also a central area for state involvement in economic affairs. Drawing increasingly on mercantilist trade theories, many of the major German principalities created special institutions to regulate trade and to organise tolls.(41) In Bavaria, for example, the patchwork of ad hoc regulation and customs levies on import and export trades was finally superseded by the relatively comprehensive Zollordnung of 1765, which remained in force until the liberal customs legislation of 1799.(42) However the extent of official involvement in the development of a commercial and tariff policy explicitly related to the positive promotion of industrial growth varied considerably between individual territories and the persistent proliferation of local customs tariffs and customs borders designed to protect indigenous producers only served to preserve a multitude of small, semi-autarchic markets.(43) The dislocation and enforced realignment of markets and trade routes during the Napoleonic wars, particularly as a result of the imposition of the continental system, was followed in the post- 1815 period by a need to re-negotiate trade treaties on a considerable scale, and to reappraise tariff policy within the context of a significant increase in British competition.(44) However, internecine conflict between the individual German states, according to Kitchen, meant that they were 'totally incapable of agreeing upon a common strategy against the influx of English manufactured goods'.(45)

One important response, both in Prussia and in other individual states, was the development of a more active economic policy designed to accelerate technological transfer and to reduce the competitive edge of British manufacturers.(46) Particularly within the context of the Prussian reform era, the state is frequently seen as creating the pre-conditions for industrial-technical innovations, either through the foundation of technical institutes and schools to supply industry with the required skilled technicians, or through the provision of travel scholarships and bursaries to facilitate the direct acquisition of the latest British manufacturing techniques.(47) In a number of specific cases, such as in steam-engine manufacturing and in the metal-working industries in general, state support may well have played a critical role in stimulating the necessary technology transfer. In Prussia, such support provided entrepreneurs with a comparative technological advantage within Germany as a whole.(48) Moreover the state continued to foster the process of technical innovation throughout the first half of the nineteenth-century, thereby enabling Germany, as a 'non-initiating country' to at least keep pace with technological change on the continent despite alleged market imperfections and political fragmentation.(49)

Rainer Fremdling's contribution to the current volume provides an important analysis of the relevance of tariff policy to the successful German borrowing of new technology. The Prussian tariff of 1818 was strongly attacked, at least in certain quarters, for its failure to provide adequate protection for indigenous industry.(50) However by treating pig-iron imports as a raw material, Prussian tariff policy effectively provided an important impulse for the long-term development of the new industrialism in Germany. The relatively liberal tariff policy of Prussia in the immediate post-Napoleonic period, as far as it affected pig-iron imports, reflected the fact that the domestic charcoal-based iron industry was still able to produce by and large at sufficiently low costs to meet British competition on its internal markets.(51) Within a broader comparative framework, Fremdling's study also serves to challenge traditional assumptions about the clear-cut differences between old and new production techniques, and illustrates a significant degree of viable co-existence between different technologies.(52) Indeed within a German context the new technology of the iron industry required considerable refining before it could finally prove its relative cost-effectiveness.

Of equal relevance for the long-term development of the German iron industry, however, was the impulse towards increased import substitution provided by the more protective tariff adopted by the *Zollverein* in 1844. Although the special privileges accorded to Belgium encouraged the continued importation of pig-iron from this particular source (53), British competition suffered a considerable restriction. The overall significance of the 1844 tariff, both for Germany's domestic iron and steel industry, and for related sectors such as the machine-construction industry, has already been established by a number of authors.(54) It was the protective environment provided by the 1844 tariff that effectively encouraged import substitution and allowed German producers to compete successfully with a British industrial sector that had served as a model for their own development.(55) However, as Fremdling clearly indicates, the viability of effective import substitution was itself predicated on the technology transfer which the relatively liberal Prussian tariff of 1818 had facilitated.

The seminal work of Rolf Dumke on the *Zollverein* provides a further important corrective to received opinion in German historiography.(56) For Blackbourn and Eley the removal of internal tariff barriers as a means of promoting freedom of trade was an important facet of the function of an economically progressive state bureaucracy serving 'almost as a kind of surrogate bourgeoisie'.(57) While recognising the financial advantages which accrued to participating states, Otto Henderson concluded that the founding of the *Zollverein* in 1834 undoubtedly stimulated German industrial development and raised expectations generally for progress in other spheres of economic life.(58) The *Zollverein* marked a 'significant step forward' in the economic growth of Germany, even if its precise weighting as a factor in contemporary development, as least according to Kitchen, cannot be adequately quantified.(59) Indeed the customs union should be viewed as part of the 'modernisation process' in central Europe as a whole, which facilitated the unification of economic laws within Germany, and led directly to the further bureaucratisation of economic policy-making.(60) In one respect such positive appraisals of the impact of the establishment of the *Zollverein* on German long-term economic development accord well with the contemporary assessments of its economic benefits. By demolishing internal trade barriers, the *Zollverein* apparently intensified inner-German economic links, contributed to the final formation of a 'national' market, provided a supportive tariff instrument, particularly in the form of the 1844 tariff, and fostered increased optimism throughout Germany as a whole.

Although it has been increasingly recognised that the policies of the separate states involved in the foundation and extension of the *Zollverein* primarily reflected political rather than narrow economic decisions, and that there was no clear linear strategy behind its evolution (61), Dumke's analysis (chapter three) undermines the assumed economic far-sightedness of German state bureaucracies. Of central importance in the establishment of the customs union were the prospective revenue gains which could be utilised to bolster the specific interests of ruling conservative elites. Most German states were patently too small to maintain an independent border tax system as an invaluable source of independent government revenue, and even in the case of the customs union between Bavaria and Wuerttemberg of 1828, 44 per cent of receipts were absorbed by administration costs.(62) Only through the establishment of a larger, more comprehensive *Zollverein* was it feasible to maximise revenue gains from such a source, and thereby, at least in the medium-term, to minimise the latent budgetary restrictions on the traditional function of the German states inherent in early nineteenth-century constitutionalism and parliamentary representation.(63) To this extent it is critical to examine the foundation and extension of the *Zollverein* within the specific context of the contemporary political economy of individual German states.

The overtly political framework for the formulation of policy relating to the formation of the *Zollverein* and the absence of any overriding objective to utilise this occasion to foster economic growth per se, also necessitates a re-appraisal of the explicit role of the customs union in German industrial development. Earlier publications frequently alluded to the possibility of a clear causal relationship. The incorporation of Baden into the *Zollverein* was followed by a new phase of industrial and commercial development and in the years immediately following 1834 there were evident indications of increased economic development in Bavaria.(64) More recent work in this field has attempted to examine the putative economic impact of the customs union on a more differentiated basis, bearing in mind the regional nature of industrialisation in early nineteenth-century Germany as a whole and the restricted data available for assessing trade flows between the participating states within the *Zollverein*.(65) Certainly in the case of the three Hessen states, although the effects of the customs union were 'not insignificant', they did not generate rapid industrialisation, nor prevent the serious socio-economic crisis of the 1840s.(66) The benefits, for Saxony of entry into the German *Zollverein* have still to be tested empirically (67), and research on other individual German states has yet to be undertaken.

Given that international trade theory generally views the possible allocation and welfare effects of customs unions as ambiguous, it is not surprising, therefore, that Dumke should conclude that the static and dynamic welfare gains generated by the Zollverein should have been relatively small. Not only were inner-German trade links already well established before 1834, despite the persistence of internal trade barriers, but the long-term growth of German trade as a whole can be assigned with a large degree of certainty to the mid-1820s, a full decade before the formal establishment of the Zollverein.(68) Moreover this important reappraisal of the economic consequences of the customs union accords well with Dumke's earlier hypothesis of German industrialisation as a case of export-led growth, with infrastructural investment and import substitution contributing significantly to the onset of substantive industrial growth.(69) But if fiscal considerations, as a means of resolving or avoiding internal political difficulties, were the predominant elements in policy formulation relating to the establishment of the customs union, and macro-economic factors, particularly rising British demand for primary products played a more critical role than the Zollverein in stimulating German industrial growth in the first half of the nineteenth-century, then it is difficult to sustain the more traditional view of the overriding significance of the gradual elimination of internal trading barriers.(70) Nor can the customs union be viewed any longer as an instrument of progressive state economic policy-making.

An equally entrenched assumption concerning the character of German industrialisation relates to the positive role of the banking mechanism in the direct promotion of industrial growth. Germany, as a relative late-comer in the development of modern industry, on the basis of Gerschenkron's general hypothesis, depended far more on banks for investible funds and entrepreneurial initiative than the earlier industrialising countries such as Britain and Belgium.(71) It is traditionally assumed that because of relative backwardness, capital accumulation remained a serious problem and that banks therefore played a critical role in supplying badly needed capital and in rectifying existing market imperfections.(72) Important developments in the banking sector, specifically the emergence of the Kreditbanken, served to lift the traditional restraints upon the flow of necessary capital to manufacturing industry and ultimately led to a situation characterised by a high degree of bank domination in industry in the immediate pre-1914 period.(73) Certainly given the pace of German industrial development in the nineteenth-century it is not surprising that the nominal capital of large enterprises rose dramatically, nor that fixed and working capital in individual sectors, such as textiles, should have multiplied considerably between 1846 and 1875.(74) Moreover by 1913, 17 of the 25 largest concerns in Germany were actually banks, a phenomenon which reinforces the view that the development and role of the banking sector was one of the most important peculiarities of the German road to industrialisation.(75)

However the central question of causality still remains to be resolved, and even the paradigmatic role of the Kreditbanken in directly fostering industrial growth in Germany has itself become subject to criticism.(76) The time series analysis by Eistert and Ringel of the relationship between investment and business activity and the provision of bank current account credits simply assigns a permissive function to the latter variable and fails to reveal a causative role for the banking mechanism as a whole in generating business activity in the period 1880 to 1913.(77) Moreover an econometric testing of Eistert's data (78), has produced a generally negative assessment of the role of German banks, arguing that an undue concentration of support for heavy industry had serious negative sectoral effects within the German economy as a whole. However such a view has been strongly contested and serious doubts surround the robustness of this analysis, particularly in view of significant data deficiencies.(79) Nevertheless the degree of support provided by the credit banks for large-scale industrial enterprises, which were frequently already in a strong economic position, may well have meant implicitly a systematic neglect of other important areas of Germany's financial business.(80)

Wilfried Feldenkirchen's essay in the present volume constitutes an important contribution to the current debate on the relative role of banks in the promotion of German industrial growth in the nineteenth-century and provides a useful corrective to traditional and over-simplistic assessments of their likely function. What emerges from Feldenkirchen's analysis is the need for a far more differentiated exploration of the changing relationships between banks and individual industries in the period under discussion. Not only is it impossible to construct a uniform model of bank-industry relations in the pre-1895 period, but the precise role of banks within the German economy clearly varied both in relation to individual industrial sectors and on the basis of the actual structure of different enterprises. Certainly even before the emergence of an efficient banking system in Germany from the mid-nineteenth-century onwards, there is little evidence of any acute shortage of capital, and existing micro-level studies of specific enterprises and industrial sectors appear to confirm the general predominance of self-financing.(81)

However external assistance from the banking mechanism may well have been of crucial importance at particular stages of development for individual concerns. As Feldenkirchen indicates the influence of the banks was clearly evident in promoting or facilitating mergers and acquisitions and thereby contributed significantly to the process of concentration evident in German heavy industry from the 1880s onwards.(82) The Kreditbanken, in particular the Deutsche Bank, played a useful role in resolving the crisis of 1903 as far as this affected the electrical engineering industry in Germany, and Tilly provides clear evidence of the willingness of the credit banks to undertake the financing of specific risky innovations.(83) In the case of the steel industry in the Ruhr, Cologne banks played an important role in company foundation and their long-standing international connections facilitated the involvement of foreign capital in sectoral development in this region.(84) However even in this case where bank-industry relations evolved in a positive fashion from a relatively early date, the geographical radius of bank influence remained very restricted.(85) Indeed it is ironic, as Feldenkirchen notes, that the decisive role of the credit banks in promoting industrial concentration at the end of the nineteenth-century only served to weaken the prospective influence of any one bank on the business activity of industrial enterprises.

It would appear, therefore, that the precise role of the Kreditbanken and the banking mechanism in general on German industrial growth must remain open. Changing market conditions and sectoral differences in the structure of individual firms were critical factors which influenced the highly differentiated nature of bank-industry relations in Germany. The marked involvement of credit banks in the heavy and electrical engineering industry was counterbalanced by a minimal role in relation to the developing chemical industry and a reinforced trend towards self-financing in the machine-construction industry.(86) It may well be that German banks, in terms of an estimated optimal portfolio diversification, were more efficient than their British counterparts in channelling additional resources into new industrial sectors (87), but the precise promotional effect of banking involvement as a whole is still difficult to identify. Although the problem of data deficiency is a significant constraint on the search for a final and conclusive solution to this issue, it is likely that new approaches examining bank-industry relations from the perspective of industrialists or focusing on the character of the different services performed by the banks for individual firms (88), will only serve to further undermine the traditional view of the role of banks in German industrial growth. The role of investment banking did not invariably conform to the original Gerschenkronian model and it would now appear to be rather rash, in the light of Feldenkirchen's research, to conclude that German banks exercised significant power with entrepreneurial implications in determining the pattern of German industrialisation.(89)

Until fairly recently the development of the 'new economic history', or cliometrics, in Germany has undoubtedly suffered from the persistence of a traditional 'neo-historicist viewpoint', which has militated against any meaningful utilisation by historians of theoretical constructs from the social sciences as a whole.(90) However in the discussion of the role of leading sectors in the process of German industrialisation, significant steps have already been taken in the utilisation of explicit economic models and the implementation of new analytical techniques. Holtfrerich's sophisticated study of the Ruhr coal industry, in seeking to test the Hoffmann-Landes hypothesis that coal-mining constituted a leading sector in German economic growth between 1851 and 1892, has revealed that all three prospective leading sectors - coal-mining, railway construction and the iron and steel industry - had limited backward linkages, but that railways played the most important role in determining the pace of industrial growth during this period.(91) As a result of increasingly effective import substitution, initially for iron rails and then for pig-iron as a whole, the continuing growth of the Prussian railway network in the 1850s actively promoted a rapid expansion in indigenous iron output, which itself necessitated an increase in Ruhr coal production.(92) According to Rainer Fremdling, on the basis of unbalanced growth theory, 'there seems to be no doubt that from the 1840s to the late 1860s the interplay between the railway and heavy industries formed a leading sector complex of German industrialisation'.(93) Even if the estimated social savings, as a proportion of German GNP remained relatively limited at no more than approximately five per cent around 1900 (94), throughout the central decades of the nineteenth-century railway development was of critical importance for economic growth. This view is reinforced by further studies of the positive effects of railway demand for the German iron industry and for specific metal-working firms.(95) Despite the fact that comprehensive development in this sector was hampered initially by territorial fragmentation (96), the recent employment of econometric analysis has finally allowed economic historians to view the impact of railway construction in a more objective perspective.

There are clearly still some reservations concerning the application of the social savings model to railway development, and the degree to which initial resource allocation, particularly in relation to both coal and iron-ore, may have retarded the potential impact of a leading-sector at a regional level.(97) However, both in terms of specific industrial sectors, and more localised economic activity, the application of econometric models has generated some important results.(98) This is equally the case in relation to Jochen Krengel's authoritative discussion of the

German pig-iron industry in the present volume. As in the case of other important branches of industry in the nineteenth-century there is no shortage of essentially descriptive monograph material, which provides an indication of the relative importance of pig-iron production.(99) During the 1850s there had been an extremely rapid technological transition in this sector, with only twelve per cent of total output charcoal-smelted by 1862.(100) German production of pig-iron rose continuously between 1870 and 1913, and the pattern of growth, if not its actual speed, remained unaffected by cyclical macro-economic changes. Germany's proportion of international pig-iron production rose from 12.3 per cent between 1871 and 1875, to 24.8 per cent between 1911 and 1913.(101) The growth of the German iron and steel industry as a whole in the second half of the nineteenth-century was facilitated by an important sequence of technical improvements, which enabled Germany to become the second largest producer of pig-iron in the world by 1914.(102)

It is not surprising, therefore, that the iron and steel industry is commonly viewed as having played a central role in the expansion of the German economy in the latter decades of the nineteenth-century, an impression which is reinforced by two more recent regional studies.(103) It is the overriding merit of Krengel's analysis that he attempts to estimate econometrically both the direct and indirect contributions of the German pig-iron industry to the growth of total employment and net national product at market prices.(104) Contrary to received opinion, this study reveals that the backward linkages of the pig-iron industry were relatively modest. Moreover the indirect contributions of this sector were clearly more important than the direct ones, with the pig-iron industry having a particularly prominent induced employment effect, even if its own employment share remained under one per cent of total employment throughout the period under consideration. Despite the fact that total pig-iron output expanded twelve-fold between the foundation of the German Empire in 1871 and 1913, this industry cannot be designated as a leading sector. But even if the performance of this sector did not accord with traditional interpretations, the pig-iron industry nevertheless remained an important feature of the German economy. Increasing urbanisation and a buoyant construction industry created a rising demand for pig-iron and the indirect effects of a rapid expansion in pig-iron output were particularly noticeable in relation to the mining and transport sectors of the economy. However it is only on the basis of a rigorous econometric analysis of the precise backward linkages of individual industries, such as the pig-iron sector, that their relative role within the developing German economy in the nineteenth-century will be more fully understood.

In recent years there has been a considerable growth of interest in the process of German urbanisation and housing development.(105) An attempt has been made to examine the economic and occupational structure of German cities during the period of rapid urbanisation in the late nineteenth-and early twentieth-centuries, particularly in relation to differentiated demographic patterns and the possible existence of specific localised housing markets.(106) Moreover the 'housing question', as such, which reflected the socio-economic impact of massive urban migration in the second half of the nineteenth-century (107), became a central focus for political debate and discussion. Political elites, both nationally and locally, were increasingly concerned that housing shortages and deteriorating housing conditions might lead to the political radicalisation of the urban working-class and the apparent failure of the unregulated house-construction industry to respond adequately to the problems of rapid urbanisation gave rise to increasing demands for a more active role for government in the general field of housing.(108) In the specific case of Hamburg the severe cholera epidemic of 1892 led to the 'housing question' taking central stage in the city's communal and social politics, whereas in Berlin substantial in-migration as early as the 1840s had accelerated a number of latent adverse processes in the housing market, and given rise to the formation of the *Berliner gemeinnuetzige Baugesellschaft* and a variety of proposals designed to alleviate the situation.(109)

According to one point of view the process of industrialisation in Germany was accompanied by a permanent housing deficiency as a result of serious constraints within the house-construction industry.(110) However research into this critical sector is still in its early stages and, as yet, there is no comprehensive analysis of the German house-construction industry during this period. Certainly the building industry was dominated by small firms with a low average level of capitalisation and few joint-stock companies were concerned with the construction of working-class housing.(111) Legal constraints on the activities of *Baugenossenschaften* (co-operative building societies), at least until 1889, inhibited the development of alternative sources of capital for house construction.(112) Despite these limitations, however, it has recently been argued that there was no long-term imbalance between supply and demand factors in the German housing market and that the absence of a persistent problem of homelessness in the *Kaiserreich* can be viewed as a remarkable achievement of the house-construction industry.(113) Although improved housing quality was associated with rising housing costs for the working-class, individual case studies have indicated that this was more than accommodated by rising real wages, with house rents in particular evincing a weaker upward trend than average per capita income.(114)

Richard Tilly's important contribution to the present volume helps to take this particular debate an important step forward. Urban development was essentially of a discontinuous character, reflecting the operation of both economic and demographic variables, and house construction was strongly cyclical throughout the period under consideration, revealing long swings with a period of fifteen years.(115) German urban population growth in the nineteenth-century is largely explicable in terms of in-migration, and pull factors, frequently income-related, were predominant.(116) Migration, in particular, was a significant determinant of urban housing investment, although the precise mechanism remains unclear. Certainly in the case of Hamburg the key demographic variables migration and marriage had no significant effect on rental levels, although this was generally the most important determinant of expected returns to housing investment. Moreover, at least in three Rhenish communities (Gemeinde) influenced by large-scale urban development, land sales, which affected both building costs and rental levels, were primarily determined by family generational cycles rather than more explicit demand-related variables.(117)

Undoubtedly the housing industry retained a strong speculative element and was not immune from serious scandals. Given the broader political implication of the 'housing question', and the increasing recognition of the need for improved housing and sanitary conditions, it is not surprising that the latter decades of the nineteenth-century should have witnessed rising pressure for remedial official intervention in this sector. Action by local authorities could well have avoided excessive land speculation and the failure of local administrations to deal effectively with the entrenched rights of existing property owners, as Niethammer has argued, adversely affected housing provision and even contributed to cultural stagnation.(118) Key factors in the process of urban development in the Ruhr from the 1880s onwards were the extension in state intervention which strengthened the internal position of city administrations and the economic upturn of the 1890s which provided local authorities with increased fiscal income for direct action in this sector.(119) Moreover the campaign for national housing legislation between 1886 and 1914 was accompanied by increasingly vitriolic attacks on Mietskasernen (tenement blocks) and the promotion of the 'cottage ideal', as the future basis for working-class housing provision.(120) The housing reform movement, in turn, encouraged the active participation of some local authorities in the field of housing provision, whether in the context of central inspection, the regulation of urban credit institutions (121), or the development of an urban land policy.

However, as Richard Tilly indicates, urban housing in Germany in the pre-1914 period remained essentially a sector dominated by private profit expectations. Despite considerable pressure for increased state intervention, the Prussian Housing Bill of 1904 was not proceeded with and new housing legislation in Hamburg in 1893, 1898 and 1907 only envisaged voluntary controls and had a limited impact.(122) Although the city of Cologne developed an exemplary policy of small-scale housing provision, despite the persistent opposition of private builders, local authority housing seldom constituted more than five per cent of the total housing stock in the years before the outbreak of the First World War.(123) In part this reflected the considerable opposition of existing interest groups to official involvement in the unregulated housing market, the persistence of the three class voting system and the domination of local politics by land and property owners.(124) However urban growth in Germany, as Tilly indicates, was discontinuous, with the second half of the nineteenth-century characterised by four similar, but essentially unique, cycles. Given the complex factors which helped to account for the failure of the housing market to stay on target, increased state intervention may well have been equally unsuccessful in predicting market movements and state-induced resource re-allocation to this sector would have been misapplied.(125) Moreover, despite the rapidity of the urbanisation process in Germany, there was a perceptible long-term improvement in housing quality and the relative absence of spatial segregation within cities would seem to suggest an easier process of urban growth than was the case in other developing economies during this period.(126) To this extent state agencies may have been even less effective than the unregulated private sector in responding adequately to the unprecedented housing demands generated by rapid urbanisation during this period.

The elucidation of the dominant role played by cyclical trends in German urban growth, however, also reflects the fact that a prominent feature of German economic history recently has been the revival of interest in the study of business cycles in the nineteenth-century.(127) Apart from discrediting the concept of Kondratieff long-waves and the so-called 'Great Depression' of 1874 to 1894, Spree's work, in particular, provides important support for a new periodisation of German take-off, with the industrial expansion of the 1850s viewed as an extension of the short-lived boom of the 1840s. Future research in this area may well be directed towards the analysis of comparative international trends (128), as the increasingly visible cyclical congruence after 1850 confirmed Germany's effective integration within the developing international economy and the emergence of the _Kaiserreich_ as a world economic power.

It is highly appropriate, therefore, that the international ramifications of economic policy within Germany, albeit in the context of post-war inflation, should be the central concern of Carl-Ludwig Holtfrerich's contribution to this volume. The traditional view of the overall effects of the inflationary spiral between the end of the First World War and 1923 has been largely negative. Although money was clearly being made during this period, the beneficiaries were the manipulators of high finance, profiteers, foreign speculators and the small Raffke (money-grubbers) and Schieber (racketeers), who directly profited from the mounting distress of others, such as the elderly, widows and those dependant on fixed incomes or savings, who were less able to survive the turmoil of hyper-inflation.(129) The apparent weakness and indecision of the German government in halting the inexorable decline of the mark's purchasing power fostered a revival of barter trade as money ceased to play a meaningful function in the economic life of the country, resulted in unexampled misery for the masses, aggravated latent middle-class alienation from the Weimar constitution, encouraged political radicalism and undermined the ability of the banking mechanism to deal with future economic crises.(130) Even if there had been a significant growth in industrial output during the inflationary period, this was merely an 'artificial blossoming' of a 'sham boom', which, in turn, helped to create an unbalanced production structure.(131) Irrespective of the precise causes of the inflationary spiral, which is viewed as having been 'quite typical' for a defeated or newly-established state characterised by government insecurity and a low level of public confidence (132), both the short and long-term effects of this experience were generally negative.

The more recent reappraisal of the impact of post-war inflation on the German secondary sector, however, has attempted to view economic policy within a contemporary political framework.(133) Not only did the traditional division of fiscal responsibility between central government and the individual states preclude any immediate resolution of the financial legacy of the First World War, but the espousal of an alternative 'correct' monetary policy in the post-war years may well have exacerbated political instability and threatened the very existence of the democratic Weimar state. Certainly inflation did provide industrialists with significant advantages. Entrepreneurs, as a whole, during this period tended to gain as debtors, as the real value of existing debts was continuously eroded by inflation, and also from the inevitable lag between prices and wages. The diffident discount rate policy of the Reichsbank reduced the real cost of credit to the secondary sector and encouraged a high rate of investment. There was a significant increase in entrepreneurial income (134), as the relative position of industrialists was strengthened by the growing scarcity of material resources and the positive effect of increased employment on aggregate demand. German GNP had fallen considerably during the war period, but with the exception of 1923, there was continuous growth between 1919 and 1925.(135) Just as inflationary trends had encouraged economic growth in the early 1950s, the post-1918 inflation period facilitated the successful shift to peace-time production, improved the capital base of German industry and promoted full employment.(136) The situation was perhaps best summed up by the General Association of German Banks and Bankers in 1923, which stated that '... thanks to the aid of the banks, German industry and commerce were given immediately after the war the means not only to preserve their resources but also to increase them in a considerable measure'. The contrast between the post-war situation of German industry and the economies of the United States and other western European countries which adhered rigidly to 'correct' financial policies could not have been more marked. Particularly during the world depression of 1920-22, the latter were characterised by high unemployment, a serious disruption to economic growth and reduced aggregate consumption.(137)

However, according to Holtfrerich's analysis, Germany's post-war inflationary boom can also be accorded a major role in facilitating an international demand-induced recovery from the cyclical downturn of 1920-21. On the assumption that relative real income growth, both in Germany and abroad, was the prime determinant of contemporary movements in the balance of trade, German trade deficits between 1920 and 1922, reflecting the increased demand for imports in a home market which was continuously expanding, would inevitably have generated stimulating effects on economic activity abroad. In particular the more than two-fold increase by volume in German primary sector imports from the United States during this period had a disproportionate impact on raw material prices internationally in view of the relatively inelastic price elasticities of demand and supply in the short run for primary commodities and American domination of world market for such products. The German economy in the immediate post-war years, fuelled by the inflationary spiral, can therefore justifiably be viewed as an important locomotive for the world economy, with the demand stimulus of the German boom equivalent to the relative size of modern demand stimuli programmes. The contrast with the international depression of 1929 to 1932, when none of the world's major economies effectively attempted to stimulate demand, could not be more marked.

In contrast to the events of 1918 to 1923, however, the Allied occupation of Germany after the end of the Second World War witnessed a radical reversal of relative economic roles, with the reconstruction of the German secondary sector in the immediate post-war years to a large degree determined by Allied occupation policy. In recent years there has been a growing interest in the economic history of the post- 1945 period and the comparative economic development of the two German states.(138) Although a central focus of this research has been an attempt to analyse the precise causative mechanism behind economic recovery, particularly in West Germany, increasing attention has been paid to such issues as zonal land reform, the attempted integration of refugees within the indigenous population, and the extent and implications of Allied dismantling of industrial plant.(139) Contemporary opinion has traditionally suggested that economic reconstruction took place 'literally from ruins', reflecting an almost complete destruction of existing industrial capacity.(140) However any explanation of West German post-war recovery predicated on such an assumption has only limited explanatory power. Once immediate production bottle-necks had been cleared, particularly in relation to the transport infrastructure, the general conditions for economic rehabilitation were relatively favourable. The extent of war damage, particularly in the three western zones has frequently been exaggerated, and did not directly necessitate any large-scale modernisation of fixed assets, as industrial buildings tended to cluster outside the range of the focal points of air raids.(141) Moreover despite the residual legacy of the original Morgenthau plan and the policy of 'industrial retrogression' still evident in the Level-of-Industry Plan of March 1946, the extent of dismantling by the western occupation powers remained limited.(142) Indeed as far as long-term economic recovery in the western areas of Germany was concerned, none of the traditional mono-causal explanations, including the currency reform of June 1948, foreign aid, the introduction of the social market economy, or even German diligence, appear to have been critical determinants of post-war industrial growth.(143) Of far greater significance in influencing the timing and pace of economic recovery, at least in the period 1945 to 1952 were indigenous supply factors, specifically the level of capital stock and the labour force potential. In conjunction with government fiscal and taxation policies designed to maximise the effective utilisation of available factors of production, even at the cost, in the short-run, of increasing social inequality and an adverse income distribution, these essentially endogenous variables provide the most convincing explanation for post-war economic growth.(144)

Within the context of examining German recovery after 1945 considerable attention has been paid to the occupation policies of the United States, and to a lesser extent, of France, but the role of the United Kingdom, despite British control of Germany's most important economic region, the Ruhr, has seldom been discussed.(145) The general picture of Allied occupation policy in the western zones is often fairly negative. Not only was there a considerable difference in terms of immediate policy objectives, but the administrative approach to economic issues on a zonal basis varied substantially.(146) Internal confusion, aggravated by changes in foreign policy as a result of the unfolding of the Cold War, was accentuated by the formation of Bizonia in 1947, and the paralysis of the occupying powers meant that there was little sense of direction in economic planning.(147)

British economic policy within its zone of occupation is a useful test case of the nature and effectiveness of the contribution of the Western Allies to German industrial reconstruction. The Ruhr, which was located within the British zone, was an important focal point for European rehabilitation as a whole, as Western Europe to a large extent depended for its economic reconstruction on fuel supplies from the coal industry.(148) From the Quebec Agreement of September 1944 onwards, the western Allies recognised that an essential feature of post-war policy would be 'the future disposition of the Ruhr', and a positive approach to industrial revival might well have been expected, given British apprehension 'that an economically prostrate Germany would create a huge vacuum in the heart of Europe, which the Soviet Union would be only too ready to fill'.(149) Indeed the initial consideration of British policy would appear to have been the rapid restoration of normal economic conditions within its zone, as in the case of the revival of a functional banking system (150), and it was this overriding objective which reinforced British reliance on existing instruments of economic control. From the start the British employed a comprehensive central administration, and although there were clearly limits to the effectiveness of 'state' planning in a context where the ownership of the means of production was retained in private hands, there was a remarkable and continuous increase in zonal industrial production from the cessation of hostilities until the summer of 1946.(151) Although the precise effect of occupation policy was mediated by the specific structure of individual industrial sectors (152), recent writers have referred to the 'constructive pragmatism' of British planning in relation to the steel industry and the 'constructive control' exercised in relation to the coal industry.(153)

However certain contemporaries were clearly less charitable in assessing British occupation policy, referring to the 'mania for destruction', 'examples of lunacy' in terms of economic planning and the negative attitude of Allied officers to the German population, which 'varies from a disgusting offensiveness, through indifference often identifiable with oblivion'.(154) Despite the moderate success of the Sparta plan in raising output from the producer goods industries, occupation policy was characterised by administrative confusion. The British authorities failed to follow a consistent line in relation to economic reconstruction and showed a marked lack of foresight.(155)

Mark Roseman's important analysis of British manpower policy in the Ruhr mines in the immediate post-war years clearly reinforces the more negative view of the role of the occupying power in zonal economic reconstruction. The fact that the general British intention in post-war Germany was to export a model of representative democracy incorporating the principle of indirect rule may, in part, explain the existence of policy and planning deficiencies (156), but Roseman's analysis reveals the absence of a clear reconstruction programme. British policy was essentially negative. Undoubtedly foreign policy considerations, including the changing nature of Anglo-French relations and the need to avoid any suspicion that the Ruhr and its industries were being built up as war potential against Russia (157), played an important role in structuring zonal economic policy. However the desire to protect British industrial interests and a latent fear of future German competition were equally significant in determining the framework of occupation policy.(158) Indeed within a broader context British policy suffered from a clear lack of direction; there was neither a commitment to fostering general economic reconstruction, nor a willingness to apply consistently punitive measures.(159) Clearly any final assessment of the effectiveness of British occupation policy must await further research on the precise nature of 'state'-industry relations in specific sectors during the immediate post-war years. On the basis of the present analysis, however, far from allowing the coal-mining sector to flourish, even in the interests of the Allies (160), British failure to effectively revive the all important coal industry of the Ruhr only served to retard economic reconstruction in Germany as a whole.

The contributions to this volume reflect a broad spectrum of issues and research interests in German economic and business history in the nineteenth-and twentieth-centuries. A number of the contributors include as part of their open agenda the central issue of the role of the state in German economic growth; other contributions help to correct some of the interpretative errors and 'erroneous beliefs' that have crept into standard German historiography.(161) This is doubly important, given that many of these traditional assumptions are implicitly incorporated into broader historical debates, such as the current concern with the German _Sonderweg_ and the interrelationship between economic and political change. Undoubtedly the 'historically unique conditions' of German industrialisation (162) may have generated a number of broader long-lasting consequences, but it would be premature to reach any definitive conclusions on the specific nature of these consequences until at least some of the missing pieces in the jig-saw puzzle of economic growth have finally been assembled.

In order to achieve this objective German historians have shown an increasing willingness to re-examine the evidence of the past with the assistance of new analytical tools. Although there still may be some concern in relation to a persistent lack of theory in the overall analysis of the causes and consequences of patterns of economic change, and the marginal impact of the 'new economic history', cliometrics has certainly enjoyed a period of lively development, at least in West Germany.(163) This is to a large extent reflected in many of the contributions to the present volume, particularly in terms of an explicit use of theory, ranging from international trade theory and the economic theory of the state in Dumke's analysis of the *Zollverein*, to Holtfrerich's use of balance of trade theory within the context of the post- 1918 German inflation. Equally a number of the present contributions attest to the increasing application of econometric techniques, as in Krengel's use of input-output coefficients in his analysis of the pig-iron industry, or in Tilly's examination of 'long swings' in German urban development in the period 1850 to 1914. By focusing on individual sectors, such as the pig-iron industry in both the first half of the nineteenth-century and in the period 1871 to 1913, the 'new industries' of electrical power and chemicals in the second phase of industrialisation from the late nineteenth-century onwards, as well as the banking and house-construction sectors, further evidence is also offered of the inherent value of micro-level studies in providing important answers to broader historical questions.

Moreover, in terms of the most appropriate level of aggregation for future research in German economic history, the value of a more sharply differentiated regional analysis is clearly evident in the contributions by Dumke, Schaefer and Roseman. Although there is an increasing recognition of the relevance of such an approach, given that a persistent characteristic of German industrialisation throughout the nineteenth-century was its regional diversity, it would be particularly productive if the deep-seated commitment to *Landesgeschichte* in Germany could develop a more overt orientation towards the central issues of international debate within the discipline.(164) Local history, in this sense, does not necessarily have to be 'written and read by those in the locality itself', of interest only to those 'who share the experience of the *Heimat*'.(165) Indeed it is perhaps only on the basis of further micro-level, sectoral studies, conducted within a broader European analytical framework that some of the central issues in German economic history in the nineteenth-and twentieth-century may ultimately be resolved.

The essays in this volume collectively reinforce the need to re-examine traditional typologies relating to modern German industrialisation and to re-assess some of the assumptions predicated on the concept of 'relative backwardness'. To this extent they may well contribute, in turn, to a necessary, 'paradigm change' in German economic history and to a re-appraisal of the fluctuating relationship between economic and political forces in moulding the historical path of German development.(166)

NOTES

1. D.Blackbourn and G.Eley. The Peculiarities of German History. Bourgeois Society and Politics in Nineteenth-Century Germany. (Oxford, 1984), p.4.

2. W.J.Mommsen. 'Gegenwaertige Tendenzen in der Geschichtsschreibung der Bundesrepublik'. Geschichte und Gesellschaft, vol.7, Heft 2, (1981), p.173.

3. R.H.Tilly. '"Soll und Haben". Recent German Economic History and the Problem of Economic Development'. Journal of Economic History, vol.29, (1969), pp.298-319; C-D.Krohn, 'Neuere Tendenzen der Wirtschaftsgeschichte', Archiv fuer Sozialgeschichte, Band XXXIV (1984), pp.589-604.

4. H.Boehme, An Introduction to the Social and Economic History of Germany. Politics and Economic Change in the Nineteenth and Twentieth Centuries, (Oxford, 1978); M.Kitchen, The Political Economy of Germany 1815-1914, (London, 1978); J.H.Clapham, The Economic Development of France and Germany 1815-1914, (Cambridge, 1921); Blackbourn and Eley. Peculiarities, pp.179,293.

5. F.B.Tipton, 'The National Consensus in German Economic History'. Central European History, vol.7, no.3 (1974), pp.195-224; J.J.Sheehan, 'What is German History? Reflections on the Role of the Nation in German History and Historiography', The Journal of Modern History, vol.53 (1981), p.13.

6. The papers by Wilfried Feldenkirchen, Jochen Krengel and Hermann Schaefer were originally presented at or submitted to the third and fourth meetings of the SSRC/DFG North West Forum on German Economic and Social History. These meetings were held at Liverpool University in 1982 and focused on the theme of 'The Paradigm of German Industrialisation'. I am grateful to the Economic and Social Research Council and the Deutsche Forschungsgemeinschaft for providing initial funding for these meetings. Preliminary versions of the papers in the present volume by Rainer Fremdling and by Rolf Dumke have already appeared in German; see R.Fremdling, 'Britische Exporte und die Modernisierung der deutschen Eisenindustrie waehrend der Fruehindustrialisierung', Vierteljahrschrift fuer Sozial-und Wirtschaftsgeschichte, vol.68 (1981), pp.305-324;

R.H. Dumke, 'Der Deutsche Zollverein als Modelloekonomischer integration', in H. Berding (ed.). Wirtschaftliche und politische Integration in Europe im 19. und 20. Jahrhundert, (Geschichte und Gesellschaft, Sonderheft 10, Goettingen, 1984), pp.71-101. An earlier article by Tilly and Wellenreuther provides a further analysis of the German building cycle in the nineteenth-century, see R.H. Tilly and T. Wellenreuther, 'Bevoelkerungswanderung und Wohnungsbauzyklen in deutschen Grossstaedten im 19. Jahrhundert', in H.J. Teuteberg (ed.). Homo habitans. Zur Sozialgeschichte des laendlichen und staedtischen Wohnens in der Neuzeit (Muenster, 1985), pp.273-300.

7. Blackbourn and Eley, Peculiarities, p.178; C. Trebilcock, The Industrialization of the Continental Powers 1780-1914, (London, 1981), p.25.

8. J. Kocka, 'Entrepreneurship in a Late-Comer Country: The German Case', in K. Nakagawa (ed.), Social Order and Entrepreneurship (Tokio, 1979), p.157; K. Borchardt, 'Die Industrielle Revolution in Deutschland, 1750-1914', in Europaeische Wirtschaftsgeschichte, Band 4 (Stuttgart and New York, 1977), p.154. See also G. Ambrosius, Der Staat als Unternehmer. Oeffentliche Wirtschaft und Kapitalismus seit dem 19. Jahrhundert (Goettingen, 1984).

9. Trebilcock, Industrialization, p.29.

10. W. Fischer, 'Das Verhaeltnis von Staat und Wirtschaft in Deutschland am Beginn der Industrialisierung', in idem., Wirtschaft und Gesellschaft im Zeitalter der Industrialisierung. Aufsaetze-Studien-Vortraege, (Goettingen, 1972), p.65 et seq.

11. Kocka, 'Entrepreneurship', p.174. See also F. Haverkamp, Staatliche Gewerbefoerderung im Grossherzogtum Baden unter besonderer Beruecksichtigung der Entwicklung des gewerblichen Bildungswesens im 19. Jahrhundert, (Forschungen zur Oberrheinischen Landesgeschichte, Bd. XXIX, Freiburg and Munich, 1979). It has also been argued, however, that Prussian education policy as a whole in the nineteenth-century was not specifically related to the developing needs of industry and that the macro-economic contribution of the educational system was marginal. See P. Lundgreen, 'Educational Expansion and Economic Growth in Nineteenth-Century Germany: A Quantitative Study', in L. Stone (ed.), Schooling and Society. Studies in the History of Education, (Baltimore and London, 1976), pp.20-65.

12. The rapid diffusion of the Bessemer process in Prussia during the 1860s, for example, was encouraged by the continuing refusal of the Prussian administration to grant patent rights to the inventor; see U. Troitzsch. 'Die Einfuehrung des Bessemer-Verfahrens in Preussen ein Innovationsprozess aus der 60er Jahren des 19. Jahrhunderts', in F.R. Pfetsch (ed.), Innovationsforschung als multidisziplinaere Aufgabe, (Goettingen, 1975), p.224.

13. See in particular the discussion on state trust capitalism and state monopoly capitalism or 'organised capitalism' within the German context in D.Baudis and H.Nussbaum, Wirtschaft und Staat in Deutschland vom Ende des 19.Jahrhunderts bis 1918/19, (H.Nussbaum and L.Zumpe, eds., Wirtschaft und Staat in Deutschland, Bd.1, Berlin, 1978), particularly pp.51-176. J.Kocka, 'Organisierter Kapitalismus oder Staatsmonopolistisch-Kapitalismus? Begriffliche Vorbemerkung', in H.A.Winkler (ed.), Organisierter Kapitalismus. Voraussetzungen und Anfaenge (Goettingen, 1974), pp.19-35. H-J.Puhle, 'Historische Konzepte des entwickelten Industrie-Kapitalismus. "Organisierter Kapitalismus" und "Korporatismus". Geschichte und Gesellschaft, 10.Jahrgang, Heft 2, (1984), pp.165-184.

14. H.Kiesewetter, 'Staat und Unternehmen waehrend der Fruehindustrialisierung; Das Koenigreich Sachsen als Paradigma', Zeitschrift fuer Unternehmensgeschichte, 29.Jahrgang, Heft 1, (1984), p.5. K.P.Harder, 'Major Factors in Business Formation and Development: Germany in the Early Industrial Period', in L.J.Kennedy (ed.), Papers of the Sixteenth Business History Conference, (1969), p.71 et seq.

15. V.Dorsch, Die Handelskammern der Rheinprovinz in der zweiten Haelfte des 19.Jahrhunderts. Eine Studie zu Funktion und Entwicklung wirtschaftlicher Interessenvertretungen, (Frankfurter Historische Abhandlungen, Bd.24, Wiesbaden, 1982), passim.

16. H.Pohl, 'On the History of Organisation and Management in Large German Enterprises Since the Nineteenth Century', German Yearbook on Business History, (1982), p.100. See also D.Swatek, Unternehmenskonzentration als Ergebnis und Mittel nationalsozialistischer Wirtschaftspolitik, (Volkswirtschaftliche Schriften, Heft 181, Berlin, 1972), p.44 et seq.

17. G.Plumpe, 'Industrie, technischer Fortschritt und Staat. Die Kautschuksynthese in Deutschland 1906-1944/45', Geschichte und Gesellschaft, Jahrgang 9, Heft 4, (1983), p.597. For a general discussion of state-industry relations during the Third Reich, see J.Gillingham, Industry and Politics in the Third Reich. Ruhr Coal, Hitler and Europe, (London, 1985).

18. G-H.Seebold, Ein Stahlkonzern im Dritten Reich. Der Bochumer Verein 1927 bis 1945, (Duesseldorfer Schriften zur neueren Landesgeschichte und zur Geschichte Nordrhein-Westfalens, Bd.3, Wuppertal, 1981).

19. Boehme, Social and Economic History of Germany, p.120.

20. See the important corrective to earlier views on this issue in I.Kershaw, The Nazi Dictatorship. Problems and Perspectives of Interpretation. (London, 1985), pp.42-60.

21. Plumpe, 'Industrie, technischer Fortschritt und Staat', p.597.

22. I.Koenig, Handelskammern zwischen Kooperation und Konzentration. Vereinigungen, Arbeitsgemeinschaften und Zweckverbaende von Industrie- und Handelskammern im niederrheinisch-westfaelischen Industriegebiet 1880 bis 1933, (Schriften zur Rheinisch-Westfaelischen Wirtschaftsgeschichte, Band 32, Cologne, 1981).

23. W.J.Reader, Imperial Chemical Industries. A History. Vol.2, (London, 1975), pp.129,179. In 1933, for example, ICI directors included a former Viceroy of India (Lord Reading), and a former Secretary of State for Air (Lord Weir).

24. It is interesting to note that on the occasion of the formation of the concern in 1925 there is evidence of a significant disapproval of centralised and authoritarian management styles, and an intention, at least on the production side, to maintain a substantial degree of decentralisation. See W.Fischer, 'Dezentralisation oder Zentralisation - Kollegiale oder autoritaere Fuehrung? Die Auseinandersetzung um die Leitungsstruktur bei der Entstehung des I.G.Farben-Konzerns', in N.Horn and J.Kocka (eds.), Recht und Entwicklung der Grossunternehmen im 19. und fruehen 20. Jahrhundert, (Goettingen, 1979), pp.476-488.

25. Plumpe, 'Industrie, technischer Fortschritt und Staat', p.594. Significantly, despite high depreciation allowances designed to stimulate the commercial production of Buna (synthetic rubber), I.G.Farben still incurred a net loss of 1-2 million Reichsmark up until the end of 1944. Only the successful conclusion of the war would have ensured long-term viability, despite the extensive degree of central government support.

26. D.Petzina, Die deutsche Wirtschaft in der Zwischenkriegszeit, (Wiesbaden, 1977), p.141. Between 1928 and 1939 undistributed profits of limited liability companies as a whole rose four-fold.

27. M.Keller, 'Public Policy and Large Enterprise. Comparative Historical Perspectives', in Horn and Kocka, Recht und Entwicklung der Grossunternehmen, pp.515-534. W.R.Cornish, 'Legal Control over Cartels and Monopolization 1880-1914. A Comparison', in Horn and Kocka (eds.), Recht und Entwicklung der Grossunternehmen im 19. und fruehen 20. Jahrhundert, (Goettingen, 1979), p.282.

28. J.Kocka, 'Family and Bureaucracy in German Industrial Management, 1850-1914 : Siemens in Comparative Perspective', Business History Review, XLV (1971), pp.133-156. Idem., 'Capitalism and Bureaucracy in German Industrialization before 1914', Economic History Review, Vol.33 (1981), pp.453-468. The expansion of the German bureaucracy itself is dealt with in J.P.Cullity, 'The Growth of Government Employment in Germany, 1882-1950', Zeitschrift fuer die gesamte Staatswissenschaft', Band CXXIII (1967), pp.201-217. See also H.Henning. Die deutsche Beamtenschaft im 19. Jahrhundert, (Wiesbaden, 1984).

29. D.F.Vagts, 'Railroads, Private Enterprise and Public Policy - Germany and the United States 1870-1920', in Horn and Kocka (eds.), Recht und Entwicklung der Grossunternehmen im 19. und fruehen 20. Jahrhundert, (Goettingen, 1979), p.615. By 1900 33,000 kilometres of the railway network in Prussia were already in public hands and only a mere 2,257 kilometres remained in private ownership.

30. M.Boeger, Die Haltung der industriellen Unternehmer zur staatlichen Sozialpolitik in den Jahren 1878-1891, (Frankfurt-am-Main, 1982).

31. See H.Wessel, 'Der Deutsche Schwachstromkabel-Verband. Vorgeschichte und Gruendung sowie Entwicklung, in den ersten Jahren seines Bestehens (1876-1917)', Zeitschrift fuer Unternehmensgeschichte, Vol.27 (1982), pp.22-44, for the important purchasing role of the Reichspost-und Telegraphenverwaltung : idem., 'Der Einfluss des Staates auf die Industrie - dargestellt am Beispiel der staatlichen Telegraphenbehoerden und der elektrotechnischen Industrie', in F.Blaich (ed.), Die Rolle des Staates fuer die wirtschaftliche Entwicklung, (Berlin, 1982), pp.203-223. For a positive assessment of the overall willingness of German entrepreneurs in the electrical industry to accept the potential benefits of state involvement, see L.Hannah, 'Public Policy and the Advent of Large-Scale Technology: The Case of Electricity Supply in the U.S.A., Germany and Britain', in Horn and Kocka (eds.), Recht und Entwicklung der Grossunternehmen im 19. und fruehen 20. Jahrhundert, (Goettingen, 1979), p.583.

32. H-W.Niemann, 'Die Anfaenge der staatlichen Elektrizitaetsversorgung im Koenigreich Sachsen', Zeitschrift fuer Unternehmensforschung, Vol.23 (1978), pp.98-117, in particular p.100. The state, in this case, would appear to have had a two-fold objective: firstly, facilitating the supply of lower unit cost energy supply to small-scale firms, and secondly, securing for its own purposes a preferential price for electricity.

33. H.Ott and Thomas Herzig (assisted by Rudi Allgeier and Philip Fehrenbach), 'Elekrizitaetsversorgung von Baden, Wuerttemberg und Hohenzollern 1913/14', Historischer Atlas von Baden-Wuerttemberg, XI, 9 (Kommission fuer geschichtliche Landeskunde im Baden-Wuerttemberg, 1982). A.Spraul, 'Ein Beitrag zur Entwicklung der oeffentlichen Elektrizitaetsversorgung in Baden', unpublished PhD thesis, University of Heidelberg, 1933.

34. W.R.Lee and E.Rosenhaft (eds.), The State and Social Change in Germany, 1880-1960. (Berg, Leamington Spa, 1988), forthcoming.

35. See Hermann Schaefer's contribution to the current volume, chapter seven. For the particular role of the Berlin city authorities in fostering the use of electricity, see

G.Henniger, 'Zu einigen Problemen der Elektrifizierung der Berliner Industriebetriebe von den Anfaengen bis zum Beginn des 20.Jahrhunderts', Berliner Geschichte, 2, (Berlin, 1981), pp.25-54.

36. H-P. von Peschke, Elektroindustrie und Staatsverwaltung am Beispiel Siemens, 1847-1914, (Europaeische Hochschulschriften, Reihe III, Band 154, Frankfurt am Main, 1981), p.345 et seq.

37. E.G.Spencer, 'Rulers of the Ruhr: Leadership and Authority in German Big Business before 1914', Business History Review, vol.53 (1979), pp.40-64. The coincidence between the development of heavy industry and German nation-building led to a high degree of mutual interdependence at least in this particular case. For the importance of regional rivalries, see Koenig, Handelskammern, passim.

38. H.Kiesewetter, 'Erklaerungshypothesen zur regionalen Industrialisierung in Deutschland im 19.Jahrhundert', Vierteljahrschrift fuer Sozial-und Wirtschaftsgeschichte, Band 67 (1980), pp.305-333. Certainly the taxation system of many German states scarcely provided an optimal basis for the promotion of effective industrial growth, although the sugar-beet industry undoubtedly benefited from fiscal policy: see W.R.Lee, 'Tax Structure and Economic Growth in Germany, 1750-1850', The Journal of European Economic History, Vol.IV, (1975), pp.153-178. J.A.Perkins, 'Fiscal Policy and Economic Development in XIXth Century Germany', The Journal of European Economic History, Vol.13, (1984), pp.311-344.

39. H.Pohl, 'Zur Geschichte von Organisation und Leitung Deutscher Grossunternehmen seit dem 19.Jahrhundert', Zeitschrift fuer Unternehmengeschichte, Band 26 (1981), p.151.

40. Pohl, 'On the History of Organization', p.96. Significantly external growth only made a relatively insubstantial contribution to overall enterprise growth and industrial concentration was not associated with a merger movement. See R.Tilly, 'Mergers, External Growth, and Finance in the Development of Large-Scale Enterprise in Germany, 1880-1913', Journal of Economic History, Vol.XLII, No.3, (1982), pp.629-658.

41. In 1689, for example, the Geheime Hofkammer was established in Prussia to regulate all tolls and trade. See F.Facius, Wirtschaft und Staat. Die Entwicklung der staatlichen Wirtschaftsverwaltung in Deutschland vom 17.Jahrhundert bis 1945, (Boppard-am-Rhein, 1959); H.Kellenbenz et al., 'Germany', in C.Wilson and G.Parker (eds.), An Introduction to the Sources of European Economic History, 1500-1800, (London, 1977), pp.204-206. For a discussion of mercantilist theory in this area, see E.Klein, 'Staatsdirigismus und Handelsfreiheit in der merkantilistischen Wirtschaftstheorie', Jahrbuecher fuer Nationaloekonomie und Statistik, Vol.180, (1967), pp.72-90.

42. E.Schremmer, Die Wirtschaft Bayerns vom hohen Mittelalter bis zum Beginn der Industrialisierung. Bergbau, Gewerbe, Handel, (Munich, 1970), pp.635-644.

43. In the principality of Hohenlohe, for example, there had been little attempt by the end of the eighteenth century to improve the chaotic state of customs stations. See W.Fischer, Das Fuerstentum Hohenlohe im Zeitalter der Aufklaerung, (Tuebinger Studien zur Geschichte und Politik, Band 10, Tuebingen, 1958), p.123.

44. See, for example, G.Ellis, Napoleon's Continental Blockade: The Case of Alsace, (Oxford, 1981). H.Berding, 'Die Reform des Zollwesens in Deutschland unter dem Einfluss der napoleanischen Herrschaft', Geschichte und Gesellschaft, Heft 4 (1980), pp.523-537. For an illustration of the post-1815 trade and tariff negotiations, see A.Zimmermann, 'Die Russisch-preussischen Handelsbeziehungen, 1814-1833', Jahrbuch fuer Gesetzgebung, Verwaltung und Volkswirtschaft, Vol.16, (1892); J.Kortmann, 'Die Niederlande in den handelspolitischen Verhandlungen mit Preussen vom Wiener Kongress bis zum Schiffahrtsvertrag von 1837', unpublished thesis, University of Muenster, 1929; F.Ruckert, 'Die Handelsbeziehungen zwischen Deutschland und der Schweiz mit besonderer Beruecksichtigung der handelspolitischen Verhaeltnisse seit dem Beginn des 19.Jahrhunderts', unpublished thesis, University of Wuerzburg, 1926.

45. Kitchen, Political Economy, p.34.

46. W.Treue, Wirtschaftszustaende und Wirtschaftspolitik in Preussen, 1815-1825, (Vierteljahrschrift fuer Sozial-und Wirtschaftsgeschichte, Beiheft 31, Wiesbaden, 1937). A.Walch, 'Die Wirtschaftliche Entwicklung unter Montgelas, 1799-1817', unpublished thesis, University of Erlangen, 1935.

47. F.Ronnenberger, 'Der Staat des 19.Jahrhunderts als Innovator', in F.R.Pfetsch (ed.), Innovationsforschung als multidisziplinaere Aufgabe, (Goettingen, 1975), p.92. W.O.Henderson, The State and the Industrial Revolution in Prussia, 1740-1870, (Liverpool, 1958), p.108 and passim. M.Schumacher, Auslandsreisen deutscher Unternehmer 1750-1851. Unter besonderer Beruecksichtigung von Rheinland und Westfalen, (Schriften zur rheinisch-westfaelischen Wirtschaftsgeschichte, Band 17, Cologne, 1968).

48. A.Paulinyi, 'Der Technologietransfer fuer die Metallbearbeitung und die preussische Gewerbefoerderung (1820-1850)', in F.Blaich (ed.), Die Rolle des Staates fuer die wirtschaftliche Entwicklung, (Schriften des Vereins fuer Socialpolitik, Band 125, Berlin, 1982), pp.99-142. F.Redlich, 'The leaders of the German Steam-Engine Industry during the First 100 Years', Journal of Economic History, (1944), p.144.

49. P.H.Wilken, Entrepreneurship. A Comparative Historical Study. (New Jersey, 1979), p.137. W.Weber, 'Innovationen im fruehindustriellen deutschen Bergbau-und

Huettenwesen (F.A.von Heynitz)', in F.R.Pfetsch (ed.), Innovationsforschung als multidisziplinaere Aufgabe, (Goettingen, 1975), p.170; idem., Innovationen im fruehindustriellen deutschen Bergbau und Huettenwesen, Friedrich Anton von Heynitz, (Goettingen, 1976).

50. W.O.Henderson, 'A Nineteenth-century approach to a West European Common Market', Kyklos, Vol.X, (1957), p.450. Opposition to the tariff was particularly strong from the mercantilist Verein deutscher Kaufleute und Fabrikanten, for which Friedrich List acted as an important spokesman.

51. R.Fremdling, 'Vergleich der Schutzzollpolitik Frankreichs und des deutschen Zollvereins in ihren Auswirkungen auf die Modernisierung der Eisenindustrie, 1815-1870', in Blaich (ed.), Die Rolle des Staates, pp.77-98.

52. R.Fremdling, Technologischer Wandel und internationaler Handel im 18. und 19.Jahrhundert. Die Eisenindustrie in Grossbritannien, Belgien, Frankreich und Deutschland, (Berlin, 1986).

53. See also H.Sydow, Die Handelsbeziehungen zwischen Belgien und dem Zollverein, 1830-1885, (Dissertationen zur neueren Geschichte, Band 4, Cologne and Vienna, 1979), Vol.1, pp.72-140.

54. Kitchen, Political Economy, pp.53-54. W.Feldenkirchen, 'Zur Kapitalbeschaffung und Kapitalverwendung bei Aktiengesellschaften des deutschen Maschinenbaus im 19. und beginnenden 20. Jahrhundert', Vierteljahrschrift fuer Sozial-und Wirtschaftsgeschichte, Band 69, Heft 1, (1982), p.40. N.J.G.Pounds and W.N.Parker, Coal and Steel in Western Europe, (London, 1957), p.227. See also the contemporary publication by J.B.Mayer, Eingangszoll auf auslaendisches Roh-und Staabeisen ist fuer Teutschland nothwendig, (Mainz, 1843), which argued that protectionism was necessary in order to facilitate an optimal utilisation of indigenous wealth and resources.

55. R.Fremdling, 'Die Eisenindustrie Grossbritaniens und Deutschlands als Indikator fuer Konjunkturschwankungen, 1821-1870', in W.H.Schroeder and R.Spree (eds.), Historische Konjunkturforschung, (Historisch-Sozialwissenschaftliche Forschungen, Band 11, Stuttgart, 1980), pp.141-159.

56. See R.H.Dumke, 'Intra-German Trade in 1837 and Regional Economic Development', Vierteljahrschrift fuer Sozial-und Wirtschaftsgeschichte, Vol.64, (1977), pp.468-496: idem., 'Die wirtschaftlichen Folgen des Zollvereins', in W.Abelshauser and D.Petzina (eds.), Deutsche Wirtschaftsgeschichte im Industriezeitalter, (Duesseldorf, 1981), pp.341-373.

57. Blackbourn and Eley, Peculiarities, pp.176-177.

58. W.O.Henderson, The Rise of German Industrial Power, 1834-1914, (London, 1975), p.40. See also the latter's magisterial and, in many senses, still unsurpassed overall survey of the evolution of the customs union: idem., The Zollverein, (London, 1984, 3rd. edn.), passim.

59. Kitchen, Political Economy, p.42.

60. H-W.Hahn, Wirtschaftliche Integration im 19.Jahrhundert. Die Hessischen Staaten und der deutsche Zollverein, (Goettingen, 1982), p.307.

61. F.B.Tipton, 'National Growth Cycles and Regional Economic Structures in Nineteenth Century Germany', in W.H.Schroeder and R.Spree (eds.), Historische Konjunkturforschung, (Historisch-Sozialwissenschaftliche Forschungen, Band 11, Stuttgart, 1980), p.31. Hahn, Wirtschaftliche Integration, p.324.

62. W.Fischer, 'The German Zollverein. A Case Study in Customs Union', Kyklos, Vol.13, (1960), p.77.

63. See also T.Ohnishi, Zolltarifpolitik Preussens bis zur Gruendung des deutschen Zollvereins. Ein Beitrag zur Finanz-und Aussenpolitik Preussens, (Goettingen, 1973), passim. This also shows the extent to which positive fiscal motivation and revenue effects were predominant in the foundation and operation of the earlier Prussian commercial union between 1818 and 1833.

64. Fischer, Wirtschaft und Gesellschaft, p.449. W.Sprekelsen, 'Die Bedeutung des Handels und der Industrie im Verfassungsleben Bayerns im Zeitraum von 1808-1951', unpublished thesis, University of Munich, 1952, p.22 et seq.

65. W.Zorn, 'Zwischenstaatliche wirtschaftliche Integration im Deutschen Zollverein, 1867-1870. Ein quantitativer Versuch', Vierteljahrschrift fuer Sozial-und Wirtschaftsgeschichte, Band 65 (1978), pp.38-76. R.H.Dumke, 'The Political Economy of German Economic Unification: Tariffs, Trade and Politics of the Zollverein Era', unpublished PhD. thesis, University of Wisconsin, 1976.

66. Hahn, Wirtschaftliche Integration, pp.156-168. Among the perceptible economic effects of the Zollverein were the acceleration of cyclical decline in those sectors already suffering from increased competition, selective benefits for the primary sector, and a greater willingness for risk-taking among entrepreneurs.

67. Kiesewetter, 'Erklaerungshypothesen', p.352, indicates that many regions of Germany, including the industrially advanced state of Saxony, may have been more strongly affected by developments in England and other parts of Europe, rather than by internal political decisions affecting the domestic economy.

68. W.Zorn, 'Binnenwirtschaftliche Verpflechtungen um 1800', in F.Luetge (ed.), Die wirtschaftliche Situation in Deutschland und Oesterreich um die Wende vom 18. zum 19.Jahrhundert, (Stuttgart, 1964), pp.106-107. M.Kutz, Deutschlands Aussenhandel von der Franzoesischen Revolution bis zur Gruendung des Zollvereins. Eine statistische Strukturuntersuchung zur vorindustriellen Zeit, (Vierteljahrschrift fuer Sozial-und Wirtschaftsgeschichte,

Beiheft, No.61, Wiesbaden, 1974). See also B.von Borries, Deutschlands Aussenhandel, 1836-1856, (Stuttgart, 1970), which indicates that German foreign trade only grew moderately up to 1850.

69. Dumke, 'Political Economy', passim: idem., 'Anglo-deutscher Handel und Fruehindustrialisierung in Deutschland, 1822-1865', Geschichte und Gesellschaft, Vol.5, (1979), pp.175-200. For a succinct synthesis of Dumke's model, see R.H.Tilly, 'A pluralistic interpretation of German Industrialization', paper for conference on Industrialization held in Florence, 1981, pp.7-8.

70. The Zollverein, in any case, was slow to develop an effective operational mode and was not functionally complete until the final adhesion of Hamburg and Bremen between 1871 and 1888.

71. For a general discussion of Gerschenkron's propositions, see P.K.O'Brien, 'Do we have a Typology for the Study of European Industrialization in the XIXth Century', The Journal of European Economic History, Vol.15, (1986), pp.316-319.

72. Kitchen, Political Economy, pp.95,224. J.Kocka and H.Siegrist, 'Die hundert groessten deutschen Industrieunternehmen im spaeten 19, und fruehen 20.Jahrhundert. Expansion, Diversifikation und Integration im internationalen Vergleich', in N.Horn and J.Kocka (eds.), Recht und Entwicklung der Grossunternehmen im 19. und fruehen 20. Jahrhundert, (Goettingen, 1979), p.91 et seq.

73. Trebilcock, Industrialization, pp.43-44.

74. Pohl. 'On the History of Organisation', p.95. In 1887 a nominal capital of 3.8 million Marks was sufficient to bring a company into the top 100 industrial enterprises, but by 1907 the lower threshold had already risen to 10 million Marks. See H.Blumberg, Die deutsche Textilindustrie in der industriellen Revolution, (Berlin, 1965), pp.43-52., for the growth of fixed capital investment in the German textile industry.

75. R.Tilly, 'Banken und Industrialisierung in Deutschland. Qauntifizierungsversuche', in F.W.Henning (ed.), Entwicklung und Aufgaben von Versicherungen und Banken in der Industrialisierung, (Berlin, 1980), p.165 et seq.

76. H.Neuberger and H.Stokes, 'German Banks and German Growth, 1883-1913: An Empirical View', Journal of Economic History, Vol.XXXIV (1974), pp.710-731.

77. E.Eistert, Die Beeinflussung des Wirtschaftswachstums in Deutschland, 1880-1913 durch das Bankenwesen, (Berlin, 1970): idem., and J.Ringel. 'Die Finanzierung des wirtschaftlichen Wachstums durch die Banken', in W.G.Hoffmann (ed.), Untersuchungen zum Wachstum der deutschen Wirtschaft, (Tuebingen, 1971), pp.93-166.

78. Neuberger and Stokes, 'German Banks', pp.710-731.

79. R.Fremdling and R.H.Tilly, 'German Banks, German Growth and Econometric History, 'Journal of Economic History, Vol.36, (1976), pp.416-424. See also the reply by H.Neuberger and H.Stokes, 'German Banks and German Growth: Reply', Journal of Economic History, Vol.36, (1976), pp.425-427.

80. R.H.Tilly, 'German Banking, 1850-1914: Development Assistance for the Strong, 'The Journal of European Economic History, Vol.15, (1986), pp.113-152.

81. K.Borchardt, 'Zur Frage des Kapitalmangels in der ersten Haelfte des 19.Jahrhunderts in Deutschland', in R.Braun and W.Fischer (eds.), Industrielle Revolution, Wirtschaftliche Aspekte, (Cologne and Berlin, 1972), p.216 et seq. For an insight into the relative importance of self-financing for individual firms and branches of industry, see J.Kocka, Unternehmensverwaltung und Angestelltenschaft am Beispiel Siemens. Zum Verhaeltnis von Kapitalismus und Buerokratie in der deutschen Industrialisierung, (Stuttgart, 1969). A.Strobel, 'Die Gruendung des Zuericher Elektrotrusts. Ein Beitrag zum Unternehmergeschaeft der deutschen Elektroindustrie, 1895-1900', in E.Hassinger et al.(eds.), Festschrift fuer C.Bauer, (Berlin, 1974), pp.303-332. V.Hentschel, Wirtschaftsgeschichte der Maschinenfabrik Esslingen AG, 1846-1918, (Stuttgart, 1977). W.Feldenkirchen, Die Eisen-und Stahlindustrie des Ruhrgebiets, 1879-1914. Wachstum, Finanzierung und Struktur ihrer Grossunternehmen, (Wiesbaden, 1982).

82. See also Tilly, 'Mergers, External Growth and Finance', pp.629-658. The capital market may also have been an important factor in determining external growth.

83. H.Neuberger, 'The Industrial Politics of the Kreditbanken', Business History Review, (1977), p.198: Tilly, 'German Banking', p.249. Typical examples would include deep-shaft coalmining, and the introduction of the Bessemer steel-making process.

84. W.Feldenkirchen, 'Banken und Stahlindustrie im Ruhrgebiet. Zur Entwicklung ihrer Beziehungen, 1873-1914', Bankhistorisches Archiv, Zeitschrift fuer Bankengeschichte, Heft 2, (1979), pp.26-52. Idem., 'Koelner Banken und die Entwicklung des Ruhrgebiets', Zeitschrift fuer Unternehmensgeschichte, Band 27, (1982), pp.81-103.

85. Similarly in a sample of 175 businessmen examined by Visser there was an overwhelming reliance on local capital, see D.Visser, 'The German Captain of Enterprise: Veblen's "Imperial Germany" Revisited', Explorations in Entrepreneurial History, Vol.6, (1969), pp.309-328.

86. W.Feldenkirchen, 'Zur Kapitalbeschaffung und Kapitalverwendung bei Aktiengesellschaften des deutschen Maschinenbaus im 19. und beginnenden 20.Jahrhundert', Vierteljahrschrift fuer Sozial-und Wirtschaftsgeschichte, Band 69, (1982), pp.38-55.

87. W.P.Kennedy and R.Briton, 'Portfolioverhalten und wirtschaftliche Entwicklung im spaeten 19.Jahrhundert. Ein Vergleich zwischen Grossbritannien und Deutschland. Hypothesen und Spekulationen', in R.H.Tilly (ed.), Beitraege zur quantitativen vergleichenden Unternehmensgeschichte, (Historisch-Sozialwissenschaftliche Forschungen, Band 19, Stuttgart, 1985), pp.45-89.

88. Neuberger, 'Industrial Politics', p.204. Tilly, 'Banken und Industrialisierung', p.173 et seq.

89. Trebilcock, Industrialization, p.95.

90. K.H.Jarausch, 'German Social History-American Style', Journal of Social History, (Winter, 1985), p.352. R.H.Dumke, 'Clio's Climacteric? Betrachtungen ueber Stand und Entwicklungstendenzen der Cliometrischen Wirtschaftsgeschichte', Vierteljahrschrift fuer Sozial-und Wirtschaftsgeschichte, Band 73, Heft 4, (1986), pp.457-487.

91. C-L.Holtfrerich, Quantitative Wirtschaftsgeschichte des Ruhr-kohlenbergbaus im 19.Jahrhundert, (Dortmund, 1973).

92. On the mechanism of import substitution, see Rainer Fremdling's contribution to the present volume, chapter two, and idem., 'Modernisierung und Wachstum der Schwerindustrie in Deutschland, 1830-1860', Geschichte und Gesellschaft, Band 5, (1979), pp.201-227. The protective tariff of 1844 was designed, in part, to stimulate the process of technological change in the iron industry; see R.Martin, Die Eisenindustrie in ihrem Kampf um den Absatzmarkt, (Leipzig, 1964), p.21. Railway investment in the 1850s is increasingly seen as a 'cycle maker', see R.H.Tilly, 'Konjunkturgeschichte und Wirtschaftsgeschichte', in W.H.Schroeder and R.Spree (eds.), Historische Konjunkturforschung, (Historisch-Sozialwissenschaftliche Forschungen, Band 11, Stuttgart, 1980), p.22.

93. R.Fremdling, 'Germany', in P.K.O'Brien (ed.), Railways and the Economic Development of Western Europe, 1830-1914, (London, 1983), p.136; idem., Eisenbahnen und deutsches Wirtschaftswachstum, 1840-1879. Ein Beitrag zur Entwicklungstheorie und zur Theorie der Infrastruktur, (Dortmund, 1975); idem., 'Railroads and German Economic Growth: A Leading Sector Analysis with a Comparison to the United States and Great Britain', Journal of Economic History, Vol.XXXVII, (1977), pp.583-604.

94. Fremdling, 'Germany', p.139. For a comparative perspective of the social savings component in other European countries, see P.O'Brien, 'Transport and Economic Development in Europe, 1789-1914', in idem., (ed.), Railways and the Economic Development of Western Europe, 1830-1914, (London, 1983), p.10 et seq.

95. H.Wagenblass, Der Eisenbahnbau und das Wachstum der deutschen Eisen-und Maschinenbauindustrie, 1835 bis 1860, (Stuttgart, 1973). J.Krengel, 'Zur Berechnung von

Wachstumswirkungen konjunkturell bedingter Nachfrageschwankungen nachgelagerten Industrien auf die Produktionsentwicklung der deutschen Roheisenindustrie waehrend der Jahre 1871-1882', in W.H.Schroeder and R.Spree (eds.), Historische Konjunkturforschung, (Historisch-Sozialwissenschaftliche Forschungen, Band 11, Stuttgart, 1980), pp.186-207.

96. See List's firm advocacy of the need for a comprehensive network of railways for the whole of Germany, cited by W.O.Henderson, 'Friedrich List. Railway Pioneer', in W.H.Chaloner and B.M.Ratcliffe (eds.), Trade and Transport (Willan Festschrift), (Manchester, 1978), pp.136-156.

97. G.E.Voelker, 'The Impact of Railroads in the German Economy in the Late Nineteenth Century', unpublished doctoral thesis, University of Nebraska, 1970, p.37 et seq. Kiesewetter, 'Erklaerungshypothesen', pp.321-322.

98. See, for example, G.Kirchhain, Das Wachstum der deutschen Baumwollindustrie im 19.Jahrhundert. Eine historische Modellstudie zur empirischen Wachstumsforschung, (New York, 1977). R.Goemmel, Wachstum und Konjunktur der Nuernberger Wirtschaft, (1815-1914), (Beitraege zur Wirtschaftsgeschichte, Band 1, Stuttgart, 1978). The latter study provides a rigorous analysis of Nuremberg's metal industry as a local leading sector.

99. H.Marchand, Saekularstatistik der deutschen Eisenindustrie, (Schriften der Volkswirtschaftlichen Vereinigung im rheinisch-westfaelischen Industriegebiet, Neue Folge, Heft 3, Essen, 1939). L.Beck, Die Geschichte des Eisens in technischer und kulturgeschichtlicher Beziehung, 5 Vols., (Braunschweig, 1890-1903).

100. A.Milward and S.B.Saul, The Economic Development of Continental Europe, 1780-1870, (London, 1973), p.408. Total output of pig-iron also rose from 211,600 tons in 1850 to 1,391,100 tons by 1870.

101. W.Feldenkirchen, 'Die wirtschaftliche Rivalitaet zwischen Deutschland und England im 19.Jahrhundert', Zeitschrift fuer Unternehmensgeschichte, Band 25, (1980), p.95.

102. G.Plumpe, 'Technischer Fortschritt, Innovationen und Wachstum in der deutschen Eisen-und Stahlindustrie in der zweiten Haelfte des 19.Jahrhunderts', in W.H.Schroeder and R.Spree (eds.), Historische Konjunkturforschung, (Historisch-Sozialwissenschaftliche Forschungen, Band 11, Stuttgart, 1980), pp.160-185.

103. For the traditionally accepted view of the significance of the iron and steel industry in German economic growth between 1871 and 1913, see W.O.Henderson, The Rise of German Industrial Power, 1834-1914, (London, 1975), pp.140-143, 235-237 and idem., The Industrial Revolution on the Continent: Germany, France, Russia, 1800-1914, (London,

1961), passim: for more recent studies, see G.Plumpe, Die Wuerttembergische Eisenindustrie im 19.Jahrhundert. Eine Fallstudie zur Geschichte der industriellen Revolution in Deutschland', unpublished doctoral dissertation, University of Marburg, 1979. Feldenkirchen, Eisen und Stahlindustrie, passim.

104. See also J.Krengel, Die deutsche Roheisenindustrie, 1871-1913. Eine quantitativ -historische Untersuchung, (Berlin, 1983).

105. See, for example, H-J.Teuteberg (ed.), Urbanisierung im 19. und 20.Jahrhundert, (Cologne and Vienna, 1983); idem., (ed.), Homo-habitans. Zur Sozialgeschichte des laendlichen und staedtischen Wohnens in der Neuzeit, (Muenster, 1985). J.J.Lee, 'Aspects of Urbanization and Economic Development in Germany, 1815-1914', in P.Abrams and E.A.Wrigley (eds.), Towns in Societies. Essays in Economic History and Historical Sociology, (Cambridge, 1978), pp.279-294. J.Reulecke, 'Sozio-oekonomische Bedingungen und Folgen der Verstaedterung in Deutschland', Zeitschrift fuer Stadtgeschichte, Stadtsoziologie und Denkmalpflege, Vol.2, (1977), pp.269-287; idem., Geschichte der Urbanisierung in Deutschland, (Frankfurt am Main, 1985); idem., (ed.), Die deutsche Stadt im Industriezeitalter. Beitraege zur modernen deutschen Stadtgeschichte, (Wuppertal, 1980).

106. H.H.Blotevogel, 'Faktorenanalytische Untersuchungen zur Wirtschaftsstruktur der deutschen Grossstaedte nach der Berufszaehlung 1907', in W.H.Schroeder (ed.), Moderne Stadtgeschichte, (Historish-Sozialwissenschaftliche Forschungen, Band 8, Stuttgart, 1979), pp. 74-111. H-D.Laux, 'The components of population growth in Prussian cities, 1875-1905, and their influence on population structure', in R.Lawton and W.R.Lee (eds.), Comparative Urban Population Development in Western Europe, (Liverpool, 1988), in the press.

107. See K.J.Bade (ed .), Population, Labour and Migration in 19th and 20th century Germany, (Leamington Spa, 1986).

108. N.Bullock and J.Read, The Movement for Housing Reform in Germany and France, 1840-1914, (Cambridge, 1985), pp.249-276.

109. C.Wischermann, Wohnen in Hamburg vor dem Ersten Weltkrieg, (Muenster, 1983), p.82. Bullock and Read, Housing Reform, p.27. During the 1840s in-migration into Berlin rose to approximately 12,000 individuals per annum and contributed significantly to increased housing density.

110. A-F.Heinrich, 'Die Wohnungsnot und die Wohnungsfuersorge privater Arbeitgeber in Deutschland im 19.Jahrhundert', unpublished doctoral dissertation, University of Marburg, 1970. R.Kastorff-Viehmann, 'Kleinhaus und Mietskaserne', in L.Niethammer (ed.), Wohnen in Wandel, Beitraege zur Geschichte des Alltags in der buergerlichen Gesellschaft (Wuppertal, 1979), pp.272-291.

111. Wischermann, Wohnen in Hamburg, pp.152-154.

112. A.v.Saldern, 'Kommunalpolitik und Arbeiterwohnungsbau im Deutschen Kaiserreich', in L.Niethammer (ed.), Wohnen im Wandel. Beitraege zur Geschichte des Alltages in der buergerlichen Gesellschaft, (Wuppertal, 1979), pp.344-362.

113. W.R.Krabbe, 'Die Anfaenge des "sozialen Wohnungsbaus" vor dem Ersten Weltkrieg. Kommunal-politische Bemuehungen um eine Loesung des Wohnungsproblems', Vierteljahrschrift fuer Sozial-und Wirtschaftsgeschichte, Band 71, (1984), pp.30-58.

114. U.Blumenroth, Deutsche Wohnungspolitik seit der Reichsgruendung-Darstellung und kritische Wuerdigung, (Beitraege zum Siedlungs-und Wohnungswesen und zur Raumplanung, Band 25, Muenster, 1975). C.Wischermann. 'Wohnungsnot und Staedtewachstum. Standard und soziale Indikatoren staedtischer Wohnungsversorgung im spaeten 19.Jahrhundert', in W.Conze and U.Engelhardt (eds.), Arbeiter im Industrialisierungsprozess. Herkunft, Lage und Verhalten, (Stuttgart, 1979), pp.215-216.

115. House construction in the first half of the nineteenth-century was also strongly cyclical, see Wischermann, Wohnen in Hamburg, p.42.

116. See also R.H.Tilly and T.Wellenreuther, 'Bevoelkerungswanderung und Wohnungsbauzyklen in deutschen Grossstaedten im 19.Jahrhundert', in H-J.Teuteberg (ed.), Homo habitans. Zur Sozialgeschichte des laendlichen und staedtischen Wohnens in der Neuzeit, (Muenster, 1985), pp.273-300.

117. H.Boehm, Bodenmobilitaet und Bodenpreisgefuege in ihrer Bedeutung fuer die Siedlungsentwicklung. Eine Untersuchung unter besonderer Beruecksichtigung der Rechtsordnung, und der Kapitalmarktverhaeltnisse fuer das 19. und 20.Jahrhundert, dargestellt an ausgewaehlten Beispielen, (Bonner Geographische Abhandlungen, Heft 65, Bonn, 1980).

118. L.Niethammer, Umstaendliche Erlaueterung der seelischen Stoerung eines Communalbaumeisters in Preussens groesstem Industriedorf, oder: Die Unfaehigkeit zur Stadtentwicklung, (Frankfurt, 1979).

119. H.Reif, 'Staedtebildung im Ruhrgebiet - die Emscherstadt Oberhausen, 1850-1914', Vierteljahrschrift fuer Sozial-und Wirtschaftsgeschichte, Band 69, (1982), pp.485-486.

120. Bullock and Read, Housing Reform, pp.74-75, 259-276.

121. As in the case of Cologne; see K.Jasper, Der Urbanisierungsprozess dargestellt am Beispiel der Stadt Koeln, (Schriften zur rheinisch-westfaelischen Wirtschaftsgeschichte, Bd.30, Koeln, 1977).

122. Wischermann, Wohnen in Hamburg, pp.88-89. M.Gruettner, 'Die Cholera als Motor der Sozialreform? Auswirkungen der Hamburger Epidemie von 1892', unpublished contribution to the conference 'Gesundheitspolitik im 19. und Fruehen 20.Jahrhundert - Deutschland und England im Vergleich', Bielefeld, 1986.

123. Krabbe, 'Anfaenge', pp.44-54. Between 1886 and 1906 the city authorities in Ulm built 267 small-scale houses, a policy which was followed by other local authorities in Strassburg, Muelhausen and Heidelberg. The city of Munich, although initially opposed to the promotion of public house-building set aside a capital provision for this purpose of 11.5 million Marks in 1913/14.

124. See Wischermann, Wohnen in Hamburg, p.89, for the role of the powerful Grundeigentuemerverein, and Reulecke, Geschichte der Urbanisierung, Tabelle 13, p.221, for evidence of the predominant control by house-owners of individual town councils.

125. The free market continued to dominate housing provision in the case of the United Kingdom; see R.G.Rodger, 'Die Krise des britischen Wohnungswesens, 1830-1920', in H-J.Teuteberg (ed.), Homo habitans. Zur Sozialgeschichte des laendlichen und staedtischen Wohnens in der Neuzeit, (Muenster, 1985), pp. 301-331.

126. C.Wischermann, 'Changes in Population Development, Urban Structures and Living Conditions in Nineteenth-century Hamburg', in R.Lawton and W.R.Lee (eds.), The Population Dynamics and Development of Western European Port Cities, (Liverpool, 1989), forthcoming.

127. K.Borchardt, 'Wirtschaftliches Wachstum und Wechsellagen, 1800-1914', in W.Zorn et al. (eds.), Handbuch der deutschen Wirtschafts-und Sozialgeschichte, Band 2, (Stuttgart, 1976), pp.204-266. R.Spree, Die Wachstumszyklen der deutschen Wirtschaft von 1840 bis 1880, (Berlin, 1977); idem., Wachstumstrends und Konjunkturzyklen in der deutschen Wirtschaft von 1820 bis 1913, (Goettingen, 1978). W.H.Schroeder and R.Spree (eds.), Historische Konjunkturforschung, (Historisch-Sozialwissenschaftliche Forschungen, Band 11, Stuttgart, 1980).

128. R.H.Tilly, 'Renaissance der Konjunkturgeschichte?', Geschichte und Gesellschaft, Vol.6, (1980), pp.243-262.

129. G.A.Craig, Germany, 1866-1945, (Oxford, 1978), pp.452-454. W.Guttmann and P.Meehan, The Great Inflation, (Farnborough, 1975), pp.121-142. See also A.Ferguson, When Money Dies. The Nightmare of the Weimar Collapse, (London, 1975).

130. Boehme, Social and Economic History of Germany, p.106. K.Hardach, 'Germany', in C-M.Cipolla (ed.), The Fontana Economic History of Europe, Contemporary Economies, Vol.6, Part 1, (Glasgow, 1976), p.192. A.Rosenberg, A History of the German Republic, (London, 1936), p.185.

131. Boehme, Social and Economic History of Germany, p.106. Hardach, 'Germany', p.192. K.Hardach, The Political Economy of Germany in the Twentieth Century, (Berkeley, 1980), p.21.

132. Hardach, Political Economy, p.20.

133. C-L.Holtfrerich, Die deutsche Inflation, 1914-1923, (Berlin, 1980): idem., The German Inflation, 1914-1923. Causes and Effects in International Perspective, (Berlin, New York, 1986). G.D.Feldman (ed.), Die deutsche Inflation : eine Zwischenbilanz, (Veroeffentlichungen der Historischen Kommission zu Berlin, Band 54, Berlin, 1982).

134. K.Laursen and J.Pedersen, The German Inflation, 1918-1923, (Amsterdam, 1964), p.81.

135. P-C.Witt, 'Finanzpolitik und sozialer Wandel in Krieg und Inflation, 1918-1924', in H.Mommsen, D.Petzina and B.Weisbrod (eds.), Industrielles System und politische Entwicklung in der Weimarer Republik, (Duesseldorf, 1974), p.402.

136. P.Czada, 'Grosse Inflation und Wirtschaftswachstum', in H.Mommsen, D.Petzina and B.Weisbrod (eds.), Industrielles System und politische Entwicklung in der Weimarer Republik, (Duesseldorf, 1974), p.387. See H-C.Wallich, Mainsprings of the German Revival, (New Haven, 1955), p.213, who refers to high prices and rising profit expectations, particularly after the outbreak of the Korean War. Laursen and Pedersen, German Inflation, p.98.

137. Holtfrerich, Die deutsche Inflation, p.297.

138. See, for example, H.Winkel, Die Wirtschaft im geteilten Deutschland, 1945-1970, (Wiesbaden, 1974). W.Abelshauser, Wirtschaft in Westdeutschland, 1945-1948. Rekonstruktion und Wachstumsbedingungen in der amerikanischen und britischen Zone, (Schriftenreihe der Vierteljahrshefte fuer Zeitgeschichte, No.30, Stuttgart, 1975). E.O.Smith, The West German Economy, (London, 1983), pp.6-31. H.Barthel, Die wirtschaftliche Ausgangsbedingungen der DDR, (Berlin, 1979). J.Roesler, Die Herausbildung der sozialistischen Planwirtschaft in der DDR, (Berlin, 1978).

139. W.Abelshauser, 'West German Economic Recovery, 1945-1951: A Reassessment', The Three Banks Review, No.135, (1982), pp.34-53. For the issue of land reform, see G.T.Trittel, Die Bodenreform in der Britischen Zone, 1945-1949, (Schriftenreihe der Vierteljahrshefte fuer Zeitgeschichte, No.31, Stuttgart, 1975); U.Enders, Die Bodenreform in der amerikanischen Besatzungszone, 1945-1949, unter besonderer Berueksichtigung Bayerns, (Ostfildern, 1982). For refugee policy and associated issues, see F.J.Bauer, Fluechtlinge und Fluechtlingspolitik in Bayern, 1945-1950, (Forschungen und Quellen zur Zeitgeschichte, Band 3, Stuttgart, 1982); S.Schier, Die Aufnahme und Eingliederung von Fluechtlingen und Vertriebenen in der Hansestadt Luebeck. Eine sozialgeschichtliche Untersuchung fuer die Zeit nach dem Zweiten Weltkrieg bis zum Ende der 50 Jahre, (Veroeffentlichung zur Geschichte der Hansestadt Luebeck, Band 7, Luebeck, 1982). On dismantling, see D.Scrivenius,

Demontagen im Land Nordrhein-Westfalen 1946 bis 1951. Spezialinventar zu den im Nordrhein-Westfaelischen Hauptstaatsarchiv Duesseldorf vorhandenen Demontage-Akten, (Veroeffentlichungen der Staatlichen Archive des Landes Nordrhein-Westfalen, Reihe C, Quellen und Forschungen, Band 9, Siegburg, 1981). This highlights the extent to which German officials and Verbaende attempted to slow down the dismantling process and to restrict the scale of this operation.

140. H.Sauermann, 'On the Economic and Financial Rehabilitation of Western Germany (1945-1949)', Zeitschrift fuer die gesamte Staatswissenschaft, Band 135, (1979), pp.301-319. R.Krengel, 'Some Reasons for the Rapid Economic Growth of the German Federal Republic', Banca Nazionale del Lavoro Quarterly Review, Vol.16, (1953), p.122.

141. Barthel, Ausgangsbedingungen, pp.37-42. See also Gottfried Plumpe's contribution to the present volume, chapter eight. In the case of I.G.Farben, strategic bombing had only severely damaged its hydrogenation plants and the company retained approximately 90 per cent of its overall capacity intact. M.Gottlieb, 'The German Economic Potential', Social Research, Vol.17, (1950), p.77.

142. Hardach, 'Germany', p.209. For details of the Level-of-Industry Plan, see idem., Political Economy, pp.92-94. Abelhauser, 'West German Economic Recovery', p.36. By 1950 only 38 per cent of industrial plants originally designated for dismantling had actually been to some extent affected by this policy, and dismantling is unlikely to have accounted for more than a five per cent reduction in the German pre-war capital stock.

143. For a discussion of the social market economy, see G.Ambrosius, Die Durchsetzung der Sozialen Marktwirtschaft im Westdeutschland, 1945-1949, (Beitraege zur Wirtschafts-und Sozialpolitik in Deutschland nach 1945, Band 1, Stuttgart, 1977). J.Leaman, 'The "Triumph" of Ordo-Liberalism in Post-War Germany - a review of the ideological origins and development of the "Social Market Economy"', paper presented to the conference Continuity and Change. German Society in Transition to the new German States, 1945-1955, Liverpool University, 1987.

144. Abelshauser, 'West German Economic Recovery', pp.34-53. W.R.Lee, 'The economic background to post-war West German recovery : myths and reality', unpublished paper presented to the Glasgow conference on 'The Foundation and Early Years of the Federal Republic of Germany', 1984.

145. See, for example, J.Gimbel, A German Community under American Occupation, Marburg, 1945-1952, (Stanford, 1961); idem., The Origins of the Marshall Plan, (Stanford, 1976). B.Kuklick, American Policy and the Division of Germany, (Cornell, 1972). F.Roy Willis, The French in Germany, 1945-1949, (Stanford, 1962). D.Petzina and W.Euchner,

'Wirtschaftspolitik in der Besatzungszeit', in idem., (eds.), Wirtschaftspolitik im britischen Besatzungsbebiet, 1945-1949, (Duesseldorf, 1984), p.7.

146. Thus, whereas economic policy in the British Zone was handled by a central administrative agency, which finally took the form of the Zentralamt fuer Wirtschaft in April 1946, the Americans relied on a more decentralised arrangement, allowing a considerable role for the Economics Ministeries of the individual Laender; see Abelshauser, Wirtchaft in Westdeutschland, pp.74-76.

147. Ambrosius, Die Durchsetzung, passim; P.Armstrong, A.Glyn and J.Harrison, Capitalism since World War II. The Making and Breaking of the Great Boom, (London, 1984), p.80. A.S.Milward, 'Grossbritannien, Deutschland und der Wiederaufbau Westeuropas', in D.Petzina and W.Euchner (eds.), Wirtschaftspolitik im britischen Besatzungsgebiet, 1945-1949, (Duesseldorf, 1984), pp.25-40.

148. R.E.H.Mellor, The Two Germanies. A Modern Geography, (London, 1978), p.148.

149. G.Stolper, German Realities, (New York, 1948), P.14. Hardach, 'Germany', p.212.

150.T.Horstmann, 'Die Angst vor dem finanziellem Kollaps', in Petzina and Euchner (eds.), Wirtschaftspolitik, pp.215-234.

151. W.Plumpe, 'Wirtschaftsverwaltung und Kapitalinteresse im britischen Besatzungsgebiet, 1945/46', in Petzina and Euchner (eds.), Wirtschaftspolitik, pp.121-152. Abelshauser, Wirtschaft in Westdeutschland, p.37.

152. The chemical industry, for example, was dominated by corporate arrangements, as had been the case in the inter-way years; see F.Stratmann. 'Strukturen der Bewirtschaftung in der Nachkriegszeit. Bas Beispiel der Chemiebewirtschaftung in der britischen und der Bizone 1945 bis 1948', in Petzina and Euchner (eds.), Wirtschaftspolitik, pp.153-172. The predominance of small and medium-sized concerns in the textile sector, on the other hand, made effective economic planning relatively difficult; see A.Drexler, 'Wirtschaftsplanung nach 1945. Das Beispiel der Textilwirtschaft', in Petzina and Euchner (eds.), Wirtschaftspolitik, pp.173-196.

153. G.Mueller, 'Sicherheit durch wirtschaftliche Stabilitaet? Die Rolle der Briten bei der Auseinandersetzung um die Stahlquote des I. Industrieplanes vom 26.Maerz, 1946', and W.Milert, 'Die verschenkte Kontrolle. Bestimmungsgruende der britischen Kohlenpolitik im Rurhbergbau 1945-1947', both in Petzina and Euchner (eds.), Wirtschaftspolitik, pp.65-86 and 105-120 respectively.

154. V.Gollanz, In Darkest Germany, (London, 1947), pp.87,89-90,94.

155. Abelshauser, Wirtschaft in Westdeutschland, p.42. Milward, 'Grossbritannien, Deutschland', pp.25-40.

156. U. Schneider, 'Grundzuege britischer Deutschland-und Besatzungspolitik', Zeitgeschichte, Vol.9, (1981); idem. Der Kampf um Demokratisierung in Wirtschaft und Gesellschaft, 1945-47, (Hefte fuer historische Oeffentlichkeit, No. 9, Hamburg).

157. Milert, 'Die verschenkte Kontrolle', p.111.

158. A similar fear of German competition accounted for British opposition to currency reform plans; see E. Wandel, Die Entstehung der Bank deutscher Laender und die deutsche Waehrungsreform 1948. Die Rekonstruktion des westdeutschen Geld-und Waehrungssystems 1945-1949 unter Beruecksichtigung der amerikanischen Besatzungspolitik, (Schriftenreihe des Instituts fuer bankhistorische Forschungen e.V., Band 3, Frankfurt am Main, 1980).

159. The French, in contrast, had no compunction over the enforcement of strict controls of production; see Willis, The French in Germany, passim, and R. Laufer, Industrie und Energiewirtschaft im Land Baden, 1945-1952, Suedbaden unter Franzoesischer Besatzung, (Forschungen zur oberrheinischen Landesgeschichte, Band XXVIII, Freiburg, 1979).

160. Boehme, Social and Economic History of Germany, p.124.

161. This is patently the case, for example, in relation to the alleged rationale for the foundation of the Zollverein, the apparent dominant role of the banks in the German economy before 1914, and the traditionally negative view of the economic effects of post-war inflation between 1918 and 1922/23. Other cases could also be cited. Webb, for example, has recently shown that the general failure by historians to examine the exact economic effects of the return to agricultural protectionism in Wilhelminian Germany has led to an overemphasis on tactical political motives; see S.B. Webb, 'Agricultural Protection in Wilhelminian Germany: Forging an Empire with Pork and Rye', Journal of Economic History, Vol. XLII, (1982), pp.309-326, particularly, p.310.

162. Tilly, 'A pluralistic interpretation', p.28.

163. It is instructive in this context to compare the two important survey articles by R.H. Tilly; see Tilly, ' "Soll und Haben" ', pp.398-319, and idem., ' "Soll und Haben" II : Wiederbegegnung mit der deutschen Wirtschafts-und Sozialgeschichte', in idem., Kapital, Staat und sozialer Protest in der deutschen Industrialisierung, (Goettingen, 1980), pp.228-251. Dumke, 'Clio's Climacteric', passim.

164. For the value of a regional approach, see R. Fremdling and R.H. Tilly (eds), Industrialisierung und Raum. Studien zur regionalen Differenzierung im Deutschland des 19. Jahrhunderts, (Historisch-Sozialwissenschaftliche Forschungen, Band 7, Stuttgart, 1979). S. Pollard (ed.), Region und Industrialisierung. Studien zur Rolle der Region in der Wirtschaftsgeschichte der letzten zwei Jahrhunderte, (Goettingen, 1980) H. Kiesewetter, 'Regionale

Industrialisierung in Deutschland zur Zeit der Reichsgruendung. Ein vergleichend-quantitativer Versuch', *Vierteljahrschrift fuer Sozial-und Wirtschaftsgeschichte*, Band 73, Heft 1, (1986), pp.38-60. For a selection of articles on the methodological problems of pursuing the history of individual territorial states within Germany, see P.Fried, (ed.), *Probleme und Methoden der Landesgeschichte*, (Wege der Forschung, Band CDXCII, Darmstadt, 1978, and E.Hinrichs and W.Norden (eds.), *Regionalgeschichte. Probleme und Beispiele*, (Quellen und Untersuchungen zur Wirtschafts-und Sozialgeschichte Niedersachsens in der Neuzeit, Band 6, Hildesheim, 1980). Apart from a few noticeable exceptions there are still comparatively few outstanding regional economic histories of single German states, but see in particular Schremmer, *Wirtschaft Bayerns*, passim, and W.Treue, *Wirtschafts-und Technikgeschichte Preussens*, (Veroeffentlichungen der Historischen Kommission zu Berlin, Band 56, Berlin, 1984).

165. Sheehan, 'What is German History?', p.11.

166. K.H.Jarausch, 'Illiberalism and Beyond: German History in Search of a Paradigm', *Journal of Modern History*, vol.55, (1983), pp.268-284.

Chapter Two

FOREIGN COMPETITION AND TECHNOLOGICAL CHANGE : BRITISH EXPORTS AND THE MODERNISATION OF THE GERMAN IRON INDUSTRY FROM THE 1820s TO THE 1860s*

Rainer Fremdling

I

The evolution of the German iron industry during the first half of the nineteenth-century cannot be comprehended by restricting oneself to internal German developments. Trade relations to the more advanced countries have to be scrutinized in order to explain both when and how a modernised German iron industry emerged. This is the main concern of this paper.

In analysing the development of this sector in its international context an issue is picked up which Pollard raised some years ago when he argued 'that the study of industrialisation in any given European country will remain incomplete unless it incorporates a European dimension'.(1) He also emphasised Britain's role in speeding up German industrialisation by delivering cheap intermediate goods, which were worked up to final goods within Germany.(2) Pollard thus corroborated the earlier view of Bowring, who had stated in his Report on the Prussian Commercial Union of 1840 the following:

> Up to the present moment the importation of articles in the early stages of manufacture, to which more labour is to be applied in Germany, is important and increasing, and serves, to a large extent, to fill up the vacuum arising from the diminished importation of wholly-manufactured articles. The various materials, the produce of our superior machinery - such as cotton, woollen, linen, silk, and other thread - metals in the earlier stages of manipulation - in a word, articles which stand almost in the situation of *raw materials* to be used in the later stages of manufacturing industry - form a very large portion of the imports of the *Zollverein* (Customs Union).(3)

The questions raised by Pollard in his brief article were to some extent carried forward by Dumke in his empirical study on the Zollverein. By using an abundance of quantitative material he also detected that 'in the decades before 1850 [there were] important increases in net imports of semi-manufactured goods'.(4) Dumke furthermore supported Pollard's view that the threat of British industrialism for German manufacturers, as expressed by Schmoller, List and others, had been greatly exaggerated.(5) It was precisely the importation of these intermediate goods which provided the key for the entry of the new industrialism into Germany.(6) Primary iron production (7), with its output of intermediate goods, may therefore serve as an appropriate example to demonstrate the beneficial effects of international trade on the modernisation of an important industrial sector in Germany.

In describing the international context in which the modernisation of German industry took place, this article will initially concentrate on the overall development of British iron exports with special reference to Germany. The next section will examine developments within Germany and outline the growth of the iron industry from the 1820s to the 1860s on a macro-economic level. To get a better understanding of the underlying forces at work, attention will be focused on the crucial period of the early 1840s. The last section will mainly deal with the particular regional development of the iron industry in the Rhineland and Westphalia.

II

At the time of the Crystal Palace World Exhibition in 1851 British iron masters dominated the world market for cheap mass-produced iron: indeed, Britain produced more iron than all other countries taken together.(8) This supremacy was mainly based on two innovations, which had revolutionised the method of smelting and refining iron: the adoption of the coke-blast furnace and the puddling and rolling process. In Britain alone, the transition from charcoal to coke or pit-coal as a fuel had already been achieved during the 18th century.(9) By 1820, the British iron industry was not only free from any real competition in her domestic market, but was increasingly able to export much of her output abroad. From 1815 to 1830, 'exports usually amounted to between one-quarter and one-third of total output'.(10) From 1830 to 1870 exports rose dramatically from one-quarter to roughly 60 per cent of total pig-iron production.

From a British point of view, on the basis of available aggregate figures, it seems quite appropriate to conclude that British iron masters 'maintained and perhaps strengthened the strong international competitive position they had established in the early part of the century'.(11) But this conclusion, drawn by Charles K.Hyde, is supported by rather crude evidence, using aggregate export figures in relation to aggregate output figures. They inevitably conceal the considerable structural changes affecting Britain's competitive position in foreign markets, which took place from the 1820s onwards. Not only did the product-mix of British iron exports shift towards the lower stages of production (from bar-iron to pig-iron, as shown in table 2.1), but above all Britain could only enlarge her export markets, especially after 1850, by diverting her incremental deliveries from her closest continental competitors, namely Belgium, France and Germany, to less developed countries such as Russia and India.(12)

During the period in question, British producers were undoubtedly the cheapest suppliers of iron internationally, but foreign producers were protected from imports, firstly by tariff barriers, and secondly by transportation costs. As a result, foreign iron industries based on charcoal, which were doomed to extinction in the long-run, despite increasing productivity, could survive and even expand well into the second half of the 19th century.(13) On the other hand this element of protection allowed the emergence of iron industries based on mineral fuel even where natural resource endowment was less favourable than in Britain. This became evident, when railway construction in countries such as Germany led to a sharp increase in demand for mass-produced iron and a modern iron industry emerged within a relatively short period. Britain herself helped her foreign competitors to accelerate the catching-up process by delivering vast amounts of cheap coke pig-iron, which was worked up in foundries and rolling mills abroad. Britain increasingly began to lose her absolute advantage in the second stage of iron production from the 1840s onwards.(14)

The bulk of British iron exports was made up of pig-iron, bar-iron and rails. Unfortunately, British export statistics subsumed rails under the category bar-iron until 1855. In subsequent years, when railway iron was registered separately, it constituted more than 50 per cent of bar-iron exports, and presumably this was also the case in the 1840s.(15) The growth of these exports between 1821 and 1870 is shown in the last columns of tables 2.A1 to 2.A3. To analyse the pace of this growth, I calculated average <u>yearly</u> growth rates between 1821 and 1870. Whereas pig-iron exports grew by a remarkable 11 per cent, bar-iron, including rails, still achieved the impressive growth rate of nearly 7.5 per cent. Both figures are well above the average yearly growth rate of British pig-iron production, which amounted to 5.6 per cent.(16) They demonstrate quite patently the growing dependency of the British iron industry on export markets. In the long-run there were considerable changes in the overseas customers for British iron. In particular bar-iron and rail exports were increasingly diverted from the European core to the periphery and the developing world. The quantitative evidence for these changes is presented in tables 2.A4 to 2.A7 (17), although I do not propose to discuss the underlying causes at this juncture. Three important customers for British iron throughout the period 1821 to 1870 were the United States, France and the German states, including Holland which was always lumped together with Germany during this period. The high shares these countries absorbed over time are shown in tables 2.A1 to 2.A3.

The fluctuating market shares of these three major customers for British iron reveal no congruity. Even the long-term development of demand for British iron was uneven, both in relation to the prominence of individual importing countries and the balance between pig-iron and bar-iron. The main clue to the fluctuations and shifts in the composition of British iron exports must therefore be found outside Britain, as her position as lowest cost producer was already established at the beginning of this period. It is the internal development of the importing countries that has to be scrutinised for an appropriate explanation of these changes.

III

The role imported iron played in the German market may be viewed from several aspects. From the standpoint of customers for finished iron products, one could argue that these imports, mainly from Britain, but also from Belgium as well, simply satisfied demands which domestic producers could not meet, because of technological backwardness, inadequate capacity, or high prices and production costs. From the standpoint of indigenous iron producers, two seemingly contradictory points can be picked out. On the one hand, British exporters competed with German suppliers in their home markets, which might very well have threatened or retarded the growth of a modernised German iron industry in some way or other. On the other hand, British exports by and large helped to speed up the diffusion of puddling and rolling and finally of coke smelting, which promoted the long-term modernisation of the German iron industry as a whole. British iron was increasingly made by employing these highly modern techniques, and the export of coke pig-iron and puddled and rolled bar-iron thereby facilitated the process of technological diffusion. Thus the trade in goods paved the way for the technology transfer. This did not mean, however, that British achievements provided the only model for German iron masters to follow. They borrowed selectively, depending on individual circumstances, by importing, imitating, adopting, altering, combining parts of the old and new technologies and thereby improving both of them. Except for railway iron, especially rails, most of the new iron products made with pit-coal or coke corresponded to traditional indigenous products made with charcoal, in such a way that they were effectively interchangeable.

In order to understand more clearly the underlying forces responsible for the changing structure of German iron imports from Britain, and the breakthrough of mineral fuel production in the German iron industry, the period from the 1820s to the 1860s has to be divided into two sub-periods with the years 1843/44 as a watershed. The earlier period was characterised from the demand side by the start of German railway construction in the mid-1830s. By the early 1840s it was clear that traditional domestic suppliers could not respond adequately, so that foreign, particularly British, iron masters satisfied this new demand. Before 1843/44 the traditional German iron industry had not been significantly or permanently damaged by the new production methods. A contemporary slump in Britain with a collapse in iron prices, coincided with the growing ability of German iron processing plants (foundries and rolling mills) to use British-produced pig-iron as an input. The sales of traditional indigenous producers fell accordingly. Iron produced with mineral fuel not only satisfied the new demands of railway construction, but also penetrated into other markets which formerly had been reserved for charcoal iron.

Prior to 1843/44 German iron production and sales had been relatively steady, and changing market conditions, such as the price decline for iron in Britain from 1825 to 1832, had hardly affected German producers.(18) However although indigenous prices had remained stable, iron importers had reacted sensitively to British price fluctuations, the price elasticity of demand being higher than one.(19) On a micro-economic level this observation is supported by evidence from letters written to the Welsh Dowlais Iron Works, which was regarded as the world's largest factory in the 1840s and 1850s. Their agent in Hamburg during the 1820s claimed that Welsh bar-iron could only compete in Hamburg by charging significantly lower prices than the high quality Swedish charcoal iron. Prices and quality therefore determined the position of Welsh iron in the important Hamburg market.(20) The rapid rise in British prices in 1836 with bar-iron rising by over 30 per cent and pig-iron by around 50 per cent (21), brought immediate losses in British iron exports. The Goldschmidt brothers in Frankfurt wrote to Dowlais: 'We regret , that the present high price of iron in your country prevents our handling new specifications of iron, as this article is now cheaper here'.(22) Indeed during 1836 German imports of bar-iron and pig-iron from Britain dropped by more than one-half and one-third respectively.(23)

After 1843/44 the situation became more complicated. German iron processing plants had now caught up with British technology and pig-iron imports into Germany no longer depended largely on differential prices. German bar-iron production, itself heavily dependent on railway demand, now determined the level of pig-iron imports; from 1843 to 1870 the elasticity of pig-iron imports with respect to bar-iron production was above one.(24)

When German railway construction began about 1835, the domestic engineering and iron industries were scarcely capable of producing the necessary investment goods, namely rails and locomotives. This was due both to technological backwardness and to inadequate capacity. In Prussia in 1837, more than 90 per cent of pig-iron and nearly 70 per cent of bar-iron was still produced by charcoal. Throughout the first years of railway construction, foreign, namely British, suppliers dominated the market and maintained their strong position into the 1840s.(25) But gradually a process of import substitution was initiated, chiefly through the backward linkage effects of railway development. An estimate of their magnitude is shown in table 2.3. Disregarding the demand for iron for locomotives, wagons, buildings, and bridges, pig-iron consumption for rails and rail fastenings amounted to between 22 and 37 per cent of domestic production, and between 16 and 26 per cent of domestic consumption of pig-iron in Germany in the period 1840 to 1859. This is well above comparable figures for the United States and Britain.(26)

During the first decade of German railway construction, between 1835 and 1845, most rails were still imported, but by the early 1840s, import substitution had begun to develop.(27) Many iron processing plants were established applying modern British technology and existing capacity was enlarged, which increasingly enabled indigenous producers to meet railway demand for rails and other finished iron products for the rest of the decade. By the 1850s, most of the rails were produced in Germany.(28) Table 2.4 shows the rapidity of this import substitution at the level of iron processing. It took no more than two decades to reverse the balance between domestic and foreign produced rails used on Prussian railways. The German iron processing industry, which had been almost incapable of producing rolled rails at the start of railway construction, experienced an enormous development up to 1860. It successfully supplied the ever-expanding domestic market for railway iron, and also exported more iron products, including rails, than were imported.(29) During the 1860s and the 1870s, the backward linkages remained extremely important, due to the further expansion of the railway network and to increasing rail replacements.

From the 1840s to the early 1860s imports of coke pig-iron continued to play a major role. In the 1840s, the production of rails depended on imported coke pig-iron, as domestic producers could not initially meet contemporary demand. The replacement of foreign rail supplies was therefore accompanied initially by an upward shift in pig-iron imports. In general, these years witnessed a stagnation of domestic pig-iron output, particularly in the charcoal-using sector. The reason for this was that railway iron required above all the cheaper pig-iron produced by coke-fired blast furnaces. At the start of railway construction the new fuel technology was both too difficult to adapt and too expensive for German conditions. Pig-iron was therefore imported from Britain and Belgium. Not before the 1850s did the production of coke pig-iron accelerate considerably and begin to dominate this sector. The 1850s saw the Ruhr, with its coal mining and iron and steel production, emerging as Germany's major industrial area. But Belgian and British pig-iron remained competitive, so that it was still imported in large quantities.(30)

Inevitably, this catching-up of the German iron industry was to impair British iron exports. Tables 2.A1 and 2.A2 reflect the process of import substitution in Germany, and they offer some insight into the importance of the German market for British iron exports. Especially in the 1840s, when Germany experienced her first railway construction boom, vast amounts of British iron were bought. Between 1840 and 1844 Germany purchased nearly 50 per cent of all British pig-iron exports, and nearly a quarter of all bar-iron exports, including rails. The following figures indicate how critical these imports were for Germany. In 1843 Britain delivered 65 per cent of her pig-iron exports to Germany (including Holland), which equalled 55 per cent of total German pig-iron production. In 1844, 33 per cent of British bar-iron exports went to Germany (including Holland), which equalled 85 per cent of total Prussian bar-iron production.(31) These export figures were never to be reached again. In addition, domestic bar-iron was made using vast amounts of imported British pig-iron. In subsequent years Germany remained an important consumer of British pig-iron, but she purchased far less bar-iron and railway iron from this source.

At this point it is worth mentioning that the timing and rapidity of German import substitution in this sector received a strong impetus from the peculiar character of the <u>Zollverein's</u> tariff policy. The tariff on iron products clearly favoured the importation of coke pig-iron. As a raw material pig-iron was free from duty until 1843, while duties on all processed iron products were designed to protect the indigenous wrought-iron industry, including rail production. The new tariff from September 1844 onwards did not represent a break with the principle of favouring pig-iron imports, although pig-iron now had to bear a duty. Special privileges, however, were granted to Belgian producers. Whereas British pig-iron was taxed at 20 marks per metric ton, the Belgian product only had to bear half this rate. It was calculated that the new tariff on pig-iron meant a price increase for Scottish products in Cologne of roughly a quarter. The existing tariff on bar-iron and rails was increased in proportion to the higher prices domestic puddling and rolling mills now had to pay for imported pig-iron. The tariff per metric ton was raised from 60 to 90 marks.(32)

However certain contemporaries, such as Oechelhaeuser (33), noticed that the pig-iron duty did not provide adequate protection, particularly for the traditional charcoal iron industry. Even after 1844, coke pig-iron was still imported in large quantities, but now the puddling and rolling mills in the Rhineland increasingly used Belgian instead of British coke pig-iron. Table 2.5 indicates the increasing Belgian share of the *Zollverein's* total pig-iron imports.(34) In 1842/43, Belgium had a share of less than 20 per cent of total pig-iron imports into the *Zollverein*, but by 1845/53 it had reached 50 per cent, which represented more than half of total Belgian exports. Even after the loss of privileged status after 1854, Belgium was still able to compete in the German market and her share did not drop dramatically until the early 1860s.(35)

The old-fashioned charcoal sector cannot be distinguished from the new iron industry based on mineral fuel, as if there had been a clear-cut separation between the two branches. In fact the old and the new techniques were combined in numerous ways. After all, the puddling process using pit-coal had already been successfully introduced into Germany by the late 1820s, in order to refine charcoal pig-iron. German puddling and rolling mills first had to learn how to use imported coke pig-iron in combination with, and finally instead of, indigenous charcoal pig-iron. This is clearly evident in a report prepared by a civil servant in the Rhineland for the Ministry of Finance in 1843. He wrote:

> The effects of low prices for foreign pig-iron grow more and more effective as the puddling plants are learning how to treat the foreign products and depend less on domestic pig-iron... Formerly the puddling plants worked on domestic charcoal pig-iron, but now they get more and more of the foreign pig-iron... At the beginning only small quantities of the latter [i.e. foreign pig-iron] could be added to produce a medium quality of rolled iron.(36)

The use of pit-coal in the refining branch of the iron industry even helped the charcoal blast furnaces to survive a bit longer. Wood and charcoal had already become rather scarce and expensive and could now be reserved for the old-fashioned furnaces as refining was increasingly undertaken with pit-coal. The Siegerland is a good example of this complementary shift. In his statistical account of the Arnsberg district (*Regierungsbezirk*) Jacobi reported in 1855/56 that refining was dominated by puddling works in this traditional stronghold of the indigenous charcoal iron industry. By using charcoal pig-iron as an input a high quality bar-iron could be produced, which was then sold at a competitive price in relation to the products of the other Rhenish-Westphalian iron masters.(37)

IV

In the end, however, both bar-iron and pig-iron, produced with mineral fuel, came to dominate the German market. There had been three channels for the diffusion of the new technology. Firstly, puddled bar-iron was simply imported, and German customers became used to working with this new product. Secondly, the refining branches of the iron industry learned how to use pit-coal in separate steps. They applied the puddling process for refining charcoal pig-iron, and later they mixed their charcoal pig-iron with imported coke pig-iron, which produced a cheaper high grade bar-iron that could be manufactured in the traditional regions of the charcoal iron industry. Thirdly, and this occurred in the Rhineland near the Belgian border and in Westphalia, puddling and rolling mills were founded, which mainly used Scottish and Belgian coke pig-iron. Initially, they still mixed it with indigenous charcoal pig-iron to produce a rather low grade bar-iron, but finally, these mills were able to make rails, which could effectively compete with foreign products. From the early 1850s onwards, numerous coke-blast furnaces were erected in the Rhineland and Westphalia, which represented a further step towards modernisation. The existing puddling and rolling mills had no problems in obtaining their pig-iron input at cheap prices from Britain and Belgium. The last step of building up a domestic coke pig-iron industry was not therefore an essential precondition for the breakthrough of mineral fuel iron production in Germany, but simply a complementary development.

Two general conclusions might be drawn from this analysis. Firstly, the new fuel technology spread continuously and gradually, with new and old techniques being interwoven in numerous combinations. Secondly, the data presented here support the thesis that foreign trade boosted rather than hindered the modernisation of the German iron industry. Furthermore, the tariff policy of the *Zollverein* effectively helped to initiate the successful process of import substitution.

* A preliminary version of this article was first presented at the Workshop on Quantitative Economic History, KUL Leuven in 1979 and at the DFG-SSRC Workshop on German Economic and Social History, Liverpool in 1980. I would like to thank the participants of these seminars for their critical and therefore helpful comments. A preliminary version of this article was published in German as 'Britische Exporte und die Modernisierung der deutschen Eisenindustrie waehrend der Fruehindustrialisiervung', Vierteljahrschrift fuer Sozial- und Wirtschaftsgeschichte, vol.68, (1981), pp.305-324.

NOTES

1. Sidney Pollard, 'Industrialisation and the European Eonomy', Economic History Review, vol.26, (1973), p.648.

2. Ibid., p.643.

3. John Bowring, 'Report on the Prussian Commercial Union', Parliamentary Papers, vol.XXI, (1840), p.435.

4. Rolf H.Dumke, 'The Political Economy of German Economic Unification: Tariffs, Trade and Politics of the Zollverein Era', unpublished Ph.D thesis, University of Wisconsin, 1976, p.151. See also Dumke's contribution to the present volume, Chapter 3.

5. Ibid., pp.172-175; see also Richard H.Tilly, 'Los von England: Probleme des Nationalismus in der deutschen Wirtschaftsgeschichte', Zeitschrift fuer die gesamte Staatswissenschaft, vol.124, (1968), pp.179-196.

6. Recently Cain and Hopkins argued that this was already generally true for the relationship between Britain and her Continental rivals from the 1820s onwards. '... the overall tendency was for Britain to become a supplier of semi-finished manufactures, such as yarn, to her industrial rivals, especially those in Europe, thus aiding their industrialization'. See P.J.Cain and A.G.Hopkins, 'The Political Economy of British Expansion Overseas, 1750-1914', Economic History Review, vol.33, (1980), p.475.

7. The primary iron industry comprises several stages of production. One can distinguish basically between two stages. First, there is pig-iron, which is smelted from the iron ore in a blast furnace. Second, there is bar-iron or wrought-iron, which is refined from pig-iron by using either charcoal or pit-coal.

8. David S.Landes, The Unbound Prometheus. Technological Change and Industrial Development in Western Europe from 1750 to the Present, (Cambridge, 1969), p.124.

9. Harry Scrivenor, History of the Iron Trade, (London, 1854, reprinted London, 1967), pp.57,87,110 et seq. The most recent publication on the industrial revolution in iron between 1700 and 1815 is Charles K.Hyde. Technological Change and the British Iron Industry, 1700-1870, (Princeton, 1977), pp.7-131.

10. Ibid., pp.144,172. The general tendency of increasing export shares was not confined to the iron industry, see Francois Crouzet, 'Toward an Export Economy: British Exports during the Industrial Revolution', Explorations in Economic History, vol.17, (1980), pp.48-93.

11. Hyde, Technological Change, p.173.

12. Before the 1860s, Belgium was only occasionally an important customer for British iron. This changed in the 1860s. At that time, the Belgian primary iron industry (compared with the British) had comparative advantages in the second stage, i.e. bar or wrought-iron production. Consequently, Belgium then imported huge amounts of pig-iron from Britain to work it up to wrought-iron. On this see my unpublished Habilitation thesis: 'Technologietransfer in der Eisenindustrie - Britische Exporte und die Ausbreitung der Koksverhuettung und des Puddelverfahrens in Belgien, Frankreich und Deutschland', Universities of Berlin/Muenster, 1982, pp.402 et seq. This has now been published: R.Fremdling. Technologischer Wandel und internationaler Handel im 18. und 19. Jahrhundert. Die Eisenindustrie in Grossbritannien, Belgien, Frankreich und Deutschland, (Berlin, 1986).

13. The iron produced with mineral fuel at that time was not a perfect substitute for charcoal iron (that is why both Swedish and Russian charcoal bar-iron still kept their customers even in Britain). The differences in quality helped to prolong the existence of iron produced by traditional methods.

14. Britain undoubtedly was the lowest cost producer during the period in question and hence possessed absolute advantages in producing primary iron products. Transportation costs and import duties, however, changed the prices of British iron consumed abroad considerably. British producers had comparatively lower absolute advantages for bar-iron and rails than at the level of smelting iron. Transportation costs diminished these absolute advantages, and adequate tariffs were even capable of undermining Britain's competitive position in foreign markets by enabling domestic producers of bar-iron to use cheap Scottish pig-iron, while at the same time raising the prices for British bar-iron and rails above the level of indigenous producers.

15. At least a hint of its former importance within the general category of bar-iron may be seen in the figures for 1856 onwards. Exports of railway iron as a proportion of total bar-iron exports were as follows: 1856/60 64.1 per cent, 1861/65 59.1 per cent, 1866/70 69.2 per cent. Source: see tables 2.A2 and 2.A3.

16. Based on the data in tables 2.A1 to 2.A3 and on Philip Riden, 'The Output of the British Iron Industry before 1870', Economic History Review, vol.30, (1977), p.455.

17. A preliminary analysis of these data may be found in Fremdling, 'Technologietransfer', pp.59-70, 340-365.

18. Max Sering, _Geschichte der preussisch-deutschen Eisenzoelle von 1818 bis zur Gegenwart_, (Leipzig, 1882), p.41.

19. On this (with the regression results) see Rainer Fremdling, 'Die Eisenindustrien Grossbritanniens und Deutschlands als Indikator fuer Konjunkturschwankungen, 1821-1870', in W.H.Schroeder and R.Spree (eds.), _Historische Konjunkturforschung_, (Stuttgart, 1981), pp.141-159, especially p.156.

20. See Glamorgan Record Office, D/DG Letter Books, Dowlais Works, Uhthoff to Dowlais, 1822 (4) F 538-545, 1823 (5) F 269-275, 1824 (4) F 436-453, 1825 (3) F 363-374.

21. See table 2.4 in Fremdling, 'Eisenindustrien', p.150.

22. See Glamorgan Record Office, D/DG Letter Books, Dowlais Works, 1836 (2) F 246, and the previous letters F 243-245.

23. See tables 2.A1 and 2.A2.

24. See footnote 19.

25. This statement is fully supported in the statistical account of all German railway companies, given by Friedrich Wilhelm Freiherr von Reden, _Die Eisenbahnen Deutschlands, Statistisch-geschichtliche Darstellung ihrer Entstehung, ihres Verhaeltnisses zu der Staatsgewalt, sowie ihrer Verwaltungs- und Betriebs-Einrichtungen_, (Berlin, 1843-1847); furthermore see, for example, Horst Wagenblass, _Der Eisenbahnbau und das Wachstum der deutschen Eisen- und Maschinenbauindustrie, 1835-1860_, (Stuttgart, 1973), pp.23 et seq.

26. Albert Fishlow, _American Railroads and the Transformation of the Antebellum Economy_, (Cambridge Mass., 1965), p.142; Robert W.Fogel, _Railroads and American Economic Growth: Essays in Econometric History_, (Baltimore, 1964), p.132; G.R.Hawke, _Railways and Economic Growth in England and Wales, 1840-1870_, (Oxford, 1970), p.240; Wray Vamplew, 'The Railways and the Iron Industry: A Study of their Relationship in Scotland', in M.C.Reed, (ed.), _Railways in the Victorian Economy_, (New York, 1968), pp.66,74; see also Brian R.Mitchell, 'The Coming of the Railway and United Kingdom Economic Growth', in Reed (ed.), _Railways in the Victorian Economy_, pp.13-32.

27. The detailed analysis provided by Wagenblass at the level of single iron processing plants supports the results presented in this article.

28. Wagenblass, _Eisenbahnbau_, pp.85,171 et seq; see also T.Banfield, _Industry of the Rhine_, (London, 1848, reprinted New York, 1969), pp.48,236 et seq.

29. Sering, _Geschichte_, pp.292,300 et seq; for rails the relation between imports and exports of the _Zollverein_ was as follows:

		Thousands of Metric Tons	
		1860-65	1866-71
1.	Imported rails	10.2	23.6
2.	Exported rails	23.6	149.9
3.	1) as ratio of 2)	0.43	0.16

30. On the quantities of pig-iron imports versus blast furnace production of the *Zollverein* from 1834 to 1879 see Sering, *Geschichte*, pp.294 et seq.

31. These calculations are based on data in tables 2.A1 and 2.A2, and H.Marchand, *Saekularstatistik der deutschen Eisenindustrie*, (Essen, 1939), pp.115,128. Without knowing the Dutch import figures it is rather difficult to assess how much of the British iron exports went to Dutch consumers. The *Zollverein* statistics do not indicate from which country the iron was imported. However, Belgian iron exports into the *Zollverein* were recorded separately at the time when they bore a lower duty than the British exports. Thus between 1845 and 1853 pig-iron imports of the *Zollverein* not originating from Belgium made up 95 per cent of British pig-iron exports bound for all Dutch and German ports. This clearly suggests that the overwhelming bulk of these British exports was worked up in rolling mills and foundries within the *Zollverein*. A similar calculation for bar-iron (including rails) reveals that roughly two-thirds of British exports went to the *Zollverein*. But this does not mean that the remaining third was consumed in Holland. First, the British category of 'bar-iron' is a broader definition than that used by the *Zollverein*, so that the extent of British exports to the customs union is biased downwards. Secondly, and more importantly, iron of this sort served a variety of purposes, and was used in ship building, railway and house construction, and in the manufacture of nails, wire and other finished wrought-iron products. Hence, the consumers of 'bar-iron' were located all over Holland and Germany, and not concentrated in the coal fields, as were the consumers of 'pig-iron'. Moreover those parts of northern Germany not belonging to the *Zollverein* at that time probably consumed as much British 'bar-iron' as Holland. Summing up, deliveries from Britain to Dutch consumers were insignificant in the case of pig-iron, but they probably amounted to well above 10 per cent in the case of 'bar-iron'. For the basic data and sources on which these calculations are based, see tables 2.5, 2.A1 and 2.A2.

32. See R.Fremdling, 'Railroads and German Economic Growth: A Leading Sector Analysis with a Comparison to the United States and Great Britain', Journal of Economic History, vol.XXXVII, (1977), pp.595-597, and Sering, *Geschichte*, p.19 et seq. The tariff rating in this case was supposed to reflect the fact that pig-iron suffered a loss in weight of one-third when being converted into bar-iron.

33. Wilhelm Oechelhaeuser (1820-1902) was the son of a paper mill owner. He worked in his father's mill until it was closed in 1848. Before becoming mayor of the Ruhr city of Muelheim (1852-1856), he held several posts, as secretary of the German association of iron masters (Verein der Eisenindustriellen des Zollvereins) and as a civil servant in the Ministry of Commerce (Reichshandelsministerium), which was created in Frankfurt in 1848. Oechelhaeuser became a prominent figure in imperial Germany. He was chairman of the big national gas enterprise "Deutsche Continental-Gas-Gesellschaft" (1856-1890), national-liberal member of the Reichstag (1878-1893) and founder and president of the German Shakespeare Association. For details see Wolfgang von Geldern, Wilhelm Oechelhaeuser als Unternehmer, Wirtschaftspolitiker und Sozialpolitiker, (Tradition, Supplement 7, 1971).

34. See also the slightly different figures presented by Wilhelm Oechelhaeuser, Denkschrift ueber den Vertrag des Zollvereins mit Belgien und die Lage der vereinslaendischen Eisenindustrie, (Frankfurt a.M., 1851), pp.6 et seq.

35. Sering, Geschichte, p.106.

36. Staatsarchiv Muenster, Oberpraesidium 1093, F 432.

37. Ludwig H.W. Jacobi, Das Berg-, Huetten- und Gewerbewesen des Regierungs-Bezirks Arnsberg in statistischer Darstellung, (Iserlohn, 1857), pp.146-149.

Statistical Appendix ; Sources and Notes to Tables 2.A1-2.A8;

1. The iron export data are to be found in the respective yearly volume of the Parliamentary Papers. For the years from 1821 to 1870 the following issues were used to compile the time series; 1825 XXI; 1829 XVII; 1830-31 X; 1831-32 XXXIV; 1833 XXXIII; 1835 XLVIII; 1839 XLVI; 1840 XLIV; 1842 XXXIX; 1843 LII; 1844 XLV; 1845 LXVI; 1846 XLIV; 1847-48 LVIII; 1849 L; 1851 LIII; 1854 LXVI; 1854-55 LI; 1856 LVI; 1857 XXXV; 1857-58 LIV; 1859 XXVIII; 1860 LXIV; 1861 LX; 1862 LVI; 1863 LXV; 1864 LVII; 1865 LII; 1866 LXVIII; 1867 LXVI; 1867-68 LXVII; 1868-69 LVIII; 1870 LXIII; 1871 LXIII p.ii.
2. British export statistics classify countries according to the sea port a cargo was sent to. For example iron imports of the Rhineland from Britain, which were sent to the Rhine, therefore appear in the British statistics as exports to Holland. That is why Holland is always included to assess British exports to Germany.
3. British iron exports to Ireland, the Channel Islands and the Isle of Man were subtracted from the total, and thereby counted as home consumption.
4. From 1853 to 1870 exports to minor customers were not specified. In these years the percentage in tables 2.A5-2.A7 do not add up to 100 per cent.

Table 2.1 : Ratio of British bar-iron exports (1) (including rails) to pig-iron exports, 1821-1870.

Year	Germany and Holland	All Countries
1821	43.4	9.3
1830	4.8	6.3
1840	1.4	3.3
1850	0.7	3.9
1860	0.3	2.7
1870	0.3	2.0

1. The figures for bar-iron were converted by a multiplier of 1.25 to make them comparable with pig-iron. The amount of pig-iron needed to produce a certain quantity of bar-iron needed to produce a certain quantity of bar-iron is not a technically fixed constant. It depends rather on the quality of the pig-iron, the desired quality of the bar or wrought-iron, and on the efficiency of the refining and finishing process. The varying combination of these three determining factors accounts for the variety of conversion rates found in the literature. The multiplier used in this case yields a lower bound estimate of the pig-iron actually used to produce the exported bar-iron. This is a realistic conversion rate for low grade bar-iron used as rails. The conversion rate assumed by the Zollverein authorities in 1844, when they raised the bar-iron duty, was quite high, implying a multiplier of 1.5. However this would have been realistic for high grade bar-iron used as an input for wrought-iron implements.

Sources: See Appendix.

Table 2.2 : Iron production in Prussia, 1836-1965, in 1000 metric tons and per cent (produced from charcoal and mineral fuel).

	Blast Furnace Output		Bar-Iron Output	
	From Charcoal		From Mineral Fuel	
Year	1000 Tons	per cent	1000 Tons	per cent
1836	88.7		50.5	32.1
1837	99.5	90.4	58.7	31.8
1842	101.0	82.0	79.3	39.5
1847	137.9		158.5	70.2
1848	127.9	83.6	115.7	51.4
1849	117.1	73.3	107.4	62.3
1850	135.0	75.1	130.4	63.6
1851	147.8	67.9	149.5	67.6
1852	167.2	58.0	183.9	70.1
1853	210.9	56.8	209.0	73.3
1854	261.5	51.9	214.3	75.3
1855	301.4	44.4	247.5	80.9
1856	363.9	36.3	274.4	83.8
1857	397.3	30.0	282.7	87.2
1858	413.3	28.6	302.9	88.1
1859	396.9	29.1	268.3	89.4
1860	394.7	24.1	265.7	89.7
1865	771.9	7.8	403.9	>95

Sources : on blast furnace output, see Hans Marchand, Saekularstatistik der deutschen Eisenindustrie, (Essen, 1939), pp.39, 88. On output from charcoal for 1837, 1842 and 1849, see Wilhelm Oechelhaeuser, Vergleichende Statistik der Eisen-Industrie aller Laender und Eroerterung ihrer oekonomischen Lage im Zollverein, (Berlin 1852), p.35. For 1848, see E. Althans, 'Zusammenstellung der statistischen Ergebnisse des Bergwerks-, Huetten- und Salinenbetriebes in dem preussischen Staate waehrend der zehn Jahre von 1852 bis 1861', in Zeitschrift fuer das Berg-, Huetten- und Salinenwesen in dem Preussischen Staate, Suppl. to vol.10, (1863), p.85. For 1850, see Wilhelm Oechelhaeuser, Die Eisenindustrie des Zollvereins in ihrer neueren Entwicklung, (Duisburg, 1855), p.14. For 1851-1860 and 1865, see Marchand, Saekularstatistik, p.39.

On bar-iron, see ibid., p.88, 128. On output from mineral fuel for 1836, see ibid., p.37. For 1837, 1842 and 1847-1860, see Althans, 'Zusammenstellung', p.101.

Table 2.3 : Railway-derived demand for iron (in pig-iron equivalents) in Germany, 1840-1859.

Years	As percent of total domestic Production (per cent)	Consumption (per cent)
1840-1844	22.1	15.9
1845-1849	32.1	24.3
1850-1854	36.5	26.2
1855-1859	31.5	22.9

Source: Rainer Fremdling, 'Railroads and German Economic Growth: A Leading Sector Analysis with a Comparison to the United States and Great Britain', '<u>Journal of Economic History</u>', vol.37, (1977), pp.590, 602 et seq.

Table 2.4 : National suppliers of the stock of rails on Prussian Railways, 1843-1863 (in per cent).

Year	Germany	Great Britain	Belgium	Austria
1843	10.2	88.1	1.8	-
1853	48.4	51.0	0.6	-
1858	61.5	37.8	0.8	-
1863	85.4	13.3	0.7	0.6

Source: Fremdling, 'Railroads', pp.590, 603 et seq.

Table 2.5 : Belgian pig-iron exports to Germany, 1841-1856, (in tons and per cent).

	Belgian Pig-iron exports to Germany (1)	As per cent of Total Pig-iron Exports	Imports of the Zollverein from Belgium (2)	As per cent of all Imports to the Zollverein (2)	(1)
1841	1,486	8.5			3.0
1842	3,779	15.6			6.3
1843	16,318	35.7			12.3
1844	21,893	39.3			30.9
1845	13,136	30.0	12,385	57.9	61.5
1846	18,224	29.0	17,846	22.6	23.1
1847	52,724	46.5	49,270	42.9	45.9
1848	28,760	48.5	29,795	41.8	40.4
1849	24,325	55.1	21,347	51.4	58.6
1850	76,158	80.1	75,857	68.4	68.7
1851	44,633	70.2	45,839	47.6	46.4
1852	39,713	60.0	35,643	38.7	43.1
1853	49,043	48.2	46,157	46.6	49.6
1854	35,438	34.0			26.6
1855	11,808	20.6			7.7
1856	14,155	22.1			7.1

Sources: (1) Ministère de l'Intérieur, Tableau général du commerce de la Belgique avec les pays étrangers, pendant les années 1831-1834, (Brussels, 1836; 1835-1856, Brussels, 1837-1857). (2) Zollverein, Verzeichniss der Commerzial-Nachweisungen fuer das Jahr ... 1845 et seq.

Table 2.A1 : British pig-iron exports to major countries, 1821-1870, per cent and metric tons.

Year	Germany per cent	Holland[a] per cent	France per cent	USA per cent	Total British Exports tons
1821	0.00	1.32	68.10	17.14	4552.00
1822	0.00	1.24	66.07	27.97	5151.00
1823	0.27	5.07	53.07	36.45	7647.00
1824	2,72	13.56	43.72	19.79	2093.00
1825	0.36	4.64	37.67	31.99	2827.00
1826	0.00	3.61	58.31	26.45	6608.00
1827	1,85	4.71	37.76	27.73	7127.00
1828	0.53	12.78	28.35	38.50	7816.00
1829	2.67	18.08	45.07	15.04	8911.00
1830	3.49	17.04	47.58	15.58	11955.00
1831	2.52	7.63	7.22	59.42	12414.00
1832	3.19	6.85	15.94	47.34	17591.00
1833	2.77	4.81	22.77	42.15	23041.00
1834	2.95	5.62	22.55	46.64	21943.00
1835	3.01	9.12	31.58	38.81	33214.00
1836	1.80	6.07	31.65	39.28	34914.00
1837	2.05	14.79	27.26	27.56	44945.00
1838	5.35	19.85	23.60	26.18	49123.00
1839	9.09	15.88	25.21	25.63	43970.00
1840	13.06	22.64	26.18	10.42	50222.00
1841	16.74	21.09	17.22	19.35	86452.00
1842	20.07	28.45	17.57	13.95	95232.00
1843	15.40	49.13	14.30	4.62	157084.00
1844	8.53	27.61	16.10	28.53	101314.00
1845	4.84	7.73	27.51	30.36	78287.00
1846	14.71	24.95	29.49	10.31	161120.00
1847	18.23	18.95	18.75	26.88	178444.00
1848	5.08	13.09	4.40	52.42	177762.00
1849	6.79	6.90	5.90	59.58	164112.00
1850	14.18	9.26	8.28	40.31	143731.00

Table 2.A1 contd.

1851	13.49	11.24	5.99	39.70	204194.00
1852	17.77	9.62	8.40	43.36	244239.00
1853	13.22	7.06	9.54	47.51	338938.00
1854	15.67	9.08	11.42	38.89	298141.00
1855	21.86	12.55	26.80	19.91	296458.00
1856	22.33	15.18	23.77	16.37	363060.00
1857	26.05	19.81	21.17	11.08	428860.00
1858	18.76	26.78	17.26	14.08	368971.00
1859	13.45	12.26	20.74	26.86	321453.00
1860	14.33	13.88	20.05	24.35	348063.00
1861	18.28	15.13	28.69	8.61	394231.00
1862	15.88	16.74	38.90	5.05	451845.00
1863	20.28	13.21	29.99	9.51	473908.00
1864	15.76	13.09	27.97	14.73	473463.00
1865	20.33	17.66	24.82	12.39	556430.00
1866	11.56	13.97	24.89	19.32	508532.00
1867	11.98	12.10	18.44	21.18	574689.00
1868	16.87	13.61	17.10	15.59	561874.00
1869	15.84	14.55	15.14	18.64	722061.00
1870	15.79	20.82	12.27	15.13	765429.00

a) Until 1832 including Belgium.

Table 2.A2 : British bar-iron exports to major countries, 1821-1870, in per cent and metric tons.

Year	Germany per cent	Holland[a] per cent	France per cent	USA per cent	Total British Exports tons
1821	1.37	4.77	33.66	6.06	33991.00
1822	1.98	4.38	7.61	15.59	33569.00
1823	1.92	7.15	7.13	9.64	33386.00
1824	2.14	7.13	5.46	11.95	25935.00
1825	0.81	3.93	5.85	14.90	25721.00
1826	2.37	6.57	8.04	10.47	33093.00
1827	3.17	6.49	3.82	17.91	45420.00
1828	4.93	5.19	4.06	16.94	51363.00
1829	5.49	6.68	3.79	12.69	56092.00
1830	6.90	8.80	3.64	15.43	60319.00
1831	5.32	6.14	1.37	23.68	64385.00
1832	5.94	8.56	2.12	20.23	74700.00
1833	6.19	5.80	1.40	36.41	75988.00
1834	4.87	5.58	2.49	26.19	71410.00
1835	5.74	5.66	2.32	30.98	95518.00
1836	2.14	3.69	1.53	55.30	89689.00
1837	8.82	7.83	0.90	34.57	87777.00
1838	6.84	8.62	1.31	37.87	130372.00
1839	4.27	7.53	1.27	44.08	125643.00
1840	5.69	9.42	1.47	20.92	130470.00
1841	12.34	5.90	1.41	32.01	172080.00
1842	18.05	9.89	2.66	23.28	174456.00
1843	14.43	9.98	2.42	12.17	178234.00
1844	19.75	13.21	1.12	28.07	234257.00
1845	35.27	4.23	1.82	16.29	155970.00
1846	26.50	6.32	1.08	21.70	147546.00
1847	24.70	2.89	1.00	30.15	217372.00
1848	8.28	2.17	0.24	50.60	325435.00
1849	2.65	2.41	0.34	60.89	381482.00
1850	2.34	1.99	0.25	58.96	449505.00

Table 2.A2 contd.

1851	4.11	1.56	0.11	64.51	524694.00
1852	7.83	1.34	0.08	60.94	557247.00
1853	6.09	0.90	0.14	63.63	654914.00
1854	1.70	3.79	1.11	55.89	614038.00
1855	4.90	3.54	11.69	37.60	527716.00
1856	9.67	4.14	6.11	24.58	272629.00
1857	7.79	4.31	4.01	25.45	276012.00
1858	6.22	4.60	5.24	23.36	230506.00
1859	4.60	2.96	1.96	35.33	271418.00
1860	4.34	2.82	2.13	32.95	280511.00
1861	5.40	4.43	7.85	9.42	239357.00
1862	5.35	4.97	9.81	15.57	279750.00
1863	5.82	2.82	6.18	18.11	291180.00
1864	4.61	1.85	0.98	26.32	251860.00
1865	6.68	3.03	1.09	10.32	221398.00
1866	3.50	2.27	1.15	23.72	237677.00
1867	3.80	2.32	2.77	14.74	262779.00
1868	4.38	2.52	1.38	13.71	261786.00
1869	3.55	3.06	2.96	14.92	301645.00
1870	3.23	2.87	1.43	16.54	282019.00

a) Until 1832 including Belgium. Until 1855 the category of bar-iron includes rails.

Table 2.A3 : British exports of railway iron to Germany, Holland, France and the USA, 1856-1870, in per cent and metric tons.

Year	Germany per cent	Holland per cent	France per cent	USA per cent	Total British exports in tons
1856	3.72	0.96	12.15	35.77	469282.00
1857	7.78	3.49	4.19	33.65	472117.00
1858	8.97	2.42	2.62	7.03	440203.00
1859	7.88	1.91	0.81	23.80	537415.00
1860	0.88	0.27	0.00	30.44	460722.00
1861	3.14	1.16	4.63	7.52	383624.00
1862	4.41	4.09	12.60	4.99	330939.00
1863	3.27	2.73	1.51	16.34	413211.00
1864	4.12	2.42	0.33	28.21	390205.00
1865	4.88	5.20	0.00	17.04	335893.00
1866	3.10	1.33	0.00	28.19	374018.00
1867	0.98	2.85	0.00	35.17	465779.00
1868	5.77	0.83	0.00	52.35	510148.00
1869	2.16	1.46	0.00	39.20	765390.00
1870	4.31	1.55	0.00	45.90	911527.00

See note to Table 2.A7.

Table 2.A4 : British pig-iron and bar-iron exports to different countries, 1821-1835, annual averages in per cent.

Receivers	Pig Iron 1821/25	Pig Iron 1826/30	Pig Iron 1831/35	Bar-iron (including rails) 1821/25	Bar-iron (including rails) 1826/30	Bar-iron (including rails) 1831/35
Russia	-	0.0	0.1	0.0	0.0	0.2
Sweden/Norway	-	0.2	-	0.0	0.0	0.1
Denmark	0.4	1.4	3.1	0.0	0.4	1.1
Germany	0.4	2.0	2.9	1.7	4.9	5.6
Holland[a]	4.2	12.3	10.1	5.5	6.8	6.5
Belgium	-	-	(5.2)[b]	-	-	(0.3)[b]
France	56.3	43.5	22.5	12.6	4.4	2.0
Spain/Portugal	0.6	2.1	0.6	7.0	6.0	3.8
Italy/Austria	0.1	4.2	2.9	17.1	15.0	11.4
South-east Europe	-	0.2	-	0.0	0.1	1.4
Europe (Total)	62.0	65.9	42.2	43.9	37.6	32.1

Receivers	Pig-iron 1821/25	1826/30	1831/35	Bar-iron (including rails) 1821/25	1826/30	1831/35
Asia (without Near East)	1.1	2.7	1.6	23.6	24.8	18.0
Near East	0.1	0.1	0.1	4.7	6.4	6.9
Africa	0.0	2.7	5.5	3.7	3.8	3.7
British North America	5.5	3.7	4.7	5.8	4.9	6.1
USA	28.4	23.4	44.9	11.4	14.9	27.8
Central and South America	2.9	1.3	0.7	6.8	7.4	4.9
Australia/Oceania	-	-	0.3	-	-	0.4
Total(1000 metric tons)	4.5	8.5	21.6	30.5	49.3	76.4

a) Including Belgium.
b) 1833-1835, these shares are included under Holland.

Table 2.A5 : British pig-iron exports to different countries, 1836-1870, annual averages in per cent.

Receivers	1836/40	1841/45	1846/50	1851/55	1856/60	1861/65	1866/70
Russia	-	0.8	1.1	0.3	1.9	1.9	3.5
Sweden/Norway	0.0	0.3	2.3	0.9	1.8	1.8	0.2
Denmark	5.5	5.4	4.3	4.5	3.8	2.2	1.7
Germany	6.6	13.5	11.7	16.4	19.4	18.2	14.6
Holland	16.6	30.2	14.8	9.7	17.8	15.2	15.4
Belgium	8.7	1.3	0.1	0.0	0.4	1.9	9.8
France	26.5	17.7	13.4	12.9	20.6	29.9	17.0
Spain/Portugal	0.5	3.3	2.4	2.7	3.7	4.3	1.7
Italy/Austria	3.3	3.4	4.3	4.2	4.8	4.8	1.7
South-east Europe	-	-	0.0	0.0	-	-	2.0
Europe (Total)	67.7	75.9	54.4	51.6	74.2	80.2	67.6

Receivers	1836/40	1841/45	1846/50	1851/55	1856/60	1861/65	1866/70
British Asia[a]	0.5	0.7	0.4	0.5	0.7	0.5	-
Rest of Asia[a]	0.1	0.4	0.3	0.1	-	0.2	-
Near East	-	0.2	0.4	0.3	0.2	0.1	-
North Africa	0.4	0.2	0.1	0.1	-	0.1	-
Rest of Africa	0.0	0.0	0.0	0.0	-	-	-
British North America	4.9	4.3	4.4	7.6	3.6	5.3	7.2
USA	24.8	17.4	38.0	37.8	18.0	10.2	17.8
Central America	0.6	0.2	0.1	0.0	-	-	-
South America	0.2	0.4	1.4	0.5	0.4	0.4	-
Australia/Oceania	0.8	0.3	0.5	0.7	1.2	1.1	1.1
Total(1000 metric tons)	44.5	103.7	165.0	276.4	366.1	470.0	626.5

a) Without the Near East.

Table 2.A6 : British bar-iron exports (until 1855 including rails) to different countries, 1836-1870, annual averages in per cent.

Receivers	1836/40	1841/45	1846/50	1851/55	1856/60	1861/65	1866/70
Russia	0.2	4.2	3.3	0.4	0.8	2.0	4.5
Sweden/Norway	0.0	0.3	0.1	0.5	0.4	0.7	0.7
Denmark	3.7	3.9	0.6	1.1	1.7	1.7	1.4
Germany	5.6	19.6	9.2	4.9	6.5	5.6	3.7
Holland	7.7	9.0	2.7	2.2	3.7	3.4	2.6
Belgium	0.2	0.0	0.0	0.0	-	0.0	-
France	1.3	1.8	0.5	2.4	3.8	5.4	2.0
Spain/Portugal	3.1	2.1	2.0	2.5	3.1	3.9	2.1
Italy/Austria	10.0	9.5	7.8	4.7	9.7	14.4	9.5
South-east Europe	0.6	0.8	1.0	0.2	1.5	2.0	3.2
Europe (Total)	32.4	51.2	27.2	18.9	31.2	39.1	29.7

Receivers	1836/40	1841/45	1846/50	1851/55	1856/60	1861/65	1866/70
British Asia[a]	9.6	9.7	5.3	6.6	14.0	13.2	14.5
Rest of Asia[a]	1.1	0.9	0.5	0.2	1.8	2.0	1.1
Near East	3.6	2.5	2.7	0.8	3.5	3.4	3.8
North Africa	0.6	0.7	0.6	0.8	0.6	1.2	0.8
Rest of Africa	1.9	1.5	0.9	0.5	1.5	1.4	-
British North America	5.6	4.9	6.6	10.5	6.4	9.4	12.1
USA	37.6	22.8	49.9	56.8	28.5	16.2	16.5
Central America	3.1	2.4	2.8	1.0	1.9	2.0	1.2
South America	2.8	2.6	2.5	2.1	5.4	5.3	7.4
Australia/Oceania	1.8	0.9	1.2	1.3	4.3	4.8	5.0
Total (1000 Metric Tons)	112.8	183.0	304.3	575.7	266.2[b]	256.7[b]	269.2[b]

a) Without the Near East.
b) Without rails.

Table 2.A7 : British exports of railway iron to different countries, 1856-1870, annual averages in per cent.

Receivers	1856/60	1861/65	1866/70
Russia	8.8	6.1	22.1
Sweden/Norway	2.0	3.8	0.5
Denmark	0.4	2.5	1.0
Germany	5.9	3.9	3.4
Holland	1.8	3.0	1.6
Belgium	-	0.0	-
France	3.9	3.6	-
Spain/Portugal	7.1	13.5	1.4
Italy/Austria	4.7	10.6	0.8
South-east Europe	-	-	2.9
Europe (Total)	34.6	47.0	33.7
British Asia[a]	23.2	18.2	9.4
Rest of Asia[a]	-	-	0.1
Near East	0.5	0.8	0.1
North Africa	2.1	3.2	1.7
Rest of Africa	0.2	1.0	-
British North America	4.2	1.8	3.6
USA	26.3	15.1	41.5
Central America	2.0	2.2	0.5
South America	2.4	5.8	3.5
Australia/Oceania	3.9	3.8	2.2
Total (1000 metric tons)	475.9	370.8	605.4

a) Without the Near East.

Railway iron includes the following categories:

1856-1861 railway iron of all sorts
1862-1864 railway rails and chairs
1865-1870 rails and tie rods.

Chapter Three

TARIFFS AND MARKET STRUCTURE : THE GERMAN ZOLLVEREIN AS A MODEL FOR ECONOMIC INTEGRATION*

R.H.Dumke

I

Thirty-four years ago Jacob Viner could still point to the *Zollverein* as the most important example and general model of a customs union: 'generalisations about the origin, nature, and consequences of unification of tariffs tend to be based mainly or wholly on the German experience'.(1) Since then the historical uniqueness of the *Zollverein* has invited numerous comparisons with more recent customs unions, in particular the European Economic Community.(2) The historical experience of Germany created certain expectations about the economic and political consequences of the EEC, which was seen as the most significant experiment in European economic integration in the twentieth-century. Indeed, the *Zollverein* arguably provided a model for the founders of the EEC, although this hypothesis still requires basic historical research. Two questions were of central importance in the analysis of the *Zollverein* experience. First, does political integration *inevitably* follow the formation of customs unions, as the German case implies, with the *Zollverein* (1834) being followed by the foundation of the *German Reich* (1871)? Alternatively was the *Zollverein* simply an exception to the general historical rule, that political union must precede successful economic integration?(3) If the latter case should be true, then, according to James Meade in 1951 'this... should have an obvious moral for those who are interested in the present attempts to build an Atlantic Union'.(4) An exception, however important, should not form the basis for generalisation, unless it is argued that rules, especially historical ones, are there to be broken and that one should learn from previous infractions.

The present standstill in the process of European political unification and the recent 150th anniversary of the successful formation of the *Zollverein* may once again lead to attempts to learn lessons from *history*. Yet, there are weighty objections against such endeavours. First, it should be emphasised that the German union evolved in a completely different historical setting compared to the EEC. Secondly, there exist several different interpretations of the history of the *Zollverein*, which hardly permit a unified view of its causes, nature and consequences. Finally, the direct comparison is fraught with the methodological problem of characterising the *Zollverein* as a prototype or general model of economic integration by tariff unification, when it may have been simply an earlier and possibly quite different case of integration.(5)

This paper suggests that an indirect comparison is to be preferred. The key issue is the degree to which the *Zollverein* and the EEC conform to a general, theoretical and timeless model or 'ideal type' of customs unions in the Weberian sense.(6) If essential dimensions of historical reality in both cases (7) are captured by the ideal type model (8), the historical occurrences of customs unions become explicable and precise comparisons between two different historical examples become feasible. The model used in this paper is derived from several important studies of customs unions in international trade theory literature and is presented in section II. Section III provides a critical overview of existing literature on the *Zollverein*. In section IV the general model is applied to *Zollverein* data, while section V discusses the results of this comparison and focuses on the chief reasons why it is so difficult to make generalisations from the *Zollverein* experience.

II

In contrast to Fischer's case study of the *Zollverein* as a customs union, which focused mainly on its institutional and operational structure (9), the present intention is to develop and apply a theoretically consistent model of customs unions to the specific case of the *Zollverein* in order to examine its economic consequences.(10) The decisive breakthrough in the development of a general theory of customs unions was Viner's study of 1950.(11) In particular, he stressed the economically ambiguous character of a customs union, which can be viewed both as an instrument of regional free trade amongst participating members and as an additional discrimination against trade with the rest of the world. The elimination of tariffs on trade with member countries, but not on that with third countries, is a partial and discriminating step towards free trade. Moreover, the establishment of a common tariff against third countries, can further impede international trade.(12) According to Viner a customs union has both positive and negative effects on trade, production and economic welfare. The positive effect, 'trade creation', is the result of the elimination of inefficient producers in a member country by competition from low cost suppliers in other member states. 'Trade diversion', the negative economic effect, results from the displacement of imports from low cost suppliers in third countries by high cost suppliers in the protected common market. In general both effects occur in any proposed new customs union, so that the economic benefits of customs unions are net benefits only; economic welfare is raised only if trade creation exceeds trade diversion. Furthermore, it is not possible to state *a priori* which effect will predominate. Thus the key question as to whether customs unions are a step towards freer trade or higher protection, can only be examined on the basis of each individual case.

In a further paper Cooper and Massell (13) demonstrated that the economic gains from customs unions derive largely from tariff reductions, but that unilateral and non-discriminatory tariff reductions would produce better allocation and welfare effects. Consequently, free trade is economically preferable to the creation of customs unions and has the additional advantage of not requiring the cooperation of partners. Customs unions should therefore be viewed as protectionist devices for which classical trade theory can provide no rationale.(14)

Since Viner's study, further positive economic effects of customs unions have been investigated, including the possible improvement in the union's terms of trade with the rest of the world, possible economies of scale in a larger common market, and the general increase in entrepreneurial efficiency due to greater competition within the union.(15) However Krauss' general verdict on customs unions still applies: 'there is ... precious little that a country cannot do for itself that it can do better with the aid of some other country along classical trade theory lines'.(16)

If the theoretical economic gains from customs unions remain so ambiguous, are there any general economic grounds for their creation? This was the concern of an important article by Harry Johnson, who argued that the problem with orthodox trade theory was 'that it puts economists in opposition to the dominant strands in the actual policy formation of international policy'.(17) According to orthodox theory all forms of protectionism must be treated as 'irrational' or 'non-economic'. However, if political considerations are the effective determinants of protectionist policies, including the formation of customs unions, economic analysis remains useful in analysing important subsidiary questions. For example, Cooper and Massell showed that tariff protection in a customs union can generate lower allocation costs than unilateral protectionism.(18) By expanding the analytical framework to include the operation of governments, Johnson provided a rationale for protection by viewing home industrial production in less developed countries as a collective consumption good or public good, whose optimal provision can only be assured by the state.(19)

Equally relevant to the present analysis is Cooper's (20) discussion of the optimal size of economically integrated regions, whether tariff unions, free trade areas, or monetary unions.(21) Like Johnson, he saw the reason for larger economic regions in the provision of an optimal amount of public goods, which can only be provided by governmental jurisdictions of different size. Among the determinants of the optimal size of a region or a governmental jurisdiction are (a) economies of scale in the provision of public goods and in governmental administration, (b) external effects, (c) the source of macro-economic disturbances (whether from within or without the planned region) and (d) the relative diversity of political preferences in a planned integrated region (the more diversity, the greater the difficulty in harmonising internal policies). Because different public goods require differently sized optimal jurisdictions, there can be no general optimal size for all governmental tasks; therefore there is no general optimal size for an integrated region. One of the central aspects of Cooper's interpretation, as applied to the EEC (22), is that economic integration involves a change in governmental jurisdictions and therefore is essentially a political process. Balassa has also argued that 'economic integration ..... appears as part of a political process the final outcome of which is determined by essentially political factors'.(23)

The outlines of the following economic model of the nature, causes and consequences of customs unions are clear and consistent: customs unions are not generally the result of economic calculations, nor do they have clear welfare effects. According to Krauss, 'the failure of economists to develop a general argument for customs unions on economic grounds, reinforces the validity of the Vinerian approach that customs unions are best viewed as non-economic institutions'.(24) It therefore makes sense to analyse them, like Cooper, using criteria derived from the economic theory of the state. Within this context of governmental and political decision-making, customs unions have the character of a positive-sum game among partner countries. A central argument of the analysis will be that customs unions can be created as acts of international cooperation and that their establishment does not necessarily require the political pressure of a hegemonic power (zero-sum or negative-sum games).

Given that customs unions are principally political institutions, it is not surprising that the estimated economic gains of the EEC and other customs unions have been relatively small. According to Krauss, 'empirical estimates of (the welfare gain) have run as low as one-twentieth of one per cent of GNP for the entire European Economic Community', while Miller-Spencer estimated the welfare gain of Britain's entry into the EEC from trade creation as one-tenth of one per cent of British GNP.(25) Denison's calculations of the contribution to the economic growth of EEC member states due to the initial elimination of trade barriers between 1955 and 1962 confirm this impression: average French growth was raised by 0.06 per cent per annum, that of Germany by 0.15 per cent, the Netherlands by 0.21 per cent and Italy by 0.16 per cent.(26) The EEC reality, therefore, conforms well to the customs union model developed above.(27)

This is not quite the case, however, with the Central American Common Market of the 1960s established between five small developing countries (Guatemala, El Salvador, Honduras, Nicaragua and Costa Rica), where the economic gains were significantly larger. Cline calculated that the welfare gains were approximately four per cent of Gross Domestic Product annually.(28) This higher economic gain can be attributed to the fact that market forces and prices in Central America did not fully reflect existing relative scarcities, as they did in the more developed EEC states. This, in turn, points to a number of new economic effects from the formation of customs union, which are potentially more significant than the usual effects of trade creation and beneficial economies of scale. In developing countries the economy is characterised by high levels of unemployment, underemployment of labour and capital, and foreign exchange constraints. Thus, distorted market prices do not reflect the relative scarcities of factors of production and of commodity imports. The opportunity costs of labour are lower than the prevailing wage rates, the cost of imported manufactures does not reflect foreign exchange scarcity and new investments occur too hesitantly, given that profit rates far exceed the cost of capital. In such a scenario trade diversion could be a rational economic policy, because the elimination of imports through new investment in manufacturing plant would save scarce foreign exchange, employ labour and utilise underemployed capital. However despite important economic gains from the Central American Common Market, war later broke out between El Salvador and Honduras and the latter country withdrew from the union protesting an inequitable distribution of regional gains.

Customs unions between developing countries should therefore be evaluated differently from those between developed economies.(29) Dynamic gains may well be more important in the former context and the impact of their geographical distribution on development disparities (30) within the union is politically sensitive. Such disparities can result in political tensions which threaten the existence of the union. These points should be kept in mind when the historical case of the Zollverein is assessed.

III

In the context of contemporary customs union theory and practice it is surprising to note that the traditional historiography of the Zollverein has continuously stressed its highly dramatic consequences. The combination of two separate historiographical traditions has produced a general interpretation of the Zollverein's history which presents it as a causal nexus (31) between German industrialisation and subsequent political unification. The Zollverein seems to have had a great impact on economic growth and significant long-term effects on political integration. One interpretive tradition was initiated by Friedrich List (32) and developed by Gustav Schmoller.(33) It has become a central trend in contemporary economic history textbooks in both the Federal Republic and in the Democratic Republic of Germany, as in works by F.Luetge (34) and H.Mottek (35). In this view the Zollverein brought about a necessary degree of protection against overwhelming British industrial competition and created a large sheltered market for German producers. It initiated German industrialisation by means of a protective umbrella for its infant industries.

But was German industrialisation decisively promoted by the Zollverein? Did the nature of Anglo-German trade have only negative consequences for the 'German' economy? Does German industrial take-off start in 1834 with the creation of the Zollverein, as Mottek (36) and Hoffmann (37) have argued? Indeed, in dealing with these central questions, a number of economic historians have been developing a more critical stance towards the Zollverein for some time. Already in 1920 A.Sartorius von Waltershausen stressed that its economic gains were not as 'transparent as the financial ones and they did not come forward so quickly in later years'.(38) J.H.Clapham also warned against a 'fallacious' argument: 'Men have often attributed economic results to the Zollverein, of which it was not really the cause .... Post hoc, ergo propter hoc. Germany began to prosper about 1835; therefore the events of 1834 caused her prosperity. The fallacious argument slides easily'.(39) The posited negative effect of British industrial competition has been questioned in newer studies by Tilly (40), Pollard (41) and Dumke (42), who see it as a positive factor in initiating German industrialisation. Finally, a number of important studies tend to support Rostow's take-off periodisation and place this important stage of German industrialisation either during the railway boom of the 1840s, or after 1850.(43) It is not my intention to argue that the Zollverein failed to provide any economic gains whatsoever but the traditional interpretation of its significance clearly needs a rigorous examination, and a detailed analysis of its economic effects is provided in section IV.

Some economic historians, however, have viewed the customs union more as a political act, than a purely economic measure with largely economic consequences. Milward and Saul have argued that 'the creation of the Zollverein depended more on political pressures than on economic ones and the long history of its successful completion is more meaningfully told by historians of diplomacy than by economic historians'.(44) This assessment also reflects the second historiographical tradition, which sees the Zollverein as a far-seeing act of Prussian diplomacy and political power. In H.von Treitschke's influential teleological vision of German history the Zollverein was the harbinger of Bismarck's Reich, and already at its inception, 'the thunder of the battle of Koeniggraetz ..... resounded from afar'.(45) This interpretation could also be properly viewed as part of the 'Hohenzollern Legend', which originated in the treatment of Prussian political and military history and was then applied to the domain of economic history.(46) Although Krueger has criticised remnants of this tradition in his analysis of Prussian industrial policy, it still seems to influence contemporary interpretations of the Zollverein. According to Huber (47) and Boehme (48) the customs union is still to be seen as part of Prussian economic power politics designed to enhance its economic dominance and political influence in German affairs.

One problem with such views is that possible long-run economic effects are implicitly used to explain the beginnings of the customs union. The standard marxist treatment of the Zollverein makes the same type of mistake, and assumes that later political and economic constellations already existed at its inception. Engels' thesis (49), that the customs union was one of the most important concessions by semi-feudal governments to the rising bourgeoisie, suffers from a lack of internal consistency. How can an influential national bourgeoisie arise before the creation of a national market? It is doubtful, in any case, whether the German bourgeoisie made its debut as a class so early in the century. Both marxist and conservative historians, like von Treitschke, seem to be writing the history of the Zollverein from an exclusively retrospective point of view. It is a problem common to such 'backward-looking historians', as Oncken said of Treitschke, that they see 'the path to economic union as the first step, even the decisive preliminary step towards the formation of political union'. And it is precisely this interpretation that Oncken warned against: 'One will certainly have to curtail such notions in the search for an interpretation of the sense of German history'.(50)

The central themes of traditional historiography which envisage a causal link between German industrialisation and a Prussian-dominated German Empire, have given rise to an unacceptable and limited interpretation of the Zollverein.

More recent studies, however, have broken out of the confines of traditional historiography and sought other reasons for its creation. Henderson's important comprehensive treatment of the Zollverein is useful in this context. In his view it represented a difficult compromise between the participating German states: 'The states concerned fought for their own narrow interests and many of them joined the Zollverein only when economic depression and empty exchequers made further resistance to Prussia impossible'.(51) Fischer has also argued that the customs union is to be seen 'not as the glorious beginning of a glorious history, but as a system of expedients set up to meet urgent needs'.(52) Since the Zollverein included a large number of states with rather different political, social and economic conditions, Berding has argued for a more differentiated analysis of its foundation: 'Conflicting political goals, economic interests and fiscal requirements have all .... influenced the decision to join in each case, although at times with a very different emphasis'.(53) The important recent investigation of the Zollverein viewed from the experience of the Hessian states by Hahn has pinpointed a variety of determinants:

> Within the Hessian states the decision to join was as a whole more the result of pressing economic and fiscal difficulties, which were recognised by both the conservative side and the liberal opposition, than the result of far-reaching political calculations by the traditional elites or a concession to a rising bourgeoisie which had sworn to follow a programme of economic nationalism à la List.(54)

These interpretations all proceed from the correct postulate that the Zollverein should be analysed within the context of the contemporary political economy, and not from a retrospective standpoint. It might well be desirable, as Berding has argued, to produce a separate analysis for each Zollverein state, but a general interpretation is also clearly necessary. Indeed, such an analysis can already be undertaken through the application of a theoretical model to the specific historical case of the customs union as a whole.

IV

The examination of the Zollverein on the basis of the general customs union model outlined in Section II, required a substantial amount of data on the volume and structure of its international and internal trade, on tariff levels and revenues, production and investment, and contemporary national income estimates. Important investigations by Kutz (55) and von Borries (56) have estimated the level and structure of

'German' international trade before the creation of the *Zollverein* and the latter's external trade during its first twenty years of operation. Ohnishi (57) and Freymark (58) have provided important data on the structure of Prussian-German trade in the 1820s, and Dumke (59) has presented a table of the *Zollverein's* internal (north-south) trade in 1837. Production and investment time series for the cotton textile sector, which was of central economic importance during this period, have been estimated by Kirchhain.(60) Calculations of Prussian per capita income by Dieterici (61) and Hohorst (62), as well as a per capita income estimate for the customs union in 1837 by Dumke (63) have also been utilised, together with the estimated average *ad valorem* tariffs in the southern and northern *Zollverein* states before 1834.

Although this data base is fragmentary, it allows, nevertheless, an analysis of the static welfare gains derived from the formation of the customs union by the southern German states and by the union as a whole in the year 1837.(64) Only an abridged form of the analysis, however, can be presented here.(65) We start with some basic economic facts: that the northern *Zollverein* member states (Prussia, Saxony, the Thuringian and Hessian states) together formed a substantially larger economic unit than the southern member states (Bavaria, Baden, Wuerttemberg) and that the North had an international and interregional comparative advantage in the production and trade of final manufactured goods, as indicated by the structure of exports to the rest of the world and to the South. Moreover, the *Zollverein* as a whole also enjoyed a comparative advantage in final manufactured goods.(66) It was assumed that trade with the North formed the preponderant part of the South's total trade, and, on the basis of internal trade data from 1837, that southern exports to the North mainly consisted of primary products. Now, in every union between a small and larger economic unit, the smaller partner gains the chief advantage, as its terms of trade improve due to the elimination of import tariffs by the larger partner in what constitutes the former's major export market. Consequently, the smaller partner can take advantage of the structure of relative prices which characterise the larger partner's markets, which it cannot normally influence significantly because of its modest economic size. Because the larger partner's major export markets lie in the rest of the world, tariff elimination by the small unit has no significant impact on the former's terms of trade. In this form of customs union, the larger partner achieves no gains: its internal and external terms of trade remain unchanged and it must even accept the loss of tariff revenues. The creation of such a customs union is, then, a redistributive act, as the smaller partner's static gains are largely neutralised by the larger partner's losses. Although the calculation was designed to produce a maximum potential welfare gain, the result indicated a relatively modest static welfare gain for the South. Its income increased at most by 4.9 million Prussian thaler, or about one per cent of south Germany's income in 1837. This was due almost exclusively to an improvement in its terms of trade, brought about by the elimination of Prussian-Hessian tariffs on imports from the South. This figure is very similar to that obtained by Huertas in his analysis of the Austro-Hungarian customs union, which revealed an increase of 1.2 per cent in Hungarian real income as a result of the elimination of Austrian tariffs on Hungarian products.(67)

What were the dynamic gains in the case of the Zollverein? Did it further the establishment of large factories, raise the degree of mechanisation and accelerate industrialisation in its member states? Thieriot (68) and von Viebahn (69) claimed such positive effects for Saxony and Prussia and according to Wysocki, 'South Germany's rise to a centre of the cotton industry is difficult to conceive without the Zollverein'.(70) During the 1830s and early 1840s this was the most rapidly mechanising sector in Germany, and if its growth can be assigned to the custom union's creation, how large was the initial dynamic gain between 1834 and 1842? The requisite production and investment data were estimated by Kirchhain (table 3.1).(71) Between 1830 and 1842 the level of gross investment did not rise significantly, although value added rose by about five million marks (three marks = one Prussian thaler) and the employment level increased by about 5,000 persons. If we assume that the rise in value added generated by this trade would not have occurred without the customs union, the apparent 'dynamic gains' from the Zollverein amounted to 1.66 million Prussian thaler.(72) These were probably the result of economies of scale in the larger market or, as Cline argued in the case of Central America, of the use of underemployed capital and unemployed labour. Welfare gains might well have been significant in a second non-traditional area. The potential employment effect of the Zollverein, or the increase in wage payments to previously unemployed workers could well have been substantial, given the evidence of underemployment in the early nineteenth-century German economy. Was the rise in employment in the cotton weaving sector attributable to the Zollverein? The increase in wage payments in this sector was more substantial than the previously calculated economic gains: between 1830/31 and 1839/41 they increased by about 6.66 million thaler and the number of workers by 84,000.(73) Yet the assumption that the expansion of the cotton weaving sector increased total labour incomes and employment by these amounts is questionable. The growth of this particular sector caused significant additional employment problems in less mechanised traditional textile branches, such as the linen industry, where domestic or proto-industrial production was still predominant. The growth of the cotton textile sector in Prussia, Saxony, Wuerttemberg and Baden was accompanied by de-industrialisation in other textile sectors in the same states. Indeed the existence of a substantial proto-industrial sector meant that the Zollverein's employment effects were noticeably different from those calculated by Cline in the Central American case. The sum of the static and dynamic welfare gains may well have been positive and have increased real incomes in south Germany. However it is questionable whether they were a decisive contribution to the region's economy. Recent regional studies of industrialisation for Wuerttemberg by Loreth (74) and Megerle (75), and Hahn's study of the Hessian states, indicate that industrial take-off in these regions only occurred decades after the 1830s.

The relatively small size of the estimated static and dynamic welfare gains from the Zollverein in its first eight years of operation is a result which accords well with the general customs union model. If the Zollverein did not generate significant economic gains, possible political consequences need to be considered in order to assess its actual nature. Once again it is important to consider whether the larger integrated area of the Zollverein constituted an optimal governmental jurisdiction. Did it result in possible economies of scale in public administration? Did it eliminate negative external effects which emanated from smaller governmental jurisdictions? The key governmental activity, which needs to be analysed in its different aspects is the taxation of foreign trade as a source of government revenue. This gives rise to a number of relevant questions. Were there economies of scale in tariff administration for revenue purposes and did revenues, net of collection costs, rise with an increase in the unit size of tariff administration? Were negative external economic effects due to the operation of numerous smaller tariff units eliminated by the customs union? Did it dampen or eliminate sources of macro-economic instability? Was the optimum tariff unit size determined by the difficulty in harmonising divergent regional views on tariff levels and structures? In other words, did problems in tariff policy harmonisation effectively limit the size of a potential tariff union?

The idea that a larger tariff region could achieve disproportionately higher net revenues was first systematically discussed by Ludwig Kuehne (76) in the context of contemporary German customs areas. He established a rule according to which the costs of customs administration rose proportionately with the length of the customs borders, and revenue increased proportionately with the size of the enclosed customs area. Given the high cost of border patrols in an age of extensive smuggling, the first part of Kuehne's rule is quite reasonable. If differences in per capita income levels, economic structure, population density, and tariff levels are ignored for the moment, then the size of the customs area would provide a proxy for the level of taxable imports. Thus the ratio of the border length of a customs area to its actual size, provides a reasonable index of its relative tax efficiency. Following a geometric law, this index of tax efficiency falls with a decline in the size of a customs administration, indicating economies of scale in the administration of a customs area. Table 3.2 provides data on the relative tax efficiency (actually, its inverse) of different customs areas at the time of the Zollverein's formation and compares these with actual administration costs as a percentage of tariff revenues. The simple border length-customs area ratio emerges as a good predictor of the actual cost ratios. It is also interesting to note that most of the German states in the early nineteenth-century were too small for the establishment of an independent border tax system as a sensible source of government revenue.(77)

The result of the unification of these states in a larger customs area was an increase in net revenues. This was due to several reasons. The optimal height of a revenue tariff could only be achieved by a union of small states. Given that the bulk of tariff revenues was derived from the taxation of colonial goods (particularly tobacco, coffee and sugar), imports and transit goods, an isolated increase in tariff levels by a typical small German state would lead to revenue losses, because trade flows would be diverted to other German states. This risk of diversion was least for the largest state, Prussia, which straddled most of the access routes between the port cities and the German hinterland. Thus, Prussia could afford to impose the highest tariffs on such goods in Germany, at a level that smaller states could not replicate. By joining the Prussian customs area and accepting the higher Prussian tariff as the common tariff, these states could now impose higher tariffs than before the union. The possibility of increasing revenue tariffs to optimal levels within the customs union, therefore, must be seen as another instance of economies of scale in public administration, in addition to the economies which involved cost reductions and net revenue maximisation. Because the ratio of border costs to customs area declined in the Zollverein, the costs of revenue collection also declined. However there was a double cost reduction involved in its creation because before 1837 there had been common interior customs borders guarded from both sides. Kuehne calculated that the Prussian customs borders in 1819 had a length of 1,073 Prussian miles [1 Prussian mile = approximately 7.5 kilometers] in comparison with the Zollverein's 1,064 miles in 1836. The customs union eliminated 781.5 miles of guarded borders, increased the customs area by 605.9 square miles and its tax efficiency was therefore greater than that of Prussia.

The impact of higher average tariff levels and lower operating costs on the finances of smaller member states was highly significant (table 3.3). During the first half of the nineteenth-century rising tariff receipts were the most important source of revenue increases in all German states. Without the customs union such revenue gains would not have been possible, except in a modest fashion for Prussia. In the case of the Hessian states the dramatic increase in tariff revenues before 1848 highlights the fundamental importance of the Zollverein.(78) Indeed, certain contemporaries were well aware of this fact, and H.L.Biersack, the director of customs for Hesse-Darmstadt, wrote in 1850, that 'the favourable financial results of the Zollverein should be seen as one of its most important and secure bonds'.(79)

The Napoleonic Wars and the Congress of Vienna had led to an epochal reorganisation of German territories and a massive reduction in their number to 39 new states. Their further political integration proved to be a fundamental problem of the early nineteenth-century. It was partly resolved by the establishment of central bureaucracies and the creation of parliaments with severely limited powers on the model of 'monarchic constitutionalism'. These new states faced the problem of carrying the increased costs of the bureaucracies and the heavy burden of war debts. Borchard (80) analysed the financial problems of the new states and showed how they attempted to solve them by new and increased taxes. The establishment of new border taxes on trade was part of the creation of a more modern form of government, as Ohnishi has shown in the case of Prussia. But the introduction of border taxes resulted in a chain reaction, because neighbouring states were directly affected. Consequently, Berding argued, 'in order to eliminate the unintended secondary effects, larger unified trade and customs regions, beyond the borders of the sovereign individual states, needed to be formed and jurisdictional rights had to be transferred to a supranational institution'.(81) This quote directly addresses the second part of the optimal jurisdiction argument: that the Zollverein eliminated negative external effects of individual government action. This argument was also part of Friedrich List's famous petition for the first Union of German Merchants and Manufacturers, presented to the German Federal Assembly on 20 April, 1819:

> Thirty-eight customs boundaries cripple inland trade, and produce much the same effect as ligatures which prevent the free circulation of the blood. The merchant trading between Hamburg and Austria, or Berlin and Switzerland must traverse ten states, must learn ten customs tariffs, must pay ten successive transit dues. Anyone who is so unfortunate as to live on the boundary line between three

> or four states spends his days among hostile tax gatherers and customs house officials; he is a man without a country.(82)

This aptly characterises the situation of many residents of the centrally located Hessian states who, not surprisingly, expected a larger customs area to lead to the elimination of burdensome intra-German customs barriers.(83) The very geographical complexity of the German states, with numerous small and sizable territories interlocked in an intricate pattern, exacerbated the negative external effects of unilaterally established border tax systems, which invariably involved a decrease in the income of other German states. Irrespective of the internal reasons behind new revenue tariffs or higher protection against British industrial imports, they had an adverse effect on other sovereign territories. Static welfare losses, however, also included the deterioration in the terms of trade of smaller, more open states, induced by larger customs areas (as in the case of the Prussian tariff of 1818), as well as welfare losses which arose out of delays in the movement of commodities occasioned by the very existence of numerous customs borders. While the latter costs were eliminated by the *Zollverein* with a resultant increase in overall welfare, this was not true in the former case. The individual static welfare effects cannot be added up, because they largely involved a redistribution of income between the German states, as was evident in the earlier discussion of the *Zollverein's* impact on South Germany. However, further so-called 'dynamic' external effects need to be taken into consideration.

The third part of the debate as to whether the customs union was an optimal jurisdiction concerns the insurance effect of a larger economic union in contrast to the instability of disunited smaller members. There are two aspects to consider. First in relation to the type of tariff utilised by the *Zollverein*, and its specific duties on import categories by weight rather than value, a decrease in the price of manufactured imports due to cyclical trends in more advanced industrial economies, particularly in Britain, would have produced an automatic increase in *ad valorem* duties. Thus, the effect of foreign business cycles would have been dampened by the *Zollverein's* tariff. The second aspect concerns the widely shared view that the higher level of tariffs on industrial goods by the customs union enhanced the economic stability of the German economy. This is a central argument in J.H.Thieriot's contemporary study, which claimed that the union diminished the influence of large 'commercial crises' (84) and augmented the inclination of factory owners to invest in fixed capital, in buildings and machines, because of a decline in investment risks.(85) He argued that 'the stable element of the Zollverein (established) the core, ... out of which the thriving development of native industry (evolved)'.(86) This is a reasonable, if largely untested, hypothesis relating to the dynamic effects of the union. I have already attempted to quantify the dynamic welfare effects in relation to the cotton industry. More significantly, for the years before 1834, the investment climate in Germany was more likely to have been affected by intra-German tariff changes and tariff wars than by possible external instability, such as the 'commercial crises' emanating from Britain. Because customs segmentation had possible negative effects on investment, new border tax systems invariably produced unintended secondary effects, which also affected future incomes. The elimination of customs segmentation by the Zollverein thus resulted in what could be termed dynamic external effects.

The optimal size of a governmental jurisdiction also depends upon the diversity of political preferences within a proposed union. The questions which concern us here are whether differences in the desired tariff levels between individual German states prevented a full tariff harmonisation - the choice of a common tariff - amongst a larger number of territories and, what factors prepared the way for tariff policy harmonisation within the Zollverein? As a matter of fact, the north German territories of Hanover, Brunswick, Oldenburg, the Mecklenburg duchies and the Hanse towns which were more inclined towards free trade, did not originally join the customs union because its tariffs were too high. The economic integration of all German states could not be realised in 1834 because of important policy differences. Nor did the proposal to establish a more protectionist German customs union in the revolutionary years of 1848/49 realise this great nationalist goal.(87) In contrast, the Zollverein tariff of 1834, which was basically the same as the Prussian tariff, did not differ significantly from the tariff preferences of its most important members. Heinrich von Treitschke argued that the Prussian tariff of 1818, which helped unite that country economically, was an important compromise between the divergent economic interests of eastern agrarians and western industrialists. For this very reason it appeared suitable for adoption by the Zollverein states in the early 1830s, as they were faced with the same problems that had confronted Prussia in 1818.(88)

However, the Middle German Commercial Union of 1828 to 1833 (89), which was established for a short period following the more protectionist customs unions between Prussia and Hessia (1828) and Bavaria and Wuerttemberg (1828), indicated that there continued to exist important and widely held preferences for low tariffs, especially by the smaller middle German states. Such a policy furthered the interests of merchants more than those of manufacturers. This split within the German bourgeoisie threatened the establishment of the Zollverein and thwarted the proposed protectionist customs union in 1848/49.(90) The switch of allegiance by a few centrally located middle German states shortly after the union's foundation was not the result of a change in tariff preferences, although a shift towards the interests of manufacturers was evident in the case of the Kingdom of Saxony.(91) The main reasons why a number of smaller middle German states joined the Zollverein were the necessity to fill empty state coffers and the desire to avoid an economically awkward geographic location surrounded by numerous customs borders.

Let us now summarise the arguments relating to the applicability of the optimal jurisdiction concept to the Zollverein. Firstly, the existence of similar tariff policies in a few of the larger key founding members before 1834 (92) facilitated tariff harmonisation in the union. Secondly, negative economic externalities, generated by the existence of numerous separate revenue tariffs within Germany, were eliminated. Customs disunity had previously increased trading costs, led to a noticeable deterioration in the terms of trade of smaller, centrally located states and increased economic instability and investment risks, particularly for smaller territories. Thirdly, the most visible advantage of the Zollverein was that it created for some of the smaller states a new and more efficient revenue source, due to increasing economies of scale in customs administration and the adoption of an optimal tariff for revenue purposes. Throughout its existence, union members, except Prussia, gained significantly from increased tariff revenues, net of collection costs. Consequently, it can be viewed as an 'optimal jurisdiction' for the purposes of taxing foreign, especially colonial, trade. Since all the basic characteristics of the general customs union model can be found in the historical case of the Zollverein, it should therefore be seen primarily as a political phenomenon, whose foundation and continued existence can be better understood within a political framework.

It is interesting to note that the 'optimal jurisdiction' approach emphasises the same types of argument which Davis and North developed in their theory of institutional change (93) as applied to American economic history. This is not surprising, since both concepts utilise basic elements from the economic theory of the state.(94) According to Davis and North, new institutions, in general, are innovations with certain economically advantageous characteristics:

> The innovation of a new institution can permit the capture of potential increases in income arising from externalities, economies of scale, risk and transaction

> costs when this income cannot be internalised within the existing institutional structure. Moreover, ... the choice between levels of institutions ... is dictated by the costs and revenues associated with each alternative. (95)

'Transaction costs' in a customs union framework refer to the costs of harmonising tariffs among prospective members. The arguments connected with the theory of institutional change are therefore essentially the same as those previously discussed in relation to the creation of the *Zollverein* as an 'optimal jurisdiction' for revenue purposes.

V

The notion that the *Zollverein*'s foundation can best be understood as a political *decision* to tap a new source of government revenue, was incorporated into an earlier discussion paper (96), which utilised the economies of scale argument implicit in the theory of institutional change. This conclusion contrasted markedly with existing interpretations of the customs union, which emphasised its economic consequences or viewed it as the result of Prussian hegemony in German affairs. By applying elements of the theory of institutional change, this approach anticipated later developments in the analysis of economic integration. This paper has attempted to utilise additional arguments from both the theory of institutional change and the concept of 'optimal jurisdiction'. It therefore provides a more complete interpretation of the *Zollverein*'s development.

This interpretation *provides* an analysis of the different regional distribution of the various advantages derived from the customs union. Although the largest member state, Prussia, obtained no evident economic gains and incurred financial losses, the smaller centrally located German territories enjoyed significant economic and financial gains.(97) For the middle-sized members, the financial gains were probably the most important. The regional distribution of the type and size of gains, therefore, seems to have been a function of the wide range in the size and location of member states, and of the interlocked geography of the *Zollverein* states, which systematically determined the *divergent gains* amongst member states, and, in turn, reflected different individual motives for joining the union. This interpretation, therefore, takes into account the historian's wish for a differentiated approach to the *Zollverein*'s creation. With the possible exception of *Prussia*, the different reasons which may have led individual states to join the union in 1834 reflected the differing emphasis on the arguments implicit in the optimal jurisdiction approach.

Because the calculated static and dynamic welfare gains from the union as a whole were so modest, it is clear that political and particularly fiscal gains inevitably played a significant role in its creation. This view is not novel. The financial aspects were already explicitly stressed in the Prussian Memorandum of 1840 which reviewed the initial period of the Zollverein's operation:

> the tariff levels of the height determined by the Union Tariff [had] only partially the purpose ... to protect the economic activity in the states of the Union as a whole, [they were], rather, largely and most importantly also levied for the satisfaction of the financial needs of the individual members.(98)

The fiscal significance of the union was unfortunately neglected by later commentators, who concentrated on the diplomatic negotiations between German states and their later conflicts concerning possible Austrian membership. This is understandable, given that the first important historical surveys of the Zollverein (99) appeared after 1860. However, they invariably stress the Zollverein's impact on inter-German rivalries, while ignoring its earlier significance for resolving or repressing political conflicts within the individual German states.

A thorough analysis of the fiscal gains from the Zollverein indicates that these were intimately related to the political development of the German constitutional monarchies in the first half of the nineteenth-century. It has been argued that constitutionalism and parliamentary representation arose in the new German states after the Congress of Vienna as a result of their contemporary financial crisis caused by the Napoleonic Wars.(100) These reform measures were designed to reassure capital markets and to restore the credit standing of individual governments.(101) The problem of the state budget, however, remained critical and assumed a central constitutional importance, since it influenced the precarious political balance between monarchial principle and parliamentarianism. Bockenforde argued that 'the budgetary rights [of parliament] were ... the essential antipode to the monarchial principle in the constitutional state'.(102) These new constitutions had thereby created for the people's representatives 'a weapon ... and an arena of action which was suited to undermine monarchial principle and ... to bring about the actual dependency of governments upon the representatives of the people'.(103) Because the significantly increased tariff revenues from the customs union were distributed to the member states on the basis of their population size, they flowed automatically into their coffers, by-passing the parliaments. The Zollverein governments could thereby avoid the necessity of paying a political price to secure the unwilling votes of parliament for increased taxes. Thus, the Zollverein revenues affected the precarious political balance within the constitutional monarchies in favour of monarchial government, strengthening its independence, and undermined parliamentary rights for over a decade after 1834. These revenues were therefore a significant factor in stabilising the German political system in the period of restoration until the mid-century.(104) The balance between monarchy and the sovereignty of the people shifted in favour of the former; the opportunity for the development of political liberalism in Germany was delayed, and perhaps permanently lost.

Certainly the conservative Prussian state had a great interest in stabilising the political system of the smaller and middle-sized German states, especially after the July revolutions of 1830/31. Because the disturbances in the southern states were seen to be related to financial and administrative deficiencies (105), Prussian help was viewed as a means of securing the desired stability. In this connection A.J.P.Taylor rightly observed that the customs union was a means of 'winning the middle classes back from Jacobinism':

> The Zollverein was not evidence that the Prussian rulers aimed at the leadership of a united Germany. It was rather witness to the sacrifices they would make to prevent a united [and liberal, or revolutionary] Germany ... The Zollverein was an 'ersatz', an economic substitute for national unification.(106)

A report of the Prussian Foreign Minister, von Werther, to the Ambassador in Munich of 13 April, 1840 supports this interpretation:

> The political idea which was the basis of the Zollverein from the Prussian point of view was, as is well known, the intention to cut the ground from under the feet of subversive political aspirations and their chimerical theories, to offer, on the one hand, to the prevailing interests a more solid direction and, on the other hand, to the desires for national unity a real and at the same time more noble foundation. This objective, for which alone the sacrifices borne by Prussia need not be regretted, has been achieved. It has been often and widely acknowledged how very much the spirit of the German population has improved since then and that the peace and unity of Germany from below has attained a new security.(107)

The political stabilisation of the German states in the 1830s through the customs union and the distribution of its revenue was, therefore, an acknowledged goal of Prussian politics.

The more one emphasises the financial distress of the governments (108) and the importance of the budget in the constitutional struggles within the German states in the first half of the nineteenth-century, the weightier is the argument concerning the *Zollverein's* fiscal significance. The financial gains can even offer a sufficient explanation for its creation: the union was founded because it was, in the final analysis, in the interest of the ruling conservative elites to obtain new tax revenues which were both politically 'neutral' from a domestic point of view and extremely necessary. I am inclined to accept this hypothesis becauses it highlights the special historical constellation within which the union was founded and because it provides the only consistent and general explanation for its creation. Moreover, this interpretation is theoretically well founded on the basis of the previously discussed general customs union model.

This last section has stressed that a prime political goal of the German states in the early nineteenth-century was the raising of revenues by taxing foreign trade. Earlier it was argued that most of these states had a size, shape and geographic location inimical to the goal of revenue maximisation. Only within a larger union could the possible economies of scale in revenue gathering be realised and the external effects on trade be eliminated. Thus, the *Zollverein's* foundation could be interpreted as the establishment of an optimal size and shape of governmental jurisdiction for revenue purposes. It is of interest to note that Friedman has attempted to establish a theory of the size and shape of nations (109), based upon essentially similar arguments, but using flimsier historical data. He argued that if the primary goal of nations was revenue maximisation (110), they would historically assume a size and shape which would allow the imposition of an optimal tax and the operation of economies of scale in raising tax revenue. If the primary revenue source was the taxation of trade, large nations would be formed. However if landownership was the basis of taxation, small states could be of optimal size, and reliance on a tax poll would promote the creation of culturally homogeneous states which could act as barriers to migration. The *Zollverein* case, therefore, seems to be one of the best *documented* historical illustrations of Friedman's first rule and provides an interesting example for the operation of a law which arguably has been in operation since classical antiquity.

Before concluding, it should be noted that the fiscal interpretation of the *Zollverein's* foundation contains arguments and assumptions which historians, in contrast to economists, generally find difficult to accept. It is important, therefore, to discuss briefly the different analytical approaches of economists and historians. The first difficulty concerns the 'functional' approach towards the *Zollverein's* creation implicit in the fiscal argument. In analysing political events, the economist is accustomed to identifing the gains and costs from such action to the relevant decision makers. Once their objectives and the political constraints of decision-making have been identified, political choices can be explained on the assumption that political actors are also rational maximisers. In the *Zollverein* case we have argued that the financial benefits had a stabilising effect on the political systems of Restoration Germany. Given the assumption that the relevant decision makers had sufficient information about the primary effects of the planned union and that they were rational and maximising calculators, the decision to form the union can be explained by its system-stabilising function. Because it can be shown that contemporaries were well aware of the projected financial gains from the union, the historians' main criticism will concern the assumption that political actors were rational. Although this is an essential element in the economists' approach, it is questioned by many historians, and the difference in approach is probably difficult to overcome. Nevertheless, it should be clear that if the pay-offs to political 'games' are not properly identified, then their actual nature must remain obscure. Because the traditional literature has largely ignored the union's financial benefits and constitutional implications, it has tended to view the *Zollverein* as a zero-sum game, where Prussia gained at the expense of other member states. Instead we have shown that it initially had clear aspects of a positive-sum game, with gains to conservative governments and elites in all member states, and corresponding losses to their respective liberal oppositions.

The fiscal interpretation of the *Zollverein's* creation has also been criticised by the historians Berding and Hahn for being one-sided and 'mono-causal'.(111) According to Hahn's study of the union from the point of view of the Hessian states: 'The *Zollverein's* occurrence was due to the most diverse economic, fiscal and political movements and incentives, and its foundation initially gave rise to the most variegated expectations and hopes'.(112) Consequently he concluded that the decision of the Hessian states to join the *Zollverein* was an example of 'partial modernisation' (113), which accurately reflected the multi-causal integration processes evident in this case. According to Rueschemeyer's general definition, partial modernisation is 'a process of social change which leads to the institution of relatively modern societal forms next to significantly less modern structures in one and the same society'.(114) In the Zollverein context this should refer to - among other aspects - the fact that an economic union was established by a partial centralisation of government jurisdictions, but in a manner which ignored political participation rights. But these are precisely the same central phenomena emphasised by the fiscal interpretation. No basic contradictions between the fiscal and the partial modernisation interpretations need arise, as the latter approach is really more of a typology or descriptive device than a causal explanation, and lends itself to the historian's favourite method of 'thick description'.(115) In contrast, the customs union model and the fiscal approach seek to identify and to critically assess the most important arguments for the Zollverein's foundation; it is, therefore, an attempt at a systematic reduction of a number of possible explanations. David Landes has provided a vivid contrast between the two methods,

> The economist seeks abstraction ... He wants sufficient explanation; and as Milton Friedman likes to say, one good explanation is enough. The historian on the other hand revels in complexity ... and generally follows the law of conservation of evidence. The explanation should try to account for as many pieces of evidence as possible ... Two good reasons are better that one, and three are better than two.(116)

This quote should make it clear that the differences in approach can be bridged by a well-understood pluralist methodology. Babel is avoidable. The historians' criticism of the fiscal interpretation of the Zollverein's foundation may in the final analysis be based solely upon a misunderstanding of the economist's methodolgy.

Let us now summarize the hypotheses derived from the application of the customs union model to the history of the Zollverein. Essential features of the Zollverein, and of the EEC today, conform to an 'ideal type' of customs union model, which was developed from recent trade literature. The most likely determining factors behind the Zollverein's creation, were not its modest static and dynamic welfare gains, but the otherwise unattainable revenue gains, which resulted from a more optimal size of customs administration. Because the newly organised German states after the Congress of Vienna experienced considerable financial difficulties with budgetary problems assuming a central position in constitutional struggles, the search for new and politically neutral revenues represented an important governmental goal. In view of the unique size distribution and interlocked geography of the German states, which ranged from very small splinter territories to states of sizable area, it was possible to realise significant economies of scale in the taxation of foreign trade for revenue purposes. Thus, the peculiar political constellation and the unusual geography of the German states in the early nineteenth-century not only helped to generate specific financial pressures, but also suggested a possible solution through the creation of the Zollverein. Moreover the financial advantages of the union retained their fundamental importance after 1834.(117)

The historical and geographical peculiarities which governed the Zollverein's creation and which explain its continued existence in the nineteenth-century also preclude any meaningful comparison with the European Economic Community.(118) Although the Zollverein and the EEC are both historical examples of an 'ideal type' of customs union and although it is useful to view both as particular examples of optimal jurisdictions, the differences between them remain large and significant. According to the present interpretation of the Zollverein, its foundation was mainly a political decision to achieve a more optimal governmental jurisdiciton which entailed, simultaneously, economic integration. The role of the Zollverein in the history of nineteenth-century Germany was, therefore, not a striking exception to Gustav Schmoller's historical rule, that economic union should follow political integration. On the contrary, it appears as an interesting modification of that rule. The history of the Zollverein, however, cannot provide any direct suggestions for the future development possibilities of the European Economic Community.

* Presented to the international conference on Economic Integration in the 19th and 20th Centuries, Schloss Rauisch-Holzhausen, July 1983 and the Faculty Research Seminar, Department of Economic History, University of Liverpool, October 1983. Useful criticism from participants on both occasions is hereby gratefully acknowledged. For further commentary I wish to thank Roger Dufraisse, Sidney Pollard, Alan Milward, Eckart Schremmer, Knut Borchardt, Scott Eddie and Richard Tilly. This is a revised and somewhat shortened version of a paper originally published in German with the title, 'Der Deutsche Zollverein als Modell oekonomischer Integration', in H.Berding, (ed.), Wirtschaftliche und Politische Integration in Europa im 19. und 20. Jahrhundert, (Geschichte und Gesellschaft, Sonderheft 10) (Goettingen, 1984).

NOTES

1. J.Viner, The Customs Union Issue, (New York, 1950), p.97.

2. Most recently by W.O.Henderson, 'The German Zollverein and the European Community'. Zeitschrift fuer die gesamte Staatswissenschaft, vol.137 (1981), pp.491-507. See also W.Fischer, 'Der deutsche Zollverein, die Europaeische Wirtschaftsgemeinschaft und die Freihandelszone', Europa Archiv, vol.5 (1961), pp.105-114; A.Weber, 'Der deutsche Zollverein als Praezedenzfall fuer die Bildung eines freien europaeischen Marktes', Schmollers Jahrbuch fuer Gesetzgebung, Verwaltung und Volkswirtschaft, vol.78 (1958), pp.45-63.

3. While J.Viner noted this rule, it seems to have originated with Gustav Schmoller, 'Die Handels- und Zollannaeherung Mitteleuropas', Schmollers Jahrbuch, vol.40, No.2 (1916), pp.529-550.

4. James Meade, 'The Removal of Trade Barriers: the Regional versus the Universal Approach', Economica (1951), p.187.

5. For such experts of the economic history of the Zollverein as Fischer and Henderson, their special knowledge of the historical case should help to avoid most of the methodological traps involved in the direct comparison - but not all of them. In this regard see note 117.

6. See M.Weber, Wirtschaft und Gesellschaft, vol.I, (Tuebingen, 1956), pp.2-5,9,10.

7. W.Fischer has already attempted such a comparison in 'The German Zollverein. A Case Study in Customs Union', Kyklos, vol.XIII (1960), pp.65-89. However, since then there have been important developments in customs union theory.

8. It is the function of the model to identify important dimensions.

9. Fischer, 'Zollverein', (1960), p.67: '... the institutions and instruments by means of which the Union operated ... are of particular interest to political economists looking for historical precedents that might serve as guides in the modern situation'.

10. Two literature surveys have been of great help for this task; M.B.Krauss, 'Recent Developments in Customs Union Theory: An Interpretative Survey', Journal of Economic Literature, vol.X, (1972), pp.413-436, and F.Machlup, A History of Thought on Economic Integration, (London, 1977).

11. It is of interest to note that this substitution of history by theory was initiated by Viner, who was one of the few international trade theorists with profound historical knowledge.

12. This depends upon whether or not the height of the common tariff exceeds that of the average tariffs of the member states before the union.

13. C.A.Cooper and B.F.Massell, 'A New Look at Customs Union Theory', Economic Journal, vol.75, (1965), pp.742-747; see also idem., 'Towards a General Theory of Customs Unions for Developing Countries', Journal of Political Economy, vol.73, (Oct.1965), pp.461-476.

14. The only exception might be the infant industry argument for protection, which Friedrich List developed for the Zollverein.

15. The last two effects have been characterised as 'dynamic' effects in the customs union literature, in contrast to the other, usual 'static' effects on economic welfare.

16. Krauss, 'Recent Developments', p.424.

17. H.G.Johnson, 'An Economic Theory of Protectionism, Tariff Bargaining and the Formation of Customs Unions', Journal of Political Economy, vol.63, (1965), p.257. According to Krauss this is 'the proper point of departure for the study of customs unions', 'Recent Developments', p.430.

18. Cooper and Massell, 'A New Look'.

19. Although Krauss and Machlup view this argument critically, Johnson's argument is of interest because it is the first time that ideas in the analysis of public goods and the economic theory of the state have been applied to customs unions:see Krauss, 'Recent Developments', and Machlup, History of Thought, pp.34-35.

20. R.N.Cooper,'Worldwide versus Regional Integration: Is there an Optimum Size of the Integrated Area'? in F.Machlup, (ed.), Economic Integration: Worldwide, Regional, Sectoral: Proceedings of the Fourth Congress of the International Economic Association held at Budapest, Hungary, (London, 1976), pp.41-53.

21. See also B.Balassa, 'Types of Economic Integration', in Machlup, Economic Integration, pp.17-36.

22. Cooper, 'Worldwide versus Regional Integration', p.52.

23. Balassa, 'Types of Economic Integration',p.30.

24. Krauss, 'Recent Developments', pp.434,430.

25. Ibid., p.430.

26. J.Denison, Why Growth Rates Differ, (Washington D.C., 1967), p.261.

27. B.Balassa calculated larger welfare gains due to the existence of dynamic effects: economies of scale and induced investments. Nevertheless, the total gains remain small - 0.65 per cent of the Gross National Product of the EEC states. See B.Balassa, 'Trade Creation and Diversion in the European Common Market', in idem., (ed.), European Economic Integration, (Amsterdam, 1965), pp.113-115.

28. W.R.Cline, 'Benefits and Costs of Economic Integration in Central America', in W.R.Cline and E.Delgado, (eds.), Economic Integration in Central America, (Washington D.C., 1978), p.110.

29. This is also emphasised by P.Robson, The Economics of International Integration, (London, 1980), chapter 10, pp.145 et seq.

30. Ibid., p.151.

31. See R.H.Dumke, 'The Political Economy of German Economic Unification: Tariffs, Trade and Politics of the Zollverein Era', unpublished PhD dissertation, University of Wisconsin, Madison, 1976, chapter I. Further useful surveys of the Zollverein literature are by H.Berding, 'Die Entstehung des Deutschen Zollvereins als Problem historischer Forschung', in H.Berding, et. al., (eds.), Vom Staat des Ancien Regime zum Modernen Parteienstaat, (Munich, 1978), pp.225-237; and the introduction to H.-W.Hahn's new study, Wirtschaftliche Integration im 19. Jahrhundert. Die hessischen Staaten und der Deutsche Zollverein, (Goettingen, 1982).

32. Friedrich List, Das Nationale System der Politischen Oekonomie, 2nd edn., (Stuttgart, 1844), p.112.

33. Gustav Schmoller, Grundriss der Allgemeinen Volkswirtschaftslehre, vol.II, (Munich, 1919), p.704.

34. F.Luetge, Deutsche Sozial- und Wirtschaftsgeschichte, 3rd edn., (Berlin, 1966), pp.467-468.

35. H.Mottek, Wirtschaftsgeschichte Deutschlands, vol.II, (East Berlin, 1964), pp.56 et seq.

36. Ibid., p.24.

37. W.G.Hoffmann, 'The Take-Off in Germany', in W.W.Rostow, (ed.), The Economics of Take-Off into Sustained Growth, 4th edn., (London, 1968), pp.95-118.

38. A.Sartorious von Waltershausen, Deutsche Wirtschaftsgeschichte, 1815-1914, (Jena, 1920), p.60.

39. J.H.Clapham, The Economic Development of France and Germany 1815-1914, 4th edn., (Cambridge, 1966), p.97.

40. R.H.Tilly, 'Los von England: Probleme des Nationalismus in der deutschen Wirtschaftsgeschichte'., in idem., Kapital, Staat und sozialer Protest in der deutschen Industrialisierung, (Goettingen, 1980), pp.97-209.

41. S.Pollard, 'Industrialisation and the European Economy', Economic History Review, vol.26, (1973) pp.636-648; see also his Peaceful Conquest. The Industrialisation of Europe 1760-1970, (Oxford, 1981), particularly 'Trade and Industrialisation', pp.164-184.

42. R.H.Dumke, 'Anglo-deutscher Handel und Fruehindustrialisierung in Deutschland', Geschichte und Gesellschaft, vol.5, (1979), pp.175-200.

43. C.-L.Holtfrerich, Quantitative Wirtschaftsgeschichte des Ruhrkohlenbergbaus im 19. Jahrhundert. Eine Fuehrungssektoranalyse, (Dortmund, 1973), p.168; K.H.Kaufhold, 'Handwerk und Industrie 1800-1850', in H.Aubin and W.Zorn, (eds.), Handbuch der Deutschen Wirtschafts- und Sozialgeschichte, vol.2, (Stuttgart, 1976), p.357. For an emphasis on the growth effects of the investment boom in the railways in the 1840s, see R.H.Tilly, 'The Take-Off in Germany', in E.Angermann, (ed.), Oceans Apart. Comparing Germany and the United States, (Stuttgart, 1981).

44. A.Milward and S.B.Saul, The Economic Development of Continental Europe, 1780-1870, (London, 1973), p.374.
45. H. von Treitschke, Deutsche Geschichte im 19. Jahrhundert, (Leipzig, 1918/20, 10th edn.), vol.4, p.379.
46. H.Krueger, Zur Geschichte der Manufakturen und der Manufakturarbeiter in Preussen, (East Berlin, 1958), p.13.
47. E.R.Huber, Deutsche Verfassungsgeschichte, (Stuttgart, 1957), vol.1, p.815.
48. H.Boehme, Deutschlands Weg zur Grossmacht, (Cologne, 1966), p.211 et seq.
49. F.Engels, 'Die Rolle der Gewalt in der Geschichte', in Marx-Engels Werke, (East Berlin, 1972), vol.21, p.421; K.Obermann, Deutschland 1815-1849. Von der Gruendung des Deutschen Bundes bis zur buergerlich-demokratischen Revolution, (East Berlin, 1967), p.99.
50. H.Oncken, 'Vorgeschichte und Begruendung des Deutschen Zollvereins. Eine Einfuehrung', in W.von Eisenhart-Rothe and A.Ritthaler (eds.), Vorgeschichte und Begruendung des Deutschen Zollvereins 1815-1834, (Berlin, 1934), vol.1, p.XCVXCVI.
51. W.O.Henderson, The Zollverein, 2nd edn., (London, 1959), p.95.
52. Fischer, 'Zollverein', p.86.
53. Berding, Vom Staat des Ancien Regime, pp.236-237.
54. Hahn, Wirtschaftliche Integration, pp.149-150.
55. M.Kutz, Deutschlands Aussenhandel von der Franzoesischen Revolution bis zur Gruendung des Zollvereins, (Wiesbaden, 1974).
56. B.von Borries, Deutschlands Aussenhandel 1836 bis 1856. Eine statistische Untersuchung zur Fruehindustrialisierung, (Stuttgart, 1970).
57. T.Ohnishi, Zolltarifpolitik Preussens bis zur Gruendung des deutschen Zollvereins. Ein Beitrag zur Finanz- und Aussenpolitik Preussens, (Goettingen, 1973).
58. H.Freymark, Die Reform der preussischen Handels- und Zollpolitik von 1800-1820 und ihre Bedeutung, (Jena, 1898).
59. R.H.Dumke, 'Intra-German Trade in 1837 and Regional Economic Development', Vierteljahrschrift fuer Sozial- und Wirtschaftsgeschichte, vol.64, (1977), pp.468-496.
60. G.Kirchhain, Das Wachstum der deutschen Baumwollindustrie im 19. Jahrhundert. Eine historische Modellstudie zur empirischen Wachstumsforschung. (New York, 1977).
61. C.F.W.Dieterici, Der Volkswohlstand im Preussischen Staate, (Berlin, 1846).
62. G.Hohorst, Wirtschaftswachstum und Bevoelkerungsentwicklung in Preussen 1816 bis 1914, (New York, 1977).
63. R.H.Dumke, 'Die wirtschaftlichen Folgen des Zollvereins', in W.Abelshauser and D.Petzina, (eds.), Deutsche Wirtschaftsgeschichte im Industriezeitalter. (Duesseldorf, 1981), pp.341-373.

64. *Ibid.*

65. For a formal treatment, see M.C.Kemp, *A Contribution to the General Equilibrium Theory of Preferential Trading*, (Amsterdam, 1969), chapter 6. The formula for the calculation of the static gains was developed from R.Jones, 'Tariffs and Trade in General Equilibrium: Comment', *American Economic Review*, vol.LIX, (1969), pp.418-424.

66. In contrast to contemporary opinion, see, for example, C.F.Nebenius, *Der deutsche Zollverein, sein System und seine Zukunft*, (Carlsruhe, 1835), p.34.

67. T.F.Huertas, *Economic Growth and Economic Policy in a Multinational Setting. The Habsburg Monarchy, 1841-1865*, (New York, 1977), pp.18 et seq.

68. J.H.Tieriot, *Welcher Einfluss auf dem Felde des saechsischen Gewerbefleisses und Handels hat der Anschluss des Koenigreichs Sachsen an den preussisch-deutschen Zollverein bis jetzt gehabt?*, (Leipzig, 1838), pp.46-48.

69. G.von Viebahn, *Statistik des zollvereinten und noerdlichen Deutschlands*, (Berlin, 1858), Part I, pp.181-182; (Berlin, 1868), Part III, p.752.

70. J.Wysocki, 'Sueddeutche Aspekte der raeumlichen Ordnung des Zollvereins', in Akademie fuer Raumforschung und Landesplanung, *Raumordnung im 19. Jahrhundert*, (Hannover, 1967), Part 2, pp.153-154.

71. Kirchhain's estimates of value added are very close to Dieterici's figures for 1842: see C.F.W.Dieterici, *Statistische Uebersicht der wichtigsten Gegenstaende des Verkehrs und Verbrauchs im Preussischen Staate und im Deutschen Zollverbande*, (Berlin, 1848), p.384.

72. In effect this is an upper-bound estimate of the welfare gains due to the increased investment in cotton mills. For a good description of the investment effect of a customs union see Cline, 'Benefits and Costs', pp.107,502 and passim, who also provides the clearest available discussion of possible static and dynamic effects. Cline's definition of the welfare gains from increased investment induced by a union's larger market has two points. The first concerns the excess of wages, w, over labour's social opportunity cost, w*. The increased investment, I, results in an increased annual stream of value added: I . incremental output-capital ratio. If labour's share is L, then the portion of the wage bill, 1-w*/w, due to the excess of wage over labour's opportunity cost is a welfare gain due to the increased investment. For example, welfare increase = (I/B)L(1-w*/w), where B is the incremental capital-output ratio. The second part of the investment effect concerns the difference in the rate of return, p, and the opportunity cost of capital, i; thus the present value of the welfare gain from extra investment in the union is I(p/i-1). In our calculation we assumed that both w* and i = 0. Since we do not have good annual investment data in

the case of the Zollverein, the basis of our calculation of the investment effect has been to take the whole increase in the annual value added in the cotton milling sector between 1830 and 1842. To compare the magnitude of this dynamic effect with the previously calculated static welfare effect, one should, further, calculate the discounted present value (in 1834, or 1837) of the investment effect which was calculated for the year 1842. This would be smaller than in the year 1842. Thus all assumptions involved in this estimate of the dynamic effect result in an upper-bound magnitude.

Generally speaking, static welfare effects are once and for all outward shifts of the production possibility frontier, while dynamic effects involve continuous outward shifts. We ride somewhat roughshod over these precise definitions and term the increase in value added in the cotton milling sector, which is 'dynamic' by definition, as the 'dynamic' effect, regardless of the real reasons for the increase, be it economies of scale, the difference between wage rates and the shadow price of labour, the difference between rates of return to invested capital and the opportunity costs of capital, etc.

73. Derived from Kirchhain, Das wachstum der deutschen Baumwollindustrie, tables 44,51,14, pp.155,166 and 73, respectively. Value added in weaving times labour's share equals labour incomes.

74. H.Loreth, Das Wachstum der wuerttembergischen Wirtschaft 1818-1918, (Stuttgart, 1974).

75. K.Megerle, Wuerttemberg im Industrialisierungsprozess Deutschlands. Ein Beitrag zur regionalen Differenzierung der Industrialisierung, (Stuttgart, 1982), p.93.

76. (Ludwig Kuehne), Ueber den deutschen Zollverein, (Berlin, 1836). This idea has also been discussed in the public finance literature: K.H.Rau, Grundsaetze der Finanzwissenschaft, (Leipzig, 1859), p.260, and A.Wagner, Finanzwissenschaft, (Leipzig, 1883), Part I, p.396. For a lengthier treatment see G.von Viebahn, Statistik des zollvereinten und noerdlichen Deutschlands, Part I: Landeskunde, (Berlin, 1858), pp.227-228, 'Grenzen, Bruttoeinnahmen und Verwaltungskosten des Zollvereins'.

77. For a lengthier treatment see my dissertation, chapter I.

78. Hahn, Wirtschaftliche Integration, p.219.

79. H.L.Biersack, Ueber Besteuerung, ihre Grundsaetze und Ausfuehrung, (Frankfurt a.M., 1850), p.186.

80. K.Borchard, 'Staatsverbrauch und oeffentliche Investitionen in Deutschland. 1780-1850,' unpublished PhD thesis, University of Goettingen, 1968.

81. H.Berding, 'Die Reform des Zollwesens im rheinbuendischen Deutschland', in H.Berding and H.P.Ullmann, (eds.), Deutschland zwischen Revolution und Restauration, (Duesseldorf, 1981), pp.102-103.

82. Quoted from W.O.Henderson, Friedrich List. Economist and Visionary, 1789-1846, (London, 1983), pp.34-35.
83. Hahn, Wirtschaftliche Integration, p.149.
84. Thieriot, Einfluss, p.65. This was used extensively by Dr.Bowring in his well-known Parliamentary Report on the Prussian Commercial Union (1840).
85. Ibid., pp.47-48.
86. Ibid., p.64.
87. See H.Best, Interessenpolitik und nationale Integration 1848/49. Handelspolitische Konflikte im fruehindustriellen Deutschland, (Goettingen, 1980).
88. H.von Treitschke, 'Die Anfaenge des deutschen Zollvereins', in idem., (ed.), Preussische Jahrbuecher, 30, (Berlin, 1872), p.402. For a comparison of the tariffs of a number of German territories before the Zollverein and of that union see Dumke 'Die wirtschaftlichen Folgen', table 4, p.247.
89. See Henderson, The Zollverein, pp.64-69.
90. See Best, Interessenpolitik, pp.149,288 and 289.
91. See W.Thieme, 'Der Eintritt Sachsens in den Zollverein und seine wirtschaftlichen Folgen,' unpublished dissertation University of Leipzig, 1914, pp.52-61. More recently see R.Muhs, 'Zwischen Staatsreform und politischem Protest. Liberalismus in Sachsen zur Zeit des Hambacher Festes', in W.Schieder, (ed.), Liberalismus in der Gesellschaft des deutschen Vormaerz, (Goettingen, 1983), pp.119-221.
92. The decade of the 1820s was marked by difficult and unsuccessful tariff conferences in south Germany before the conclusion of a customs union between Wuerttemberg and Bavaria in 1828. They are an indicator of how difficult and costly tariff harmonisation could be. Still, this should be seen as a learning process, whose 'transaction' costs were, in the final event, not incurred in vain because they facilitated the establishment of the later Zollverein. Concerning this process of clarification see A.H.Price, The Evolution of the Zollverein. A Study of the Ideas and Institutions leading to German Unification between 1815 and 1833, (Ann Arbor, 1949).
93. L.E.Davis and D.C.North, Institutional Change and American Economic Growth, (Cambridge, 1971).
94. For example, see J.M.Buchanan and G.Tullock, The Calculus of Consent. Logical Foundation of Constitutional Democracy, (Ann Arbor, 1969); W.J.Baumol, Welfare Economics and the Theory of the State, 2nd edn., (Cambridge Mass., 1967).
95. Davis and North, Institutional Change, p.25.
96. R.H.Dumke, 'The Political Economy of Economic Integration: The Case of the German Zollverein of 1834', Discussion Paper No.153, Institute for Economic Research, Queen's University, presented at the Canadian Economics Association's eighth annual meeting, Toronto, June 5, 1974. The Discussion Paper later became chapter I of my dissertation.

97. Because small economies are relatively open, i.e., the share of foreign trade in total income is large, they are more susceptible to trade restrictions by their customers compared to larger economies and the elimination of those restrictions will result in larger gains to the smaller economies.

98. Denkschrift ueber den Einfluss der Zollvereinigungs-Vertraege auf die preussischen Staats-Einnahmen, (Berlin, 1840), Part II, p.20.

99. For example, A.Weber, Der deutsche Zollverein, (Leipzig, 1867); von Treitschke, 'Die Anfaenge', passim.

100. H.Obenaus, 'Finanzkrise und Verfassungsgebung. Zu den sozialen Bedingungen des fruehen deutschen Konstitutionalismus', in G.A.Ritter, (ed.), Parlament und Regierung. Zur Geschichte des Parlamentarismus in Deutschland, (Duesseldorf, 1974), p.67. More recently see H.-P.Ullmann, 'Ueberlegungen zur Entstehung des oeffentlichen verfassungsmaessigen Kredits in den Rheinbund Staaten (Bayern, Wuerttemberg und Baden)', Geschichte und Gesellschaft, vol.6, (1980), pp.500-522; for Baden see H.-P.Ullmann, 'Badische Finanzreformen in der Rheinbundzeit', and for Prussia see H.Schissler, 'Preussische Finanzpolitik nach 1807. Die Bedeutung der Staatsverschuldung als Faktor der Modernisierung des preussischen Finanzsystems'; the last two articles are in Geschichte und Gesellschaft, vol.8, (1982), pp.333-366 and 367-385, respectively.

101. See Obenaus, 'Finanzkrise', p.71, as well as the articles by Ullmann and Schissler cited in the previous footnote.

102. E.-W.Bockenforde, 'Der Verfassungstyp der deutschen konstitutionellen Monarchie im 19. Jahrhundert', in idem., (ed.), Moderne deutsche Verfassungsgeschichte (1815-1918), (Cologne, 1972), p.155.

103. Ibid., p.156.

104. For a more extensive argument see my Discussion Paper, or chapter I of my dissertation. Evidence for the thesis that the Zollverein revenues stabilised the political systems of the Hessian states is provided in Hahn, Wirtschaftliche Integration, pp.239 et seq., 308; and idem, 'Zwischen deutscher Handelsfreiheit und Sicherung landstaendischer Rechte. Der Liberalismus und die Gruendung des deutschen Zollvereins', in Schieder (ed.), Liberalismus, pp.269 et seq. The argument that new types of state finances stabilise the political system has also found a very promising application in Prussian history: see, for example R.Braun, 'Taxation, Sociopolitical Structure, and State-Building: Great Britain and Brandenburg-Prussia', in Ch. Tilly, (ed.), The Formation of National States in Western Europe, (Princeton, 1975), p.326: 'The Prussian tax reforms of the nineteenth century serve as examples of how changes of tax systems could

be connected with the limitation of franchise, the graduation of political participation, and the preservation of privileged political positions'.

The stability of the Zollverein states also increased because the elimination of tariffs on internal German trade got rid of one of the main reasons for social protests in the middle German states: see H.Volkmann, 'Soziale Innovation und Systemstabilitaet am Beispiel der Krise von 1830-1832 in Deutschland', in O.Neuloh, (ed.), Soziale Innovation und sozialer Konflikt, (Goettingen, 1977), pp.59-65.

105. See the resumé of a Prussian report in R.H.Tilly, 'Germany', in Ch. Tilly, L.Tilly and R.Tilly, The Rebellious Century, 1830-1930, (Cambridge Mass., 1975), p.220: 'An interesting report on turbulance in southern Germany during these years (1830-1832), prepared in 1832 for Prussian officials (possibly by a professional informer), commented on the relative calm of Prussia and attributed the difference to financial-administrative causes. Governments in these regions not only avoided heavy spending because of the taxes and democratic concessions that they would necessitate, but, because of their small size, relative administration costs were higher (and/or the quality of administration lower)'.

106. A.J.P.Taylor, The Course of German History, (London, 1945), pp.61 and 63.

107. Quoted in Hahn, Wirtschaftliche Integration, p.399.

108. Further investigations of the trend in the ratio of government expenditures and taxes to national income in the early 19th century are required. While a graph in H.C.Recktenwald's survey, 'Oeffentliche Finanzwirtschaft I: Allgemeines', in Handwoerterbuch der Wirtschaftswissenschaft, 26/27 Lieferung, (Stuttgart, 1980), Graph 2, p.151, indicates a decline in the nominal per capita government expenditures in Germany between 1821 and 1862, this conflicts with the data on Prussia, Bavaria and Baden between 1820 and 1850 in Borchard's study, Staatsverbrauch: see Dumke, 'Political Economy of German Economic Unification' pp.33 and 100-103 which attempts to include important extraordinary government expenditures; a recalculation of the per capita expenditures for these states showed no decline, rather, an increase during those years. Because prices fell during the first half of the century, real per capita government expenditures most probably rose during that period. See also the discussion concerning the government ratio in Ullmann, 'Badische Finanzreformen', pp.351-352.

109. D.Friedman, 'A Theory of the Size and Shape of Nations', Journal of Political Economy, vol.85, (1977), pp.59-77. I would like to thank Dan Usher for pointing out this study.

110. The insight that the historical process of nation building in western Europe was intimately related to the problem of maximising government revenues is central to the

analysis in Ch. Tilly, (ed.), The Formation of National States in Western Europe, (Princeton, 1975), passim. The perceptive comments in W.W.Rostow's review in the Journal of European Economic History, vol.5, (1976), pp.256-259 are helpful here. Rostow characterises an essential viewpoint of the studies in this volume as follows: 'the heart of the political process lies in the extractive-coercive activities of the state'. This is also a main assumption of Friedman, who attempts to uncover economic laws which might lie behind the process of nation building.

111. Berding, 'Die Entstehung', pp.236,237; Hahn, Wirtschaftliche Integration, p.18.

112. Hahn, Wirtschaftliche Integration, p.307.

113. Ibid. pp.19,307.

114. D.Rueschemeyer, 'Partielle Modernisierung', in W.Zapf, (ed.), Theorien des sozialen Wandels, 3rd edn., (Cologne, 1971), p.382.

115. See R.W.Fogel, 'Circumstantial Evidence in 'Scientific' and Traditional History', in D.Carr, et. al., (eds.), Philosophy of History and Contemporary Historiography, (Ottawa, 1982), pp.61-112.

116. D.S.Landes, 'On avoiding Babel', Journal of Economic History, vol.38, (1978), p.9.

117. For archival evidence that the financial advantages retained their fundamental importance in the later decisions prolonging the union in 1854 and 1866 see H.Boehme, Vor 1866. Aktenstuecke zur Wirtschaftspolitik der deutschen Mittelstaaten, (Frankfurt a.M., 1966). The fiscal bonds of the union proved durable. Thus, it is not necessary to explain the Zollverein's longevity by appealing to an evolving political dynamism in favour of political unification. The union was financially stable from its inception. For remarks about the political dynamics of the union see Fischer, 'Zollverein', p.113; Hahn, Wirtschaftliche Integration, p.312.

A further important bond in the case of the union can be derived from Paul Streeten's interesting criticism of the 'fallacy of symmetry', an assumption implied in most customs union analyses. Streeten pointed out that '... the economic gains from joining may be small or negligible, yet the losses from staying out could be substantial'. See his 'Common Fallacies about the Common Market', Weltwirtschaftliches Archiv, vol.90/2, (1963), pp.276-91, here p.278. In the case of the Zollverein this argument would apply specifically to the last few central German states which joined the union after all other commercial alternatives, especially the Middle German Commercial Union, had collapsed. The argument applies equally to any individual middle German state entertaining the thought of leaving the union once it had been established. In both instances the foreseeable disruption of trade flows and the loss of usual export markets would have led to substantial terms of trade and welfare losses. Thus, penalising the last to join and the first to leave, the *Zollverein's* geography helped cement the union while the *decision to* join the *Zollverein* was a *bilateral* agreement with Prussia, leaving the union would have necessitated some other viable *multilateral* arrangement for most members.

118. In the 1950s, as is still the case today, the interpretation of the role of the *Zollverein* in German history in French historical texts was largely influenced by H.von Treitschke's views which emphasised the rise of Prussian hegemony in Germany. French opponents of a European Economic Community in the 1950s were afraid of possible German political ascendancy in an economic union with this potentially stronger economic partner. (I am indebted to Roger Dufraisse for these interesting references). It is, therefore, conceivable that lessons from history were applied during the EEC's beginnings, but these were based upon an inadequate, one-sided interpretation of the *Zollverein*. Furthermore, it would be an interesting irony of history if the proponents of the EEC were influenced by unrealistic expectations about the economic and, especially, the political consequences of an economic union; in other words, if the foundation of the EEC was furthered by an inadequate understanding of history, as well. In this instance historical research can help to establish a more sober view of the European Economic Community's future development chances.

Table 3.1 : Investment, output and employment in German cotton mills, 1830-1842.

Year	Gross Investment (1,000 Marks)[a]	Value Added (mill. Marks)[b]	Employment[c]
1830	570	6.67	13,600[d]
1834	634	5.52	15,400[e]
1837	2,018	7.34	18,200[f]
1840	907	8.90	19,500[g]
1842	402	11.31	18,500[h]

Source: G. Kirchhain, <u>Das Wachstum der deutschen Baumwollindustrie im 19. Jahrhundert</u>, (New York, 1977).

a. Table 25, pp.109-110.
b. Net of depreciation costs. Table 42, pp.146-147.
c. Table 14, p.73.
d. Average of the years 1830/1831.
e. Average of the years 1834/1836.
f. Average of the years 1836/1838.
g. Average of the years 1839/1841.
h. Average of the years 1844/1848.

Table 3.2: Costs of tariff collection in German customs areas.

Region	Ratio Border Length to Customs Area[a]	Actual Administration Costs as a per cent of Tariff Revenues
Zollverein	0.129	14.7[b]
Prussia	0.21	15 - 20[c]
Bavaria without the Palatinate	0.24	25[d]
Palatinate	0.48	150[e]
Wuerttemberg	0.47	43[f]
Kurhessen	0.77	around 100[g]
Hessen-Darmstadt	0.91	around 100[h]
Baden	0.75	...[i]
Nassau	0.67	...[j]
Saxony	0.59	...[k]

a. G. von Viebahn, Statistik des zollvereinten und noerdlichen Deutschlands, Erster Teil I: Landeskunde, (Berlin, 1858), pp.519-520: 'Grenzen, Bruttoeinnahmen und Verwaltungskosten des Zollvereins'.
b. K.H. Rau, Grundsaetze der Finanzwissenschaft, (Leipzig, 1859), p.260; for the year 1836.
c. T. Ohnishi, Zolltarifpolitik Preussens bis zur Gruendung des Deutschen Zollvereins, (Goettingen, 1972), p.35; for the year 1818.
d. Rau, Grundsaetze, p.260; for the year 1826.
e. Ibid, p.260; for the year 1830.
f. A. Sartorius von Waltershausen, Deutsche Wirtschaftsgeschichte, 1815-1914, (Jena, 1920), p.59; and F.W. von Reden, Allgemeine Vergleichende Finanzstatistik, Vergleichende Dartstellung des Haushalts, des Abgabewesens und der Schulden Deutschlands und des uebrigen Europas, I. Band, (Darmstadt, 1851), II. Band (Darmstadt, 1854/56), p.228.
g. von Waltershausen, Deutsche Wirtschaftsgeschichte, p. 59. See also von Viebahn, Statistik, p.149. '... the administration in relation to revenues became mightily expensive...': H-W. Hahn, Wirtschaftliche Integration im 19. Jahrhundert. Die hessischen Staaten und der Deutsche Zollverein, (Goettingen, 1982), p.218: '... in view of the high administration costs hardly any revenues remained in the year 1831...'

h. von Viebahn, Statistik, p.145.

i. For the following areas no information on administration costs is available. However, arguments which emphasize the impact of geography upon administration costs and, therefore, upon the type of customs system employed can be frequently found. For example, von Waltershausen, Deutsche Wirtschaftsgeschichte, p.60: '... the long-stretched Baden almost turned to free trade because it could not carry the costs of protecting the border'. See also von Viebahn, Statistik, with a similar point, p.173.

j. von Viebahn, Statistik, p.174; Nassau had low tariff levels.

k. Ibid p.162: for the Thueringian splinter states he remarked, p.167, that 'the size and the geographic location of these states made the introduction of a system of enclosed customs impossible.

Table 3.3 : The Structure of Central Government revenues[a] in several *Zollverein* member states, 1820-1850 (per cent of total net revenues).

Revenue Source	Prussia[b] 1821	1829	1841	1849	Bavaria[b] 1819	1825	1837	1849	Baden[b] 1820	1830
A. State Domains, Forests, Fisheries	17.5	15.2	12.3	11.9	27.4	26.9	27.1	22.0	24.5	18.1
B. State Enterprises	10.8	14.2	14.9	12.6	10.9	12.0	13.4	10.7	9.2	14.5
C. Direct Taxes	32.8	36.2	30.3	28.4	28.4	28.4	20.5	22.8	35.8	34.8
D. Indirect Taxes	35.4	33.3	36.4	37.0	29.0	33.0	35.0	43.0	30.5	32.6
Tariffs	14.5	14.0	17.8	17.3	8.1	7.1	10.3	15.8	9.4	8.4
E. Other	3.5	1.1	6.1	9.9	4.3	0.6	4.0	1.5	-	-

Revenue Source	1840	1850	Wuerttemberg[c] 1819/20	1830/31	1839/42	Hessen-Darmstadt[d] 1820	1824/26	1830/32	1839/41	1848/50
A. State Domains, Forests, Fisheries	16.5	12.5)	38.0	33.7	40.0	32.8	26.6	24.3	26.7	20.9
B. State Enterprises	10.7	12.0)				...	...	...	...	...
C. Direct Taxes	28.5	28.5	30.9	31.9	22.6	46.0	40.0	33.4	27.3	25.7
D. Indirect Taxes	43.9	46.1	31.1	34.4	37.3	19.3	31.9	39.0	39.6	44.4
Tariffs	16.1	19.6	6.2	7.4	14.6	2.2	5.8	7.9	9.9	13.6
E. Other	0.4	0.9	-	-	-	1.9	1.5	3.3	6.4	9.0

Revenue Source	Hessen-Kassel[d,e] 1831	1833	1841/42	1846/48	Nassau[d,f] 1830	1836	1840	1846
A. State Domains								
Forests, Fisheries	32.7	33.4	33.0	31.0	...	...	...	...
B. State Enterprises	18.5	17.3	18.9	19.3	17.3	15.2	14.7	19.9
C. Direct Taxes	19.8	19.7	15.9	15.8	48.0	38.3	37.7	35.2
D. Indirect Taxes	20.6	22.5	24.9	26.7	...	...	...	...
Tariffs	9.4	12.1	14.7	17.9	13.8	23.8	27.1	26.4
E. Other	4.6	4.2	5.1	4.9	...	...	...	...

a. Net revenues. The costs of collection have been subtracted in the revenue date for Prussia, Bavaria, Baden, Wuerttemberg. Gross revenues are the basis of the calculations for the Hessian states and Nassau, with the exception of tariff revenues since 1834.

b. Sources: K. Borchard, Staatsverbrauch und oeffentliche Investitionen in Deutschland 1780-1850, unpublished dissertation, University of Goettingen, 1968, pp.31 and 33. For Prussian tariff revenues see T. Ohnishi, Zolltarifpolitik Preussens bis zur Gruendung des Deutschen Zollvereins, (Goettingen, 1972), pp.122-123.

c. Sources: J.D.G. von Memminger, Wuerttembergische Jahrbuecher, (Stuttgart, 1826), with data for 1819/20; Memminger's Beschreibung von Wuerttemberg, vol.3, edited by the Koeniglich Statistisch-Topographisches Buereau, (Stuttgart, 1841) with data for 1839/42; Verhandlungen der Kammer Abgeordneten des Koenigreichs Wuerttemberg, Erstes Heft, (Stuttgart, 1830), Anlage VII, Haupt-Finanz-Etat 1830-33.

d. Source: H.-W.Hahn, Wirtschaftliche Integration im 19. Jahrhundert. Die hessischen Staaten und der Deutsche Zollverein, (Goettingen, 1982), Anhang, tables 2-5, pp.317-325.

e. Capital incomes from the state wealth have been added to the revenues from state enterprises.

f. Revenues from the state salt monopoly have been added to revenues from state enterprises. Since revenues from the domains were not subject to the control of the parliament, they have not been included here.

Chapter Four

BANKING AND ECONOMIC GROWTH : BANKS AND INDUSTRY IN GERMANY IN THE NINETEENTH CENTURY AND THEIR CHANGING RELATIONSHIP DURING INDUSTRIALISATION*

Wilfried Feldenkirchen

I

German industrialisation which started rather slowly at the beginning of the nineteenth-century, but gained momentum after the introduction of railways, was considerably influenced by the banks. Despite variations in concentration, according to region and type of branch, the banks acted as investors and lenders of capital during the three main stages of German industrialisation.(1) The growth of large-scale enterprises and the close connection between credit banks and industrial enterprises are generally regarded as characteristic features of German industrialisation, which helped to overcome the competitive disadvantages that can be traced back to Germany's relative backwardness.(2) Until the First World War eight German joint-stock banks had developed into Grossbanken (big banks) of which the Schaaffhausen'sche Bankverein, the Bank fuer Handel und Industrie (Darmstaedter Bank), the Disconto-Gesellschaft and the Berliner Handelsgesellschaft were initially the most important, before being joined by the Deutsche Bank, the Dresdner Bank, the Nationalbank fuer Deutschland and the Commerz- und Disconto-Bank from the 1870s onwards.(3) Measured by their balance sheet total as well as by their share capital, the three biggest German enterprises in 1913 were banks, and among the 25 biggest enterprises were 17 banks.(4)

The close connection between the banking system and German industry has interested scholars since the end of the nineteenth-century. Sombart saw a close relationship from the cradle to the grave between banks and joint-stock companies. Hilferding had a strong influence on contemporary attitudes when he claimed in 1910, that there was a strong dependence of industrial enterprises on the banks.(5) More recent publications on the subject are often based on econometric models but lack empirical data, as Helmut Boehme correctly emphasised a few years ago.(6) E.Eistert, Neuburger and Stokes, and Richard Tilly came to different results, when they looked at the influence of the banks on German industrialisation. Even though Eistert rejected the existence of a causal relationship between developments in the banking sector and the growth of the German economy, he stressed the growth-promoting influence of the banks. The provision of funds by banks grew faster than the indicator for overall economic growth, namely net national product at current prices.(7) As Eistert confined himself to an analysis of financing undertaken with the help of money provided by the banks, he did not look at the influence that the banks exercised on the expenditure of industrial enterprises, and therefore could not pass any general judgement on the importance of banks for the growth of the German economy. Neuburger and Stokes, however, viewed as the central issue the question as to whether the amount of bank capital flowing into industry was influenced by its supply or by its demand.(8) They argued that the banks favoured heavy industry at the expense of light industry, thereby reducing the efficiency of the economy. Leaving methodological misgivings aside, which have already been discussed by Tilly and Fremdling (9), I would like to stress that Neuburger and Stokes do not sufficiently take into consideration the different enterprise structure in pre-1914 Germany. They wrongly assume that enterprises in the light industry sector had a demand for bank capital that was as high as that of the large-scale enterprises in the heavy and electro-technical industries, and that the banks failed to meet these requirements. Richard Tilly, however, has developed in a number of articles an increasingly refined assessmemt of the relationship between banks and industrial enterprises and the commonly assumed dependence of the latter on the former.(10) The latest publications on banking history by Manfred Pohl, on the other hand, do not pay very much attention to this particular aspect.(11)

The archive material of the big banks seems to be lost for the pre-First World War period, and there is hardly any useful material in state archives that appears relevant for a study like this. I would like therefore to look at the problem from the credit-seeking side, based on the primary and secondary sources of the industrial enterprises themselves. The intention of the analysis is to show whether, and, if so, to what extent, the established variations in the growth rates of individual industrial sectors (12), differences in fixed assets (13), or the extent of cartelisation were significant in determining the nature of capital funding and the relationships between banks and industrial enterprises. The paper will also explore the alternative hypothesis, that irrespective of type of industry, the nature and extent of capital procurement was decisively determined by the date of a firm's incorporation, its size, profitability, and share-holder composition. I will confine myself to joint-stock companies, where business archive material is available, because joint stock companies became increasingly important in the economy towards the end of the nineteenth-century. Indeed in certain branches of industry they had achieved a position of dominance well before this period.

II

For a long time it was generally thought that the German economy lagged behind English development in the first half of the nineteenth-century because of a lack of capital. More recent publications have shown that the level of savings had as little effect in restricting investment in the first decades of the nineteenth-century as it did later on.(14) Very high levels of investment in agriculture, trade and in the infrastructure were successfully financed, and fiscal surpluses and the liquidation of state debts contributed to a superfluity of capital, so that the interest rate on public loans was lowered from 4 to 3.5 per cent in the 1830s.(15) We cannot speak of a general lack of capital in Germany in the first half of the nineteenth-century, but there certainly was a problem of distribution, as the Prussian capital market had a pronounced regional character right from the start, because of poor transport facilities and territorial divisions.(16) As the most important industries of this period produced durable mass consumer products and would have required a buoyant growth in demand in order to have achieved faster growth, the funds needed for industrial investment were small. According to Tilly before 1849 the share of net investment in industry in relation to overall investment remained below five per cent.(17) If we take Hoffmann's calculation of gross national product, the textile industry, which constituted the largest industrial sector by the mid-nineteenth-century, only had a capital stock that could have been raised on the basis of an annual savings rate of seven per cent.(18) Among the 102 joint stock companies founded in Prussia between 1826 and 1850, with an overall capital of 638 million marks, there were only 19 industrial enterprises with a combined share capital of 9.5 million marks.(19) Undoubtedly there was a financing problem for some branches of industry in reconciling specific new investment demands, connected with profitable technological change, with the requirements of capital lenders for security, liquidity and the divisibility of invested capital.(20) However the capital demand of most companies was small and could be met mostly by the owners, or by their partners.(21) Bank credits were of minor importance when raising the initial capital, although in the case of existing firms they had already assumed in part an important dimension.(22) Some banks, such as the Cologne banking houses of Schaaffhausen, Oppenheim, Stein and Herstatt with substantial indigenous capital reserves, were already able to grant high overdraft credits before 1850. The overdraft credits granted by the Cologne banking houses to industrial enterprises rose from 2.5 million talers in the mid-1830s to 12 million talers in 1847, with credit limits very often being considerably exceeded in agreement with the banks.(23) Capital imports were of minor importance until the 1840s, although the significance of foreign risk capital in some pioneer enterprises cannot be denied.(24)

As a result of the revised Prussian mining law (1851), the growing demand of the railways, as the Rostowian leading-sector in Germany, the possibility of coke smelting, and the discovery of blackband in the Ruhr, the first *Gruenderperiode* (foundation period) in relation to heavy industry occurred between 1852 and 1857.(25) Most of the enterprises founded after 1850 could no longer be financed by single entrepreneurs, so that new ways of financing had to be found. Many of the newly established enterprises in heavy industry were joint-stock companies which existed alongside mining companies of the old and new type.(26) Whereas only three concessions for mining companies and iron and steel works, with an authorised capital of 3,306,367 talers, had been granted in the Ruhr area in the 1840s, 44 concessions with an authorised share capital of 41,238,333 talers were granted in the 1850s.(27) Daebritz estimated the capital demand of both the new and recently expanded existing companies in the mining and metallurgical sectors in the 1850s at approximately 100 million talers.(28) Despite the fact that capital requirements in other branches of industry were considerably lower, and that joint-stock companies were not very numerous even in fast growing sectors such as mechanical engineering (29), the demand on the capital market took on vast dimensions, clearly exceeding the capacity of existing financing methods. The growing capital demand of industry was brought about by far-reaching technical and economic changes. In contrast to Great Britain, industrialisation in Germany did not start in the consumer goods industries, but in the capital-intensive heavy goods industries, where a strong tendency towards large-scale enterprises already existed because of new technology.(30)

The foundation of joint-stock companies on a scale which effectively reflected demand and the contemporary expansion of industrial production would not have been possible if there had not been a corresponding change in the banking structure. Indeed in hardly any other field of the German economy in the mid-1850s was there such a general degree of backwardness as in the banking sector.(31) Even though the business and credit connections of banks to traditional industrial enterprises should not be underrated, we cannot speak of an efficient banking system existing in Germany before the middle of the nineteenth-century. Before 1848 there was no banking company, as such, until a fundamental change took place with the foundation of the A. Schaaffhausen'sche Bankverein as the first German joint-stock bank.(32) Prussia, in the first instance, refused to licence any more joint-stock banks out of regard for the agricultural interest, despite the growing demand for large-scale financing institutions generated by the industrial upswing.(33) The Disconto-Gesellschaft and the Berliner Handels-Gesellschaft were therefore established as limited partnerships in order to get round these regulations. (34) Outside Prussia the growing demand for loans and the commercial success of the French Crédit Mobilier after 1850 led to the foundation of joint-stock banks, of which the Bank fuer Handel und Industrie, promoted by nearly all existing Cologne banks (35), was the most important.

Although the foundation of joint-stock banks changed German banking fundamentally in the long run, private bankers retained their predominant position in dealings with the industry during the 1850s. The Cologne banks alone, of which only Schaaffhausen was a joint-stock bank, provided up until 1857 about 25 million talers for industrial financing.(36) These banks refused to accept larger deposits for a fixed period , and generally they only helped with the foundation of enterprises and subsequently preferred to conduct regular banking business. In 1863 Simon Oppenheim in his last will explicitly forbad his heirs to tie up bank capital in industrial shareholdings.(37) Therefore most of the shareholdings of the Cologne banks were due to non-liquid loans. In the 1850s the Cologne banks were the principal money lenders to the new companies in heavy industry in the Ruhr, as there were no serviceable banks in that area at the time.(38) By and large the Cologne banks did not act directly as founders of industrial enterprises, but as agents for the founding entrepreneurs in placing part or all of the available shares. As the Schaaffhausen'sche Bankverein always endeavoured to resell industrial shares in order to maintain its own liquidity, the bank took part in many transactions. As early as the 1850s the bank already held the leading position in both the coal and iron and steel industries of the Ruhr which it was to retain until 1914.(39). The Bankverein took part in the conversion of Hermannshuette into the Hoerder Bergwerks-und Huettenverein, in the foundation of the Koelner Bergwerks-Verein, the Koeln-Muesener-Bergwerks-Aktiengesellschaft and the Harpener Bergbau AG.(40) In other branches of industry the role of the Bankverein is worth mentioning in the foundation of the Koelnische Baumwollspinnerei-und weberei and the Koelnische Maschinenbau AG.(41)

Among the private banking houses in Cologne it was the Oppenheim bank in particular that developed its business relations with heavy industry in the Ruhr, through investment participation in the firm of Detillieux Frères & Cie., and in the mining companies Koenigin Elisabeth, Langenbrahm, Concordia and Pluto.(42) Even more important was the foundation of the Phoenix company in 1852, which was planned as the first mixed concern in the heavy goods sector of the Ruhr and thus required a high level of capital investment. Oppenheim took over 1.1 million talers, i.e. 73 per cent of the initial capital: 700,000 talers were to be offered for sale on the Paris stock exchange, while 400,000 talers were taken up by the bank on its own account.(43)

The Cologne banks continued to develop their existing comparatively close relationship with industry after 1850, particularly in those industrial sectors which underwent economic growth in the region around Cologne. By contrast the private banking houses in the other German states maintained their cautious attitude, or only expanded their industrial interests relatively slowly.(44) As the industrial expansion in Germany exceeded the capacity of the private banks interested in industrial financing, the new joint-stock banks were soon able to assume a significant role in the foundation of companies and in investment banking. Up until 1857 the Bank fuer Handel und Industrie, which had the declared intention of promoting 'sound and big enterprises by investing the bank's and other people's money' (45), had founded seven companies in the south-west German textile industry with a nominal capital of 2,580,000 guilders with approximately one-third of the share capital (813,160 guilders) retained by the bank itself. Well into the 1870s nearly all the bank's profits originated from stock-exchange transactions and shareholdings in industrial companies, and it was only after 1890 that the bank realised most of its profits through regular banking activities.(46) The Berliner Handels-Gesellschaft, founded with the help of Gustav Mevissen, Abraham Oppenheim and the Berlin banks S.Bleichroeder, Robert Warschauer & Co. and Gebr. Schickler, on the other hand, was an investment bank right from the start.(47) The Disconto-Gesellschaft was also founded 'to grant credit to solid smaller industrialists who previously had only been able to obtain it on unfavourable terms, if at all'.(48) The Disconto-Gesellschaft played an important role in the founding of new enterprises, and although initially it limited itself to current account transactions, it increasingly became actively involved in companies it had helped to set up, as considerable new funds flowed into the bank as a shareholder. Besides some smaller enterprises, the Disconto-Gesellschaft had shareholdings in the newly established Henrichshuette, Bleialf and Vereinigte Praesident.(49) The Henrichshuette, founded in 1851, was transformed in 1863 into a limited partnership after the bank had incurred considerable losses.(50) Between 1860 and 1863 the Disconto-Gesellschaft successfully reorganised the Phoenix metallurgical enterprise which had run into financial difficulties. In this case it was important to refloat illiquid loans as shares, although the transfer process in cases of industrial reorganisation had been a problem ever since the initial founding of joint-stock companies.(51)

The insufficient willingness of banks to provide industrial investment and the heavily decentralised character of the Prussian capital market also explain why more than one-third of the issued share capital in the 1850s came from outside Prussia.(52) Thirty-seven per cent of the share capital in heavy industry came from other German states or from foreign countries. In the remaining branches of industry, which had a smaller capital demand, the non-Prussian share was lower, although it constituted approximately 25 per cent in textiles.(53) In as far as it was not a question of direct foreign investment, the Cologne banks, and in particular the banking house of Oppenheim, were able to act as an intermediary in securing French and Belgian capital, on account of their contacts in Paris and Brussels. The Deutsch-Hollaendischer Aktienverein fuer Bergbau und Huettenbetrieb was financed by Dutch investors and by the banking houses Herstatt and Hueck. Dutch investors also had substantial shareholdings in the AG Vulcan.(54) Hibernia and Shamrock were completely financed with English and Irish capital (55), although English capital became increasingly less important in comparison with French or Belgian capital.(56)

We cannot dispute the pioneering role of the banks in founding and financing enterprises in the heavy industry sector, but we should not overrate the influence of the banks on the economy in general or even on the secondary sector in this first phase of German industrialisation. Within the secondary sector, whose share of net national value added was 20.7 per cent in 1850, joint-stock companies only dominated a few branches of industry. In 1857 overall share capital in industry only amounted to seven per cent of industry's total capital stock.(57) But joint-stock companies together with joint-stock banks were a pre-requisite for the procurement of investment capital. If the banks had not fulfilled this function, investible savings would not have been channelled into industries with an increasing capital demand. After the Preussische Bank had progressively raised its discount rate between 1848 and 1857 from 4 to 7.5 per cent, the capital demand of industry dropped sharply in the following slump. In the 1860s there was no significant strain on the capital market either. The number of cases involving an increase in capital stock was low, and if external capital was raised it was mostly done by issuing bonds.(58) Because of the investors' diminishing confidence in Germany's economic outlook, it very often turned out to be difficult to place bonds between 1857 and 1863.

III

The upswing in the economy from the late 1860s onwards, the abolition of the licensing requirement for joint-stock companies, the victorious outcome of the war with France, which had to pay substantial reparations, (even if their effect is sometimes overrated), led to an unprecedented economic boom in the early 1870s. This was reinforced by the inflationary effect of the German currency reform, as new gold coins were introduced before the old ones had been called in.(59) In heavy industry a second *Gruenderperiode* followed the surge of promotional activity of the 1850s and its effects were further enlarged by the rapid expansion of existing companies.(60) In mechanical engineering (61), in textiles and in the fast-growing chemical industries, joint-stock companies became more numerous, although they did not become as predominant as in the case of heavy industry.(62) Between 1871 and 1873, 2,781 million marks were invested in newly founded joint-stock companies (see figures 4.1 and 4.2), which was about half a billion more than in the years from 1851 to 1870.(63) The banks, which themselves became objects of speculation (64), acted as company promoters and capital lenders particularly in heavy industry, while in other branches of business they had a more limited function, frequently restricted to facilitating technical development. This reflected the fact that most of the new joint-stock companies were actually reorganised family enterprises, whose funds were no longer sufficient to meet the increased requirements for fixed and working capital.(65)

Although the figures differ greatly according to company and branch of business reflecting divergent development processes (66), the need for capital on the part of firms and the procurement of capital by banks generally rose between 1870 and 1913. In this period the net value added of the secondary sector grew by four per cent annually.(67) However, there were strong fluctuations over time in the growth rate of industry's demand for capital. In this context the possibilities of auto-financing and the nature of economic growth were more important than the capital market.(68) If we take the balance sheet total as an indicator of a company's growth (table 4.1), we find periods of slow and strong or even erratic growth correlating closely with market conditions. The only exception to this is the textile industry. During the so-called *Stockungsspanne* (slack phase) (69), which lasted until 1895 and was characterised by long recessions and short and weak upswings, the growth rate of most companies' balance sheet totals was low. This was especially true for heavy industry which suffered from excess capacity and a dramatic fall in prices. The high investment levels of the early 1870s, the resulting excess capacity and the financial difficulties

Fig. 4.1 JOINT STOCK COMPANIES FOUNDED BETWEEN 1871 AND 1913

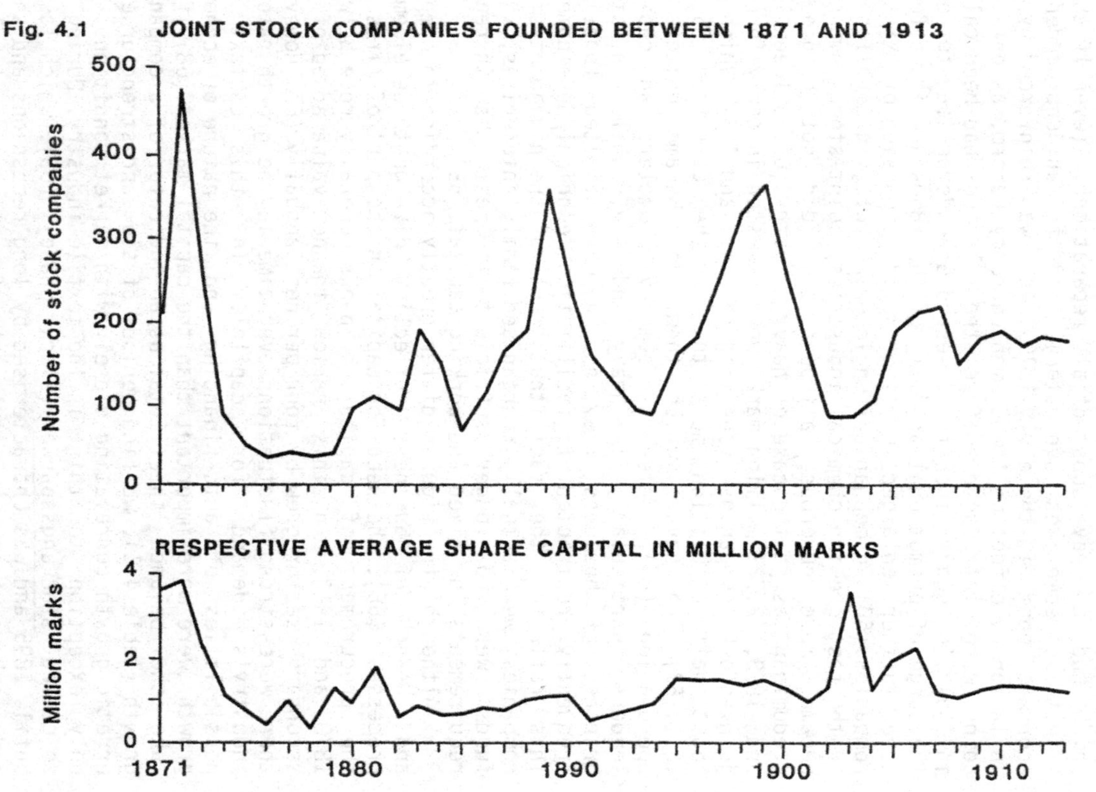

Fig. 4.2 SHARE CAPITAL OF NEWLY FOUNDED JOINT STOCK COMPANIES, 1871–1913 AND ISSUE OF STOCKS IN INDUSTRY, 1883–1913

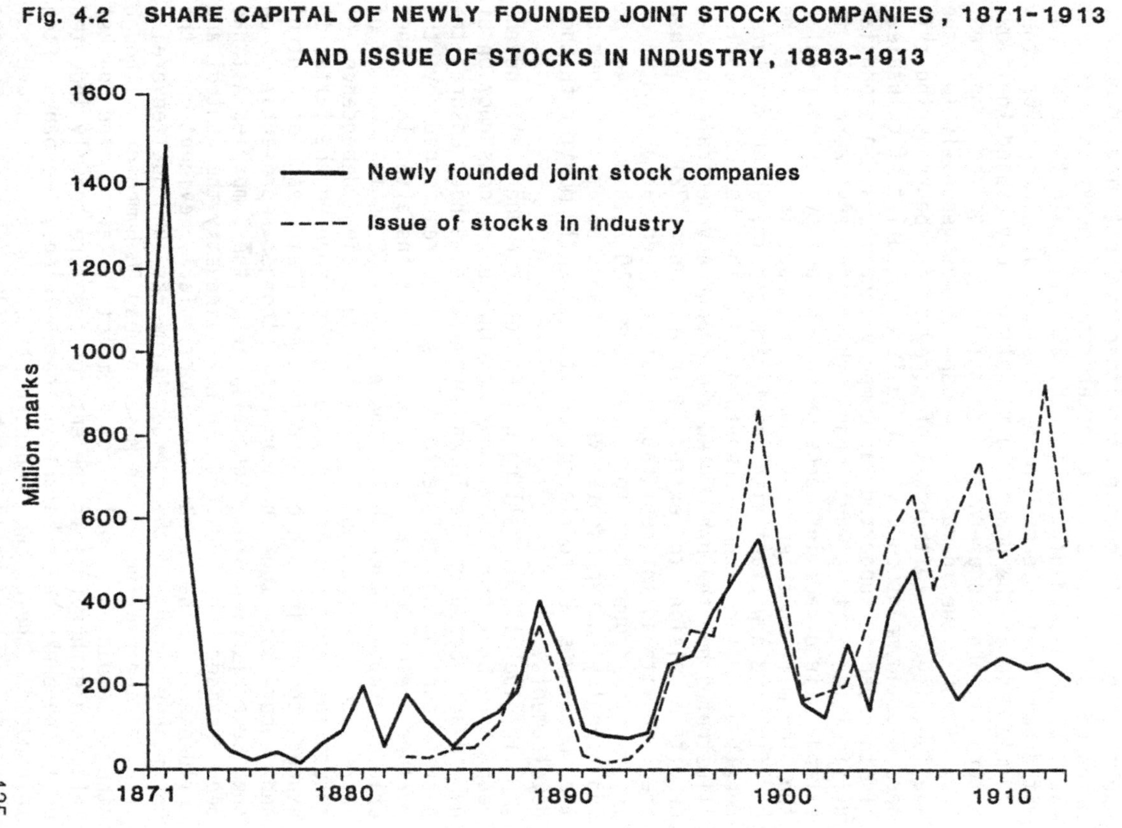

which often led to industrial mergers, all contributed to the slow growth of this sector.(70) At the same time the cyclical downswing of the years 1873 to 1879 which had not been expected by most companies either in its timing or extent, affected severely a lot of enterprises in heavy industry and made them dependent on the banks.(71) While the banks had withdrawn their loans in the crisis of the late 1850s, they now made use of the downswing to deliberately expand their own interests and to exercise direct influence on the companies. Even though the demand for capital was generally low, the availability or withdrawal of money by the banks during this period often meant survival or failure for a lot of companies. If the banks supported a company that was in financial difficulties, it always meant that the banks were able to extend their direct influence on company policy. In particular the ten million taler loan granted to Krupp in 1874, after he had financed new plant with short-term credit, which was later recalled after the down-turn in the business cycle, illustrates how the banks used the dependency generated by new credit provision to extend their influence.(72) They issued the loan with an interest rate of six per cent at a premium of 86, while Krupp had to repay it at 110 within nine years. Additionally a representative of the banks became a member of the company's board in order to directly monitor further developments.

In the 1880s falling prices for iron and coal, and the need for bank credit in order to finance the construction of new plant based on the Thomas production method, ensured the banks' continuing influence. This was reinforced by the further deterioration in market conditions after 1882, when prices dropped even below those of the 1870s in a period of increasing production.(73) The resulting dependence of industrial enterprises on the banks enabled the latter to expand their influence even further. Their means of control and supervision took the form of a stronger representation on the supervisory board, especially after the Companies Act had been revised in 1884.(74) In heavy industry the control and influence of the banks was particularly evident in the Dortmunder Union and the Hoerder Bergwerks- und Huettenverein, and in engineering in the Maschinenbau AG Humboldt, although other companies could not completely avoid the banks' influence either.(75) If the enterprises were heavily indebted or if the banks had substantial shareholdings, the banks often introduced their own representatives onto the board of directors as indicated in table 4.2.(76) In some enterprises exceptional events led to a stronger bank influence on their supervisory bodies. The Bochumer Verein's unsuccessful investments in Italy and Spain led to the Berliner Handels-Gesellschaft and the Schaaffhausen'sche Bankverein sending two representatives on to the supervisory board in

1892.(77) In the 1880s the banks increasingly demanded that their clients should have no contacts with other banking houses, so that they were better able to control the company's finances and external borrowing. The banks were able to demand such an exclusive connection as the relatively limited capital needed by industrial enterprises did not yet surpass the financing capacity of individual banks. In 1891 the Hoerder Bergwerks-und Huettenverein agreed at a creditors' meeting not to initiate any commercial dealings with other banks. Because of that guarantee the Schaaffhausen'sche Bankverein and Deichmann & Co., which had granted extensive loans in the 1880s unsecured by mortgages, declared that they were willing to fundamentally reorganise the firm and to save it from bankruptcy.(78)

The banks tried to use their increased influence to secure greater concentration within industries and higher company profitability. Since the late 1870s the banks had been eager to promote output agreements and price cartels in heavy industry. As it had been impossible to enforce such agreements in the 1880s, the banks, with the Disconto-Gesellschaft in the lead, promoted the expansion of big enterprises such as the Gelsenkirchener Bergwerks AG and the Harpener Bergbau AG, expecting to achieve their aims more easily once industrial concentration had taken place.(79) The number of collieries in the *Oberbergamtsbezirk* (superior mining district) Dortmund, for example, dropped from a peak of 277 in 1879 to 170 in 1890.(80)

Prior to 1895, there is no uniform model of the relations between banks and industry and of the importance of banks in raising industrial capital. In those branches of industry where relatively small enterprises were predominant, the banks' influence was generally small. But even in the heavy and electro-technical industries there were both companies which were unable to reach important decisions without consulting the banks, and companies which could freely determine their entrepreneurial objectives on the basis of a relatively good financial position. If we look at those companies which were not dependent on financing by the banks, there was clearly a pronounced hostility towards borrowed capital in the 1880s. This was due in part to the experience of individual firms and also reflected their reaction to the plight of other companies in the *Gruendungskrise*[a] when the banks had repeatedly withdrawn loans and endangered their existence. Other firms were afraid that their scope for decision-making would be more or less severely restricted by borrowing external capital. Hostility towards external capital in many firms still largely owned by individual families often went as far as a conscious renunciation of possible expansion and the potential advantages of borrowing capital.

Eisen-und Stahlwerk Hoesch, the Gutehoffnungshuette and Krupp were three major firms which took into account the ability of family members and associated share owners to provide funds, in determining the growth of share capital. The share capital of Hoesch and the Gutehoffnungshuette remained unchanged until 1896. The desire of the principal shareholders to keep their share of stock and to retain their influence, in this context encouraged significant self-financing. The supervisory board of Hoesch decided on 2 April, 1897, 'to continue to keep the commanding position' and to retain its influence even when there was an increase in share capital. A take-over bid for the new shares by a group of banks was to be avoided, 'as it is not desirable that outside elements come on to the supervisory board or even the board of directors'.(81) In order to retain a dominant position, the members agreed among themselves not to sell their shares without the express consent of the other board members. When the premium for the new shares was fixed, consideration was given to the sums to be raised by individual family members.(82) In the electro-technical industry it was Werner Siemens' adoption of this business attitude that promoted or at least made possible the rise of the AEG.(83) Nearly all the firms in the textile industry, as well as the smaller, mostly family-owned firms in the chemical industry, only fell back upon borrowed capital when essential investments seemed necessary to keep the company going. Less urgent projects were simply dropped, if they were dependent on external borrowing. In the less capital-intensive branches of industry such a controlled policy of expansion by the owners was still possible up until the outbreak of the First World War. On the other hand after 1895 technological change, cartelisation and the aggressive growth policy of managerial enterprises forced traditional entrepreneurial firms in the heavy and electro-technical industries to develop at a pace that could no longer be accommodated on the basis of the financing potential of shareholders.(84)

After the <u>Gruendungskrise</u>[a] investment banking and underwriting became less important and were replaced by regular banking business. Many firms, however, were forced to accept bank credits for the initial funding of plant and working capital, so that between 1882 and 1895 the banks financed almost half of all net investment.(85) In mechanical engineering the foundation of joint-stock companies became more frequent in the 1880s in comparison with the preceding decade, but the capital demand of these new firms was rather low. The increases in share capital in the industrial sectors under examination during the 1880s were also not very significant in extent.(86) The demand for share capital was generally low because of the slow growth in production, excess capacity and the resultant modest investment propensity. If some companies raised or had to raise their share capital, this was frequently preceded by a merger and the new shares were issued as priority shares. A lot of the coal mines ran at a loss, which had to be covered by additional payments. In particular the Essener Credit-Anstalt, with its close ties with the mining companies of the Ruhr, frequently had to provide credits for this purpose.(87) In the 1880s, regardless of industrial sector, share capital made up a very big, if not the biggest part, of the total working capital of individual firms.

Between 1850 and 1873 the German banks had often been initiators in founding joint-stock companies and had frequently invested their own capital in such enterprises. In the 1880s, however, the banks tried to avoid direct shareholdings in firms as far as possible. The reason for this new attitude can be found in the experience of the 1870s, when the banks often had to undertake substantial value adjustments, on account of significant reductions in the share value of individual firms.(88) If a bank remained as a major shareholder, it was mostly due to the fact that the shares could not be disposed of at all, or only at unfavourable rates. In some cases, however, banks kept these shares to promote concentration and cartelisation in those branches of industry in which they were interested.(89)

IV

In the upswing period after 1895 the average annual growth of the balance sheet total was higher than in the earlier slack phase of economic activity, regardless of industrial sector (table 4.1). The growth rates were particularly high in the case of the big chemical companies, in the electro-technical and heavy industries.(90) Because of the resulting higher demand for capital, the relations between banks and industry intensified, but it does not seem justified to conclude from this, or from the stronger bank representation on company supervisory boards, that industrial enterprises had become more dependent on the banks. Instead there was a growing emancipation of companies from the banks from the beginning of the twentieth century onwards.

In mechanical engineering, in the textile and chemical industries, and in the electro-technical industry there were only relatively infrequent increases in share capital after 1895, so that chronological turning points are difficult to identify. Share increases, nevertheless, increasingly occurred at the end of the upswing or at the start of a downturn in market conditions (see figure 4.3). Yet in heavy industry there was a temporal concentration of increases in share capital. The extent and timing of the increases in capital were strongly influenced by the adoption of cartel agreements

Fig. 4.3 PLACEMENT OF SECURITIES IN GERMANY, 1883-1913

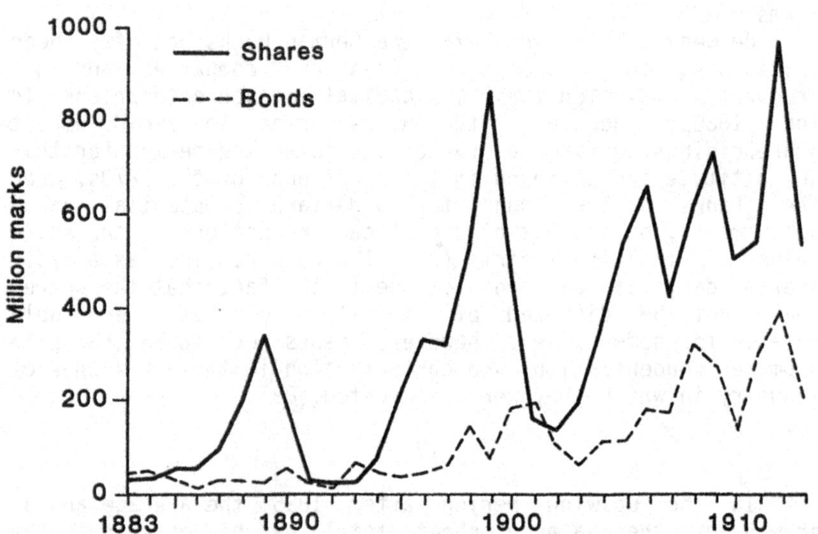

particularly after 1893. In the iron and steel industry the big increase in share capital in 1910 was due to the fact that the Steel Works Association, founded in 1904 and prolonged in 1907, was running out at the beginning of 1912. According to the regulations of the Association, the companies' production quotas were calculated on the basis of existing plant. As a result the construction of new plant and the direct purchase of quotas were regarded as appropriate means to expand one's own quota allocation.(91)

The growing long-run importance of short-term borrowed capital was also characteristic of the way capital was raised, particularly by the bigger companies. The individual enterprises in the recession of the 1880s had tried to keep the amount of borrowed capital as low as possible, primarily because of low profitability. Indeed the average annual growth rate of equity capital during this period had sometimes been higher than that of borrowed capital. However from the 1890s onwards the bigger companies purposely used short-term borrowed money for the initial financing of new plant, as this actually represented long-term credit through the process of constantly renewed substantial current account advances.(92) The share of overdraft credit in all credit provision rose from 50.8 per cent in 1895 to more than 70 per cent after the turn of the century.(93) As the banks thereby provided companies with sufficient means to carry out necessary and immediate investments, the enterprises were able to postpone a formal approach to the capital market until a time when either high stock discounts were possible or favourable borrowing conditions existed. The banks were willing to grant overdraft credit, as this could lead to an increase in share capital or to the issue of bonds, and other business transactions from which they could profit.(94) The banks' willingness to grant high overdraft credits is also understandable, as the big companies could offer adequate surety on account of their substantial holdings of stock exchange securities. The banks also considered that the risk in granting credit to big enterprises was negligible in comparison with their supply of capital to smaller firms.(95) The banks could supply these funds as there had been a general separation of bank capital and credit, following the example of the Deutsche Bank. Until the 1870s the amount of the bank's own capital had set the limit for the supply of credit. After 1900 the bank's share capital had more or less a guarantee function, but no longer limited the banks' volume of business.(96)

Even though in the long run the ratio of indebtedness to capital rose in the case of nearly all companies, most firms consciously did not make full use of the funding potential of external capital, despite the increase in capital rentability as a whole. As a result of their concern to preserve independence and self-sufficiency, they rejected any increased influence of outsiders in the firm and preferred to dispense with a broader capital basis and attendant faster growth and higher profits.(97) If expanding companies could dispense with external capital or do without borrowed funds in order to limit the influence of banks, this was due to a number of individual factors. Capital was accumulated internally, profits were retained, reserves were formed, for example for pensions, the proceeds from the depreciation of plant were released, or firms were able to benefit from other forms of asset restructuring. In the earlier period this internal accumulation of capital was a major, if not sole, source of fund-raising for many companies. Its overall importance, however, can only be calculated from the earnings situation of individual companies and the amount of distributed profits.(98)

A look at distributed and retained profits reveals remarkable differences between individual firms, which can apparently be attributed to the composition of the share-owning body. The calculation of the dividend and the possibility of retaining profits were evidently dependent on the expectations and demands of shareholders, which very often did not accord with the general attitude of directors in big enterprises to dividend payments. The managing directors wanted to expand their freedom of action through increased self-financing.(99) Companies in which the family still held the majority of shares tended to retain a higher proportion of net profits, as private and company interests largely coincided. This tendency was influenced by the fact that extensive internal procurement of equity capital helped these firms to dispense with non-family shareholders for a relatively long time. Besides these family enterprises, the big companies in the chemical industry also retained a high proportion of net profits. Generally the absolute amount of funds available to companies from retained earnings rose after the turn of the century. Some companies used their retained earnings for extraordinary depreciation; they often put them in special reserve funds or dividend supplement funds or carried them as a surplus brought forward for a period of years. In addition to retaining earnings by such means, almost all the companies examined in this study also made considerable provisions for sickness and pension funds as part of their social welfare policy. Technically, this represented internally financed borrowed capital, but it could also be regarded as a form of financing comparable to the use made of the company's own funds. Provision was for longer-term needs, disbursement was not at a specific date and no interest had to be paid on the funds. Most of the companies under review were thus able to finance their internal growth solely by self-financing.(100) For the banks the increasing level of self-financing meant a reduction in their influence.(101)

Besides the more frequent use of overdraft credits, the substantial growth in the liquidity of practically all companies after 1895 shows how they endeavoured to react as quickly as possible to any investment requirements. Even though the liquidity ratios were not as high as they are nowadays, they had increased significantly in comparison with the period from 1873 to 1894.(102) First degree liquidity was generally higher in the case of smaller enterprises, than for very large firms. This can be explained by the fact that relatively smaller firms needed to be equipped to deal with sudden demands for new investment, whereas the very large companies were able to provide such funds more effectively and more quickly through asset restructuring.

During the so-called period of stagnation up to 1894 almost all the companies had considerable short-term debts with the banks. In the upswing after 1895, however, a lot of them maintained very considerable bank balances, sometimes reaching a proportion of 50 per cent of all current assets in several cases in the years before the First World War as indicated in table 4.3. The fluctuations in bank balances during these years were due to the investment behaviour of individual firms.(103) If there was heavy investment, the level of the balances maintained with the banks fell accordingly; if investment was low, the level rose again. In the period from 1900 to 1913 the industrial joint-stock companies enlarged their securities by 744 million marks and their bank balances by 531 million marks.(104) The highly liquid assets accumulated by firms further reduced their dependence on the banks. These funds could be used as the company management desired, without the knowledge of the banks or even, if necessary, against their will. The change in the position of enterprises in relation to the banks can also be seen in their negotiations on interest rates for short or medium-term deposits of company funds with the banks.(105)

The process of industrial concentration which was greatly strengthened by the formation of cartels, further limited the influence any one bank could exercise on industrial enterprises. Mergers often brought several big banks on to the supervisory boards, and the competition and rivalry between banks ultimately limited their influence, even if numerically there were more bank representatives on the boards.(106) At the same time the investment sums required by the new large-scale concerns grew to such an extent that they were beyond the financing power of any one bank.(107) The share issues almost always had to be handled by a consortium. Emil Kirdorf, General Director of the Gelsenkirchener Bergwerks-Gesellschaft, was able to state at the meeting of the Verein fuer Socialpolitik (Social Policy Association) in 1905, with clear justification, that:

> In case it should be pointed out again that there is already something like a state monopoly, because the great banks dominate our industry, I would wish to dispute such an assertion in the strongest possible terms. The influence of the major banks on heavy industry in Rhineland-Westphalia has never been as low as it is at present.(108)

In the electro-technical industry the foundation of holding and financing companies since the mid-1890s, which did not involve the use of banking capital to any large extent, effectively reduced dependence on the banks.(109) Thus it was the increasing concentration process, which the banks had encouraged and helped to finance, which generally restricted their influence.(110) The Dresdner Bank commented in its Annual Report for 1908 that the wave of concentration and the formation of industrial associations, particularly in heavy industry, had undeniably made these companies less dependent on the banks.(111) In some branches of industry concentration had already progressed so far in the years before the First World War that it actually endangered the continued existence of cartels.(112)

The banks' influence, however, can clearly be traced in mergers and acquisitions. The higher the share of external growth in the overall growth of an enterprise, the more easily could the banks influence the extent and direction of growth because of the greater sums of money involved. Among the mining companies this was especially true for the Gelsenkirchener Bergwerks AG, whose acquisitions of other firms were almost all planned and prepared by the Disconto-Gesellschaft.(113) In other branches of industry mergers and acquisitions were also facilitated and encouraged when the same bank or group of banks were interested in the two companies concerned. The representatives of the banks on the supervisory boards of these companies, with their wide-ranging business contacts, were in a position to see which firms were possible candidates for mergers or take-overs. The examples of the Duesseldorfer Roehren- und Eisenwalzwerke AG in 1910 and the Bergmann-Elektrizitaets-Werke in 1911 show that the banks were able to force enterprises, which were financially less sound, to undertake a merger or incorporation with another firm. New credits would only be granted in these cases if the firms agreed to the merger.(114)

In heavy industry the banks had decisively promoted concentration since the 1880s, but this was particularly the case after the turn of the century. In the electro-technical industry the Berliner Handels-Gesellschaft encouraged the expansion of AEG, just as the fusion of Siemens-Schuckert and Bergmann can be partly attributed to the role of the Deutsche

Bank.(115) In the chemical industry technical reasons were decisive in promoting concentration and the initiative always remained with the industrial enterprises themselves. In other branches of industry, however, increasing concentration in industry and in banking was mutually reinforcing. There was no such interdependence in the chemical industry.(116)

V

To summarise we can say that there were big differences in the relations between the banks and industry, depending on the branch of industry concerned, market conditions and the composition of the share-holding body. The level of capital requirement and its rate of growth in each branch of industry were decisive factors in determining the sectoral diffusion of joint-stock companies. In the heavy and electro-technical industries the banks' influence was greater, while it was hardly noticeable in the engineering and chemical industries, Yet we cannot speak of a dependence of industrial enterprises on the banks, but rather of a mutual interdependence, the causes and effects of which cannot be isolated.(117) Already in 1910, when Hilferding spoke of a dependence of industrial enterprises on the banks as a general characteristic of the German economy, he was patently no longer correct.(118)

* This is a slightly extended version, with additional footnotes, of a paper held at the SSRC/DFG conference in Liverpool University in May 1982.

a The crisis following the 'foundation period' of 1871-73.

NOTES

1. O.Jeidels, Das Verhaeltnis der deutschen Grossbanken zur Industrie, (Leipzig, 1905); Jacob Riesser, Die deutschen Grossbanken und ihre Konzentration, 3rd enlarged and revised edition, (Jena, 1910).

2. Alexander Gerschenkron, Economic Backwardness in Historical Perspective, (Cambridge/Mass., 1962), p.18 et seq.; David S.Landes, 'The Structure of Enterprise in the Nineteenth Century. The Cases of Britain and Germany', in XIe Congrés International des Sciences Historiques, (Uppsala, 1960), Rapport V, p.116; Juergen Kocka, 'Entrepreneurs and Managers in German Industrialisation', in P.Mathias and M.M.Postan (eds.), Cambridge Economic History of Europe, (Cambridge, 1978), vol.7.1, p.536 et seq.; Lars G.Sandberg, 'Ignorance, Poverty and Economic Backwardness in the Early Stages of European Industrialisation: Variations on Alexander Gerschenkron's Grand Theme'. The Journal of European Economic History, vol.11, (1982), pp.675-98. There is nevertheless no uniform picture of how important joint-stock companies really were for starting German industrialisation.

3. Karl Erich Born, Geld und Banken im 19. und 20. Jahrhundert, (Stuttgart, 1977), p.166. The Deutsche Bank, however, had not been very much interested in investment banking in its early years. The bank wrote in its Annual Report for 1885: 'In the course of industrialisation many firms have been reorganised into joint-stock companies. Yet, we stayed away from that and rather preferred to work in our old fields: overdraft credit, deposits, bonds.'

4. Richard H.Tilly, 'Banken und Industrialisierung in Deutschland. Quantifizierungsversuche', in F.W.Henning (ed.), Entwicklungen und Aufgaben von Versicherungen und Banken in der Industrialisierung, (Berlin, 1980), p.165.

5. Rudolf Hilferding, Das Finanzkapital. Eine Studie ueber die juengste Entwicklung des Kapitalismus. Unchanged reprint of the 1910 edition (Berlin, 1947).

6. Helmut Boehme, 'Bankenkonzentration und Schwerindustrie 1873-1876. Bemerkungen zum Problem des Organisierten Kapitalismus', in Sozialgeschichte heute. Festschrift fuer Hans Rosenberg, (Goettingen, 1974), p.432 et seq.

7. Ekkehard Eistert, Die Beeinflussung des Wirtschaftswachstums in Deutschland von 1883 bis 1913 durch das Bankensystem. Eine theoretisch-empirische Untersuchung, (Berlin, 1970).

8. H.Neuburger and H.Stokes, 'German Banks and German Growth', The Journal of Economic History, vol.34, (1974), pp.710-731.

9. Rainer Fremdling and Richard H.Tilly, 'German Banks, German Growth and Econometric History', The Journal of Economic History, vol.36, (1976), pp.416-424.

10. Richard H.Tilly, Kapital, Staat und sozialer Protest in der deutschen Industrialisierung, (Goettingen, 1980), passim.

11. Manfred Pohl, Konzentration im deutschen Bankwesen (1848-1980), (Frankfurt a.M., 1982); idem, 'Die Entwicklung des deutschen Bankwesens zwischen 1848 und 1870', in Deutsche Bankgeschichte, vol.2, (Frankfurt a.M., 1982), pp.143-220; idem, 'Festigung und Ausdehnung des deutschen Bankwesens zwischen 1870 und 1914', in Deutsche Bankgeschichte, vol.2, (Frankfurt a.M., 1982), pp.221-356.

12. Wilfried Feldenkirchen, 'Wirtschaftswachstum, Technologie und Arbeitszeit von der Fruehindustrialisierung bis zum Ersten Weltkrieg', in H.Pohl (ed.), Wirtschaftswachstum, Technologie und Arbeitszeit im internationalen Vergleich, (Beiheft 24 of the Zeitschrift fur Unternehmensgeschichte, Wiesbaden, 1983), tables 32 and 33.

13. In 1913 the ratio between fixed and current assets in the following sectors of industry was as follows:

Pit- and coal-mining	3.03
Iron and steel industry	1.12
Engineering	0.56
Chemical industry	1.28
Textile industry	0.63

14. Knut Borchardt, 'Zur Frage des Kapitalmangels in der ersten Haelfte des 19. Jahrhunderts in Deutschland', in Rudolf Braun and Wolfram Fischer (eds.), Industrielle Revolution, Wirtschaftliche Aspekte, (Cologne and Berlin, 1972), p.216 et seq.

15. Arthur Spiethoff, Die wirtschaftlichen Wechsellagen, vol.I, Erklaerende Beschreibung, (Tuebingen and Zurich, 1955), p.113.

16. Kurt Boesselmann, Die Entwicklung des deutschen Aktienswesens. Ein Beitrag zur Finanzierung gemeinwirtschaftlicher Unternehmen, (Berlin, 1939), p.29.

17. Richard H.Tilly, 'Banken und Industrialisierung in Deutschland, 1850-1870', in idem, Kapital, Staat und sozialer Protest, (Goettingen, 1980), p.35; Richard H.Tilly, 'Capital Formation in Germany in the 19th Century', in P.Mathias and M.M.Postan (eds.), Cambridge Economic History of Europe, vol.7.1, (Cambridge, 1978).

18. Borchardt, 'Frage', p.218.

19. Boesselmann, Entwicklung, p.199 et seq.

20. Walter Obenaus, 'Aktiengesellschaften in der Bayrischen Wirtschaftgeschichte des 19. Jahrhunderts', unpublished thesis, University of Munich, 1976, p.206.

21. Peter Coym, 'Unternehmensfinanzierung in fruehen 19. Jahrhundert - dargestellt am Beispiel der Rheinprovinz und Westfalens', unpublished PhD thesis, University of Hamburg, 1971, p.38 et seq.; Karl Heinrich Kaufhold, 'Handwerk und Industrie 1800-1850', in W.Zorn (ed.), Handbuch der deutschen Wirtschafts- und Sozialgeschichte, (Stuttgart, 1976), vol.2, p.343; in M.Kellenbenz (ed.). 'Zur Frage der Industriefinanzierung im fruehen 19. Jahrhundert', in: Oeffentliche Finanzen und privates Kapital im spaeten Mittelalter und in der ersten Haelfte des 19. Jahrhunderts, (Stuttgart, 1971), p.123 et seq.

22. Boesselmann, Entwicklung, p.34.

23. Wilfried Feldenkirchen, 'Koelner Banken und die Entwicklung des Ruhrgebiets', Zeitschrift fuer Unternehmensgeschichte, vol.27, (1982), p.93.

24. Heiner R.Schramm, 'Die Kapitalbildung in der fruehen Industrialisierung des Raumes Essen - Muelheim/Ruhr im Spiegel der Notariatsurkunden 1810-1870', unpublished PhD thesis, University of Bonn, 1969, p.135.

25. Paul Wiel, Wirtschaftsgeschichte des Ruhrgebiets. Tatsachen und Zahlen, (Essen, 1970), p.113; Wilfried Feldenkirchen, Die Eisen- und Stahlindustrie des Ruhrgebiets 1879-1914. Wachstum, Finanzierung und Struktur ihrer Grossunternehmen, (Wiesbaden, 1982), p.22 et seq.

26. Leo Kluitmann, Der gewerbliche Geld- und Kapitalverkehr im Ruhrgebiet im 19. Jahrhundert, (Bonn, 1931), p.14.

27. Boesselmann, Entwicklung, p.201; Kluitmann, Geldverkehr, p.48.

28. Walther Daebritz, 'Entstehung und Aufbau des rheinisch-westfaelischen Industriebezirks', Beitraege zur Geschichte und Technik der Industrie. Yearbook 1 of the Verein deutscher Ingenieure, p.44.

29. Wilfried Feldenkirchen, 'Kapitalbeschaffung und Kapitalverwendung bei Aktiengesellschaften des deutschen Maschinenbaus im 19. und beginnenden 20. Jahrhundert', Vierteljahrschrift fuer Sozial- und Wirtschaftsgeschichte, vol.69, (1982), p.42; Horst Thieme, 'Statistische Materialien zur Konzessionierung von Aktiengesellschaften in Preussen bis 1867', Jahrbuch fuer Wirtschaftsgeschichte, (1960), part II, p.286 et seq.

30. Knut Borchardt, 'Wirtschaftliches Wachstum und Wechsellagen 1800-1914', in W.Zorn (ed.), Handbuch der deutschen Wirtschafts- und Sozialgeschichte, (Stuttgart, 1976), vol.II, p.239.

31. Richard H.Tilly, 'Verkehrs- und Nachrichtenwesen, Handel, Geld-, Kredit- und Versicherungswesen 1850-1914', in W.Zorn (ed.), Handbuch der deutschen Wirtschafts-und Sozialgeschichte, (Stuttgart, 1976), vol.II, p.588.

32. Helmut Boehme, 'Gruendung und Anfaenge des Schaaffhausenschen Bankvereins, der Bank des Berliner Kassenvereins, der Direktion der Disconto-Gesellschaft und der Darmstaedter Bank fuer Handel und Industrie. Ein Beitrag zur preussischen Bankpolitik', Tradition, vol.10, (1965), pp.189-212 and Tradition, vol.11, (1966), pp.34-102. See also Gustav Mevissen's Report at the Annual Meeting of the Bank fuer Handel und Industrie in 1853: 'The inefficiency of the existing banks has been a fact and was increasingly realised the faster German industry expanded'.

33. Walther Daebritz, Gruendung und Anfaenge der Disconto-Gesellschaft, (Berlin, Munich and Leipzig, 1931), p.9; Landes, 'Structure', p.117; Richard H.Tilly, Financial Institutions and Industrialization in the Rhineland 1815-70, (University of Wisconsin Press, Madison, 1966), p.115.

34. Riesser, Grossbanken, p.362.

35. Bernhard Hilgermann, Das Werden und Vergehen einer bedeutenden Provinzbank: A. Schaaffhausenscher Bankverein AG 1848-1929, (Cologne, 1973), p.16 et seq.

36. Feldenkirchen, Koelner Banken, p.93.

37. Archives of the Oppenheim Bank, No.18.

38. Friedrich Wilhelm Klinker, Studien zur Entwicklung und Typenbildung von vier rheinisch-westfaelischen Provinzaktienbanken, (Volkswirtschaftliche Abhandlungen der badischen Hochschulen 22, Karlsruhe, 1913), p.13.

39. Jacob Riesser, _Zur Entwicklungsgeschichte der deutschen Grossbanken mit besonderer Ruecksicht auf die Konzentrationsbestrebungen_, (Berlin, 1905), p.56.

40. Archives of the Dortmund-Hoerder Huetten-Union (DHHU), No.51; Alfred Krueger, _Das Koelner Bankiergewerbe vom Ende des 18. Jahrhunderts bis 1875_, (Essen, 1925), p.159.

41. Riesser, _Entwicklungsgeschichte_, p.57 et seq.

42. Oppenheim-archive No.204.

43. Oppenheim-archive No.198.

44. Pohl, _Konzentration_, p.49 et seq; Boesselmann, _Entwicklung_, p.27; Alfred Blumenberg, 'Die Konzentration im deutschen Bankwesen', unpublished PhD thesis, University of Heidelberg, 1905, p.9.

45. The Annual Report for 1853. For the business policy of the bank, see Albert Salzmann, 'Ursprung und Ziel der modernen Bankenentwicklung', unpublished PhD thesis, University of Leipzig, Dresden, 1904, p.13.

46. Pohl, 'Festigung', p.280.

47. Daebritz, _Gruendung_, p.64; Hellmut Gebhardt, 'Die Berliner Boerse - Von den Anfaengen bis zum Jahre 1896', unpublished PhD thesis, University of Erlangen, 1928, p.48; Albert Blumenberg, 'Die Konzentration im deutschen Bankwesen', unpublished PhD thesis, Universities of Heidelberg and Leipzig, 1905, p.43.

48. Harald Winkel, 'Kapitalquellen und Kapitalverwendung am Vorabend des industriellen Aufschwungs in Deutschland', _Schmollers Jahrbuch fuer Wirtschafts- und Sozialwissenschaften_, vol.90, (1970), p.282.

49. Pohl, 'Entwicklung', p.270.

50. Daebritz, _Gruendung_, p.165.

51. Oppenheim-archive No.198.

52. H.Blumberg, 'Die Finanzierung der Neugruendungen und Erweiterungen von Industriebetrieben in Form von Aktiengesellschaften waehrend der 50er Jahre des 19. Jahrhunderts in Deutschland, am Beispiel der preussischen Verhaeltnisse erlaeutert', in H.Mottek (ed.), _Studium zur Geschichte der industriellen Revolution in Deutschland_, (East Berlin, 1960), p.192.

53. Walther Daebritz, _Denkschrift zum fuenfzigjaehrigen Bestehen der Essener Credit-Anstalt in Essen_, (Essen, 1922), p.42.

54. Schramm, 'Kapitalbildung', p.316.

55. Agnes M.Prym, _Staatswirtschaft und Privatunternehmung in der Geschichte des Ruhrkohlenbergbaus_, (Essen, 1950), p.24 et seq. - Hibernia was founded in 1854 by the Irishman William Thomas Mulvany.

56. Richard H.Tilly, 'Die Industrialisierung des Ruhrgebiets und das Problem der Kapitalmobilisierung', in idem, _Kapital, Staat und sozialer Protest in der deutschen Industrialisierung_, (Goettingen, 1980), p.75.

57. Tilly, 'Banken und Industrialisierung', p.51.

58. Blumberg, 'Finanzierung', p.203.

59. Martin Gehr, 'Das Verhaeltnis zwischen Banken und Industrie seit der Mitte des 19. Jahrhunderts bis zur Bankenkrise 1931 unter besonderer Beruecksichtigung des industriellen Grosskredits', unpublished PhD thesis, University of Tuebingen, 1959, p.5.

60. Feldenkirchen, Eisen- und Stahlindustrie, p.39 et seq.; see also diagram 4.1.

61. In engineering 131 joint-stock companies were founded and the stock capital of the existing companies became seven times as high as before 1870, see Feldenkirchen, 'Maschinenbau', p.42.

62. Ernst Engel, 'Die erwerbsthaetigen juristischen Personen im preussischen Staate, insbesondere die Aktiengesellschaften', Zeitschrift des Koeniglich Preussischen Statistischen Bureaus, vol.15, (1875), p.453.

63. Hans Rosenberg, Grosse Depression und Bismarckzeit. Wirtschaftsablauf, Gesellschaft und Politik in Mitteleuropa, (Munich, 1967), p.41: between 1871 and 1873 more than 2,781 million marks were invested in joint-stock companies, which was 500 million marks more than in the period from 1851 to 1870.

64. Boehme, 'Bankenkonzentration', p.435.

65. Of the 353 existing joint-stock companies in engineering, 100 had a stock capital of between 0.5 and 1 million marks, 98 had a stock capital of between 1 and 2 million marks and only 17 had a stock capital of more than 5 million marks. The average stock capital of all the 6,631 joint-stock companies founded between 1886 and 1912 was 1,325 million marks, see E.Freiberger, 'Die deutsche Maschinenbauindustrie', unpublished PhD thesis, University of Wuerzburg, 1913, p.31; Pohl, 'Festigung', p.231; Obenaus, 'Aktiengesellschaften', p.136.

66. See Wilfried Feldenkirchen, 'Industriefinanzierung im 19. Jahrhundert', in K.Duwell and W.Koellmann (eds.), Westfalen im Industriezeitalter, (Wuppertal, 1984), vol.2, pp.189-211.

67. Walther G.Hoffmann, Das Wachstum der deutschen Wirtschaft seit der Mitte des 19. Jahrhunderts, (Berlin, Heidelberg, New York, 1965), p.454.

68. Richard H.Tilly, 'Zur Entwicklung des Kapitalmarktes und Industrialisierung im 19. Jahrhundert unter besonderer Beruecksichtigung Deutschlands', Vierteljahrschrift fuer Sozial- und Wirtschaftsgeschichte, vol.60, (1973), p.156.

69. As I do not hold Rosenberg's term 'Great Depression' to be justified for the period from 1873 to 1895, I have used Spiethoff's term 'Stockungsspanne' (slack phase), see Spiethoff, Wechsellagen, p.124.

70. Both the Gutehoffnungshuette and the Hoerder Bergwerks-Verein among the more established firms, and the Rheinische Stahlwerke and the Dortmunder Union among the newly founded iron works, had to reduce their capital. Schalker Gruben- und Huettenverein had to write off all its capital and was reorganised into a cost book company, see Feldenkirchen, Eisen- und Stahlindustrie, p.237.

71. This was especially true for the companies that had to reduce their capital, see Gehr, 'Verhaeltnis', p.26.

72. Krupp-archive WA IV 1641; WA II 13.

73. Emil Muessig, Eisen- und Kohlenkonjunkturen seit 1870. Preisentwicklung in der Montanindustrie unter Einwirkung von Technik, Wirtschaft und Politik, 2nd edn., (Augsburg, 1919).

74. After 1884 the supervisory board hired the directors of the company and had the right to call an extraordinary general meeting.

75. DHHU-archive No.51,818,1193; Archives of Kloeckner-Humboldt-Deutz. See also the minutes of the Schaaffhausen'sche Bankverein.

76. DHHU-archive No.113.

77. Archive of the Bochumer Verein 142 04 No.5.

78. Minutes of the Schaaffhausen'sche Bankverein; minutes of the extraordinary general meeting of the Hoerder Bergwerks- und Huettenverein.

79. Boehme, 'Bankenkonzentration', p.437; Gehr, 'Verhaeltnis', p.49; Bruno Simmersbach, Wirtschaftliche Entwicklung der Gelsenkirchener Bergwerks-Aktiengesellschaft von 1873 bis 1904, (Freiberg, 1906), p.5. For a listing of the coal mines acquired by Gelsenkirchen, Harpen and Hibernia, see Fritz Schlueter, 'Das Verhaeltnis von Gewerkschaft zur Aktiengesellschaft im Ruhrkohlenbergbau, die Verschiebungen und inneren Ursachen', unpublished PhD thesis, University of Cologne, 1940.

80. Prym, Staatswirtschaft, p.27 et seq.

81. Hoesch-archive A3 b2 p.63.

82. Hoesch-archive A3 b2 p.77.

83. Juergen Kocka, 'Siemens und der aufhaltsame Aufstieg der AEG', Tradition, vol.17, (1972), p.125.

84. Kocka, 'Entrepreneurs', p.559.

85. E.Eistert and J.Ringel, 'Die Finanzierung des wirtschaftlichen Wachstums durch die Banken. Eine quantitativ-empirische Untersuchung fuer Deutschland 1850-1913', in Walther G.Hoffmann (ed.), Untersuchungen zum Wachstum der deutschen Wirtschaft, (Tuebingen, 1971), p.100.

86. Feldenkirchen, Eisen- und Stahlindustrie; idem., Maschinenbau.

87. W.Lindsiepe, 'Die Essener Credit-Anstalt im Zusammenhang mit der wirtschaftlichen Entwicklung des rheinisch-westfaelischen Industriebezirks', unpublished PhD thesis, Essen, 1914, p.53.

88. Hilgermann, Werden, p.24; Kocka, 'Entrepreneurs', p.566; Riesser, Grossbanken, p.265.

89. Boehme, 'Bankenkonzentration', p.439; Daebritz, Gruendung, p.164.

90. See table 4.1.

91. Feldenkirchen, Eisen- und Stahlindustrie, p.240.

92. Examples are given in Wilfried Feldenkirchen, 'Kapitalbeschaffung in der Eisen- und Stahlindustrie des Ruhrgebiets', Zeitschrift fuer Unternehmensgeschichte, vol.24, (1979), p.53; idem., 'Kapitalbeschaffung' p.49.

93. Eistert and Ringel, 'Finanzierung', p.156. The capital market did not play a major role in the financing of industry's investments.

94. G. von Schulze-Gaevernitz, Die Deutsche Kreditbank, (Tuebingen, 1922), p.121; Phoenix-archive P 125 35.

95. Feldenkirchen, Eisen- und Stahlindustrie, tables 32,74 and 114.

96. Riesser, Grossbanken, p.64.

97. Feldenkirchen, 'Kapitalbeschaffung'.

98. Walther G.Hoffmann, 'Die unverteilten Gewinne der Kapitalgesellschaften in Deutschland 1871-1957. Trend, Konjunktur und branchenmaessige Unterschiede', Zeitschrift fuer die gesamte Staatswissenschaft, vol.115, (1959) p.271.

99. Feldenkirchen, Eisen- und Stahlindustrie, p.277 et seq.

100. In the iron and steel industry the percentage of distributed profits in family-owned companies was as follows:

Krupp	65.3 per cent
Gutehoffnungshuette	63.3 "
Hoesch	73.2 "

Rheinische Stahlwerke and Bochumer Verein retained only five per cent of their profits. The example of Hoesch shows that retained profits depended on the structure of ownership. When the family was in complete control of the shares, Hoesch retained 44 per cent of its profits. Later on it was considerably less.

101. W.Hagemann, Das Verhaeltnis der deutschen Grossbanken zur Industrie, (Berlin, 1931), p.175.

102. Riesser, Grossbanken, p.541.

103. See for instance the balance sheets of the big chemical companies.

104. Tilly, 'Kapitalmarkt', p.88.

105. Hoesch-archive A3 b5; BV-archive 129 00/24; RSW-archive 123 00/15.

106. Krupp-archive WA IV 1264; FAH IV C 116; Thyssen-archive, Personenarchiv August Thyssen No.1.

107. That was certainly one of the reasons why the Dresdner Bank and Schaaffhausen formed an _Interessengemeinschaft_ (community of interest) in 1904.

108. Quoted in F.A. Freundt, _Emil Kirdorf_, (Essen, 1922), p.48.

109. Hagemann, _Verhaeltnis_, p.113 et seq.

110. Riesser, _Grossbanken_.

111. See the bank's Annual Report for 1908.

112. Feldenkirchen, _Eisen- und Stahlindustrie_, p.118 et seq.

113. Simmersbach, _Entwicklung_, p.5 et seq.

114. Phoenix-archive P 1 25 24 3. Although there was no actual fusion between Siemens-Schukert and Bergman, by 1912 Siemens had a controlling influence.

115. Pohl, _Konzentration_, p.269.

116. Riesser, _Grossbanken_, p.549.

117. Tilly, 'Banken und Industrialisierung', p.184.

118. Juergen Kocka, _Unternehmer in der deutschen Industrialisierung_, (Goettingen, 1975), p.103.

Table 4.1 : Average annual growth rates of balance sheet totals of enterprises in selected industrial sectors (in per cent), 1879-1913.

Company	1879-1894	1894-1913
Gelsenkirchener Bergwerks AG (1)	7.52	10.32
Harpener Bergbau AG (1)	16.44	5.87
Hibernia (1)	5.90	6.74
Gutehoffnungshuette	0.79	8.51
Krupp	2.14	7.26
Phoenix	1.15	12.32
Rheinische Stahlwerke	3.97	11.55
Hoesch	3.70	13.38
Deutsch-Luxemburg (2)	-	17.14
Gewerkschaft Deutscher Kaiser (3)	-	14.26
Farben-Fabriken Bayer (4)	4.89	10.74
Badische Anilin- und Soda-Fabrik (5)	2.88	6.80
Farbwerke Hoechst vorm. Meister Lucius & Bruening (6)	3.96	8.38
AEG (7)	17.32	14.30
Siemens & Halske (8)	-	3.35
Bergmann-Elektrizitaetswerke (9)	-	22.24

1. 1882-1913
2. 1901/2-1913/14
3. 1892-1913
4. 1881/82-1913
5. 1881-1913
6. 1881-1913
7. 1883-1913/14
8. 1899/00-1913/14
9. 1900-1913

Table 4.2 : Representation of the 'Big Banks' on the supervisory boards of German joint-stock companies by sector*: number of seats (chairmen/vice-chairmen).

	Number of Seats on Supervisory Boards	Mining	Stoneworks	Metal-Working
Bank fuer Handel und Industrie	101(19/16)	10(1/1)	4(1/2)	2(-/1)
Berliner Handels-gesellschaft	101(11/18)	18(3/3)	1(-/-)	8(-/2)
Commerz- und Disconto-Bank	35(4/3)	1(-/-)	2(-/1)	2(-/-)
Deutsche Bank	134(25/20)	13(1/3)	1(-/1)	3(1/1)
Disconto-Gesellschaft	125(12/8)	21(3/-)	2(-/-)	2(-/-)
Dresdner Bank	102(19/14)	13(1/1)	2(-/-)	3(-/1)
Nationalbank fuer Deutschland	102(3/3)	13(1/-)	4(-/1)	3(-/-)
Schaffhausen'scher Bankverein	113(26/16)	26(6/-)	2(-/1)	4(1/2)
Total	813(119/98)	115(16/8)	18(1/6)	27(2/6)

Bank	Engineering	Chemical Industry	Textile Industry	Foodstuffs Industry
Bank fuer Handel und Industrie	16(2/2)	3(1/1)	5(1/2)	7(2/1)
Berliner Handels-gesellschaft	10(3/3)	7(-/3)	-	3(-/2)
Commerz- und Disconto-Bank	8(1/1)	1(-/-)	1(-/-)	3(-/-)
Deutsche Bank	27(5/3)	1(-/-)	6(-/2)	3(-/-)
Disconto-Gesellschaft	10(-/2)	7(1/1)	-	1(-/-)
Dresdner Bank	14(2/2)	1(1/-)	2(-/1)	2(-/-)
Nationalbank fuer Deutschland	18(-/-)	3(1/-)	-	7(-/1)
Schaafhausen'scher Bankverein	16(3/1)	2(-/1)	5(2/1)	1(-/-)
Total	119(16/14)	25(4/6)	19(3/5)	27(2/4)

*Compiled acording to: J. Riesser, Die deutschen Grossbanken und ihre Konzentration im Zusammenhang mit der Entwicklung der Gesamtwirtschaft in Deutschland, 3rd completely revised edition, (Jena 1910), pp.603-624.

Table 4.3 : Share of bank balances in current assets, 1894/95-1913/14, in per cent

Year	GHH(1)	KRUPP	PHOENIX	RSW(2)	HOESCH
1894/95	5.9	1.7	7.3	0.3	*
1895/96	11.4	10.8	17.9	0.7	*
1896/97	5.4	0.6	12.4	3.1	*
1897/98	8.5	4.6	30.8	1.2	*
1898/99	16.7	6.2	26.0	23.7	32.8
1899/00	13.9	10.2	17.1	44.2	36.1
1900/01	14.0	9.8	*	*	21.6
1901/02	22.0	11.5	*	2.7	11.9
1902/03	22.7	11.5	12.4	25.3	46.2
1903/04	0.6	5.6	24.0	12.4	49.9
1904/05	6.7	4.5	23.0	*	55.2
1905/06	6.8	4.4	27.2	30.4	45.5
1906/07	12.9	4.5	32.2	29.8	47.9
1907/08	29.8	4.8	27.3	19.3	51.8
1908/09	24.4	7.0	29.6	*	51.0
1909/10	17.0	11.7	40.0	44.8	59.8
1910/11	16.1	16.7	35.7	48.9	58.4
1911/12	18.5	18.5	33.9	45.2	64.6
1912/13	23.7	17.2	30.7	38.0	54.7
1913/14	8.1	12.4	29.0	43.3	30.4

* No bank balances available

1. Gutehoffnungshuette.
2. Rheinische Stahlwerke.

Chapter Five

CYCLICAL TRENDS AND THE MARKET RESPONSE : LONG SWINGS IN URBAN DEVELOPMENT IN GERMANY, 1850-1914*

Richard Tilly

I

In spite of an already rich and progressively growing body of literature (1), the historiography of Germany's urban development contains room for further improvement. One important but undeservedly neglected aspect of that development concerns its timing and especially its discontinuous character. Surges of very rapid growth alternated with phases of stagnation, but in an irregular and unpredictable pattern. Each phase engendered plans which only imperfectly fitted the conditions which followed, though over time, no doubt, a learning process of sorts was taking place. This development reflected two major sets of change, demographic and economic. It reflected above all the interaction of decisions generating urban-bound migration and urban population growth with decisions to invest in urban housing which, ultimately, would accommodate that population growth. The relevance of the concept of 'long swings' to understanding such processes lies in the fact that it was specifically developed to deal with them. And yet it has rarely been applied to Germany's urbanisation history.(2) This paper attempts such an application. After a brief discussion of the 'long swings' concept, it considers the evidence on long swings in German urban development - in effect defined as population growth and housing investment - and then passes on to a brief discussion of migration and to an evaluation of the role of demographically induced demand and autonomous supply factors in explaining urban housing investment. A few general remarks conclude the paper.

II

According to one of the concept's most recent proponents, Brinley Thomas,

> long swings are fluctuations in the rate at which the whole network of urban infrastructure is developed, whereas the short business cycles are fluctuations in investment in producer durables and inventories.(3)

The merit of this definition is that it identifies one important reason for the concept's development, namely the recognition that the notion of the normal or 'major' cycle which economists had 'discovered' and perfected in the heyday of business cycle analysis did not cover observed fluctuations well enough to be left unamended. Two variants of amendment have been developed. One of these involves analysis of the 'building cycle', in which construction activity - mainly but not exclusively urban residential construction - is examined and found to have a period or swing of from 12 to 25 years.(4) This research has included studies of the building industry in general and/or of building activity in particular cities. The second variant focuses on swings in aggregate economic relationships, in which urban construction activity is seen as a major part of aggregate capital formation and is related to aggregate swings in population growth, migration and family formation. These swings, which can involve international migration and synchronous international capital movements, may also have a period of from 12 to 25 years.(5)

Empirical work on long swings has generated a vast literature, much of it concerned with the development of sophisticated techniques for identifying and measuring fluctuations.(6) As part of this development, two major hypotheses have been advanced to explain long swings: 1) the 'household demand' hypothesis, and 2) the 'investor's expectations' hypothesis. According to the household demand hypothesis, 'long swings' are created by swings in population growth and especially in the size of age groups entering the life-cycle phase of family formation, for it is the size of such cohorts which determines the stimulus of effective demand for housing and thus investment in housing and related social overhead capital. The duration of such swings is determined largely by cohort size and the length of life cycle phases. The 'investor's expectations' hypothesis, on the other hand, sees long swings as caused mainly by the supply side of the building sector. Housing is seen as a long-lived capital good whose supply should be geared to long-run demand. However, long-run demand changes are not easy to forecast, and in an industry of small-scale producers such as the building industry, response to change was slow to get started and slow to correct itself when proven 'wrong'. As A.Cairncross has shown, for example in the case of Glasgow, such supply conditions could generate long swings under plausible assumptions 'without any change in demand whatever'.(7)

Of course, both explanations can be combined, and it is not unlikely that both demand and supply factors were at work.(8) This is a point which will be taken up again further below.

III

The first question to raise is an empirical one. Can we find long swings in German urban development in the nineteenth-century? More precisely, are there long swing-type movements in urban population variables and housing investment?

1. The answer to the question is a qualified yes. The 'yes' refers largely to the evidence on housing investment. Figure 5.1, taken from M.Gottlieb's important study, applies major turning points as its criterion and identifies three long swings with peaks in the mid-1870s, late 1880s to early 1890s, and mid-1900s. Most of the other figures also reflect long swings in housing. Figure 5.2, for example, depicts the course of growth in the number of residential buildings over the entire nineteenth-century in Prussia and identifies troughs in the early 1830s, late 1840s, early 1860s and early 1880s. Figure 5.3 is an attempt to provide empirical support for the claim that long swings in housing investment in different cities were synchronous, i.e., frequently in harmony with one another and with 'national' swings. Note here the common expansion of the late 1830s and early 1840s, of the 1870s and late 1880s. These measurements are crude, to be sure, for the absence of annual data for the first half of the century, made resort to averages of five-year periods necessary. Figures 5.4 and 5.5 provide a visual presentation of data for the two cities of Hamburg and Berlin, applying, as a sorting-out device, three-year moving averages. Figures 5.6 and 5.7 round off the discussion of evidence for long swings in housing by displaying, first, the raw data on the rate of growth of housing and, second, its cyclical pattern, as measured by its autocorrelation. Applying the 'Box-Jenkins' test, long swings with a period of 15 years become apparent.(9) It should be added that this test has been applied to other housing growth series as well (including those for Berlin, Frankfurt, Munich, Duisburg, and Dortmund, as well as to Hoffmann's German-wide series) and in virtually all cases it has identified cycles with a duration of from 13 to 19 years.(10)

2. The qualification to the positive answer to our original question refers to the demographic side of the matter. Table 5.1 and Figure 5.2, for example, show fluctuations in population growth which overlap and in part coincide with the swings in housing investment (the boom of the 1840s and the late 1890s), but the periodicity is fairly dissimilar. Figure 5.2 reveals less synchronous movement in population than in housing investment. Figures 5.4 and 5.5 reflect some overlapping and hint at interesting lagged relationships between population and net migration and building growth, but

Fig. 5.1 INDEX OF ANNUAL URBAN HOUSING INVESTMENT IN GERMANY, 1867-1913 (1900 = 100)

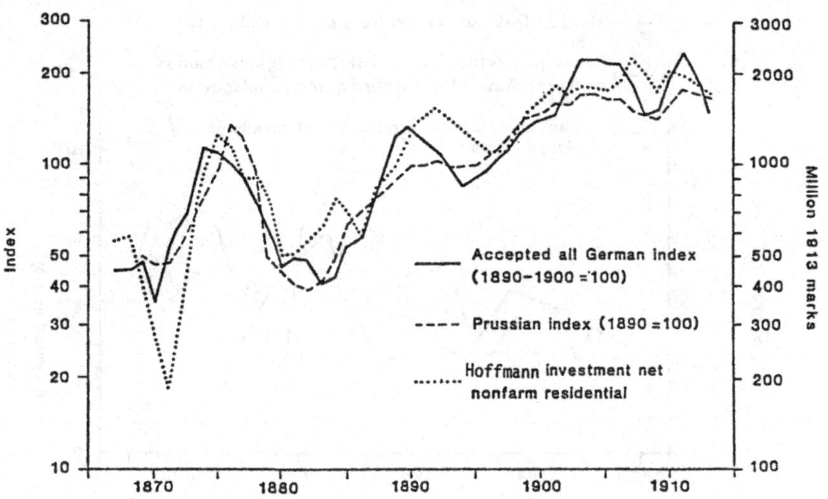

Source: M. Gottlieb, Long Swings in Urban Development, New York 1976, Appendix H, p. 325

Fig. 5.2 ANNUAL GROWTH RATE OF HOUSING STOCK AND URBAN POPULATION IN PRUSSIA, 1816-1913

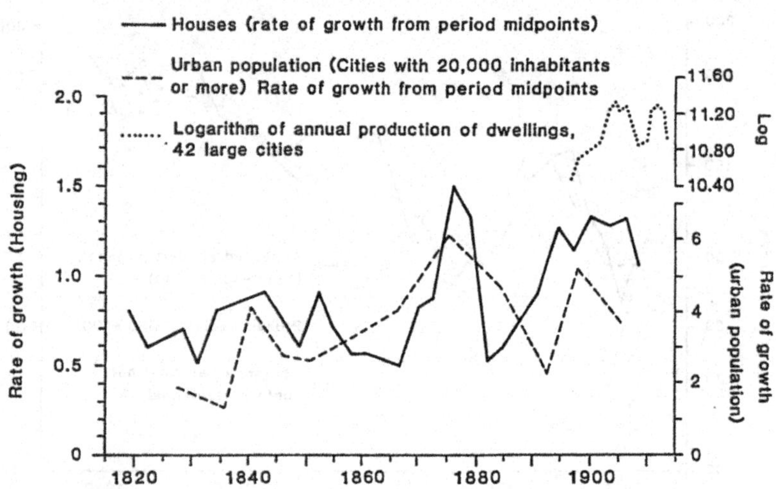

Fig. 5.3 ANNUAL GROWTH RATE OF STOCK OF DWELLINGS AND POPULATION IN THREE CITIES, 1815-1913

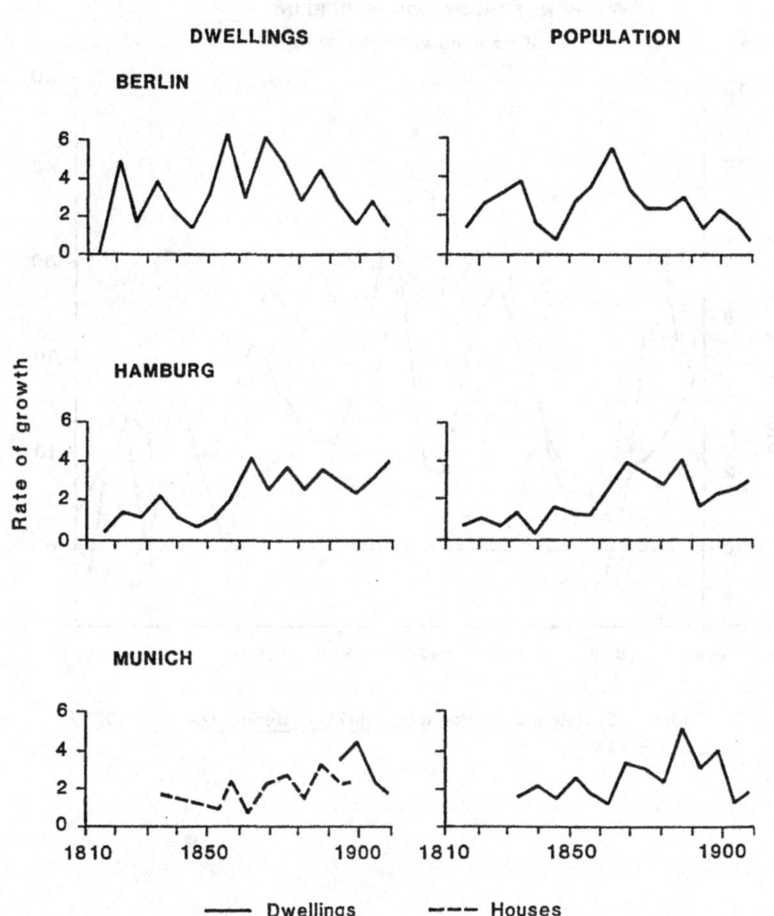

Fig. 5.4 ANNUAL GROWTH RATE OF STOCK OF DWELLINGS AND NET MIGRATION IN BERLIN, (3 year moving averages)

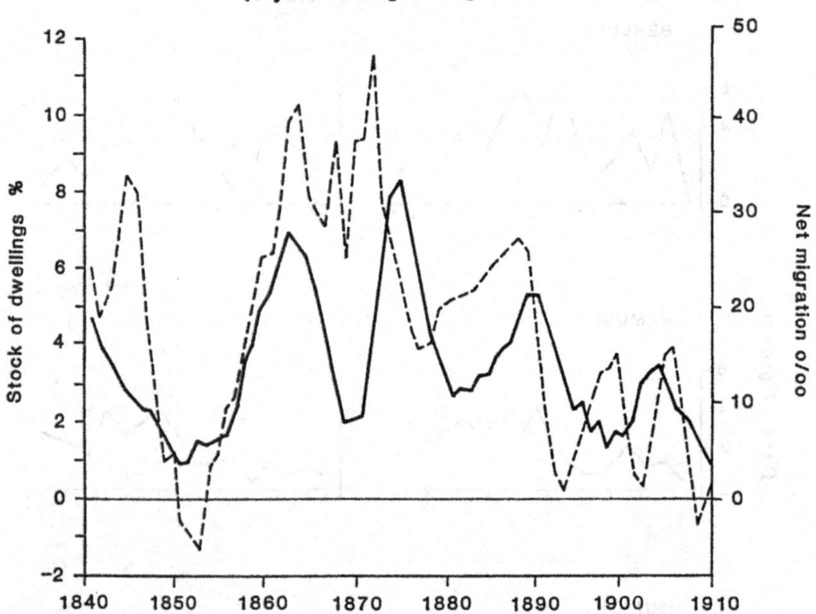

Source: E. Reich, Der Wohnungsmarkt in Berlin, 1840–1910, Leipzig 1912

Fig. 5.5. ANNUAL GROWTH RATE OF STOCK OF DWELLINGS, POPULATION AND NET MIGRATION, HAMBURG, 1871-1913

(3 year moving averages)

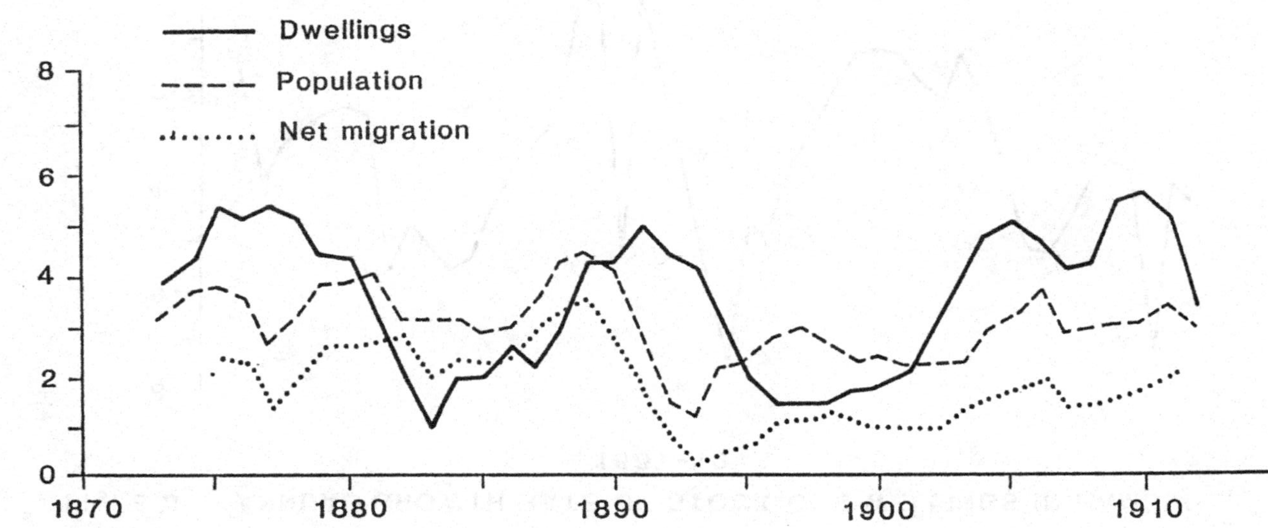

Fig. 5.6 ANNUAL GROWTH RATE OF STOCK OF DWELLINGS IN HAMBURG, 1867-1912

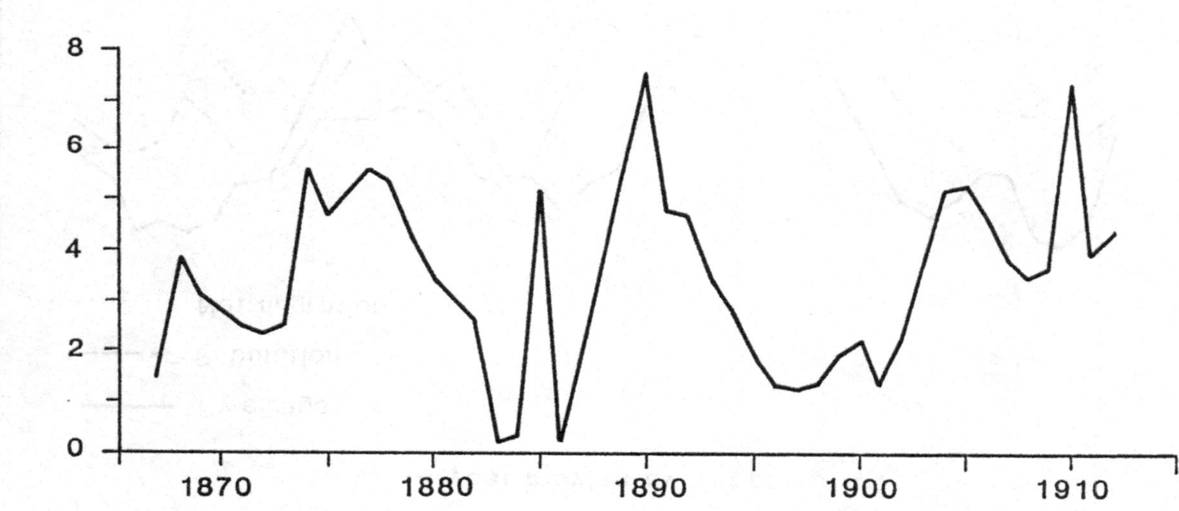

Source: Statistisches Handbuch fur den Hamburgischen Staat 1885, 1891 and 1920 (1867–1883 p.78) (1884–1889 p.88) (1890–1912 p.132)

Fig. 5.7 AUTOCORRELATION, ANNUAL GROWTH RATE OF STOCK OF DWELLINGS IN HAMBURG, 1867-1912

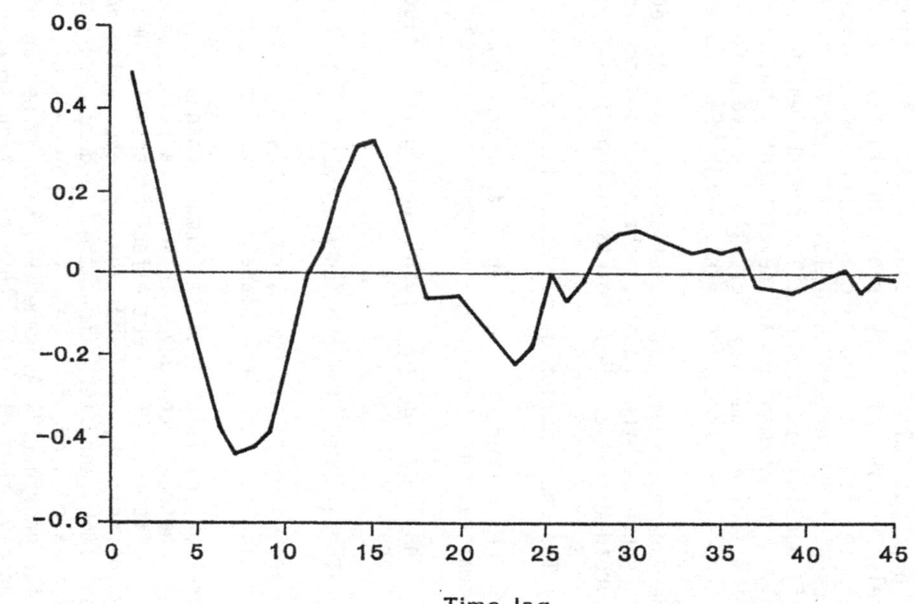

See footnotes 9 and 10

visual inspection, once again, suggests that the periodicities were different. The 'Box-Jenkins' test for autocorrelation applied to these and other urban series failed to uncover, with two exceptions, a clear pattern of long demographic cycles.(11) This qualified result suggests that there is a significant relationship between population growth and migration, on the one hand, and urban housing investment, on the other, but also that visual inspection of graphs cannot adequately uncover it. My reaction to that result in this paper is to step back and take a closer look at migration and urban population growth and its relationship to the supply side of housing investment. The remarks which follow apply generally to German urban development, but the present exposition relies heavily for illustrative purposes on data drawn from the history of the North Sea port city of Hamburg.(11a)

The second empirical question to be raised in this context concerns the causes, character and consequences of German urban migration. Four points will be taken up:

1. The contribution of migration to urban growth.

2. The connection between urban migration and overseas migration.

3. The question of 'push' and 'pull' influences upon urban migration.

4. The effects of migration upon housing investment.

This fourth point, to be sure, takes us into a general consideration of possible explanations of housing investment.

1. Migration explains most of German urban population growth in the nineteenth-century. This is a result of direct and indirect effects. The <u>direct</u> effect of positive net migration is, by definition, an addition to the native population. Between 1865 and 1905 for the largest Prussian cities migration accounted for nearly 75 per cent of the recorded population growth.(12) And <u>when</u> Prussian or German cities grew more rapidly, they did so <u>because</u> migration grew, not because of natural increase. For those same Prussian cities migration 'explained' over 90 per cent of the rate of population increase over nine periods between 1865 and 1905.(13)

For the important city of Hamburg, net migration accounted for around 60 per cent of total population growth between 1867 and 1913 and it explained almost three-quarters of <u>annual</u> changes in population growth rates over the period (equation 1).(14)

$$P_{to} = \underset{(0.002)}{1.42 + 0.85} M_{to} \qquad R^2 = 0.74 \quad DW = 1.04 \qquad (1a)$$

or in first-difference form (T-statistics in parentheses):

$$P_{to} = \underset{(3.970)}{7.107} + \underset{(3.378)}{0.005} M_{to} + \underset{(2.916)}{0.245} T \qquad R^2 = 0.502 \quad DW = 2.277 \qquad (1b)$$

The indirect contribution of migration to urban population growth lay in its effect on the number of marriages and births. Urban migrants were heavily concentrated in the age group 20-30. For samples taken from Berlin, Hamburg and Frankfurt between 1870 and 1900, a concentration of migrants in the age group 19-21 could be observed. The median age at marriage was probably around 26-28 for men and between 23 and 25 for women.(15) Waves of net migration would tend to produce, after a lag of four or five years, waves of marriages and more births. It is well known that the marriage market of large German cities in the period 1870 to 1913 tended to be dominated by migrants. In Hamburg in the 1880s, for example, migrants accounted for over 80 per cent of all marriages.(16) Equations 2 and 3 are a crude attempt to capture this effect for the city of Hamburg over the period 1871 to 1913. The data are three year averages of annual rates of change. The use of such averages reflects the belief that influences on social change of the kind investigated here do not follow the calendar as closely as annual time series data imply. In equation 3 an estimate of the effect of short-run income change lagged one period is added to that of migration. The improved estimates confirm expectations about the independent, positive effect of income upon marriage rates.(17)

$$E_{to} = 8.72 + \underset{(0.11)}{0.24} M_{t-5} \qquad R^2 = 0.26 \qquad (2)$$

$$E_{to} = \underset{(0.07)}{8.15} + \underset{(0.09)}{0.31} M_{t-5} + \underset{(0.04)}{0.11} Y_{t-1} \qquad R^2 = 0.51 \quad DW = 1.56 \qquad (3)$$

And if we look again at the growth of the 19 largest Prussian cities between 1865 and 1905 (table 5.2), we find clear evidence of a positive relationship between net migration gains and natural increase four or five years later. In five of the eight cross-sectional correlations the statistical relationships were significant at the five per cent level, although no attempt was made to transform the data and work out optimal lags.

2. There seems to have been a kind of inverse relation between overseas migration from Germany on the one hand and internal migration and urban growth on the other. For example, there was a rise in emigration in the late 1840s and early 1850s which coincided with a slackening of urban growth. In the 1850s emigration increased significantly along with rural net migration losses and with a rising rate of urban growth. In the 1860s and particularly in the early 1870s emigration slowed down, probably because a still higher rate of urban growth could absorb the growing net outflow from rural regions.(18) In the 1880s emigration at first soared to new heights and then fell back, thus displaying an almost perfectly inverse connection with internal migration into cities. These connections deserve closer attention because they suggest a switching process among migrants, possibly having long swings characteristics reminiscent of British history.(19)

3. No clear connection could be found, however, between the timing of urban migration waves and either the delayed effects of population pressure or contemporaneous effects of agrarian depression. Correlations between emigration from agrarian regions and birth surpluses 20 years earlier and also between emigration and the growth rate of agricultural net output are not significant.(20) This would seem to indicate that the timing of migration out of rural areas was clearly not the product of push factors. However a somewhat different conclusion can be drawn from cross-sectional comparison. If we examine the case of the East Elbian provinces, as the major source of Prussian migrants in the period 1870 to 1913, a roughly positive link can be found between demographic and institutional push factors on the one hand, and net migration on the other.(21) This observation is a useful reminder that distinguishing between push and pull influences upon migration only makes sense within the context of a particular hypothesis.(22) In this paper interest centres on the timing of urban migration, for which a push explanation does not seem to apply.

On the contrary, waves of migration can be effectively explained by the changing force of attraction of cities, i.e., by pull factors. Periods of rapid urban expansion are associated, at least initially, with an overall increased level of economic activity driven mainly by industrial production and concentrated largely in urban centres.(23) In this connection it is worth noting that throughout the period there is a significant and possibly growing gap in real income levels between the agrarian regions losing migrants and the cities gaining them, while the trend of per capita income in both was upward, at least from 1850 onwards.(24) For Hamburg, where income estimates are available, we have a test of this relationship, which suggests that migration was indeed a pull phenomenon. Drawing on the estimates of regional per capita income cited in footnote 24, we can observe a marked differential between Hamburg and its principal catchment areas, Schleswig-Holstein and Hanover, against the background of a rising trend.(25) But when income in Hamburg rose and fell sharply, migration to that city did likewise. Equation 4 estimates this relationship for the period 1874 to 1913:

$$M_{to} = 0.745 + \underset{(0.058)}{0.254}\, Y_{t-1} \qquad R^2 = 0.435 \quad DW = 0.21 \qquad (4)$$

The estimate would be barely satisfactory even if there were no serial correlation.(26) Because of this, and because visual inspection of the series showed a break in the relationship in the early 1890s, two estimates were made for the periods 1874 to 93 (5a) and 1894 to 1912 (5b).

$$M_{to} = 1.16 + \underset{(0.058)}{0.256}\, Y_{t-1} \qquad R^2 = 0.673 \quad DW = 0.48 \qquad (5a)$$

$$M_{to} = 0.25 + \underset{(0.065)}{0.39}\, Y_{t-1} \qquad R^2 = 0.704 \quad DW = 0.22 \qquad (5b)$$

The problem of serial correlation unfortunately remains, but the pull hypothesis does seem to be supported. Systematic investigation of other cities has not been undertaken, as far as I know, although there are hints of a similar relationship between Berlin and its hinterland and a roughly similar test confirms the pull effect for the industrial city of Duisburg.(27)

4. The last question to be raised in this paper begins with a consideration of the effects of net migration upon urban housing investment. A good deal of corroborative evidence on the side of a positive relationship exists, ranging from Lee's observation on the initiating effect of migration waves on urban housing swings (in the 1870s, late 1880s, late 1890s, and in the years 1903 to 1906 and 1909 to 1911), to the individual city studies of E.Reich on Berlin, F.-W.Henning on Cologne and Duesseldorf, and C.Wischermann on Hamburg.(28) However, this evidence is largely of a casual kind. For the city of Hamburg, a survey of possible links, direct and indirect, was conducted, the results of which are displayed in table 5.3.

Quite a few significant connections can be seen here, but the most significant are those between building investment, on the one hand, and marriages and migration on the other. This is particularly interesting since an a priori case can be made for the relevance of both marriages and migration gains, which represent additional households with a likely influence on local housing demand. These two variables were thus selected for the attempt to 'explain' housing investment, the result of which appears in equations (6a and 6b). Only in equations (6b and 6c), which utilize annual changes in the variables (or first differences), is the variance 'explained' satisfactorily. Moreover in both equations only the migration coefficient is significant. This supports the hypothesis that migration contributed significantly to urban housing investment, but the mechanism remains unclear.

$$G_{to} = 2.224 + \underset{(.154)}{.314\, M_{t-2}} + \underset{(.137)}{.048\, E_{t-3}} \qquad R^2 = 0.12 \quad DW = 0.38 \qquad (6a)$$

$$G_{t} = \underset{(.001)}{.0032M} + \underset{(.011)}{.010E_{t-1}} + \underset{(1.309)}{0.351T_{t-3}} - \underset{(31.681)}{34.287} \qquad R^2 = 0.534 \quad DW = 1.31 \qquad (6b)$$

Only in equation (6c) is the problem of serial correlation satisfactorily 'solved' through the use of the dependent variable, housing investment (=G), as an independent variable, lagged one period. However it must be noted that in this formulation the variable migration (=M) is just barely significant at the five per cent level of confidence:

$$G_{t} = \underset{(0.165)}{0.492\, G_{t-1}} + \underset{(.001)}{0.002M_{t-1}} + \underset{(1.194)}{0.911T} - \underset{(.011)}{0.001E_{t-2}} - \underset{(30.577)}{1.411} \qquad (6c)$$

$$R^2 = 0.623 \quad DW = 2.018$$

However, some serious problems remain, apart from statistical ones. The above formulation does not include any 'market' variables. It implies that migration somehow created effective demand which was then supplied, albeit with a lag. Since German urban housing was allocated almost exclusively through local urban markets in the nineteenth-century, demographic factors, in order to have influenced housing investment, must have also influenced market variables, such as the level of rents, or the number and relative importance of empty houses. In the case of Hamburg, we noted that zero-order correlations, focusing on demographic variables, show no direct noticeable effects on these two market indicators, which were, however, significantly related to housing production. For example, the level of vacant dwellings in a given period, which was closely related to the level of rents, is hardly affected by either marriage or migration rates in the same or previous period (taking each of those variables individually.(29)

It would therefore seem useful at this point to take a brief look at the supply side of urban housing, before drawing conclusions about the importance or unimportance of demographic demand variables. In general, we may characterise the production side of the German housing market as marked by small-scale enterprises and a high degree of competition. As late as 1907, more than two-thirds of the enterprises in Germany's construction industry employed fewer than five workers. This was equally true of large cities such as Hamburg and Berlin.(29a) Of course, urban building land was itself not infrequently held in large blocks, by private capitalists, large financial institutions or state and local governments. Its availability could depend on political decisions about space allocation, building codes, etc., and could thus reflect non-market forces in individual instances. However, such decisions would presumably have no temporal pattern themselves and are thus excluded from consideration here. In any case, once the typically small-scale builders acquired the land, they built largely multiple dwelling units for rental. By the 1870s single-family, owner-occupied dwellings were the exception in larger towns and almost all dwellings were built largely in advance of demand.(30) The building itself, which took from one to two years, was financed mainly from local sources, secured by a mortgage on the property. On completion the builders sold the property and repaid their creditors with the proceeds, frequently immediately initiating further new projects. It was at this point, but not before, that institutional investors such as the mortgage banks, savings banks and insurance companies entered the financial picture, joining forces with the ultimate investors themselves, namely private capitalists who would generally have raised something like one-quarter to two-fifths of the purchase price in cash. There are thus grounds for believing that the capital market did not determine the timing of urban housing investment, or at least not the exact timing of 'starts'. Of course, it may well have influenced both the duration and amplitude of expansionary and contractionary phases already underway. According to Gottlieb, there are long swings in the supply and yield of mortgage credit during this period in Germany which could have curtailed or even hastened upswings, and the question certainly deserves further attention.(31)

An interesting and important feature of housing investment movements between 1870 and 1913 concerns the behaviour of building costs, house prices and rents. These magnitudes overlap to a great extent, suggesting that competitive links between the different parts of the housing market were at least partly effective. Land prices were the most volatile of all and at certain times and places could account for a considerable share, perhaps 40 to 50 per cent, of given increases in urban property values. Over the cycle as a whole, however, and in the long run, land prices represented a minor share of finished house prices, ranging from ten to as much as 25 per cent. In general, according to M.Gottlieb, 'average prices of improved property tended to fluctuate with greater amplitude but in close correspondence to building cost'.(32) This could explain the otherwise curious phenomenon in German housing markets: namely, that changes in building costs led the investment swings, rising and falling before the latter (see figure 5.8).(32a) If, in fact, such changes indicated expected prices for improved property (finished houses and lots), then the cyclical position of costs is plausible. This fact itself suggests the need for any 'modelling' of the market to include finished house prices. Unfortunately, however, this is another variable about which too little is known.(33)

It is worth emphasising that the housing market in Germany, as elsewhere in the nineteenth century, was marked by its inability to 'stay on target' which produced considerable swings in the number and share of empty dwellings, possibly reflecting 'overproduction' and inefficiency in the social sense. As one German investigator (Hunscha) put it: between 20 and 40 per cent of new housing demand was concurrently either underprovided or overprovided, with a lag between new demand and new supply running from one to two years.(34) In fact, long swings may be seen as the result of market interaction in which vacancies - clear signals of excess supply - are the principal generating force.

For Hamburg, once more, we have some statistical support for such assertions. There are long swings in empty dwellings and they are positively related to the swings in production. In the period from 1874 to 1913 there were years in which more than half of current production went into the stock of vacancies and for the period as a whole, close to one-tenth did so.(35) This is evident in the auto-correlation data on Hamburg discussed earlier and can also be detected in the regression equation (7a), (in which V = share of total dwellings vacant, D = rate of growth of number of dwellings and standard error in parenthesis):

$$V_{to} = 0.51\,D_{to} - 1.65 \qquad R^2 = 0.79 \qquad (7a)$$

$$(0.10) \qquad DW = 0.67$$

In equation (7b) migration is then added:

Fig. 5.8 INDICES OF HOUSING INVESTMENT, BUILDING COSTS AND RENTS, GERMANY 1870–1913

(Annual Data, Trend Removed)

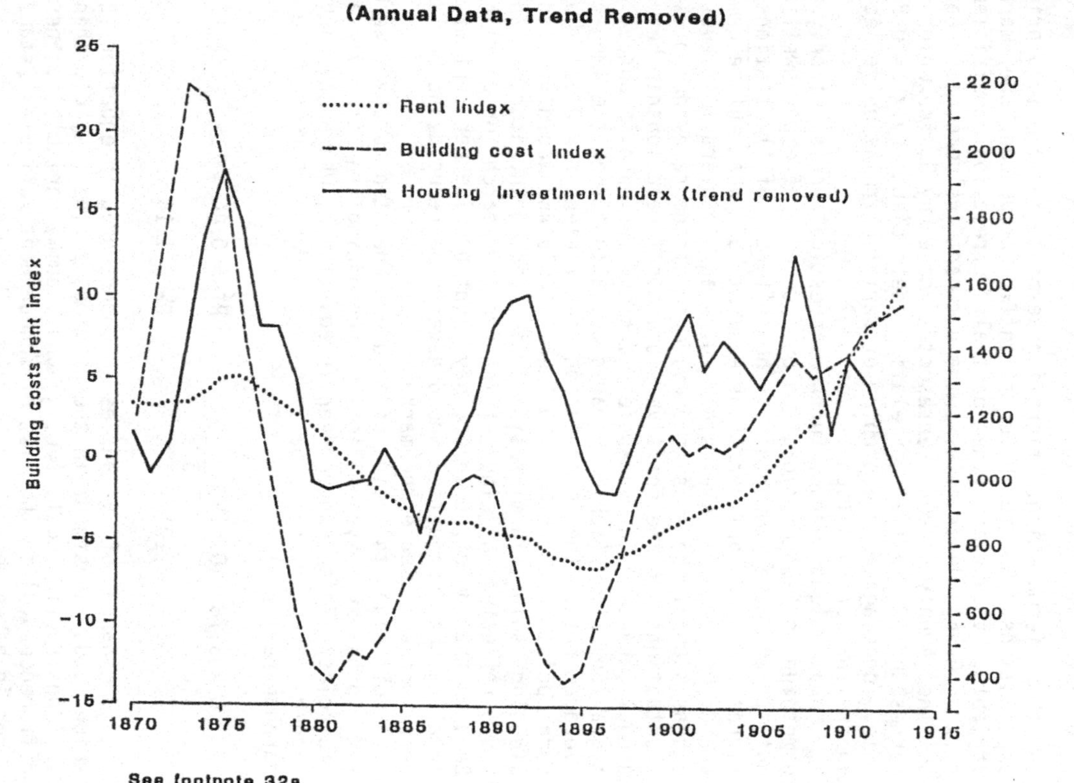

See footnote 32a

$$V_{to} = 0.52\, D_{to} - .21M_{to} - 1.28 \qquad R^2 = 0.81 \qquad (7b)$$
$$(.04) \quad (.08) \qquad DW = 0.70$$

In this formulation, migration seems to conform to <u>a priori</u> expectations and to have slightly influenced the market variable, vacancies (the partial correlation coefficient, $ry.x^2 = 0.56$). Nevertheless, the dominant influence is clearly on the supply side (represented here by D, for which the corresponding partial correlation coefficient, $ry.x^2 = 0.83$). Note, once again, the problem of serial correlation reflected in the low Durbin-Watson values.

What might warrant further investigation is not only the dampening effect of migration on the level of empty dwellings but, even more important, the effects of <u>fluctuations</u> in migration upon builders' assessment of what future demand would be and on what constituted an 'intolerable' level of excess supply. There is some evidence of the relevance of such fluctuations in the positive statistical relationship between annual changes in vacancies and the variance in annual net migration flows (taking squared deviations from the long-term average rate, the correlation coefficient $r = 0.52$). Up to some point, it seems, builders could and would respond to widening swings in migration by increasing inventories, which thus reflected a kind of information search (or cost).(36) Beyond that point, however, say eight or nine per cent of the total stock, production would have to be reduced and builders were forced to leave the market.

Following this line of argument one step further, we may see producers systematically responding to the variable vacancies. This can be seen in equation 8, where the link is lagged over three periods (standard errors are in parentheses):(37)

$$G_{to} = 5.78 - 0.51V_{t-3} \qquad R^2 = 0.44 \qquad (8)$$
$$(.10) \qquad DW = 1.14$$

The dominance of vacancies is underscored in equation (9a), which adds investment in the previous period ($=G_{t-1}$), changes in construction costs ($=C_{t-2}$) and a dummy variable for period differences (D) to the list of independent variables (standard error in parentheses):

$$G_{to} = 31.153 + 0.743G_{t-1} + 0.095C_{t-2} - 3.102V_{t-2} - 0.018D \qquad (9a)$$
$$(12.645) \quad (.113) \quad (.478) \quad (1.912) \quad (2.901)$$
$$R^2 = 0.583 \qquad DW = 2.305$$

The regression coefficients are only significant for investment in the previous period and for vacancies. Note that changes in construction costs do not function here as a significant variable in the way they do in the equation of footnote 32a. An interesting further formulation adds average rental returns (=REN) to the explanatory model, improving the estimate considerably (standard error in parentheses):

$$G_{to} = 0.240G_{t-1} + 0.595REN_{t-2} - 6.512V_{t-2} - 310.517 \qquad (9b)$$

(.150) (.135) (1.612) (77.089)

$R^2 = 0.741$ DW = 2.133

This variant was the best performer in a long list of tests.(37a) A case can thus be made for a model of the urban housing market in which vacancies and rents serve as crucial signals of scarcity and profitability.

However, an alternative formulation of these relationships may be preferable, particularly if we are searching for a specification of the relationship between housing investment and its expected profitability. Vacancies are an indirect indicator of such profitability, but so are rents, with which vacancies are highly and negatively correlated (38), interest rates, and building costs. Two possibilities present themselves. First, the above-mentioned determinants may be combined to form a proxy for expected profits to house ownership and this proxy inserted into a regression model purporting to explain investment. This approach is the subject of a story told elsewhere.(39) For present purposes it can be illustrated for the important capital city of Berlin, with the help of equation 10 (in which RI = real housing investment, RR = expected rate of return, RZ = real rate of interest, and T = Time, with T-statistics in parentheses):

$$RI_{t} = 0.296 + 0.721RI_{t-1} + .001T + 2.534RR_{t-1} - 3.642RZ_{t-1} \qquad (10)$$

0 (8.267) (0.327) (3.521) (3.296)

$R^2 = 0.671$ DW = 2.152

Apart from past investment, expected profits are the most significant variable. However for reasons discussed elsewhere, this approach does not function too well in explaining housing investment in Hamburg. We therefore resort to the second possibility mentioned above, and seek to explain investment in terms of determinants which one may assume to influence significantly expectations of profitability. Equation 11, which utilises an alternative real investment variable based on fire insurance returns, illustrates this approach by linking investment to the determinants cited above: interest rates (Z), rents (=REN), and building costs (=C) with T-statistics in parentheses:

$$RI_{t} = \underset{(8.79)}{2.22REN_{t-2}} + \underset{(4.55)}{3.13C_{t-2}} - \underset{(-4.10)}{119.65Z_{t-2}} - 767.18 \qquad (11)$$

$$R^2 = 0.69 \qquad DW = 1.77$$

All three variables are statistically significant and the estimate seems to be econometrically acceptable.(40)

From the point of view of this paper one of the most interesting features of the results just discussed only emerges when one begins to examine the determinants of expected returns to housing investment. For it turns out that in both Hamburg and Berlin rents are the most important determinant of all, and in both cases rents themselves are significantly influenced by a demographic factor, namely marriages.(41) Taken in conjunction with the links between vacancies and migration discussed earlier, this adds authority to the argument that population change and housing investment, in Germany as elsewhere, were closely connected parts of that large-scale process we call urbanisation.

IV

Long swings in Germany's urban development in the nineteenth century deserve attention not only because they add yet another case to the 'long swing' chapter of econometric history, but because the interaction of population change and housing investment emphasised by such swings is so central to our understanding of German urbanisation. Although German historians have long stressed the serious social and political problems raised by the country's rapid urban growth, until recently the importance of the 'housing question' as an element of the larger 'social question' has been overlooked and underplayed.(42) In this concluding section of the paper, therefore, attention is drawn to some important connections between the focus of this paper and the late-nineteenth-century 'housing question'.

The main structural features of the 'housing question' are easily sketched. Massive migration into cities in the second half of the nineteenth century transformed the latter into production centres with large concentrations of working-class populations which had to be housed.(43) This represented an economic problem with social and political implications, for housing was an important element in working-class living conditions, and an issue of potentially great significance for working-class politicisation. The 'housing question' posed to Germany's conservative political leaders and opinion makers the danger of a political radicalisation of the working-class population, in opposition to the political and social institutions of the second German Kaiserreich. This danger had to be weighed against the potentially enormous costs which any solution of the 'housing question' inevitably implied. The universal provision of adequate housing for the working-class would necessitate a significant redistribution of income away from the propertied classes.

The objects of the 'housing question' were mainly working-class dwellings and their potential working-class inhabitants. Its subjects, that is, those who asked the often rhetorical questions and supplied the answers, can be divided into two general groups representing contrary positions which continually collided with one another. On the one hand, we may identify a group consisting of representatives of urban property owners, land developers, real estate investors and a small but articulate following of economically informed scholars and journalists who placed their hopes in a 'free-market' solution and economic liberalism. They meant by this a minimum of restrictions on private property rights in urban land and building and the development of standardised facilities for transfers and the financing of urban real estate. From such a clear set of rules, they felt, sufficient investment in new construction and housing improvements would be forthcoming to more than solve the housing problem. On the other side we have the 'social reformers', including representatives of the government bureaucracy at the state and particularly the municipal level, journalists, and probably a strong majority of politically engaged social scientists, particularly many members of the ascendant 'historical school of economics'. This group placed their hopes in government intervention and restrictions on private property rights in urban land use and building activity.

It is useful to view the relationship between these two positions in a true historical perspective, although for this purpose an initial and arbitrary leap into the 'seamless web' of history is essential. By the early 1870s market criteria dominated the production and distribution of housing in German cities. In the first great wave of urban growth in the 1870s, an investment boom coincided with widespread complaints about housing shortages and 'rent gouging' (Wuchermiete), but this phase was quickly succeeded from around 1875 onwards by a wave of failures of private builders and of foreclosures, accompanied by the exposures of sharp and even fraudulent practices in the real estate business. This generated public criticism of 'free market' housing provision and led to some of the first semi-scholarly investigations into the housing question.(44) It also gave rise to articulated demands for government intervention. This marked the origins of the group of 'social reformers', a group which was not wholly homogeneous, but which nevertheless tended to return to two main points:

1. The recommendation that a high priority be accorded to a construction programme of working-class or 'small housing' (Kleinwohnungen), to be financed or at least subsidised by state and municipal governments. The main beneficiaries of such a programme would be low-income groups.

2. The emphasis on the necessity of restricting, or even eliminating, 'free market' price formation in urban real estate. This reflected their belief that monopoly power in urban land markets led to rising land rents which inevitably led to rising housing rents and priced the lower-income groups out of the market for all but sub-standard housing.

It is only against the background of this attack on the deficiencies of 'free market' arrangements that the position of the defendants of economic liberalism in urban housing can be understood. Their position was basically negative, a 'critique of the critique', so to speak, which rested on three main arguments:

1. Critics of the 'free market' assumed a strong demand for 'suitable housing' and examined only the shortfall on the supply side. However it was excessive demand which led to higher rents for urban dwellings which, in turn, generated rising urban land prices. Higher land prices, as a result of monopoly power, did not generate higher rents.

2. The 'social reformers' who recommended that the government should build or subsidise the construction of 'small dwellings' did not discuss the costs of such a programme, nor its limits. From which socio-economic groups were the necessary funds to come, by what financial means, and to which social groups were they to flow? They argued that the implicit redistributive effects of such a programme and its probable dampening effect on private housing investment deserved public discussion. The 'free marketeers' also assumed that any such discussion would be certain to sow disunity among the circle of potential beneficiaries and payees.

3. If the cause of the urban 'housing problem' lay in population migration to Germany's cities running ahead of supply, for whatever reasons, and if rents were to be seen as a price which potentially served to regulate this excess demand, government intervention to reduce that price would act as a stimulant of demand. Unless government intervention took

place uniformly and proportionately across all of Germany, the net result would be an increase in urban-bound migration. According to this view, the German 'housing question' suddenly appeared as an 'urban migration question', where urban-bound migration was insufficiently based on the effective urban demand for labour and hence on the supply of income necessary to finance adequate housing.

The interesting result of this part of the story of distributional struggles in Germany's Kaiserreich is the triumph of the 'free market' position. Urban housing remained until 1914 a sector dominated by private profit expectations. To be sure, important changes did take place. Co-operative housing was well established by World War One, the Mortgage Bank Law of 1899 did affect the supply of finance to urban residential construction and municipal zoning laws were not wholly impotent.(45) On the whole, however, German urban housing remained a market product. Why? No doubt a plurality of factors deserve to be elucidated in providing an answer to this question. Surely the pervasive political influence of property owners and private capitalists must have played an important role; and quite possibly the clear evidence of improvements in the country's urban housing conditions had some effect. But in concluding this paper, we would like to return to its point of departure and single out the phenomenon of discontinuity as a factor of major significance. Urban growth, we have seen, was discontinuous. Phases of 'excess demand', with shortages calling forth explanatory theories and related policy recommendations, led chronologically into phases of excess supply, which called for new theories and new policy solutions, rendering previous ones obsolete. That is to say, the discontinuity of urban growth confronted not only private investors, but also public planners and potential planners with considerable uncertainty, with shifting targets, and costly risks. Viewing the second half of the nineteenth-century as a whole and through the spectacles of modern statistical methods, we can identify at least three, and possibly four major swings in urban residential construction (see figures 5.1 to 5.8). But despite some similarities, each swing was unique. No periods were precisely identical and the amplitudes varied considerably. Moreover, movements in those activities which might reasonably have been related to swings in residential construction, were subject to still greater irregularity. Given the historical uniqueness of changes in such phenomena as building costs or urban migration, contemporary investors in the residential construction industry would have had difficulties in predicting the market's movement, even if they had had full access to the economic historian's data on the relevant period, which they certainly did not. Indeed even if they had been equipped with such knowledge, individual builders might still have been unable to anticipate or influence the behaviour of their competitors. Despite considerable information, they might well have chosen a probabilistically unpromising course of action as long as there was a slight possibility of success.(46) Under such circumstances - assuming cost-consciousness to be an important part of policy-making - it is not easy to argue that political decision-makers in Germany's Kaiserreich were wrong, on balance, in leaving the bulk of such uncertainties and risks to private actors in a relatively free market.

* The author wishes to thank the Deutsche Forschungsgemeinschaft for financial support of the research embodied in this article. He also gratefully acknowledges the cooperation of colleagues in the Special Research Group for Comparative Urban History at the University of Muenster (Sonderforschungsbereich 164), particularly the help of Professor Dr. H.-J.Teuteberg and Dr.Clemens Wischermann. Finally, thanks are due to Thomas Wellenreuther, Muenster, for research assistance and especially for the 'Box-Jenkins' estimates of serial correlation.

NOTES

1. For a recent survey see the editor's introduction by H.-J. Teuteberg in H.-J.Teuteberg (ed.), Urbanisierung im 19. und 20. Jahrhundert, (Cologne and Vienna, 1983).

2. The first serious attempt to my knowledge is that of M.Gottlieb, Long Swings in Urban Development, (New York, 1976), where German experience is discussed bit by bit and largely on a comparative basis.

3. B.Thomas, Migration and Urban Development, (London, 1972), pp.4-5.

4. A classic formulation is A.Burns, 'Long Cycles in Residential Construction' in The Frontiers of Economic Knowledge, (National Bureau of Economic Research, New York, 1954).

5. Prominent spokesmen for this variant are S.Kuznets, Capital in the American Economy. Its Formation and Financing, (National Bureau of Economic Research, Princeton, 1961) and R.Easterlin, Population, Labor Force and Long Swings in Economic Growth, (National Bureau of Economics Research, New York, 1968). 'Long Swings' have frequently been dubbed 'Kuznets' Cycles', so prominent was Kuznets's role in identifying them.

6. For a survey and an additional estimating technique see C.Franks and W.McCormick, 'A Self-generating Model of Long Swings for the American Economy, 1860-1940', Journal of Economic History, vol.XXXI, (1971). It should be added that this article makes no attempt to survey the vast 'long-swings'

literature. For another article in the Franks-McCormack vein, but focusing on the swings in international migration, see L.Neal, 'Cross-Spectral Analysis of Long Swings in Atlantic Migration', in P.Uselding (ed.), Research in Economic History, vol.I (Greenwich, Conn., 1976), pp.260-97.

7. A.Cairncross, Home and Foreign Investment, 1870-1913, (Cambridge, 1953), pp.30-31.

8. Ibid. 'But it is doubtful whether if it were not fed by fluctuations in demand, it would give rise by itself to cycles so pronounced as those observable in buildings'.

9. See G.Box and G.Jenkins, Time Series Analysis, Forecasting and Control, (San Francisco, Cambridge, London, Amsterdam, 1970).

10. Copies of this evidence, compiled by Thomas Wellenreuther, Muenster, can be made available upon request.

11. The exceptions are: 1) the growth of the 25-30 age group in the capital city, Berlin, between 1870 and 1910; and 2) the number of births in the city of Hamburg, from 1866 to 1913.

11a. The author is grateful for having been able to draw on the highly informative study on Hamburg housing by Clemens Wischermann. Wohnen in Hamburg vor dem Ersten Weltkrieg. (Studien zur Geschichte des Alltags, vol.2, edited by H.-J.Teuteberg and P.Borscheid, Muenster, 1983).

12. The data are from A.Steinhart, Untersuchungen zur Geburtigkeit der deutschen Grossstadtbevoelkerung, (Berlin, 1912).

13. See table 5.2 which is the basis for this claim. With the average rate of net migration as one variable and the rate of population increase as the other, $R^2 = 0.91$ (N = 9).

14. In equation (1a) P = population growth and M = net migration rate, both as annual rates of growth based on the population of the previous period (standard errors are in parentheses). The data are taken from the Statistische Handbuecher fuer den Hamburgischen Staat, 1885, 1891 and 1920. They apply a broad definition of city borders and thus under-estimate migration to some extent.

15. This sample is a casual one and should be understood as a plea for further research into this important question. It is taken from the following works: P.Mombert, Studien zur Bevoelkerungsbewegung in Deutschland, (Karlsruhe, 1907), especially p.64 et seq.; Steinhart, Untersuchung zur Geburtigkeit, passim.; H.Bleicher, 'Die Bewegung der Bevoelkerung in Frankfurt a.M. im Jahre 1891', Beitraege zur Statistik der Stadt Frankfurt a.M., NF2. (1983), and J.Jackson, 'Wanderungen in Duisburg waehrend der Industrialisierung', in W.H.Schroeder (ed.), Moderne Stadtgeschichte, (Historisch-Sozialwissenschaftliche Forschungen vol.8, Stuttgart, 1979).

16. See, for example, *Statistisches Handbuch fuer den Hamburgischen Staat*, 1891.

17. See some aggregative evidence for Germany in R.Spree, *Wachstumstrends und Konjunkturzyklen in der deutschen Wirtschaft von 1820 bis 1913*, (Goettingen, 1978), especially p.119. In equation (3) Y = income and in both equations E = marriage rate (standard errors, once again, are in parentheses under the regression coefficients). The income data are from W.Hoffmann and J.Mueller, *Das Deutsche Volkseinkommen, 1851-1957* (Tuebingen, 1959), pp.86-87.

18. Evidence on urban rates of growth is in table 5.1 above and also in G.Hohorst, J.Kocka, G.A.Ritter, *Sozialgeschichtliches Arbeitsbuch II. Materialien zur Statistik des Kaiserreiches, 1870-1914*, (Muenchen, 1975). This source also contains an annual series on German emigration. For the earlier period a similar series can be found in W.Fischer, J.Krenzel, J.Wietog, *Sozialgeschichtliches Arbeitsbuch I, Materialien zur Statistik des Deutschen Bundes, 1815-70*, (Muenchen, 1982). Data on rural net migration can be computed by assuming that administrative districts (*Regierungsbezirke*) can be classified as 'rural' or 'urban' and examining the Prussian data presented in A.Markow, *Das Wachstum der Bevoelkerung und die Entwicklung der Aus- und Einwanderung*, (Tuebingen, 1889) and in R.A.Dickler, 'Labor Market Pressure Aspects of Agricultural Growth in the Eastern Region of Prussia, 1840-1914', unpublished Ph.D. thesis, University of Pennsylvania, 1975. See table 5.4.

19. See, for example, the works of Thomas, *Migration and Urban Development* or Cairncross, *Home and Foreign Investment*. See also table 5.4 of this article, for an array of relevant indicators. In addition to data mentioned in the previous note, it presents a version of the index of German industrial production published by W.Hoffmann, et al. *Das Wachstum der deutschen Wirtschaft seit der Mitte des 19. Jahrhunderts* (Berlin, Heidelberg, New York, 1965), table 76.

20. The experiment mentioned in the text applied the data and assumptions cited in note 18. For nine periods between the years 1826 to 1885 and for eight 'agrarian' districts of Prussia the regression of net migration on the surplus of births 20 years earlier yielded $R^2 = 0.06$. A correlation between net migration out of agrarian districts and agricultural production, drawing on the data in Dickler, 'Labor Market Pressure', and in Spree, '*Wachstumstrends*', for 18 periods was r = 0.15.

21. Dickler, 'Labor Market Pressure', especially chapter VI,C.

22. See the useful comments on this point by L.Neal, 'Cross-Spectral Analysis of Long Swings'.

23. Hoffmann's index of industrial production correlates positively with urban growth in the period from 1850 to 1913,

see Hoffmann et al., Das Wachstum der deutschen Wirtschaft, table 76. For eleven of the periods defined in table 5.4 the coefficient $R^2 = 0.34$.

24. Regional per capita income estimates are in G.Hohorst, Wirtschaftswachstum und Bevoelkerungsentwicklung in Preussen 1816 bis 1914, (New York, 1977), chapter 7. Data on rising per capita output levels in East Elbian Prussia are in Dickler, 'Labor Market Pressure'.

25. The situation outlined in the text can be illustrated by the following index of per capita income for the years:

	1871	1883	1913
Kingdom of Prussia	100	100	100
Hamburg	256	229	179
Schleswig-Holstein (province)	78	77	105
Hanover (province)	88	89	92

Over this period Prussian per capita income grew by approximately 117 per cent according to Hoffmann and Mueller, Das Deutsche Volkseinkommen, pp.86-87. The other income data are from Hohorst, Wirtschaftswachstum, chapter 7.

26. The low Durbin-Watson value derives partly from the use of three-year moving averages. This may be the point at which one should concede that least squares linear regression techniques have their limits, particularly where time series are being analysed. Where swings in the series running over several years occur, the Durbin-Watson test may be irrelevant. On this see A.Koutsoyiannis, Theory of Econometrics, 2nd. edn. (London, 1977), chapter 10. But given the use of regression techniques, the low Durbin-Watson statistic is a cause for concern.

27. See, for example, L.Baar, Die Berliner Industrie in der Industriellen Revolution, (East Berlin, 1966), p.167 et seq., especially pp.189-90; also M.Haines, Economic-Demographic Interrelations in Developing Agricultural Regions. (New York, 1977), pp.431,469 et seq., and J.Jackson, 'Wanderungen', especially tables 2-4.

28. J.J.Lee, 'Aspects of Urbanization and Economic Development in Germany, 1815-1914', in P.Abrams and E.A.Wrigley (eds.), Towns in Societies, Essays in Economic History and Historical Sociology (Cambridge, 1978), pp.279-294; F.-W.Henning, 'Die Stadterweiterung unter dem Einfluss der Industrialisierung (1871 bis 1914)', in H.Kellenbenz (ed.), Zwei Jahrtausend Koelner Wirtschaft, 2 vols., (Cologne, 1975), vol.II, pp.267-337; F.-W.Henning, Duesseldorf und seine Wirtschaft. Zur Geschichte einer Region, 2 vols, (Duesseldorf, 1981), pp.542-556; E.Reich, Der Wohnungsmarkt in Berlin von 1840-1910, (Berlin, 1912); Wischermann, Wohnen in Hamburg, passim.

29. The correlation coefficients between vacant dwellings and the other named variables in the case of Hamburg in the period from 1874 to 1913 were as follows: rents = 0.94 (current period); marriages = 0.06 (previous period); migration = 0.17 (current period).

29a. *Statistik des Deutschen Reiches* (Gewerbliche Betriebsstatistik) vols.216,218 und 219, (Berlin, 1909-1910).

30. The literature is quite unanimous on these characteristics of the urban building sector. For Hamburg, see Wischermann, *Wohnen in Hamburg*, especially pp.147,148-71; for Berlin, Reich, *Der Wohnungsmarkt in Berlin* and also V.von Carthaus, *Zur Geschichte und Theorie der Grundstueckskrisen in deutschen Grossstaedten*, (Jena, 1917).

31. Gottlieb, *Long Swings*, pp.29-30,99-100 and 165.

32. *Ibid.*, *pp.179-180*, see in addition A.Voigt, 'Die Bedeutung der Baukosten fuer die Wohnungspreise', *Schriften des Vereins fuer Sozialpolitik*, vol.XCIV, (1901), where for Berlin a ratio of 3 or 4 to 1 between building costs and land acquisition is given for the period from 1875 to 1898; and A.Schleiss, *Die Gruende der Mietsteigerung der Wohnungen in Hamburg im letzten halben Jahrhundert*, (Leipzig, 1906), especially p.36 et seq.

32a. The investment index is in millions of marks in 1913 prices. The trend-removed estimates were added to the mean value for the period from 1870 to 1913. All of the data are from Hoffmann et al., *Das Wachstum der deutschen Wirtschaft*, passim. It is worth adding that these data form the basis for a statistically significant estimate of housing investment for Germany as a whole during the period from 1870 to 1913:

$$I_{to} = 1219.52 + \underset{(2.751)}{29.513C_{t-2}} - \underset{(6.346)}{35.852R_{t-2}} \qquad R^2 = 0.75 \quad DW = 1.22$$

where I = investment in 1913 prices (as in figure 5.8), C = index of building costs and R = index of rents, with T - statistics in parentheses. Given the emphasis in this article on migration, the result for Germany as a whole is rather surprising.

33. See also my paper 'Wohnungsbauinvestitionen waehrend des Urbanisierungsprozess im Deutschen Reich 1870 - 1913' in H.-J.Teuteberg (ed.). *Stadtwachstum, Industrialisierung, Sozialer Wandel. Beitraege zur Erforschung der Urbanisierung im 19. und 20. Jahrhundert.* (Berlin and Munich, 1986), pp.61-100.

34. See especially K.Hunscha, 'Die Dynamik des Baumarktes', *Vierteljahreshefte zur Konjunkturforschung*, Sonderheft 17. (Berlin, 1930), p.16.

35. The annual average increase in the number of dwellings in Hamburg between 1874 and 1913 was 4848, that of vacant dwellings 334; but the standard deviations were high and are telling: 3297 for the former and 1645 for the latter.

36. The urban housing market would seem to be paradigmatic for 'disequilibrium analysis' of the kind J.Kornai has propagated, see J.Kornai, Anti-Equilibrium, (Amsterdam, 1971), passim.

37. Pioneering econometric work on housing investment in Hamburg for the period under discussion here was done years ago by none other than Jan Tinbergen in his book Statistical Testing of Business Cycle Theories, (New York, 1968: reprint of League of Nations, Geneva, 1939). He used Hamburg as a case representative of Germany, having a long run of data. He tested an equation explaining building activity in terms of rents, vacancies, building costs and interest rates, but vacancies lagged three periods were the main factor. This paper attempts to build on Tinbergen.

37a. The tests involved all possible combinations of the following independent variables with housing investment defined as annual changes in the number of dwellings (Gelasse) in all cases:

$$G_{to} = f\,(G_{t-1},\ REN_{t-2},\ V_{t-2},\ Y_{t-1},\ T)$$

38. See footnote 29. This does not hold for 'real' rents, i.e., nominal rents per dwelling deflated by the wholesale price index in Hoffmann et al. Das Wachstum der deutschen Wirtschaft, passim.

39. As cited in footnote 33 above.

40. This estimate and much more on the housing market in Hamburg and elsewhere has been developed by Thomas Wellenreuther, University of Muenster (see also footnote 10).

41. Wellenreuther's work on Hamburg has identified marriages as one key variable. For Berlin in the period 1870 to 1913 we have the following (with E = Marriages and T - statistics in parentheses):

$$REN_{to} = 5.923 + 0.148T + 0.482REN_{t-1} + 7.410E_{t-1} + 127.817C_{t-1}$$

$$(.881) \quad (5.651) \quad (2.826) \quad (4.373)$$

$$R^2 = 0.749 \qquad DW = 2.223$$

42. One of the classic statements of the problem is by W.Koellmann, 'Industrialisierung, Binnenwanderung und "Soziale Frage"' in idem., Bevoelkerung in der industriellen Revolution, (Goettingen, 1974), pp.106-124, first published in Vierteljahrschrift fuer Sozial- und Wirtschaftsgeschichte, vol.46, (1959). H.-J.Teuteberg and a group of young historians whose work he has stimulated have made the most significant newer contributions to the analysis of the 'housing question'; see the first five footnotes of this paper, footnote 11a (where C.Wischermann's study on Hamburg is cited), and also

the contributions by Teuteberg and Wischermann to the volume cited in footnote 33: H.-J.Teuteberg. 'Die Debatte der deutschen Nationaloekonomie im Verein fuer Socialpolitik ueber die Ursachen der "Wohnungsfrage" und die Steuerungsmittel einer Wohnungs-reform im spaeten 19. Jahrhundert, and C.Wischermann, 'Wohnungsmarkt, Wohnungsversorgung und Wohnmobilitaet in deutschen Grossstaedten, 1870-1913', both in Teuteberg, Stadtwachstum, pp.13-60, and pp.101-134 respectively.

43. It can be shown that the most rapidly growing cities and most rapidly urbanising districts in Germany in the period from 1867 to 1907 (or from 1871 to 1910) were those cities and districts in which the industrial labour force was growing most rapidly. That is, German urbanisation in this period was a function of the industrialisation of the labour force. In Prussian districts, between 1867 and 1907, $R^2 = 0.77$ (N=11). An obvious point, perhaps, but one worth making.

44. As several historians have pointed out, (e.g. Wischermann, Wohnen in Hamburg, pp.16-24), concern with the housing problem antedated the 1870s and the first major scholarly investigation, by the Verein fuer Sozialpolitik, came in the 1880s. Nevertheless, the 1870s had a special role to play. It may be necessary to add that the sweeping generalisations being made here are based on a reading of the 'social reformers' such as Huber, Faucher, Schmoeller, Fuchs, Eberstadt, Wagner, etc. (cited by Teuteberg and Wischermann in their contributions listed above) and the 'critique of the critique' as published in the Deutsche Oekonomist, a Berlin weekly, in the period between 1883 and 1913.

45. For discussion of some of these measures and their background see U.Blumenroth, 'Deutsche Wohnungspolitik seit der Reichsgruendung'. (Beitraege zum Siedlungs- und Wohnungswesen und zur Raumplanung, vol.25, Muenster, 1975). See also W.Krabbe, 'Die Anfaenge des "sozialen Wohnungsbaus" vor dem ersten Weltkrieg', Vierteljahrschrift fuer Sozial- und Wirtschaftsgeschichte, vol.71 (1984), p.30 et seq., for examples of intervention.

46. That is, entrepreneurs might have either associated high psychic costs with leaving the industry or have had relatively high fixed costs which induced them to continue to produce as long as some part of such costs could be met, or both.

Table 5.1 : Annual average rates of growth of population in Prussian cities with 20,000 or more inhabitants, 1819-1910.

Year	Population (in 000's)	Growth Rate	Annual Growth Rate
1819	637		
1834	838	32	1,8
1837	875	4	1,3
1843	1.114	27	4,0
1849	1.319	18	2,7
1852	1.423	8	2,6
1861	1.866	31	3,1
1871	2.712	45	3,9
1880	4.610	70	6,1
1890	7.189	56	4,6
1895	8.091	13	2,3
1900	10.480	30	5,1
1910	14.941	43	3,7

Source : author's calculations.

Table 5.2 : Population growth and natural increase in Prussian cities, 1865-1905. (per 1000 inhabitants per year).

Cities	1865/67	1868/71		1872/75		1876/80		1881/85	
	R I	RN I	R I	RN I	R I	RN I	R I	RN I	R I
Krefeld	6,20	4,94	6,90	10,58	16,40	15,47	27,90	15,74	40,00
Aachen	7,89	6,60	15,70	8,54	16,10	12,26	14,80	11,28	19,50
Elberfeld	15,20	7,73	14,70	13,66	22,30	14,02	29,20	14,83	55,20
Barmen	28,50	11,95	23,90	10,80	30,90	18,16	26,70	13,75	18,20
Koeln	3,80	4,63	5,70	10,33	8,00	11,46	11,70	8,76	18,60
Duesseldorf	51,60	4,47	46,60	11,70	26,10	13,62	34,80	13,79	39,20
Dortmund	39,90	14,34	56,10	16,35	62,40	20,24	43,30	18,13	33,30
Essen	75,90	16,95	56,00	25,87	30,60	17,94	10,10	14,83	18,40
Halle	13,40	7,34	14,00	10,99	22,80	14,00	33,30	11,50	32,60
Magdeburg	15,90	1,80	19,20	6,33	11,50	9,29	15,20	6,91	77,20
Breslau	17,00	3,07	26,20	7,22	35,30	6,82	29,00	3,31	23,70
Danzig	7,60	-2,63	-1,50	7,12	9,70	5,83	20,90	6,50	16,30
Koenigsberg	11,90	-6,63	10,20	4,01	5,80	5,24	34,50	1,96	21,60
Stettin	13,70	1,62	7,60	11,70	9,70	8,03	19,70	5,33	21,50
Berlin	26,20	3,00	28,80	8,45	34,60	11,48	33,10	8,55	33,40
Frankfurt	3,10	-0,26	16,80	8,02	29,40	11,23	47,10	7,80	42,80
Hanover	21,70	9,69	27,90	11,57	40,50	16,01	36,20	11,41	28,80
Kiel	-	8,91	56,70	11,98	34,30	15,98	34,30	14,72	35,60
Wiesbaden	46,70	5,59	31,30	12,69	41,50	11,00	37,40	4,98	25,10
Correlation Coefficient	0,62		0,63		0,62		0,02		0,03

Cities	1886/90 RN I	1886/90 R I	1891/95 RN I	1891/95 R I	1896/1900 RN I	1896/1900 R I	1901/05 RN I	1901/05 R I	X[a)]
Krefeld	16,44	38,40	13,70	17,40	10,28	1,40	11,85	b)	0,66
Aachen	10,60	19,80	11,07	14,90	12,88	29,70	11,85	27,30	0,34
Elberfeld	14,60	32,70	16,09	27,90	15,56	23,40	13,84	15,90	0,48
Barmen	14,81	20,30	15,67	21,80	15,94	21,20	15,38	21,60	0,01
Koeln	12,16	89,40	13,10	72,30	14,84	30,10	15,58	30,90	0,50
Duesseldorf	15,38	46,70	16,75	46,80	19,32	43,10	17,44	39,70	0,04
Dortmund	17,03	31,90	18,78	39,00	20,89	52,80	21,38	50,70	0,47
Essen	16,35	35,70	10,07	43,20	20,94	45,90	26,51	125,80	0,44
Halle	11,68	39,00	13,20	37,40	9,94	50,70	9,71	27,50	0,15
Magdeburg	13,67	81,40	12,59	30,30	11,55	13,20	8,75	11,80	0,72
Breslau	4,99	21,70	6,71	23,20	8,07	24,70	7,04	24,60	0,25
Danzig	6,39	10,50	7,44	9,20	8,71	16,40	10,98	25,60	0,23
Koenigsberg	4,53	7,40	4,56	20,90	4,50	16,60	5,59	28,10	-0,02
Stettin	6,44	25,60	8,18	56,70	8,78	53,80	10,65	47,50	0,31
Berlin	9,60	37,40	9,00	25,20	8,52	19,00	7,36	20,30	0,53
Frankfurt	6,58	29,60	7,59	44,70	11,92	53,30	11,49	40,80	0,72
Hanover	11,78	31,00	14,56	45,90	14,17	38,70	9,44	18,20	0,49
Kiel	13,36	53,70	17,76	56,20	15,91	50,10	16,09	80,70	0,09
Wiesbaden	5,86	27,30	7,44	31,10	8,42	30,90	7,50	33,50	-0,06
Correlation Coefficient		0,39		0,35		0,43			

a) Correlation coefficient
b) Change in city boundaries
R I = Rate of Increase
RN I = Rate of Natural Increase

Table 5.3 : Zero-order correlations, housing stock and selected variables (rates of growth) Hamburg, 1874-1913.

Variable	Time Lag	Coefficient (Pearson)	Number of Observations
A. Annual Averages			
1. Number of Marriages	t-4	0,31	35
"	t-3	0,43	36
"	t-2	0,17	37
"	t-1	0,10	38
"	to	0,17	39
"	t+1	-0,18	38
"	t+2	-0,43	37
"	t+3	-0,38	36
"	t+4	-0,20	35
2. Number of Births	t-4	0,24	35
"	t-3	0,37	36
"	t-2	0,56	37
"	t-1	0,28	38
"	to	0,39	39
3. Net Migration	t-2	0,27	41
"	t-1	0,18	42
"	to	0,26	43
B. 3-Year Moving Averages			
1. Number of Marriages	t-3	0,58	36
"	t-2	0,48	37
"	t-1	0,32	38
2. Number of Births	t-2	0,48	37
3. Net Migration	t-2	0,51	39
"	t-1	0,46	40
"	to	0,36	41
4. Income	t-3	0,27	37
"	t-2	0,21	38

Table 5.4 : Indicators linking German urban growth and emigration, 1819-1910, (annual average rates of change in per cent).

Periods	Urban Population (Prussia)	Industrial Production (Germany)	Emigration[c] (Germany)	Rural Net Migration[a] (Prussia)	Rural Net Migration[b] (Prussia)
1819-34	1.8		.015	+ .057	
1834-37	1.3		.066	+ .161	
1837-43	4.0		.080	+ .151	
1843-49	2.7		.165	- .318	- .05
1849-52	2.6	1.8	.294	+ .066	- .04
1852-61	3.1	3.1	.320	- .069	
1861-71	3.9	4.6	.218	- .170	- .34
1871	6.1	2.7	.147		- .46
1880-90	4.6	4.4	.288		- .73
1890-1895	2.3	4.1	.159		- .458)
1895-1900	5.1	4.7	.047		
1900-1910	3.7	3.4	.046		- .22
	(Germany)				
1871-75	6.0	7.6	.190	- 1.057	- .986
1875-80	3.2	- 1.0	.140	- .523[1])	
1880-85	3.4	3.4	.375	- 1.154[2])	- 1.578[2])
1885-90	5.0	5.4	.200		- 1.558[3])
1890-95	3.8	4.2	.159		- 1.376[4])
1895-1900	5.2	5.2	.047		- 2.004[5])
1900-1905	3.8	2.7	.050		- 1.321[6])
1905-1910	3.3	4.1	.042		- 1.351[7])

a) Data from A. Markow, *Das Wachstum der Bevoelkerung und die Entwicklung der Aus-und Einwanderung*, (Tuebingen, 1889).

b) Data from R.A. Dickler, 'Labor Market Pressure Aspects of Agricultural Growth in the Eastern Region of Prussia', 1840-1914, unpublished Ph.D. thesis, University of Pennsylvania 1975.

c) Data from W. Fischer, J. Krengel, J. Wietog, *Sozialgeschichtliches Arbeitsbuch I, Materialen zur Statistik des Deutschen Bundes, 1815-70*, (Muenchen, 1982), and G. Hohorst, J. Kocka, G.A. Ritter, *Sozialgeschichtliches Arbeitsbuch II, Materialen zur Statistik des Kaiserreiches 1870-1914*, (Muenchen, 1975).

1. 1876-80
2. 1881-85
3. 1886-90
4. 1891-95
5. 1896-1900
6. 1901-1905
7. 1906-1910
8. 1891-1900

Note: The discrepancy between Markow's and Dickler's estimates could not be easily traced and so was allowed to stand. It should be pointed out that aggregating net migration figures for East Elbia from the individual districts can easily produce an overestimate of the total urban-industry-bound migration. For the latter, the decadal figures in the table's upper half are rather more appropriate.

Chapter Six

SECTORAL PERFORMANCE AND ECONOMIC DEVELOPMENT : THE BACKWARD LINKAGES OF THE GERMAN PIG-IRON INDUSTRY, 1871-1913, AS A FACTOR IN MACRO-ECONOMIC GROWTH

Jochen Krengel

I

In the 1860s Germany produced annually approximately one million tons of iron, in the form of pig-iron, bar-iron, cast-iron, wire and steel. By 1870 pig-iron and steel production had risen to 1.4 million tons and 170,000 tons respectively and output at this stage was already greater than that of France or Belgium. Between 1871 and 1913 output of pig-iron increased twelve-fold, so that by the outbreak of the First World War Germany was the second largest producer of pig-iron in the world. The expansion of the iron and steel industry is regarded as having been of fundamental significance to the expansion of the German economy in the latter decades of the nineteenth century. It was Keynes who argued that 'the German empire was built more truly on coal and iron, than on blood and iron', and the iron and steel industry as a whole is frequently accorded a special role in German economic development, constituting throughout the period under consideration one of the backbones of the German economy. Moreover it was also a sector influenced by the development of cartels and other organisational issues. Pig-iron itself was an intermediate product, of central importance in the expansion of iron and steel production. However the traditional view of the fundamental importance of the pig-iron industry to German economic development is in need of revision and reappraisal. The following paper will seek to reassess the role of the pig-iron industry on the basis of an econometric analysis of this sector's backward linkages. Despite certain data limitations, the material provided from the Imperial Statistical Office is particularly suitable for the application of this type of analysis.(1)

Before analysing the demand of the German pig-iron industry for its inputs between the years 1871 and 1913, it is necessary to make some remarks on the subject of pig-iron itself and on the statistical methods used in describing and measuring this demand. Pig-iron is an initial product of steelworks and foundries. It differs from steel and finished cast-iron products in an economic sense and metallurgically from steel as well. Pig-iron has a much higher percentage of carbon than steel: approximately 3 per cent as opposed to 0.5 to 1 per cent. This higher percentage of carbon makes pig-iron unforgeable; to convert it into wrought-iron, normally called steel, it has to be decarbonised. Thus we can call pig-iron carbonised steel. The difference in economic terms between pig-iron and steel or the foundry products which are metallurgically similar to pig-iron, is also clear: as it is an input for those two branches of the iron and steel industry, it is only used and traded within the iron and steel sector itself. Other industries which use finished iron and steel products as an input only have dealings with steelworks and foundries, not with pig-iron works. Thus we may also call pig-iron in an economic sense unfinished iron.(2)

II

The statistical method of measuring the backward linkage effects is very similar to the standard input-output-calculation. I have constructed three and four year averages for various sets of data, relating mainly to the input demand of the German pig-iron industry for the years 1871 to 1873 and 1908 to 1911.(3) Only in these years was there sufficient data to attempt an interlacing analysis of some sectors of the German economy by way of comparison.

I have concentrated this analysis on the direct and indirect contributions of the pig-iron industry to the growth of net national product at market prices and to total employment. Because of the statistical construction of the sectoral value added of the pig-iron industry, I have had to fall back on net national product instead of the normally employed gross national product, as the sectoral value added of pig-iron production contains no allowance for depreciation.

If we now look at table 6.1, which gives the direct contributions of the pig-iron industry to these two macro-economic indicators, we can see, besides evidence of absolute growth, that the relative importance of this branch of industry was remarkably small. The share of employment remained stable at one-seventh per cent of total employment, and the share of value added increased slightly from one-seventh to nearly one-half per cent of net national product. Such a result is quite surprising if we call to mind the prominent role of this industry in German historiography and its possible position as a key-industry.(4)

But it would nevertheless be incorrect to conclude from these findings that this industrial sector was completely unimportant in the German economy. McCloskey has previously stated in his analysis of the British iron and steel industry that pig-iron production needed a large amount of material inputs and in my opinion his remarks accurately reflect the real function of this industry for macro-economic growth.(5) Its importance lay not so much in its own share of various macro-economic indicators, but rather in the value added and employment which it induced through its demand effects on other branches of the economy. These indirect contributions were arguably much higher than its own economic significance. In the period under consideration, pig-iron production in Germany involved the use of iron-ore, coke and some additional mineral products such as limestone, as well as transportation services. That iron-ore and coke are necessary for pig-iron production is self-evident, but what were these additional mineral products and transportation services needed for? The former were used to keep the slag and cinders, inevitable by-products of pig-iron smelting, in a fluid state. Because of their specific gravities, pig-iron collected at the bottom of the furnace, slag and cinders at the top. If the whole process of reduction was not to come to a quick end by blocking up the furnace, slag had to be removed and this was only technically possible if it remained fluid, and could therefore be taken from the blast furnace in the same manner as fluid pig-iron. Transportation services, mainly by rail, were necessary for another reason. During the period in question all the great German pig-iron producing regions were located geographically where only one of their basic inputs, either coke or iron-ore, was available in sufficient quantities. The Saar-Lorraine district had some coke and a lot of iron-ore; the Ruhr and the Upper-Silesian districts had large deposits of coal and very little iron-ore. Due to these geological characteristics the missing inputs had to be imported. Thus the use of transportation services was indispensable for the individual regions. Railway transportation, although not a material input, in contrast to the other factors under consideration, was nevertheless of the greatest significance for this branch of German industry.(6)

Table 6.2 presents the proportion of output in various sectors of the German economy generated through supplying the pig-iron industry. If we rely only on these linkages, however, the total effect of growth induction is underestimated for two reasons. Because of unsolveable data problems it was impossible to quantify the demand for products of the machine contruction industry and the construction sector as a whole, although both supplied large parts of the capital stock of the pig-iron industry. For the same reason the quoted linkage between the railways and the pig-iron industry is too low, as it was impossible to even guess at the level of demand for transportation which was induced by transporting finished pig-iron. According to the results given in table 6.2, approximately ninety per cent of the production of the iron-ore mines was dependent on demand generated by the pig-iron industry. The corresponding figures for the coal-mining industry, other mining industries supplying limestone and the railway sector were fifteen per cent, ten per cent and five to six per cent respectively.(7) These percentages seemed to be quite stable over the whole period, with the one exception of iron-ore mining, which reduced its dependency by an increase in exports to Belgium and France. This trend was reinforced by a fall in domestic demand from the pig-iron industry itself, which attempted to substitute better quality foreign ores for indigenous supplies.(8)

The mining sector of the German economy in particular was affected to some extent by the growth of the pig-iron industry, as dependency rates, ranging between ten and ninety per cent for three selected sub-branches of this industry show. In my opinion these results demonstrate the correctness of McCloskey's assessment of the role of this sector in macro-economic growth. However, in order to arrive at a more exact calculation of induced macro-economic growth on the basis of the available figures, we have to introduce the assumption that the share of output absorbed by the pig-iron industry was equal to the share of employment induced by its demand. Only if we accept this seemingly realistic hypothesis can we use the output shares given in table 6.2 as indicators of induced employment growth.

Table 6.3 shows the basic data on employment in the relevant industrial sectors and in the German economy as a whole. If we compare the average annual growth rates of sectoral employment with the growth rate of the total economy, we can identify growth-accelerating and growth-decelerating sectors. In particular the growth rates of employment in the coal-mining and railway sectors of 3.6 per cent and 3.4 per cent respectively seem to have positively affected the growth in total employment, which grew by a rate of 1.4 per cent within the same period. Employment within the pig-iron industry itself must have had a more or less stabilising effect, with only a very moderate growth rate of 1.6 per cent. Sectors which had a relatively inhibiting effect on the growth in total employment included iron-ore mining and other mining branches, with employment growth rates of only 0.3 and 1.1 per cent respectively. If we now weight the absolute figures of table 6.3 with the relative shares of output in table 6.2 we obtain the estimate of induced employment which is given in table 6.4.

The 35,000 employees in the German iron-ore mines between 1871 and 1873 represented men who worked indirectly for the pig-iron industry. By the period 1908 to 1911, this figure had risen to 36,000 and the induced employment had therefore only increaed absolutely by 1,000 men. This was a much slower growth than that of total employment within the iron-ore mines, which grew from 37,000 to 41,000 during the same period. This decelerating growth of induced employment reflected the diminishing output dependency of the iron-ore mines which fell from about 96 per cent between 1871 and 1873 to 88 per cent between 1908 and 1911 for the reasons stated above. If we look at the annual growth rates of induced sectoral employment, they differ in the same manner as in table 6.3, but with a slightly higher variation. Thus, induced employment increased within coal-mining and railways with growth rates of approximately 4 per cent, in contrast to an annual growth rate of 3.5 per cent for total employment. Induced employment within the iron-ore mining sector remained practically stable, in contrast to a very slow growth of 0.3 per cent in total employment. Induced employment within the other mining industries also grew by a rate of 0.9 per cent, slightly slower than total employment in this sector. It would appear that these varying growth rates explain to a certain degree the differing growth intensity of the sectors concerned. How could employment within the iron-ore mines have grown faster than it did, at a time when the pig-iron industry, which constituted its main market, was reducing its relative demand? Certainly the very good position of the coal-mining sector within the growth process was at least positively influenced by induced employment which grew faster than total employment. The same line of argumentation can be used in relation to the growth processes of the other mining industries and the railways, but as the importance of the pig-iron industry for the sectoral outputs in question was less important, the effect was accordingly more limited.

We can now attempt a rough estimation of the total contribution of the pig-iron industry to employment in Imperial Germany. The relevant data are collected in table 6.5. The second column shows the employment within the pig-iron industry itself, i.e., its direct contribution to total employment. The third column shows the induced employment representing the sum of sectoral employments listed in table 6.4. Certainly this induced employment is underestimated, due to the reasons stated above, and also due to the omission of the cumulative effects of demand variations. These cumulative effects become apparent if we bear in mind that the highly dependent growth of iron-ore mining also created a demand for investment goods which affected other sectors of industry, for example machine construction. The variations in demand associated with the pig-iron industry were therefore felt within the most distant parts of the German economy, although we are not able to quantify these effects during this period. For this purpose we need complete input-output tables which cannot be constructed at the present time, because of the continuing absence of detailed information.(9) Therefore the so-called 'total contribution' of the pig-iron industry, column 4 of table 6.5, represents only the barest minimum contribution. If we look specifically at the years 1871 to 1873, the demand generated by the pig-iron industry created, in addition to 25,000 jobs in its own sector, a further 72,000 jobs within the German economy as a whole. At a minimum about 100,000 people worked directly or indirectly for this industry. In the years from 1908 to 1911 the respective figures were 45,000 and 180,000, so that the total contribution of the pig-iron industry to employment was approximately 225,000 jobs. The employment multiplier (induced employment divided by direct employment) had increased from approximately three in the years from 1871 to 1873 to four in the years from 1908 to 1911. Therefore induced employment grew faster than direct employment (2.5 per cent per annum in comparison to 1.6 per cent per annum). Although the relative share of direct employment remained relatively stable at about 0.15 per cent of total employment throughout the entire period, the overall employment contribution (both direct and induced) of the pig-iron industry rose perceptively from 0.6 per cent of total employment between 1871 and 1873, to 0.8 per cent between 1908 and 1911. This confirms the accuracy of my major hypothesis in relation to the high importance of the pig-iron industry for induced growth during this period.

However, can we regard this branch of the economy as a major factor in macro-economic growth given that it only registered an employment share of under one per cent? Even if we take into account that in this period approximately one-third of all those gainfully employed in Germany still worked in agriculture (10) and that the relative shares of individual industries in total employment were accordingly always quite low, the pig-iron industry, irrespective of its possible growth-inducing role within some branches of heavy industry, does not seem to have been a key industry in terms of the general growth process of the German economy after 1871.

III

This judgement becomes more conclusive, if we look at the development and growth dependencies of sectoral value added. The figures listed in table 6.6 provide the basis for this part of the analysis. They represent the data on induced employment from table 6.5, rearranged according to the sectoral classification in Hoffmann's study, which constitutes the main source of information on net sectoral production.(11) It is clear from table 6.6 that the importance of the pig-iron industry for the entire mining sector was declining during this period. The proportion of induced employment in mining as a whole which can be attributed to the pig-iron industry fell from about 22 to 23 per cent to about 17 per cent. At the same time the interconnection between transportation services and the pig-iron industry increased slightly from three to four per cent. In order to estimate the increase in value added induced by the demand of the pig-iron industry, on the basis of the data contained in table 6.6, we have to assume that the share of induced employment was equal to the share of induced value added. On the basis of this highly plausible assumption we may proceed to examine table 6.7. This contains the sectoral value added data for selected branches of German industry, expressed in million marks and in constant 1913 prices. We can see that all the industrial branches concerned, including pig-iron, were clearly growth industries. Their annual growth rates ranged from 4 to over 5 per cent in comparison with a growth rate for the German economy as a whole of 2.5 per cent. By weighting the complete value added of the total mining sector and transportation services with the shares given in table 6.6 we can obtain the induced value added figures given in table 6.8. In the total mining sector the annual growth of induced value added was slower than the growth of the entire sector (3.2 per cent as opposed to 4 per cent). Just the opposite was true in the case of transportation services, where the induced value added grew at a slightly faster rate than was the case for this sector within the economy as a whole (6.1 per cent as opposed to 5.3 per cent). This result complements the outcome of the employment analysis: the differing growth rates of mining as a whole and transportation are explained, with varying accuracy, by the demand variations of the pig-iron industry. The declining connection between this industry and the mining sector generally led to a relative fall in the growth of induced value added, while the increasing growth of induced value added within transportation was responsible to a certain extent for the quite extraordinary growth rate of this entire sector.

Table 6.9 shows in the same manner as table 6.5 the direct and indirect contributions of the pig-iron industry to net national product. In the years around 1872 this sector contributed not only its own 26 million marks but also induced at least 100 million marks of income in connected branches of the economy. The total contribution was therefore 126 million marks in absolute terms or 0.7 per cent of net national product. The value added multiplier which stood at about four had nearly the same dimension as the employment multiplier. In the years from 1908 to 1911 the pig-iron industry produced, besides its own contribution to net national product of 184 million marks, 403 million marks of induced value added, thus bringing the total effect to nearly 600 millions, or 1.25 per cent of net national product. However the value added multiplier had fallen from four to two, in clear contrast to the registered trend in the employment multiplier, which rose from three to four. A comparison of the annual growth rates of the relevant indicators produces the same result: while induced employment (table 6.5) increased between the periods 1871-73 and 1908-11 at an annual rate of 2.5 per cent, employment within the pig-iron industry itself only rose at a rate of 1.6 per cent. The growth of induced value added, on the other hand, as table 6.9 indicates, was clearly slower than the annual growth rate of total value added for the pig-iron industry itself (5.4 per cent for pig-iron: 3.8 per cent for induced value added).

I would like to argue that the reason for this lay in the different development of sectoral labour productivities. In particular the mining sector could not compete with the rising productivity levels in the pig-iron industry. To quadruple its net production, the mining industry had to increase overall employment three-fold, while the pig-iron industry achieved a seven-fold increase in value added through an approximate doubling of total employment.(12) These results are quite reliable, because the relative rigidity of the production functions and the low rate of technical progress within the mining sector as a whole have already been established by Holtfrerich in his study of the coal-mining industry of the Ruhr region.(13) Nevertheless it is difficult to regard the pig-iron industry as an important factor in macro-economic growth during the period from 1871 to 1913. The relative share of pig-iron's contribution to total employment was under one per cent and its share of sectoral value added in net national product was only around one per cent. On this basis the contribution of the pig-iron industry to German economic growth was relatively restricted. The development of net sectoral production therefore confirms the thesis already formulated in the earlier section of this paper connected with the analysis of the employment multiplier.

IV

The results of the analysis of the backward linkages generated by the German pig-iron industry in the period from 1871 to 1913 are therefore as follows:

1. The direct contribution of this industry to employment and net national product was remarkably low, in contrast to the predominant role assigned to it in traditional German historiography.

2. The indirect contributions of this sector were much more important than the direct ones, but not important enough to warrant a classification of this industry as a major factor in German national economic growth during the last decades of the nineteenth-century. However its importance for heavy industry, especially mining, was certainly much greater.

3. The results of growth inducement were clearly different in relation to employment and net national product. The relative retardation in the improvement of productivity within the entire mining sector accounted for a measurably larger multiplier effect in relation to employment than sectoral value added.

4. In addition the analysis has provided an important methodological lesson. It is clearly both dangerous and misleading to assess the performance of branches specific of industry only by their direct contributions to macro-economic indicators. Only on the basis of a comparative analysis of sectoral outputs and demand variations can we possibly obtain results closer to historical reality.

NOTES

1. For the traditional view of the role of the iron and steel industry in German economic development in the period 1871 to 1913, see W.O.Henderson, The Rise of German Industrial Power 1834-1914, (London, 1975), pp.140-43,235-37, and idem., The Industrial Revolution on the Continent: Germany, France, Russia, 1800-1914, (London, 1961), passim.

2. On this see Jochen Krengel, 'Die deutsche Roheisenindustrie 1871-1913. Eine quantitativ-historische Untersuchung', unpublished PhD thesis, University of Berlin, 1982, p.11 et seq., since published as J.Krengel. Die deutsche Roheisenindustrie 1871-1913. Eine quantitativ-historische Untersuchung. (Schriften zur Wirtschafts und Sozialgeschichte, Bd.34, Berlin, 1983); Ludwig Sinzheimer, 'Der volkswirtschaftliche Charakter der technischen Entwicklung des deutschen Eisenhuettengewerbes 1865-1879', unpublished PhD thesis, University of Munich, 1892, p.14 et seq.

3. For the problems arising from the application of the modern method of input-output calculation see Jochen Krengel, 'Zur Berechnung von Wachstumswirkungen konjunkturell bedingter Nachfrageschwankungen nachgelagerter Industrien auf die Produktionsentwicklung der deutschen Roheisenindustrie waehrend der Jahre 1871-1882', in Wilhelm Heinz Schroeder and Reinhard Spree (eds.), Historische Konjunkturforschung (Historisch-Socialwissenschaftliche Forschungen vol.11, Stuttgart, 1981), p.187 et seq., and Krengel, 'Roheisenindustrie', p.171 et seq.

4. The reader may obtain a bibliographical summary in Wilfried Feldenkirchen, Die Eisen- und Stahlindustrie des Ruhrgebiets 1879-1914, (Wiesbaden, 1982), p.588 et seq.; Krengel, 'Roheisenindustrie', p.280 et seq.; Hans Marchand, Saekularstatistik der Deutschen Eisenindustrie, (Essen, 1935), p.143 et seq.

5. Donald N.McCloskey, Economic Maturity and Entrepreneurial Decline. British Iron and Steel 1870-1913, (Harvard Economic Studies, vol.142, Cambridge/Mass., 1973), p.74 et seq.

6. Krengel, 'Roheisenindustrie', p.23.

7. This quota is only a very rough approximation; it represents the relative share of limestone consumption by the German pig-iron industry to the gross production of the so-called 'Other Mines' in W.G.Hoffmann's Das Wachstum der deutschen Wirtschaft seit der Mitte des 19. Jahrhunderts, (Berlin, Heidelberg, New York, 1965), p.194.

8. Krengel, 'Roheisenindustrie', p.175.

9. Krengel, 'Roheisenindustrie', p.204.

10. G.Hohorst, J.Kocka, and G.A.Ritter, Sozialgeschichtliches Arbeitsbuch II, Materialien zur Statistik des Kaiserreiches 1870-1914, 2nd edn. (Muenchen, 1978), p.66.

11. Hoffmann, Wachstum, p.454.

12. Hoffmann, Wachstum, p.194 and Tables 1 and 7.

13. Carl-Ludwig Holtfrerich, Quantitative Wirtschaftsgeschichte des Ruhrkohlenbergbaues im 19. Jahrhundert, (Dortmund, 1973), p.108.

Table 6.1 : The absolute and relative contributions of the German pig-iron industry to net national product and total employment, 1871-73, 1908-11.

Period	Work Force Employed (in 1,000)	Value Added (in million marks at constant 1913 prices)
1871-73	25 (0,14%)	26 (0,14%)
1908-11	45 (0,15%)	184 (0,39%)

Source: J.Krengel, 'Die deutsche Roheisenindustrie 1871-1913. Eine quantitativ-historische Untersuchung', unpublished PhD. thesis, University of Berlin, 1982, pp.199, 202.

Table 6.2 : The demand of the pig-iron industry as a share of the output of selected industrial sectors, 1871-73, 1908-11.

Period	Iron-ore mines	Coal-mines	Other mines	Railways
1871-73	95,5%	13,5%	10,9%	4,9%
1908-11	88,3%	15,1%	10,3%	6,2%

Source: Krengel, 'Roheisenindustrie', p.200.

Table 6.3 : Total employment in selected industrial sectors and in the German economy (in 1,000), 1871-73, 1908-11.

Period	Iron-ore mines	Coal-mines	Other mines	Railways	Pig-iron industry	Total economy
1871-73	37	164	47	202	25	17.657
1908-11	41	613	72	698	45	29.142
Annual Growth Rate (AGR)	+0,3	+3,6	+1,1	+3,4	+1,6	+1,4

Source: W.G. Hoffmann, Das Wachstum der deutschen Wirtschaft seit der Mitte des 19. Jahrhunderts, (Berlin, Heidelberg, New York, 1965), p.194 et seq.

Table 6.4 : Induced employment (in 1,000) created by the demand of the pig-iron industry, 1871-73, 1908-11.

Period	Iron-ore mines	Coal-mines	Other mines	Railways
1871-73	35	22	5	10
1908-11	36	93	7	43
AGR	+0	+3,9	+0,9	+4,0

Sources: Calculated with data given in tables 6.1 and 6.2.

Table 6.5 : The direct and indirect contributions of the pig-iron industry to employment, in absolute terms (in 1,000), and as a proportion of total employment, 1871-73, 1908-11.

Period	Pig-iron industry	Induced employment	Total contribution
1871-73	25 (0,14%)	72 (0,41%)	97 (0,55%)
1908-11	45 (0,15%)	179 (0,61%)	224 (0,76%)
AGR	+1,6	+2,5	+2,3

Sources: Tables 6.1 and 6.4

Table 6.6 : Induced employment generated by the pig-iron industry rearranged in absolute terms (in 1,000), and in relation to total sectoral employment, 1871-73, 1908-11.

Period	Total Mining	Transportation
1871-73	62 (22,5%)	10 (3,1%)
1908-11	136 (16,8%)	43 (4,1%)

Sources: Hoffmann, Wachstum, p.454 and table 6.4.

Table 6.7 : Total value added in selected industrial branches and net national product in million Marks and in constant 1913 prices, 1871-73, 1908-11.

Period	Total mining	Transportation	Pig-iron industry	Net National Product
1871-73	388	419	26	18.765
1908-11	1.696	2.878	184	47.522
AGR	+4,0	+5,3	+5,4	+2,5

Sources: Hoffmann, Wachstum, p.454 et seq., and table 6.1.

Table 6.8 Induced value added generated by the pig-iron industry in mining and transportation, in million Marks and in constant 1913 prices, 1871-73, 1908-11.

Period	Total Mining	Transportation
1871-73	87	13
1908-11	285	118
AGR	+3,2	+6,1

Sources: Calculated with data given in tables 6.6 and 6.7.

Table 6.9 : The direct and indirect contributions of the pig-iron industry to net national product, in absolute terms (in million Marks in constant 1913 prices), and in per cent, 1871-73, 1908-11.

Period	Pig-iron industry	Induced value added	Total contribution
1871-73	26 (0,14%)	100 (0,53%)	126 (0,67%)
1908-11	184 (0,39%)	403 (0,85%)	587 (1,24%)
AGR	+5,4	+3,8	+4,2

Sources: Tables 6.6 and 6.8.

Chapter Seven

'NEW INDUSTRIES' AND THE ROLE OF THE STATE : THE DEVELOPMENT OF ELECTRICAL POWER IN SOUTH GERMANY FROM c.1880 TO THE 1920s

Hermann Schaefer

I

Electricity was, as Joseph A.Schumpeter wrote, 'the dominant factor' of the industrial boom period from the mid-1890s onwards.(1) It was a characteristic of the economic development of all industrial nations during the second industrial revolution in a similar way to the role of the steam engine in the first industrial revolution. However an international comparison reveals a remarkable difference. The late-comer nations, the United States and Germany, were now outpacing England, the world's first industrial nation.

The first public power stations in Europe had indeed been established in Britain. A pioneer water-powered station had been established in 1881 in Goldaming (Surrey) by the German company Siemens and a pioneer steam station had been set up by Edison in January 1882 at Holborn Viaduct in London. However Britain in the long run was unable to take the lead in international electricity supply or in the development of the electro-technical industry.(2) The United States and Germany became the world-wide leading nations in the development of electricity, and other European states only realised 'a decade or more later'(3) many of the possibilities first achieved in Germany. While the performance of the British entrepreneur in the field of electricity supply could be justifiably regarded as 'inadequate'(4), Germany, despite a belated start, rapidly rose to a very strong position in world markets.

It is the aim of this essay to provide a survey of the rise of the electrical industry and the development of a state-controlled system of electricity supply in Germany before the First World War. The main task will be to contrast the role and significance of the activity of private enterprise, with the developing role of the state in the field of electricity supply. The multitude of different forms in which electricity supply undertakings appeared during the years of 'high industrialisation' around the turn of the century, does not permit a detailed description of all the different regions of the German Empire. In order to tackle the issues at stake, I have therefore concentrated on the South German federal states, Baden, Wuerttemberg and Bavaria. The circumstances in Baden will often be compared to those of its neighbour, Wuerttemberg. The example of Bavaria will be treated briefly at the end of the paper since it differs from the other two states in a significant way.(5)

II

Of all the federal states of the German Empire at the end of the nineteenth-century, in which electricity was produced by water power, Baden and Wuerttemberg had experienced a particularly early and dynamic start in this sector. As a matter of fact, Baden and Wuerttemberg had only small quantities of mineral resources, and anthracite had to be shipped to south-west Germany from the Ruhr or Saar areas. The supply of water, however, was unevenly distributed between the two states. Baden offered by far the better possibilities for the production of electricity, mainly because of the presence of the Rhine and its tributaries originating in many cases in the Black Forest and providing a relatively steady flow of water. Conditions in Wuerttemberg were less favourable. The supply of water from the river Neckar, the main river in the region, and from its tributaries, was only moderate and subject to great seasonal changes. Natural circumstances, such as the existence of water power or suitable mineral resources, however, were important for the location of the production of electricity, particularly for the construction of power plants. They also largely determined the possible use and sale of the final product.(6)

A broad range of possibilities for using electricity, as well as great prospects for the future, only opened up after Thomas A. Edison had invented in 1879 an easily used light-source, namely the incandescent filament lamp. Edison demonstrated this invention to the European public at the first fair for electrical engineering in Paris in 1881. Several engineers realised at the same time the potential usefulness of this new electric light bulb. In Stuttgart, for instance, Paul Reisser was the first to install electric lamps in his business premises as well as in the post office situated in the same house. The current was provided by a dynamo driven by a gas engine and set up in the cellar of the building. At the same time the Studiengesellschaft (research company), founded by Rathenau and Edison in 1882, established the first Edison system of any considerable size in Berlin. Its power output of 25 kilowatt-hour (kWh) was used solely for lighting purposes. In December 1882, the Wilhelmstrasse in Berlin was used to test electric lighting. This experiment was greatly welcomed by the inhabitants of Berlin and served as a powerful advertisement for electricity. In 1883, Rathenau founded the Deutsche Edisongesellschaft fuer angewandte Elektrizitaet (DEG) (German Edison Company for Applied Electricity) as the successor to the earlier Studiengesellschaft. Its explicit purpose was to exploit Edison's patents in Germany.

Rathenau made an agreement on the division of the market with the firm of Siemens and Halske, which dominated the electro-technical sector at that time. Siemens was to retain his interests in the manufacture of machines for the generation of electricity and the production of cables and other accessories, while the German Edison Company was to take over the production of bulbs and the supply of equipment. Reisser's firm in Stuttgart, mentioned above, received the general agency of the Edison Company for Wuerttemberg. Among Reisser's first customers was the King of Wuerttemberg who ordered electrical lighting for the royal court theatre in Stuttgart. In 1884, the Edison Company set up the first block station in Berlin, providing electricity to a group of houses situated at the corner of Friedrichstrasse and Unter den Linden. This was then one of the busiest areas in the city centre. A well renowned cafe, several shops, and two restaurants belonged to this block and were supplied with electricity by a generator in the cellar of the building. A number of problems showed up at the beginning. It was reported, for example, that the ice that should have served to cool champagne in the cafe had to be used on the engines which were frequently running hot. Flickering lamps and other difficulties, which attracted the ridicule of the inhabitants of Berlin, were soon dealt with, and the system continued to be in use for ten years without any intermission.

At that time, the block unit, i.e. the small electric power station restricted in operation to a self-contained group of houses, appeared as the power station of the future. Rathenau, however, kept developing plans which went well beyond this concept. He wanted to supply whole districts of individual cities through one big power station. In 1884-5 the first public power station in Germany was set up in Berlin, and in 1888 the first station was set in operation in Hamburg.(7)

The biggest problem at that time was the transport of electric current from the power station to the electric lamps. Apart from a number of specific difficulties in the construction of the grid, in the load that cables could carry and in the wiring system, the problem that gave rise to most concern was the drop in voltage resulting from the transport of electric current. In most cases, areas of supply were limited to a radius of three kilometers. Similarly, the first local stations, based on the system of direct current, had to be erected within the consumer areas, i.e. within the respective urban centres. As a result the possibilities of supplying electric current were initially limited, and electricity generation in the big cities depended almost exclusively on the use of steam power. A more general use of water power, which depended on the location of specific sites, only became possible after the problem of transporting current over relatively long distances had been solved. It was thus an epoch-making event when, in 1891, for the first time polyphase alternate current was transmitted over a distance of 175 kilometers. This was from Lauffen on the river Neckar, where water power was used, to Frankfurt-am-Main. From then on, the large scale generation of current by water power seemed possible, together with the widespread supply of electricity within large areas.(8)

Local authorities and individual states, however, were reluctant to risk the investment of large sums of capital in this kind of new energy. Indeed, the risks involved in electrical engineering could not easily be assessed at that time. There was a confusing variety of electrical systems, including direct, alternate, and three-phase current. In addition, many towns were afraid that the construction of local power stations would lead to competition with the gas works which were already owned by the same municipal authorities.(9)

These were the main reasons as to why private initiative became responsible for the building of electricity supply systems at the beginning of this period. Above all, private industrial enterprises, using small and even extremely small generators (the latter mostly located in mills and saw-mills), were responsible for the initial generation of electric current by water power. In the last decade of the nineteenth-century, many mills and saw-mills had to struggle in order to maintain production at the level of existing capacity, so that the owners became interested in the generation of current as an additional source of income. Usually they simply had to exchange an efficient turbine for an old mill-wheel, since they already held the licence to use available water supplies for business purposes. The current produced in this way could be sold to surrounding villages.(10)

The construction of the first European power station on a large river, namely at Rheinfelden on the Upper Rhine, between 1894 and 1898, furnishes an extremely significant example of the commitment on the part of industrial enterprises to the exploitation of water power. Emil Rathenau, manager of AEG (Allgemeine Electricitaets Gesellschaft: General Electricity Company) was the initiator of this project and the driving force in founding a 'preparatory company' under the control of AEG.

Since the end of the 1880s, there had been considerable discussion about the exploitation of water power in this area, where the fall in the level of the river Rhine was particularly favourable. 'Quantities of energy', Rathenau said, 'which in other places have to be wrenched out of the earth with great efforts are freely available here. All we have to do is to seize on them and exploit them'.(11) Realising this idea, however, was not as easy as it might appear from this quote. There were various difficulties to be overcome by the company before it was possible to start with the construction of the power station. The Rhine at this place formed the border between Switzerland and the Grand Duchy of Baden. Difficult negotiations with both states about licensing became necessary. In 1894, a concession for common exploitation was finally granted. Then, however, Emil Rathenau's ambitious project was endangered by financing problems. The cost of the plant was estimated at twelve million Swiss francs. Only after its projected output had been reduced to half of what was originally planned and only after the future profitability of the plant had been secured through agreements with prospective customers, was it possible to form a company to finance the project. In reality, this meant that the Aluminium Aktiengesellschaft Neuhausen/Switzerland agreed by contract to transfer part of its production to Rheinfelden and to take as a subscriber 30 per cent of the current generated there. Similarly, the Elektrochemische Werke Bitterfeld agreed to establish a branch which would consume 20 per cent of the current. In other words, about 50 per cent of the current from the planned power station had to be 'sold', before the banks involved in the project were willing to accept the investment risk. It is generally known that the banks at that time felt doubtful about industrial enterprises in the field of electrical engineering. Their attitude towards the project at Rheinfelden was by no means exceptional. It can be explained by the fact that the market for electricity generators often seemed very insecure and undertakings, such as the Rheinfelden project, appeared to possible investors as extremely speculative.(12)

The plant started operation in 1898. The construction costs amounted to 8.3 million marks or 12.2 million marks including the grid. It produced up to 70 million kWh a year.(13) In order to attract industrial customers, the power station at Rheinfelden had acquired land in its immediate surroundings. It was to a certain extent successful in achieving this objective. Apart from the two electro-chemical firms mentioned above, which consumed large amounts of electricity, several other industrial plants were established at Rheinfelden, including various textile factories and the sodium factory DEGUSSA. Nevertheless, the construction of an extensive grid became necessary in order to supply current to other customers, including the factories in the nearby Wiesental, and in Lorrach, Wyhlen and Grenzach. A big carbide factory, founded on the initiative of the power station itself, contributed to a better exploitation of the night current supply. What Rathenau had predicted in 1896 quickly became true after only a few years, at a time when the power station was still being built. As he had correctly remarked:

> Up to now, the industry of the Upper Rhine has been living a calm and complacent life. This was because a vital element of modern life, namely coal was lacking. Now, however, electricity will step in and create busy places of industry around a natural centre of gravitation in Rheinfelden. All the prerequisites for their development have been fulfilled by the construction of this power station.(14)

It soon became evident that Rathenau's plans had been realistic, both in general terms as well as in regard to the original projected size of the plant. There was now a higher demand for current, so that the building of another similar power station, a few kilometers upstream, was already being considered. However negotiations with the relevant authorities, including the government of Baden, and three bordering Swiss cantons, went on for such a long time that the power station at Rheinfelden had to install a steam-powered generator to supplement its normal output of 12,000 kilowatts.

The actual goal of the electrical manufacturing firms was to produce electrical appliances. They themselves, however, had to create the demand for this new kind of commodity in the first place. They had to ask for municipal concessions, and had to build the plants and run them. They were thus able to secure for themselves sales monopolies. Utility companies founded by individual electrical manufacturing firms to supply electricity, were obliged contractually to buy their electro-technical equipment from the same firms. The restriction of competition produced by the establishment of sales monopolies undoubtedly reinforced the tendencies towards concentration within the electrical manufacturing industry itself. Due to the activities of these firms, which pioneered the establishment of generating plants, the initial distrust and scepticism towards the unknown possibilities of high-voltage technology were quickly dispersed. As a result, the way was prepared for a continual increase in demand.(15) There are numerous examples which illustrate the sceptical attitude of many local authorities towards electric power until far into the 1890s. The authorities in Stuttgart, for example, refused for almost ten years a licence for a generating plant. Finally in 1895, the Schuckert company received the sole concession for the construction and running of a plant, but the firm was also to carry all the risks associated with such an undertaking.(16) The reluctance of the local authorities can be neatly characterised by a statement of Mr. Duncker, mayor of Berlin at that time. In a debate within the city council about the licensing of the DEG (German Edison Company), which later became the AEG, he stated: 'The company has all the risk, the city the financial advantages'.(17)

One should not forget, however, that there were a few cities which were among the pioneers of the electrical industry. Among these were Luebeck and Elberfeld, which set up generating plants in 1887, and Darmstadt which did so in 1888. Triberg, a small town and tourist centre in the Black Forest, was also the site of the earliest plant in Baden that served as a supplier to the public. Its waterfalls and market place were lit by arc-lights as early as 1881. In 1888, a mill was bought by the Triberg city council and transformed into a power station, in order to create an adequate and safe supply of electricity for street lighting. These examples, however, are isolated cases. The majority of local authorities only gradually abandoned their hesitant stance. This change in attitude was conditioned by the positive experience of private enterprises in this sector, as well as by the projected profitability of supplying electricity for the municipal budget.

By 1889/90 there were power stations in at least eight German cities. Seven of these stations were municipal undertakings. The number increased markedly around the turn of the century. The big cities set the pace, and middle-sized and small ones followed. In 1904/5 there were power stations in 55 cities, and 43 of them were municipal ones. The procedure of establishing electricity supply systems within the big German cities, however, was by no means uniform. There were vivid discussions whether one should license private enterprises or found municipal undertakings. On the whole, it seems as if three-quarters of all generating plants by 1907 were run by municipal authorities. In cities with a population in excess of 100,000 inhabitants the proportion was over 80 per cent.(18)

One of the exceptions, however, was the power station of the city of Mannheim. As in the case of Stuttgart, after hesitating for some time, the municipal authorities gave the license to a private firm in 1898, namely the Swiss-owned Brown, Bovery Company (BBC). As compensation, so to speak, BBC had to agree to open up an electro-technical factory in Mannheim and to transfer their German business headquarters from Frankfurt-am-Main to Mannheim. BBC built a steam powered generating plant for Mannheim and leased it from the city, until it was finally taken over by the municipal authorities themselves in 1906.(19)

III

The number of electric power plants constructed in Germany reached its peak in the first decade of this century, so that there were more than 4,000 individual plants in Germany on the eve of the First World War. In Baden, for example, 521 out of a total of 1,557 municipalities, i.e. about one-third, were supplied with electricity by 1914. In other words, 1.3 million out of a total of 2.1 million inhabitants, (approximately two-thirds of Baden's population), lived in areas where electricity was available. As indicated above, the reason for this was that generating plants were established primarily in urban centres. Rural regions were less well supplied, because electricity in these areas was used almost exclusively for lighting purposes and building the grid in the countryside was much more costly. So-called Ueberlandzentralen (overland power stations), designed to transmit electricity to the countryside, came into existence as early as the turn of the century. However the price of current supplied by these stations was considerably higher than in densely populated areas, and this in turn acted as an obstacle to any effective expansion of sales and the recruitment of new customers.(20)

It is interesting to note the way in which the Ueberlandzentralen, designed to cater for an extensive electricity supply to large areas, developed before 1914. The pattern of development differed greatly between Baden and Wuerttemberg.(21) In Baden, the supply was primarily in the hands of private enterprises. AEG, Siemens and Halske, and BBC, as well as their subsidiary companies, focused on specific areas which combined agriculture with industry and trade. They were scarcely interested in areas which were secluded and clearly dominated by agriculture, such as the Odenwald and the Tauber region, since these areas did not appear to offer the opportunity for high profits. In Wuerttemberg, too, the electrical manufacturing industry shrank from investing in an extensive grid within regions that were without large-scale industry. They concentrated on the industrial areas of the middle Neckar around Stuttgart, where they found a ready market. The small communities, villages and towns whose needs were ignored took refuge in self-help. They founded co-operative associations of different districts and municipalities, the most important of which was the Oberschwaebische Elektrizitaetswerke (OEW) (Association of Generating Plants in Upper Swabia) founded in 1909 in Tettnang, Ravensburg and Wangen. These associations were able to provide a sufficient supply of electricity before 1913 in almost all the areas concerned. The big industrial enterprises dominated the Stuttgart area, but on the whole they did not monopolise electricity supply. In Baden, however, industrially less developed areas continued to depend on individual generators (Odenwald, the Tauber region, Stockach, and Ueberlingen), as well as on small private Ueberlandzentralen, early municipal power stations and private hydro-electric plants in small communities.

In clear contrast to Wuerttemberg, however, private enterprises were beginning to cover large areas. The power station at Rheinfelden supplied the southern area of the Upper Rhine, the Wiesental with its textile industry, the Kandertal, the southern parts of the Markgraeflerland, and a number of Swiss villages. It also provided part of the current consumed by Basel. From 1912 onwards, the power station at Laufenburg took over the supply of the area to the east and provided current to large parts of the Upper Rhine, the south of the Black Forest up to the region around Lake Constance and the Baar area.

The Breisgau, with Freiburg as its most important city, was supplied with electricity from 1911 onwards by the Badische Kraftlieferungsgesellschaft Freiburg (BaKaGe) (the Energy Supply Company of Freiburg). This company had been founded by the power stations Rheinfelden, Laufenburg, and Muelhausen/Alsace in order to supply and distribute current generated by these individual plants. There was also an overland power station and a few industrial generators which supplied current to a number of villages. Most of these power stations exploited water power as their primary source of energy. In the north of Baden, however, steam power played the dominant role. Here, the reliance on coal as the primary source of energy was a consequence of the fact that most power stations were located close to river ports.

Before the First World War, Baden had been divided into two electricity supply areas which were completely different from each other.(22) To the north of the Lahr - Wolfach line, power stations were mostly based on coal, to the south they depended on water power. In Wuerttemberg coal was predominant. Here, only 26 per cent of the maximum output came from water power, while it was almost 50 per cent in the case of Baden. A further difference between Baden and Wuerttemberg can be seen in the fact that in Baden there was an early tendency towards the construction of large power stations, while in Wuerttemberg small generators remained dominant for some time. As late as 1913, 28 per cent of the current in Wuerttemberg was generated by these small plants, in contrast to only 14 per cent in Baden.

IV

The characteristic features of the way Baden's electrical industry developed can be summarised as follows: topographical factors (the water power of the Upper Rhine) and the transport possibilities generated by the ports of Mannheim, Karlsruhe etc., encouraged the development of business interests, particularly in electrical manufacturing and in the electro-chemical industry.

Although it was not until the 1920s that total electricity coverage was provided for whole states by regional generating companies, the origins of the so-called unified power system (Verbundwirtschaft) can be found before the First World War.(23) Pooled or unified supply systems meant that various power stations, using different sorts of primary energy combined to supply particular areas. The region around the Upper Rhine and the southern Upper Rhine may be regarded as the nucleus of today's European pool system for the supply of electricity. The first unified power system was formed in this region as early as 1908 by the power stations at Beznau on Aare and Loentsch, both run by a company affiliated to the Swiss BBC. From the technological point of view, the type of combination practised in this case still appears very efficient. The power plant Beznau, exploiting the water power of a river, supplied the basic load. It constantly provided a relatively fixed amount of current, which could only be slightly increased through an auxiliary steam-powered generator. Loentsch, situated in the Alps, supplied the peak load, which significantly exceeded the normal basic load. This was only possible for limited periods of time and was dependent on the amount of water stored in its reservoir. Both plants supplied their current into the same grid and, despite high costs for the connecting lines, worked more efficiently in combination, than on their own. This unified power system may indeed be called international, since part of the current generated in Loentsch-Beznau was exported to Germany, or more specifically to the Upper Rhine area. Another significant example of an early pool system is furnished by the combination of the power stations Rheinfelden, Beznau and Loentsch. In 1912, they combined to supply a high level current equivalent to the later output of the power station at Laufenburg. Laufenburg, which was still under construction at that time, started power generation in 1913. The pool was formed mainly to develop a market for electricity, even before the Laufenburg plant, with its relatively high output level, was set in operation. The early formation of pooled systems, without doubt, was supported by the complicated interconnections between the leading electrical manufacturing corporations (AEG, Siemens, and BBC), which also cooperated with each other in international financing companies for the construction of new power plants.

In Wuerttemberg a kind of pool system also came into existence before 1913. The Interessengemeinschaft Wuerttembergischer Elektrizitaetswerke (the Combination of Electricity Generating Plants in Wuerttemberg) was intended to furnish support in cases of power failure and overloading. The state's two biggest generators, the generating plant at Stuttgart and the Neckarwerke AG Esslingen, operated jointly as early as 1911. The number of cooperating companies increased in the following years and there were plans, developed during the First World War, for forming a combination of all important power stations in order to counteract the disadvantages of heterogeneous supply systems. The most important reason for the formation of unified power systems lay in the fact that a combination of different generating plants yielded better ratios of exploitation, than individually run power stations.

Some explanations are now necessary in order to understand the technological basis for efficient power generation and electricity supply. Even today current has to be generated according to demand, since the storage of current is practically impossible, at least in the quantity necessary for public supply. Generation and supply have to take place the moment current is needed and have to be adapted to consumption fluctuations.(24) This means that a basic operating condition of the electricity industry is that plant generating capacity, or power output, must be able to meet peak demand at any time, while retaining a certain generating reserve. It is evident that a power station becomes more efficient, the more regularly it is employed to full capacity. Having to install generators with an output far beyond average demand, simply because of a few minutes of maximum demand, is clearly not profitable. The efficiency of a power plant is increasingly reduced, the more demand fluctuates during the day, as well as during the year. Plant efficiency is positively related to minimal demand fluctuations and a regular output approximating to maximum capacity. In the period before the First World War, power plants were often generating power far below their actual capacity. The main reason for this can be seen in the prevailing mode of decentralised generation by a multitude of small and medium-sized generators catering for restricted areas of supply. Only after various power stations combined and amalgamated their supply areas by connecting their grids into a unified power system (Verbundsystem), did the possibility arise for an individual plant to have recourse to other stations with excess supply, whenever its own capacity was exhausted.

Thus the power plants were able to raise their efficiency. Furthermore, the amalgamation of different supply areas had the advantage that the larger and more advanced power plants could take over responsibility for basic current supply, while the smaller and less modern plants functioned in an auxiliary capacity for periods of peak demand. It should be noted, however, that it was not until the 1920s that a considerable number of combinations covering large areas came into existence. From this perspective, the development on the Upper Rhine in south-west Germany appears as a pioneering example of energy supply, initiated by the big electrical manufacturing corporations. These firms were willing to innovate and were aiming at improved efficiency. Although the different areas of supply gradually began to cooperate with each other, there was no controlled planning of the electricity industry's development. The concept of concentrated power generation in big plants had not yet been accepted. Despite the development of overland power stations, other small local plants were still being built or enlarged. Moreover, the general supply of large geographical areas was far from complete before the First World War.

V

In Baden, a political controversy concerning the electricity industry arose at an early stage. On the one hand, the discussion centred on the political objective of state-wide supply. On the other hand it focused with far greater emphasis on the dangers of a monopoly of public supply by the big corporations, whose predominant role in Baden was a characteristic feature of the industry's development.(25)

There are two clear periods in the development of political attitudes towards the development of the electricity industry in Baden. In the first period private enterprise was dominant. The second period began around 1911, when the state became more active. In the following section, I will focus on the circumstances in Baden, as the development of an active policy in regard to the electricity industry in Wuerttemberg only occurred after 1914. It was only then that attempts were made to provide a uniform supply of electricity for the whole country.

In the first period up until 1911, the state of Baden willingly left the initiative to private enterprise. State intervention was limited to the legal procedures connected with the issuing of licences necessary for the construction of electricity plants and grids. State licences were especially important in cases where water power was utilised for generation and where public roads were crossed by electricity cables. A participation by the state in the construction of power plants was rejected by the Second Chamber of Parliament in Baden in 1892. Ten years later, however, some members of Parliament became afraid that private companies might monopolise the utilisation of water power on the Upper Rhine. In 1902/3, the Second Chamber called upon the government to intervene actively in the electrical power sector of Baden's economy and to limit any further expansion of private enterprise. The government, however, did not agree to this demand and continued negotiating with private firms over new concessions for water power utilisation, despite unanimous criticism by Parliament in 1906. In 1907/8, the government gradually came over to the Parliament's point of view. The electrification of different sections of the state-owned railway network and the installation of electric lighting in railway stations was then under consideration, and this prompted the government to order an official study of possible locations for water power utilisation. The interest of the state-owned railway company in exploiting the new energy source for the operation of trains and also for the supply of villages and cities, was a critical factor.

Parallel to this development, the state began restricting the autonomy of local authorities to grant concessions for electricity generation and supply. In 1910, a municipal reform act denied local authorities with less than 4,000 inhabitants the right to issue concessions on their own. Rules were also established which affected contracts relating to the supply of current and the government introduced clear procedures for the issue of such contracts. In 1912, the *Oberdirektion des Wasser- und Strassenbaus* (the General Administration for Waterway and Road Construction) created a special section for water power and electricity. This section had the task of supervising contracts between local authorities and electricity supply undertakings, and was to control current prices and tariffs, and to give advice on current supply to local authorities. These government measures were meant to protect the interests of local authorities. It was increasingly felt that the public interest as a whole was endangered by extended contracts, overpriced current and in cases where contracts allowed a supply monopoly for both current and generating equipment. Private enterprise was undoubtedly hampered by these measures and this led, in turn, to certain delays in the provision of electricity to smaller communities. From the point of view of the national economy, however, these regulations provided significant advantages. They brought about a uniformity in the supply of electricity to local authorities at a time when, technologically, the centralised supply of large geographical areas had become possible. These regulations also prevented capital investment being directed into the construction of small and less profitable generating plants.

The government finally had to establish firm policy principles relating to the electricity industry over the decision on the construction of a power station on the river Murg in the north of the Black Forest. There had been an increasing discussion in relation to this projected plant from 1904 onwards. The final decision clearly showed that the government was now very concerned over the possibility that AEG could control monopolistically both electricity supply and the price of current throughout the country. Large parts of southern Baden were already exclusively supplied by AEG, which partly owned the big power plants of Rheinfelden and Laufenburg and exercised considerable influence over the plant at Muelhausen/Alsace, which supplied the Breisgau. The Secretary of the Interior, Herr von Bodman, stated in a crucial parliamentary debate on October 23rd, 1912:

> It has to be acknowledged explicitly that, in accepting high risks, the power plants on the Upper Rhine have shown the possibility of utilising and exploiting enormous amounts of water power. They thus became pioneers and gave new life to large parts of our country's economy. But the danger exists that, as soon as competition between individual companies has disappeared, prices will be raised as high as possble, to whatever level is possible without losing customers. The economy of the whole country will suffer, if this danger becomes a reality. Viewed from this perspective the nature of the problem justifies the government's decision to take parts of the country's electric supply into its own hands.

It was therefore decided that the state should construct the Murg power plant. This was a decisive step towards increasing state involvement in regard to the electricity industry. The Murg power plant was set in operation in 1918 and added considerably to the amount of current available in Baden.(26)

The trend towards state-wide electricity supply was continued in the 1920s with Baden developing more rapidly than Wuerttemberg. In 1921 an electricity supply undertaking for the whole country was founded as a joint-stock company later known as the Badenwerk AG, with the state holding all the shares. Wuerttemberg, however, remained the most decentralised area of electricity supply in Germany for a long time, with an enormous multitude of separate and independent electricity supply undertakings. This may have been of some advantage to the consumers in Wuerttemberg, where relatively low current prices persisted during the Weimar period. An electricity supply company for the whole country did not come into existence until 1934.(27)

Finally I would like to outline the situation in Bavaria, the third federal state of southern Germany. Bavarian policy in regard to the electricity industry is often seen as a paragon of state influence on the industrial structure of this sector. Even if it is correct to say that the Bavarian goverment, in order to protect public interests, 'tried to find ways and means for establishing a uniform system that was to supply the whole country with current for lighting and industrial purposes' (28), this statement only represents half the truth. There was a fierce controversy in the decade before the First World War between different interest groups, particularly between industry, parliament and the government. It was only in 1914, that the state of Bavaria decided to take over the exploitation of water power on the basis of an official plan for electricity development. On the surface, the construction of the Walchenseekraftwerk (Walchensee power station), a government-owned plant which came into operation in February 1924, was simply designed to supply the state-owned railway network. Behind this decision, however, was the expectation that public electricity supply undertakings would be able to provide current to all the country at lower costs and more safely than private ones. Overland supply was to be left to the initiative of private enterprise. The Bavarian state therefore took a considerable time to decide on the most appropriate form for electricity supply undertakings, despite early plans for the supply of the whole country. In the meantime, cities and villages were able to decide on their own form of electricity supply. The activity of private enterprise, however, was probably muffled by the insecurity generated by state policy towards electricity supply and the hesitant attitude of investors.

The situation in Baden, on the other hand, was quite different. The very early initiative of private enterprise in the field of electricity supply was accompanied by high rates of investment. The early success of private enterprise, as well as oligopolistic and monopolistic tendencies in the sphere of electricity supply for the whole country, acted both as a catalyst and a challenge, and eventually forced the administration to decide on the precise form of state participation in the electricity industry.(29)

VI

I have tried in this paper to present three more or less detailed studies of policies applied by different states in southern Germany towards the developing electricity industry before the First World War. The three examples represent three different concepts of energy supply. The Bavarian model represented an officially planned structure of power generating undertakings whose location was determined on the basis of a strict scheme. This structure, however, was enforced relatively late. Wuerttemberg, on the other hand, represented a totally different approach. Electricity supply was decentralised, because municipal authorities or their associations, which represented the lowest level of state administration, retained a dominant role over a relatively long period, while the Government of Wuerttemberg refrained from interfering in policy matters. The Baden model falls somewhere between the other two. In Baden, the early and successful dominance of private enterprise gradually gave ground to the concept of state involvement, which meant that the state began to take over the role of the entrepreneur and actively created an electricity supply system. In the northern states of Germany, strict state schemes concerning the structure of enterprises in the electricity supply sector seldom existed. Public authorities usually tried to enforce their views in policy areas relating to the supply of electricity by joining private electricity supply undertakings and influencing their internal decision-making.(30)

What were the implications of the different approaches to energy policy by the South German states? What consequences did this have on the process of regional economic and industrial development? Of the South German states, Baden and Bavaria had the richest supply of water suitable for transformation into electrical power. In the case of the Grand Duchy of Baden, the early establishment of power plants provided a certain push towards industrialisation. In areas which benefited from the early establishment of power plants, the developing electro-chemical industry quickly responded with the creation of factories and industrial capacity. This, in turn, had a multiplier effect on a regional basis. Investments in this new field of industrial production were invariably capital-intensive, which prompted further investment in other sectors and branches of industry, resulting in a regional 'take-off'. To this extent the establisment of electrical power plants facilitated the development of densely industrialised areas dependent on this new source of energy supply.(31) A similar push towards industrialisation also occurred in Bavaria. However, in this case this impulse was delayed by the hesitancy of state policy in the field of energy supply. In the pre-1914 period state policy in this field remained under the dominant influence of the state railway interests, which in the medium-term had an adverse effect on industrial development, particularly in the sphere of 'new' industries. It was without doubt the comprehensive and systematic planning introduced by Oskar von Miller which enabled Bavaria to overcome its relative backwardness in the general field of energy supply, with important consequences for the pace and pattern of later industrialisation. However, before the First World War, it was the Grand Duchy of Baden which remained the pace-maker in this field.(32) Indeed it could be argued that state participation in the planning and financing of early power plants in Baden, and the concern for an effective distribution of energy supply to consumers in general, was the forerunner of modern state energy policy.

NOTES

1. Joseph A.Schumpeter, Business Cycles. A Theoretical, Historical, and Statistical Analysis of the Capitalist Process (2 vols., McGraw-Hill, New York and London, 1939), vol.1, p.438.

2. David S.Landes, The Unbound Prometheus. Technological change and industrial development in Western Europe from 1750 to the present (Cambridge, U.P., Cambridge, 1969), p.285; Leslie Hannah, Electricity before Nationalisation. A Study of the Development of the Electricity Supply Industry in Britain to 1948 (John Hopkins U.P., Baltimore and London, 1979), p.7; Ian C.R.Byatt, The British Electrical Industry 1875-1914. The economic returns to a new technology (Clarendon Press, London, 1979), pp.15-28.

3. Landes, Unbound Prometheus, p.287.

4. Schumpeter, Business Cycles, p.432.

5. This contribution is part of a research project, which is supported by the Deutsche Forschungsgemeinschaft and carried out under the leadership of Prof.Dr.Hugo Ott at the Institute for Economic and Social History in the University of Freiburg. The author wants to express his thanks for the good cooperation with members of the project team, especially to his colleague Thomas Herzig who is preparing a PhD thesis on this topic and to whom he owes useful hints and advice. For a first report on the research project see Hugo Ott, Rudi Allgeier, Philipp Fehrenbach and Thomas Herzig, 'Historische Energiestatistik am Beispiel der oeffentlichen Elektrizitaetsversorgung Deutschlands. Eine Zwischenbilanz', Vierteljahrschrift fuer Sozial-und Wirtschaftsgeschichte, vol.68, (1981), pp.325-348. See also Hugo Ott (ed.), (compiled by Rudi Allgeier). Bibliographie zur Geschichte der Energiewirtschaft in Deutschland. (Quellen und Forschungen zur historischen Statistik von Deutschland, vol.1., Scripta Mercaturae Verlag, Stuttgart, 1985). Hugo Ott (ed.), (compiled by Thomas Herzig). Statistik der oeffentlichen Elektrizitaetsversorgung Deutschlands 1890-1913. (Quellen und Forschungen zur historischen Statistik von Deutschland, vol.2., Scripta Mercaturae Verlag, Stuttgart, 1985).

6. Substantial information on this can be found in Hugo Ott and Thomas Herzig (assisted by Rudi Allgeier and Philipp Fehrenbach), 'Elektrizitaetsversorgung von Baden, Wuerttemberg und Hohenzollern 1913/14', Historischer Atlas von Baden-Wuerttemberg XI,9, (Kommission fuer geschichtliche Landeskunde in Baden-Wuerttemberg, 1982). A fundamental reference is Theodor Wessels, 'Elektrizitaetswirtschaft', Handwoerterbuch der Sozialwissenschaften, (Stuttgart, Tuebingen, Goettingen, 1961) vol.3, pp.184-189.

7. Rudolf Wissell, 'Von der Blockzentrale zur Drehstromversorgung', in Das Zeitalter der Elektrizitaet. 75

Jahre Vereinigung Deutscher Elektrizitaetswerke, (Frankfurt a.M., 1967), pp.7-14: Heinrich Bueggeln, Die Entwicklung der oeffentlichen Elektrizitaetswirtschaft in Deutschland unter besonderer Beruecksichtigung der sueddeutschen Verhaeltnisse, (Stuttgart, 1930), pp.1-39.

8. Heinrich Calliess, 'Uebergang zum Drehstrom - Beginn der Ueberlandversorgung', in Zeitalter der Elektrizitaet, pp.15-19; Hans Christaller, 'Der Ausbau der Wasserkraftwerke', in Zeitalter der Elektrizitaet, pp.39-41.

9. A.Riedler, Emil Rathenau und das Werden der Grosswirtschaft, (Berlin, 1916), pp.78-79; Albrecht Strobel, 'Die Gruendung des Zuericher Elektrotrusts. Ein Beitrag zum Unternehmergeschaeft der deutschen Elektroindustrie 1895-1900', in E.Hassinger, J.H.Mueller and H.Ott (eds.), Geschichte - Wirtschaft - Gesellschaft. Festschrift fuer Clemens Bauer zum 75. Geburtstag (Duncker & Humblot, Berlin, 1974), pp.306-7: Hannah, Electricity before Nationalisation, p.8.

10. Ott and Herzig, 'Elektrizitaetsversorgung von Baden, Wuerttemberg und Hohenzollern', pp.3-4: Helmut Groener, Die Ordnung der deutschen Elektrizitaetswirtschaft (Nomos, Baden-Baden, 1975), p.46 et seq.

11. Alfred Spraul, 'Ein Beitrag zur Entwicklung der oeffentlichen Elektrizitaetsversorgung in Baden', unpublished PhD thesis, University of Heidelberg, 1933, pp.44 et seq. See also Elektrotechnische Zeitschrift, Berlin, 1896, p.402; Bernhard Mohr, 'Rheinfelden (Baden). Siedlungsentwicklung und ihre Bestimmungsfaktoren, raeumliches Wachstum und Bautraeger einer Industriestadt am Hochrhein', Regio Basiliensis, vol.19, (1978), pp.97-142.

12. Strobel, 'Zuericher Elektrotrust', p.310 et seq.

13. Christaller, 'Wasserkraftwerke', pp.40-41.

14. Spraul, Oeffentliche Elektrizitaetsversorgung in Baden, pp.45-46; Emil Rathenau, 'Die Kraftuebertragungswerke zu Rheinfelden', Elektrotechnische Zeitschrift (1896), pp.402-409; Mohr, 'Rheinfelden'.

15. Groener, Ordnung der Elektrizitaetswirtschaft, p.47 et seq.

16. Ott and Herzig, 'Elektrizitaetsversorgung in Baden, Wuerttemberg und Hohenzollern', pp.3-4.

17. Groener, Ordnung der Elektrizitaetswirtschaft, pp.50-51.

18. Ibid., pp.50,87; Spraul, 'Oeffentliche Elektrizitaetsversorgung in Baden', p.16.

19. Ott and Herzig, 'Elektrizitaetsversorgung in Baden, Wuerttemberg und Hohenzollern', pp.3-4; for another interesting case see Hugo Ott, 'Privatwirtschaftliche und Kommunal(staats)wirtschaftliche Aspekte beim Aufbau der Elektrizitaetswirtschaft dargestellt am Beispiel des Strassburger Elektrizitaetswerkes', in Aus Stadt- und

Wirtschaftsgeschichte Suedwestdeutschlands. Festschrift fuer Erich Maschke zum 75. Geburtstag (Kohlhammer, Stuttgart, 1975), pp.255-280.

20. Spraul, 'Oeffentliche Elektrizitaetsversorgung in Baden', pp.51-52; Ott and Herzig, 'Elektrizitaetsversorgung in Baden, Wuerttemberg und Hohenzollern', pp.6-7.

21. Ibid., p.10; Bueggeln, Oeffentliche Elektrizitaetswirtschaft in Deutschland, p.75 et seq.

22. Spraul, 'Oeffentliche Elektrizitaetsversorgung in Baden', p.51 et seq; Geschaeftsbericht des Grossherzoglich Badischen Ministeriums des Innern fur die Jahre 1906-1912 (Karlsruhe, 1912), vol.2, pp.448-463 and a map on electricity supply in Baden 1913 in the appendix.

23. Generally see Georg Boll, 'Nationale und internationale Verbundwirtschaft auf Hoch- und Hoechstspannungsleitungen' in Zeitalter der Elektrizitaet, pp.77-89: Christaller, 'Wasserkraftwerke', pp. 41-42; for details see Ott and Herzig 'Elektrizitaetsversorgung in Baden, Wuerttemberg und Hohenzollern', pp.7-10.

24. Die deutsche Elektrizitaetswirtschaft, in: Ausschuss zur Untersuchung der Erzeugungs- und Absatzbedingungen der deutschen Wirtschaft. Verhandlungen und Berichte des Unterausschusses fuer Gewerbe: Industrie, Handel und Handwerk. III. Unterausschuss (Berlin, 1930), p.16 et seq; Bueggeln, Oeffentliche Elektrizitaetswirtschaft in Deutschland, p.49 et seq.

25. Spraul, 'Oeffentliche Elektrizitaetsversorgung in Baden', p.60 et seq; Geschaeftsbericht des Badischen Ministeriums des Innern, pp.448-463.

26. Spraul, 'Oeffentliche Elektrizitaetsversorgung in Baden', p.66; Amtliche Berichte ueber die Verhandlungen der Badischen Staendeversammlung No.129 (Karlsruhe 25. Oktober 1912), Zweite Kammer, 107. oeffentliche Sitzung am 23. Oktober 1912. For some aspects during World War One see Hermann Schaefer, Regionale Wirtschaftspolitik in der Kriegswirtschaft. Staat, Industrie und Verbaende waehrend des Ersten Weltkrieges in Baden, (Stuttgart, 1983), passim.

27. Ott and Herzig, 'Elektrizitaetsversorgung in Baden, Wuerttemberg und Hohenzollern', pp.10-12; see Die deutsche Elektrizitaetswirtschaft, p.90 et seq. for Wuerttemberg, and p.92 et seq. for Baden; Klaus Teichert, Die staatlichen Einwirkungen auf die Elektrizitaetswirtschaft in Baden, dargestelt insbesondere am Beispiel der Badenwerk AG, unpublished law dissertation, University of Freiburg, 1953; Hans Eggers, Reich und Laender in der Elektrizitaetswirtschaft Badens und Wuerttembergs, unpublished PhD thesis, University of Freiburg, 1923.

28. For Bavaria an important work is Fritz Blaich, Die Energiepolitik Bayerns 1900-1921, (Lassleben, Kallmuenz Opf., 1981).

29. Ott and Herzig, 'Elektrizitaetsversorgung in Baden, Wuerttemberg und Hohenzollern', pp.20-22.

30. For a survey on other plants and regions see Die Elektrizitaetswirtschaft im Deutschen Reich. Entstehung, Aufbau, Werke, Arbeits- und Interessengebiete, Statistik, Finanzen (Berlin, 1934).

31. Hermann Schaefer, 'Gewerbelandschaften: Elektro, Papier, Glas, Keramik', in Hans Pohl (ed.), Gewerbe- und Industrielandschaften, (Stuttgart, 1985).

32. Only Saxony started with a similarly early energy policy, see Hans-Werner Niemann, 'Die Anfaenge der staatlichen Elektrizitaetsversorgung im Koenigreich Sachsen', Zeitschrift fuer Unternehmensgeschichte, vol.23, (1978), pp.98-117; Johannes Buechner and Otto Bittmann, 'Der Kampf um die Vorrangstellung in der saechsischen Elektroenergieversorgung (EEV) von 1911 bis 1916', Jahrbuch fuer Wirtschaftsgeschichte (1981), pp.25-50. According to the research project mentioned in note 5, a prevailing opinion now needs to be corrected, see Blaich, Energiepolitik, p.174 et seq.

Chapter Eight

THE POLITICAL FRAMEWORK OF STRUCTURAL MODERNISATION : THE I.G. FARBENINDUSTRIE AG, 1904-1945

Gottfried Plumpe

I

THE FORMATION OF THE I.G. FARBENINDUSTRIE AG

The German chemical industry always has had and still has today an important position in the international economy. In 1980, ahead of the American chemical industry, it was the world's greatest exporter and despite two lost wars and immense losses of productive capacity, especially in central Germany, it has maintained its traditional leading role.(1) Even after the dissolution of I.G. Farben as a result of the Allied Control Office law number nine of November 1945, the three great successor-firms, the Badische Anilin- und Soda-Fabrik AG, Ludwigshafen (BASF), the Bayer AG (Farbenfabriken vorm Fr. Bayer) Leverkusen (FFB), and the Farbwerke Hoechst AG, Hoechst (FWH) are some of the most important companies in the world's chemical industry.(2)

However, the exceptional predominance of the German organic chemical industry in the domain of dyestuffs and pharmaceuticals and its general lead in the acceptance of modern science-based technologies has disappeared. The myth of modern chemistry as an exclusive German speciality has passed away. In the course of the first half of this century chemical industries of at least equivalent standing developed in other countries. Wars and political interventions were not the cause of this development, but simply accelerated it and thereby disturbed the natural process of adjustment to economic and technological change. The history of the German chemical industry, particularly her outstanding firm, the I.G. Farben, was closely connected with this process.

In 1925 eight of the biggest chemical firms in Germany amalgamated into the I.G. Farbenindustrie AG. Their respective managers decided that the BASF, as the largest enterprise, should take over the capital of the FFB, the FWH, the Aktiengesellschaft fuer Anilin Fabrikation, Berlin (AGFA), the Chemische Fabrik Griesheim-Elektron, Frankfurt (Griesheim) and the Chemische Fabriken vormals Weiler-ter Meer, Uerdingen (Uerdingen). The newly constituted firm was to be known as the I.G. Farben AG. Leopold Cassella & Co., GmbH, Frankfurt

(Cassella) and Kalle & Co. AG, Biebrich (Kalle) were incorporated as subsidiaries.(3) This merger concluded a concentration process which had started at the beginning of the century. When it became evident that further expansion in the chemical industry would lead to increasing conflicts and costly rivalry between the great firms, the proposal of Carl Duisberg, manager of the FFB and one of the most important leaders of German industry at that time, to form a great combination, immediately attracted the support in principle of his colleagues. Hence in 1904 the two biggest firms, the BASF and the FFB created an *Interessengemeinschaft* (combine), which was joined by AGFA in the same year. Only the non-participation of the FWH hindered a complete merger at this time, and this was due to the latter's insistence on a disproportional share in the profit-pool, in relation to its comparative size. It therefore expected greater gains outside the *Interessengemeinschaft*, and in 1907 formed another combination with Cassella and Kalle. But relations between these two groups, called respectively the *Dreibund* (Triple Alliance) and the *Dreierverband* (Triple Union), generally remained friendly and cooperative.(4)

Together they dominated the international dyestuffs trade and had successfully expanded into the pharmaceutical and photographical business on the eve of the First World War. In 1913 the BASF achieved the synthesis of ammonia by high-pressure catalytic hydrogenation of nitrogen, produced by fixation out of the atmosphere. Due to an increasing demand for nitrogen fertilisers this success promised great profits. In 1912 the FFB failed to develop a satisfactory process of rubber synthesis, but gained a valuable experience in this promising field of organic chemistry.(5) In addition the firms which were later to form I.G. Farben also possessed very modern facilities for producing heavy chemicals. Since 1890 they had operated the new contact-process for producing sulphuric acid, and Griesheim, which joined I.G. in 1916 was the market leader in the field of electro-chemistry.(6) In nearly every country the German firms maintained sales organisations and agencies. In countries where effective trade barriers and import duties had been introduced, branch plants were set up. The largest number of such subsidiaries were established in Russia, which besides the United Kingdom and the United States was the most important market for German chemicals. Plants also existed in France, America, Belgium and the United Kingdom, but they only produced special products. Their main purpose was to guarantee the validity of patents and trade marks.(7)

The predominance of the German chemical industry, however, also implied a significant degree of market dependence for the importing countries. On the other hand, the German manufacturers were also dependent on imported materials, particularly sulphur, sulphurores, saltpetre, phosphates, coal-tar derivatives and organic products. In this way there existed a multilateral inter-dependence. This did not amount to a strategic dependence on the part of western industrial countries. The British industry still dominated the heavy chemical trade, and the most productive plants for explosives were in the United States (du Pont) and the United Kingdom (Nobel). Moreover British and American capital controlled the most important source of nitrogen, the Chilean saltpetre deposits, and their navies controlled the sea routes.(8) Without the success of the ammonia synthesis, the technological advantage of the German chemical industry would have been lost under war conditions, because nearly all modern explosives contain nitrogen compounds which were then produced from the Chilean nitrate of soda. Therefore the German government, having recognised the decisive importance of the supply of nitrogen for warfare, supported the construction of large synthesis plants, particularly on the basis of the BASF's Haber-Bosch process. As a result of this combined I.G.-government activity, the dependence on saltpetre imports completely disappeared and by the early twentieth century I.G. had developed an annual capacity of 300,000 tons of nitrogen. The government contributed more than 51 per cent of the total investment of 1.1 milliard Reichsmark (about £55 million).(9) The total capital of the entire I.G. amounted to about £21 million in 1914. This constituted the most important expansion of plant during the war and resulted from cooperation with the government, but there were other significant developments.

After the outbreak of hostilities the firms expected a short campaign and sharply reduced their business activities. When the war dragged on and industrial mobilisation became indispensable, the chemical industry of all belligerent countries inevitably became involved in the production of war materials. The increasing demand necessitated an enormous enlargement of plant, the introduction of new activities including the synthesis of organic acids (acetone), rubber (methylene rubber), and staple rayon, and the development of new processes to facilitate import substitution.(10) Inevitably the same process occurred in countries which previously had imported German chemical products. Since German imports had to be replaced, these states attempted to diversify their chemical industries into dyestuffs, organic intermediates, and pharmaceuticals.(11) These developments were extensively supported financially by national governments and the indigenous chemical industry, as the biggest producer of explosives and poison-gas became a keystone of modern warfare.

With the growth in capacity and product diversification, the chemical industries internationally realised immense profits and developed great financial strength. The I.G. firms were able to purchase many lignite deposits and built up impressive reserves. Du Pont invested millions of dollars in dyestuffs research and in the purchase of important subsidiaries. The employed capital of the British Nobel Dynamite Trust Company grew from £4.2 million in 1913 to £15.9 million by 1919. The capital of the I.G. companies increased from £8.7 million (1913), to £19.5 million (1917) and to £35 million (1924), and the number of employees increased from 39,625 in 1913 to 82,980 by July 1918.(12) However this rapid expansion of capacity created serious long-term problems. The allied governments made it clear that they would continue to restrict access to world markets after the war, in order to protect their own chemical industries and to avoid German competition. The situation was aggravated by the seizure by all belligerent states of their enemies' property, including patents, trade marks, subsidiaries and sales organisations.(13)

Even in the case of a German victory, the chemical industry expected substantial difficulties in re-entering vital export markets. The two combines of 1904 and 1907 therefore decided in 1916 to amalgamate into a larger _Interessengemeinschaft_, and Griesheim, Uerdingen and two smaller firms also joined the I.G. This merger did not affect the basic independence of the individual companies, but provided a profit-pool and an institutional framework for harmonising common business interests. Post-war expectations, however, were not the only reason for the amalgamation. It was also intended to enable the firms to avoid unnecessary competition in responding to the large public demand of the war economy, and to resist any political intervention in their freedom of trade. It was therefore designed to strengthen the firms' position in relation to the state bureaucracy.(14)

The defeat of Germany and the Versailles peace-treaty, which embodied many of the Allies' economic war aims, aggravated the problem of Germany's re-entry into the international economy. Chemical plants which had produced war materials were to be destroyed, while one-quarter of the industry's production was to be placed at the disposal of the victorious allied powers. Free access to international markets was to be restricted and Germany was forced to grant the Allies unilateral trade preference which made it impossible to develop an independent trade policy.(15) Post-war social and political unrest seemed to threaten the existing economic order and endanger private property, until the stabilisation period of 1923/4. The I.G. management, therefore, welcomed the allied occupation forces in Leverkusen, Frankfurt and Ludwigshafen, which at least guaranteed law and order. But the occupation also created artificial inner-German frontiers and transportation difficulties and strikes disrupted production and raw material and energy supplies, particularly coal shipments from the Ruhr.(16)

Germany's weak international position made private economic strength all the more important. The I.G. group, therefore, successfully tried to re-establish agreements with its international competitors, and their significance is well illustrated by the I.G.-French nitrogen agreement of 1919. Although the French army insisted on the destruction of the BASF ammonia plants, the French government tolerated the agreement in return for information on the synthesis technique.(17) Until the outbreak of the Second World War, these agreements between the great chemical enterprises were more important in determining the conditions of international trade than national trade policies. Moreover it was largely the relative strength of individual firms which determined their share of international markets, a factor which more than justified the formation of the I.G. in 1916. International agreements, however, were not the only factor behind the final drive towards complete concentration in the 1920s, as I.G. was strengthened in 1920 by the incorporation of the Leuna-Werke, and its great nitrogen plants, which had hitherto been outside the pool.(18)

By the beginning of the 1920s, despite poor expectations, I.G. sales had increased and even exceeded those of 1913. The classical dyestuffs business shrank, but new products, especially nitrogen fertilizers, made growth possible. After the stabilisation of the German currency in 1923/4, the nitrogen business contributed to an immense upswing.(19) However growth was unequal and dyestuffs suffered heavily from the change in the international chemical trade. In 1924 about 158,000 tons of dyestuffs were produced in the world, the same quantity as in 1913, but Germany's share had dropped from 81 per cent to 46 per cent. Overcapacity, surplus stocks and the maintenance of separate sales organisations by all I.G. members, threatened the profitability of the dyestuffs section. The additional cost of producing the same dyes at different I.G. plants alone amounted to £100,000 a year.(20) Rationalisation was absolutely necessary and that involved a fundamental re-distribution of shares in the pool and a loss of production for most plants. A closer relationship between the various I.G. firms seemed indispensable. However, it was not this immediate need for rationalisation that led to complete amalgamation.

In contrast to the events of 1904, the chairman of BASF, Bosch, insisted in 1925 on immediate and complete amalgamation. BASF was then engaged on an ambitious development programme. In 1923/4 BASF, following its success with ammonia synthesis, had developed a process for synthesising methylalcohol and was pursuing the possibility of gasoline hydrogenation with the final aim of producing hydrocarbons. This programme required immense investments and involved many potential risks. It severely stretched the resources of BASF and was the decisive factor behind the formation of I.G. in 1925 and the final amalgamation process in the chemical industry. It was, therefore, mainly the challenge of technological progress and not rationalisation requirements that led to the creation of I.G. Farben.(21)

II

THE ORGANISATION OF THE COMPANY

The formation of the new joint-stock company required a new organisation because the institutional framework of 1916 was no longer sufficient. After much debate a compromise was found, which combined the necessary central management, with considerable independence for the large firms involved in the creation of the new I.G. (see diagram 8.1). So-called _Betriebsgemeinschaften_ (BG) or works' communities were constituted, which effectively comprised the former units of the large I.G. firms.(22) The different works' communities were not geographically based, but contained all the works of the larger firms wherever they were located in Germany. The BG managed the daily business of the plants, but they could not decide anything of general importance without the consent of the board of directors. The size of I.G's first board was not particularly satisfactory, as all members of the executive boards of the founding firms were made directors. Therefore a smaller _Arbeitsausschuss_ (AA) or working-committee was formed, with only 26 members. In this committee the real power of decision-making was restricted to a very small group, which consisted of Carl Bosch, the chairman of the executive board, and the other leaders of the various works' communities and important central committees.(23) According to German joint-stock company law, the stockholders' general meeting elected a supervisory board to control the management. But this board also was too large after the merger, and a _Verwaltungsrat_ (governing council) was formed of seven members of the supervisory board. All the chairmen of the founding firms, excluding Bosch himself, joined this committee and Duisberg became its head. The general council looked after the interests of the stockholders, selected the leading management and controlled the company's finances. However I.G. did not have a large number of stockholders, and the composition of the general council showed that the company actually controlled its own affairs.(24)

Only the general council and members of the working-committee received all vital information and made important decisions. The quality of information provided to both these bodies was a critical factor in their operation. For this purpose I.G. constituted a far-reaching network of committees for all administrative, technical and research

Figure 8.1

I.G. Farbenindustrie : AG Organisation Plan (1931)

Share Holders' Meeting

Board of Directors

Central Committee

Working-Committee

	Technical Comm.	Financial Comm.	Commercial Comm.	
	Main Group I	Main Group II	Main Group III	Central Administration (Berlin/Frankfurt)
Group of Works - Hydrogenation Oberrhein (BASF) Mittelrhein (Hoechst) Niederrhein (Bayer)	Production - Inorganics - Nitrogen - Mining	Production - Photographics - Organics - Intermediates - Solvents - Plastics - Dyestuffs - Pharmaceuticals - Plant Protection	Production -Artificial Silk -Essential Oils	Central Financial Administration Book-keeping Purchasing Social Department Law and Patents Traffic Advertising etc.
Mietteldeutschland Berlin	Sales - Nitrogen - Oil - Coal/Lignite	Sales - Chemicals - Dyestuffs - Pharmaceuticals	Sales -Photographics -Artificial Silk -Essentials	

purposes.(25) The most important unit was a central Technischer Ausschuss (Tea) or technical committee, which discussed all technical problems with special reference to their economic importance and the company's investment policy. The Tea could not make final decisions, but the working-committee generally confirmed its proposals. It had a great number of sub-committees, dealing with research, production and product application. The daily business of the Tea was to prepare the multitude of investment decisions necessary for individual plants, to discuss technical innovations and to plan technical development.(26) Its members were all chemists, while the executive board contained a few non-technicians, such as economists and lawyers. The Kaufmaennische Auschuss (KA), or sales committee, discussed sales questions and general economic issues, but its remit overlapped with the activities of both the working-committee and other committees representing important company interests.(27) Therefore the KA was suspended in the post-1929 depression, when strong rationalisation was required.

Besides the technical committee a number of administrative committees were established, including a purchasing committee (for managing the entire purchase of raw materials, intermediates etc.), an energy committee, a legal and patents committee, and a central accounting and tax committee. The most important administrative office was the central financial board under the leadership of Hermann Schmitz, who became chairman of the company when Bosch became a member of the governing council in 1935. This office dealt with the company's structure, its relationship with German and international subsidiaries, the raising of capital and the daily financing of business. Although the company's head office was located in Frankfurt-am-Main, its central financial administration was situated in Berlin, with easy access to many of the major banks and the stock exchange. The necessary linkage between the committees and the board of directors, particularly the working-committee, was provided by both a constant exchange of information and through close personal contacts. The membership of the working-committee, the leadership of the individual works' communities and the other important committees was identical.

Although the I.G. administration was a large apparatus, comprising more than a thousand employees and many offices, the organisation was not a bureaucratic one.(28) Although bureaucratic tendencies existed, the organisation retained an innate flexibility, because of the need for a fast and effective response to dynamic technological change. Normative career structures could not be developed in the absence of management study courses, and the nature of contemporary economic and political development did not encourage the emergence of a rigid bureaucratic institution.

However the original organisation proved to be inadequate in the face of the post-1929 depression. This was particularly the case in relation to controlling new developments. In August 1929 Duisberg, as head of the finance committee, wrote: 'Well, I cannot conceal it, I have had sleepless nights knowing the state of expenditure for investment laboratories and especially for research'.(29) Together with Bosch he set up a three-man committee to control investment. To achieve this the entire company was divided up on technical grounds into three divisions which represented the main activities of the company. Although the original works' communities continued to function, they were now subordinated to the new structure.(30) The committee clearly had a limited task, but it did provide an effective technical control of existing plants, which had hitherto been missing. During the depression years the company had to rationalise other administrative structures. A smaller, and more effective central committee replaced the working-committee, and, as it was only composed of seven members in 1931, it constituted an inner circle.(31) Because of the depression, the huge board of directors was also further reduced with its membership declining from 84 in 1929 to 43 by 1931. The entire staff of leading managers was reduced from a peak of about 700 in 1930 to 552 by the end of 1931. As a result, the ratio of senior staff to employees fell from 1:133 (1925) to 1:126 (1931) and the ratio of sales to administration costs (primarily wages) grew from 68.6:1 in 1926 to 123.4:1 in 1932. The depression, therefore, led to a necessary rationalisation which had been largely neglected in the immediate post-1925 period.(32)

The organisation remained unchanged until 1937/8 (see diagram 8.1). The introduction of a _Betriebsfuehrer_ or works manager on the basis of the Nazi law on the organisation of national work (1934) hardly affected the company's management, and the 'social commission' (soko) continued to deal with social welfare matters.(33) In 1937/8 a reform of company law strengthened the position of the head of the firm (on the basis of the _Fuehrer_ principle) and of the entire board of directors. The importance of some central committees accordingly declined after 1938. The same reform changed the position of the chairman of the supervisory board and the _Verwaltungsrat_ was therefore dissolved. The most significant changes in company management, however, were not due to Nazi reform legislation. The period of immense growth during the armaments boom of the 1930s was accompanied by a shift away from authoritarian leadership, and towards a collegial management style, with increasing interdependence between individual managers in the different branches of company activity. Moreover the chairman, Schmitz, was an economist and unable to judge all the relevant technological issues.(34)

Growing involvement in government economic programmes connected with the war economy did not pose any fundamental questions. It simply reinforced a tendency towards a more technocratic form of management. This was also reflected by the emergence of the third generation of leaders within the company, following the death of Duisberg and Bosch's retirement in 1935. The assumption of not being politically responsible for the consequences of industrial production was a fateful component of this technocractic behaviour. But this managerial attitude was not something unique to the I.G. leadership, or to German industrialists alone.

III

FROM BOOM TO DEPRESSION: I.G. FARBEN 1926-1932

The merger happened at a favourable time, as a minor downturn in 1926 had been followed by a general upswing. From 1926 sales grew at an average rate of 9.4 per cent, which was equivalent to the general growth rate in industrial sales and superior to that of the chemical industry as a whole.(35) I.G.'s share of chemical sales increased from 28 per cent (1926) to 31 per cent (1929), although its share of total industrial sales remained at about two per cent.(36) This growth was accompanied by further changes in the company's product range (table 8.1). Dyestuffs sales tended to decline, as new products increased in importance. After a peak in 1928 the sale of nitrogen products also started to fall, although throughout the 1920s both home and export demand from agriculture for nitrogen fertilisers was a key factor in stimulating growth. Their average share of total sales amounted to approximately 40 per cent between 1926 and 1928. The importance of diversification is well illustrated by the fact that by 1929, six per cent of sales came from new fields such as metals, artificial silk, and gasoline. But company growth was also boosted by modifications to traditional products, where technological progress facilitated a multitude of minor improvements. More than seven per cent of pharmaceutical sales in 1929 and four per cent of dyestuff sales in 1930 were improved products. The most famous new products, however, were synthetic methylalcohol, improved light washing-dyes, 'indanthrene', vulcanisation-accelerators, new solvents, such as butadiene, and the special lubricant 'oppanol'.

In contrast to Svennilson's view (38), the international chemical trade did not stagnate in the late 1920s, although the diversification of the chemical industries in Britain, America and France led to increasing national self-sufficiency. The growth and expansion of new markets and the enlargement of old ones made possible a growing export business.(39) Between 1926 and 1929 I.G. exports rose at an average rate of 7.9 per cent and exports in 1926 exceeded those of 1913 by 65 per cent. Although domestic sales grew at an average rate of 11.1 per cent during the second half of the 1920s, I.G.'s export quota still exceeded 50 per cent.(40) The company's growth continued to depend on foreign demand after the war, although to a slightly lesser extent.(41) However the composition and direction of exports did change (table 8.2). Exports to the three great industrial countries, Britain, America and France fell dramatically, and although Europe as a whole became the most significant export region, markets in Asia and Latin America grew considerably in importance. The most important single markets in 1929 were China (60 million RM) followed by the United States (45 million RM), Japan (44 million RM), British India (33 million RM) and Italy (31 million RM).(43) In 1913 the five leading markets had taken about 75 per cent of total exports, while in 1929 the equivalent markets only took 27 per cent of all I.G. exports.(44) This shows an increasing regional diversification of exports. Post-war development was also characterised by a considerable alteration in the composition of exports (table 8.3). Although dyestuffs still remained the most important export, growth would not have been possible without the nitrogen business. The share of dyestuffs declined sharply, and chemical exports stagnated, due to increasing international self-sufficiency. The export of pharmaceuticals and photographical products rose, as did their importance in I.G.'s international trade.

However one cannot discuss chemical exports in the inter-war period without reference to international industrial agreements and cartels. The world's chemical industry was one of the most cartelised sectors of the international economy.(46) Because I.G. was the largest German company, it had a crucial position in international business relations. In the inter-war period these international arrangements between the great chemical companies were more influential than national trade policy. Moreover the respective share of international business was primarily a function of the strength of individual firms.

In the early 1920s I.G. immediately tried to establish close relations with French and British companies. But protectionist policies in the chemical field in both countries prevented any general agreement, and contemporary expansion in the short-run made such agreements unnecessary.(47) It was not until after 1927 that an agreement was finally reached. The first instance of cooperation between anglo-american companies and I.G. followed its take-over in 1926 of the Dynamit Aktiengesellschaft (DAG), the German part of the old Nobel Trust. Since 1924/5 close connections had existed between DAG, Brunner, Mond & Co. and du Pont, involving a general marketing agreement for Latin America and a 20 per cent participation by the two foreign firms in DAG.(48) In 1926 I.G. took over all of DAG's preferential shares and 27.7 per cent of its capital, and DAG became one of its subsidiaries. I.G. thereby entered into contractual agreements with du Pont and Imperial Chemical Industries (I.C.I), which were important for regulating the dyestuffs trade.(49)

A Franco-German dye-cartel was also set up in 1927, comprising I.G. and C.M.C. (Compagnie Nationale de Matières Colorantes et Manufactures de Produits Chimiques du Nord Réunis, Établissements Kuhlmann, Paris).(50) This envisaged a complete merger between the two firms, which was not realised, however, until the Second World War. Two years later, the so-called Swiss I.G. joined the cartel, which was particularly important as Switzerland was the second largest exporter of dyestuffs.(51) A year later I.C.I. also joined this continental cartel (52), which meant that it absolutely dominated the dyestuffs trade with a market share of at least 80 per cent. The cartel's importance was enhanced by the incorporation of the cartel-partners' subsidiaries, which reinforced its market domination particularly in Italy and Spain. Additional agreements consolidated its position. Although the great American producers, du Pont, the National Aniline and Chemical Corporation, and General Aniline (an I.G. subsidiary), could not join the cartel owing to legal regulations, supplementary agreements between I.C.I. and du Pont guaranteed their goodwill.(53) But the cartel did not enable I.G. to reconquer its pre-war market share. The cartel effectively guaranteed I.G. a quota of 65.4 per cent, whereas in 1913 its share of international dyestuffs exports had been 85 per cent.(54)

The international nitrogen trade was similarly regulated after 1930. After 1918 I.G. and the Norsk Hydro Kvaelstoff AS (NH) were the only important exporters of synthetic nitrogen, sharing the market with Chilean saltpetre. The military importance of an independent nitrogen supply, however, led to increasing government support for the construction of ammonia plants in most major countries. In addition the rapid growth in demand for nitrogen fertilisers contributed to a nitrogen boom, with production of synthetic nitrogen rising from 141,000 tons to 1,019,000 tons between 1920 and 1930.(55) In 1919 only Germany had a large synthetic capacity, but by the 1930s 19 countries, mainly in Europe, had nitrogen plants with a total capacity of 2.3 million tons. Germany, however, had 46 per cent of the world's capacity, and I.G.'s share of this was 71 per cent (or 1.055 million tons).(56) This represented 33 per cent of world capacity. By the mid-1920s only Germany, Norway, Belgium and the United Kingdom were net exporters of nitrogen. Germany's share of total nitrogen exports by 1928 stood at 68 per cent, but growing competition threatened this position.(57)

I.G. was aware of this trend and tried to regulate the nitrogen market from the early 1920s. But Brunner, Mond & Co. and the French chemical industry were neither amenable, nor prepared to be I.G.'s junior-partners. The first step towards market regulation was only taken in 1927, when I.G. took over the export business of Norsk Hydro (NH), which in return received information on I.G.'s ammonia synthesis. I.G. now held 25 per cent of NH's capital, which was a sign of a good understanding between I.G. and the French chemical industry, as NH was in fact a French company.(58) In the face of severe problems at the start of the depression, I.C.I. changed its mind and agreed in 1930 to an export cartel. This led to the creation of the German-English-Norwegian Group (DEN), which became the core of the later general nitrogen cartel.(59) The DEN-group controlled over 90 per cent of nitrogen exports in 1930, but new competition arose. A general European cartel (CIA) was therefore formed in 1930.(60) The CIA did not comprise all producers and was initially limited to one year, but costly competition illustrated its value and the cartel continued until the outbreak of war.(61) It was completed by a network of contracts with outsiders, particularly Japan, and in 1938 a formal cartel contract was concluded between the CIA and the Chilean saltpetre exporters.(62) These contracts confirmed the leading position of I.G., but the company also lost a great deal. Its share of world nitrogen production dropped from 29 per cent (1928) to ten per cent (1932).(63) This development reflected an important adjustment process for the German chemical industry, as its earlier predominance in the nitrogen field could clearly not be maintained. These cartels for dyestuffs and nitrogen meant that about 67 per cent of I.G. exports were regulated. The remaining export business was covered by other contracts.

In addition, the general relationship between I.G. and other great firms in this sector was very good. A famous example of industrial cooperation was the 'Division of Field Agreement' of 1929 between I.G. and Standard Oil of New Jersey, which divided responsibility for chemicals and oil between the two firms and provided a common procedure in areas of overlapping activity, including hydrogenation, and rubber synthesis from oil derivatives.(64) A Joint American Study Company (JASCO) was formed a year later to develop common research and both firms wanted to avoid mutual competition. Agreements were also made in 1933 in the fields of magnesium and glycols with other American firms, including the Aluminium Company of America (ALCOA) and the Union Carbide & Carbon Chemical Corporation.(65) One year earlier I.G. had reported with some justification that: 'relations between us and the great American firms are absolutely friendly' (66), and this also typified the company's relationship with British and French chemical firms.

Another important element in I.G.'s foreign relations was the re-establishment of overseas plants. This was particularly important in the United States, where trade barriers were most effective and market regulation officially prohibited. Moreover the starting point was unfavourable. During the war German property had been seized and considerable anti-German feeling hindered post-war reconstruction. I.G., therefore, tried to rebuild its business with American partners on the basis of its advanced technological expertise. In 1923 an agreement was initialled with the Weiss-group, as owners of the Sterling Incorporation, which had purchased in 1918 the former Bayer assets in America, and retained their profitable aspirin business and trademark rights for the American continent and Britain. The agreement provided for the formation of a common pharmaceutical firm in America, the Winthrop Chemical Company, to control the indigenous market. Sterling was to retain the American aspirin business, a profit-pool was to be set up in Latin America, Canada and Britain, and I.G. was to control the remaining international aspirin-markets. The loss of the profitable American aspirin-market seems to have been accepted by I.G. as a means of avoiding lengthy legal proceedings and costly competition.(67) A year later a contract was signed between the Grasselli Chemical Company and I.G. Again a joint company was formed to produce dyestuffs and intermediates, and in this case I.G. succeeded in gaining absolute control over this company in 1928. After the take-over, the company's name was changed to General Aniline, which soon became the third largest American dyestuffs producer.(68) In 1928 a further joint company (AGFA- Ansco) was created to produce photographical products between the old Ansco-Corporation and I.G.(69)

I.G.'s investment reconstruction in America was concluded in 1929 with the formation of a holding company (the American I.G. Chemical Corporation), which took over the shares of the Winthrop Co., the General Aniline, the AGFA-Ansco and a Kalle subsidary, the Ozalid Co.(70) In the same year these shares were transferred to a Swiss holding company (I.G. Chemie, Basel) (71), which had been formed in 1928 to provide a neutral platform for the company's international activities. Although I.G. did not actually own the Swiss company's capital of 290 million Swiss francs, effective mechanisms existed which ensured absolute control. The Swiss holding company dealt with all I.G.'s American interests, as well as 50 per cent of the Norsk Hydro shares. The close relations between I.G. and I.G. Chemie remained unaffected until the outbreak of war, when they were legally terminated in order to neutralise the company's American property. Even now this procedure remains controversial.(72)

Other important foreign connections were developed in Central Europe, Spain and Italy. In the former case, through its ownership of DAG, I.G. held a 51 per cent share in Dynamit Nobel Bratislava (DNB), a holding company with multifarious activities, that provided substantial influence over the chemical industries of Czechoslovakia, Hungary, Austria and Yugoslavia. Important minority holdings existed in the Yugoslavian Stickstoffabrik Ruse, the Hungarian explosives company Ipari Robbanoyag and the Prima Societate Romana de Explozivi.(73) I.G. was directly involved in the Spanish companies Sociedad Electroquimica de Flix (Barcelona), and the 50 per cent subsidiary Fabrication Nacional de Colorantes y Explosivos S.A. (Barcelona).(74) In Italy I.G. held a 50 per cent share in the Societa Chimica Lombarda and jointly operated ACNA with Montecatini.(75)

In Germany I.G. consisted of numerous subsidiaries, mainly in the field of explosives and mining, but several chemical plants also belonged to the group. Table 8.4 lists the most important companies in which I.G. was involved. This amounted to a share value of 373 million RM. Apart from those cases where I.G. had total control, the company's interests were mainly located in explosives and combined fields such as cellulose and mining. The most important share-holding was in the so-called 'explosives concern' (Sprengstoffkonzern), where I.G. actually possessed total control.(77) The capital of the Sprengstoffkonzern, at approximately 137 million RM, exceeded the capital of the second largest German chemical company, the Oberschlesische Kokswerke und Chemische Fabriken AG, Berlin.(78)

During the First World War the I.G. group had been Germany's greatest producer of explosives but it had relinguished this line after 1918. In 1926 I.G. 'reconquered' the German explosives trade, taking over not only DAG, but the Rheinisch-Westfaelische Sprengstoff AG, the Westdeutsche Sprengstoff AG, Wolff & Co. etc. The agreed regulation of the explosives market secured I.G. a 65 per cent share, in addition to an important export trade which had also been regulated by the agreement in 1924/5 between DAG, Brunner, Mond & Co. and du Pont.(79)

Until the 1950s coal, as well as coal-tar and its derivatives, remained the most important raw material of the German chemical industry. By 1914 the Dreibund (AGFA, BASF, FFB) had begun to secure an independent source of coal supplies by purchasing the Auguste Victoria mine, north of the Ruhrgebiet. During and after the war I.G. purchased all available mines and coal deposits, especially in central Germany, and took over the Riebeck'sche Montanwerke from the broken Stinnes trust and the coal interests of the Rheinische Stahlwerke.(80) As a result I.G. became almost self-sufficient in coal supplies, but continued to depend for energy-supply on both public and private power stations. I.G.'s mining interests remained limited to a nine per cent share of national lignite production and a 1.7 per cent share of coal output.(81) This did not give rise to any conflict of interest between I.G. and the big mining companies or German heavy industry as a whole.(82) The mining companies might have preferred to sell coal, coke and coal-tar to I.G., but generally individual interests were respected and the expansion of the mining companies into the field of chemicals remained strictly limited. Moreover, industrial groups, contrary to popular opinion, did not exist as socio-political units outside the sphere of separate industrial associations.

The business policy of I.G. tended to avoid conflicts and competition and instead sought contracts, mutual agreements and cartelisation. Although I.G. was the most important German enterprise during this period, with unparalleled strength, it nevertheless did not constitute a monopoly. However by 1937 I.G. was the sole producer of methylalcohol, magnesium, nickel, synthetic tanning agents, sera and cellophane and had a dominating position in dyestuffs (98 per cent), photographics and organic intermediates (90 per cent), solvents (70 per cent), plastics and plasticisers (90 per cent) and nitrogen (70 per cent).(83) But besides I.G. there were numerous other chemical enterprises, some of which were of considerable importance.

The list in table 8.5 clearly reflects I.G.'s predominance, which was reinforced by important connections with three of the other major companies in this sector.(85) The German market was thus almost completely regulated by conventions, cartels, and syndicates, and the large enterprises generally respected each other's interests. However, the supply-side could not fix prices and control demand. Animosity sometimes developed against I.G. particularly in relation to its pricing policy, and this also reflected growing anti-capitalist feelings within Germany. Extreme nationalists attacked the company as a multinational enterprise, pursuing the interests of 'international finance capital' instead of German interests.(86)

In 1929 the economic upswing came to a halt and in the following years Germany passed through its worst depression in modern history. The end of the boom was marked by a collapse in prices, stagnant investment and production, and a fall in share values. 1929 also marked the end of I.G.'s great investment programme. The first sign of the economic change was a general stop in company recruitment in June 1929 (87), followed by a steady reduction in staffing levels. Two months later the three-man committee was established to reduce investment and research expenditure. The impact of general economic conditions on business policy is difficult to assess. Independent of the general situation, a period of expansion had come to an end in 1929, which inevitably led to reduced investment. The general downturn, however, initiated a decline in the nitrogen business, which reduced the company's earnings considerably. These factors, in turn, accentuated the contemporary macroeconomic trend in Germany as a whole. To deal with these problems, management cut investment and research, and reduced staffing levels in this policy of retrenchment (table 8.6). A reduction in investment, however, was the most important element. At the bottom of the depression in 1932 investment was only 28 per cent of its 1928 level, whereas personnel costs were 46 per cent of their 1929 level. Moreover the structure of investment underwent a considerable shift. In the years 1930-33, 21 per cent of new investment was for the creation of new capacity, in contrast to 50 per cent in 1927-29.

The company's financial liquidity was not seriously threatened during the depression and the fall in sales was the main determinant of managerial policy.(89) This began in 1929, with a fall in nitrogen sales, while I.G.'s other markets continued to grow. This decline was caused by a fall in agricultural incomes and increasing international competition. In 1929 nitrogen sales fell by 10 per cent and continued to fall by an average of 19 per cent per annum until 1933. During the depression average fertiliser sales were only 45 per cent of the annual average for the years from 1926 to 1929.(90) In 1932 the nitrogen division registered a substantial loss of 25 million RM., not least because of a price war between the DEN-group and other producers, and because of important losses in the gasoline sector.(91) Problems were not limited, however, to the nitrogen division. The artificial silk business also operated at a loss during the depression, but this was compensated by a buoyant photographic business after 1932. This division (<u>Sparte III</u>) only incurred a deficit (1.3 million RM.) in 1929.(92) The remaining immense profits of the dyestuff, pharmaceutical and chemical sectors not only outweighed the losses in nitrogen, gasoline and artificial silk, but preserved the financial liquidity of the entire company. Even in the worst year of the depression, in 1931, I.G. earned more than 93 million RM., despite losses of 39 million RM. in nitrogen and artificial silk.(93) The published balance sheet showed a profit of 44.5 million RM. Table 8.7 also shows that sales in all sectors suffered during the depression, except for the export of pharmacueticals and gasoline sales.

By 1932 I.G. had mastered the depression, mainly by reducing investment and staff. However the decision to curtail research investment, although understandable, was arguably a mistake, particularly in the field of organic chemistry, rubber, modern plastics and fibres. The company certainly had enough money to continue the development of these important fields, and deferred expenditure meant that I.G. increasingly lost its technological superiority in the 1930s. Commercial rubber and synthetic fibre were first marketed by du Pont in 1932 (95) and 1938 (96) respectively. These were both fields where I.G. had drastically reduced investment during the depression. Moreover, the share of research investment continued to decline after 1933, indicating that the depression brought an end to the earlier period of intensive research. A final effect of the depression was the further loss of export markets. Bruening's deflationary policies were ostensibly designed to increase Germany's exports, but I.G.'s exports declined at a faster rate than domestic demand.(97) This did not, however, represent an intentional retreat from export markets or a trend to self-sufficiency.(98)

In terms of the controversy over the role of German industry in the collapse of the Weimar Republic and the installation of the Third Reich, I.G. does not appear to have played an important part.(99) During the Weimar period I.G. had considerable political influence and supported Stresemann's policy of rapprochement with the Western states. In the depression years it initially supported Bruening's deflationary policy, but after the financial collapse of 1931 favoured government intervention to combat unemployment. This position was reflected in the participation of Warmbold, a former director of I.G., and a close friend of Schmitz, in the governments of von Papen and Schleicher. Significantly when the first Hitler government was formed, many so-called bourgeois ministers were included, but Warmbold was not one of them.(100)

IV

I.G. DURING THE THIRD REICH

Today few people would doubt that the Nazi state from its inception was intent on expansion by force. Many contemporaries were also aware of the potential consequences of Hitler's policy.(101) The German bourgeoisie welcomed rearmament, as a step towards regaining national honour and equality with other powers. German industry correctly saw it as means to overcome the depression. Public investment and a rising demand for armaments, rather than employment policies and work procurement reinforced the upswing.(102) The famous autarchic economy, initiated by Schacht's New Plan (1934), was intended to secure Germany's independence of raw material imports in case of a war blockade and to finance the increasing demand for such imports which resulted from the armaments boom.(103) Rearmament, therefore, meant the preparation of a self-sufficient war economy. Following the experiences of the First World War, military planners appreciated the critical importance of the chemical industry, and its significance had subsequently been reinforced by the increasing role of tanks, aircraft, submarines and motor transport in military tactics. Modern warfare was impossible without petrol, light and alloy metals, rubber, lubricants, high octane propellants, rayon, and cellulose, not to mention explosives and their intermediates. In Germany I.G. Farben was the only company which could produce most of these materials in satisfactory amounts and was able to develop new products and processes. It is not difficult to understand therefore why I.G. occupied a key economic position in the Third Reich, nor why I.G. accepted its role and cooperated with the state in preparing the German war economy. Cooperation with the state, with the provision of price and sales guarantees, assisted procurement of resources, and investment credits, would facilitate substantial company expansion and further product diversification, without the usual financial risks. Moreover, the state did not conscript I.G., but 'purchased' its cooperation. There was accordingly no economic reason for refusing to cooperate. Indeed it also promised long-term benefits under normal market conditions. The management clearly recognised that economic planning was intended to enlarge Germany's military power, but it probably entertained the illusion that Germany would not start a major war. After the actual outbreak of war, economic ambition and a fateful sense of patriotic duty, led to an increasing entanglement in the history of the Third Reich.(104)

At the beginning of Nazi rule I.G. was sceptical about certain forms of government intervention.(105) But this position changed when effective cooperation between I.G. and the government started in 1933 with a contract on petrol production. This involved a price and sales guarantee to I.G. for 300,000 tons of petrol, which enabled a full use of existing capacity and an end to losses in this field.(106) Further contracts followed designed to enlarge capacity in light and alloy metals, intermediates, heavy chemicals, high octane spirit, rayon and other artificial fibres. Long before the Four Year Plan of 1936, the enlargement of industrial capacity to achieve self-sufficiency had already begun. However it was badly coordinated between competing authorities, as in the case of rubber synthesis.(107) Through frequent planning discussions, close contacts inevitably developed between I.G. and the state authorities, particularly the Air Ministry. The political leaders were impressed by the ability of I.G.'s management and when Goering, who, besides many other offices, commanded the German Air Force, became the political head of economic planning in 1936, he entrusted research and development within the Four Year Plan to the head of I.G.'s nitrogen division, Carl Krauch.(108) In 1938 he became the Plenipotentiary for Special Questions relating to

Chemical Production and de facto minister of the chemical industry. His office developed the plans for increased chemical production and the allocation of raw materials. As head of the research and development board he was in charge of research both in industry and universities and also planned product development in areas such as textile fibres, rubber, modern plastics, tanning materials, resins, mineral oil and fats. Krauch held this position until the end of the Third Reich. Although he resigned from his divisional post in 1938, he remained a member of I.G.'s board of directors and became chairman of the supervisory board in 1940.(109)

Some historians have argued that this effectively represented an amalgamation between I.G. and the state. Others have claimed that the firm's dominance was the result of inter-industry competition and Goering's political influence. The cooperation between I.G. and the state is also alleged to have been a symbol of state monopoly capitalism.(110) However none of these arguments are convincing. The Nazi state was not solely concerned with economic planning, nor was this its final aim. The relationship between I.G. and the state represented a form of close cooperation with strictly limited aims. These reflected key elements in Nazi rule, especially in relation to the expansion of 'living space' by military force. Economic factors could affect political planning at any time, and any amalgamation state of the interests of I.G. and the Nazi remained partial and superficial. However one cannot doubt the importance of the chemical industry for the war economy and for German self-sufficiency. Raw materials constituted the decisive bottle-neck in both cases, and these could only be procurred from the chemical industry. I.G.'s dominance, therefore, was not the result of a mysterious competition between industrial groups, but of technical necessity. Nor does cooperation between industry and the state in this case represent an extension of state monopoly capitalism. It was not the Nazi's ultimate objective to secure the profitability of private monopolistic enterprises (111); this was merely an important means of guaranteeing industry's necessary cooperation.

After 1933 and the end of the depression, the company began to expand production. Investment, mainly due to government economic planning, underwent three distinct stages. There was a slow increase of 22 per cent between 1933 and 1936 with average annual investment at 225 million RM., followed by an enormous growth from 1936 to 1939, when average annual investment amounted to 628 million RM. This was accompanied by a shift towards new capacity and a steady decline in research investment (table 8.6). This trend continued during war time, when investment rose again, to an average of 928 million RM. By 1942, 60 per cent of investment went into new capacity and only 10 per cent into research. The bulk of investment was directed towards securing national self-sufficiency (table 8.8).

As a result the company's productive capacity was enormously enlarged (table 8.9). By 1939 I.G. produced 72 per cent more heavy chemicals (chlorine, caustic soda, sulphuric acid) than at the peak of the boom in 1929 and production in this field rose by a further nine per cent by 1943. Increasing diversification reflected the immense growth of solvents, as output rose by 166 per cent between 1927/29 and 1939, and by a further 91 per cent by 1943. Expansion was almost universal and only the dyestuffs section declined after the outbreak of war. A lot of new products were introduced, particularly modern plastics, synthetic rubber, fibres, detergents and fatty-acids.(114) All these products were important for German self-sufficiency, as well as for the development of modern chemical technology. As a result of extensive investment programmes, Germany secured an adequate supply of these materials and the company accordingly grew rapidly. Since 1933, six complete new Grosswerke (large-scale plants) had been constructed, representing an investment of over 1.6 milliard RM.(115)

The drive towards economic self-sufficiency also accelerated the shift from export to domestic markets. After 1933, for the first time in the company's recent history, less than 50 per cent of its output was exported and during the war, when overseas exports virtually ceased, the figure fell to 20 per cent. The long-term trend towards a concentration on european markets continued and by 1938 Europe, excluding the United Kingdom and France, accounted for 48 per cent of total exports. Asian exports fell from the early 1930s onwards as a result of the Japanese-Chinese war, while Latin America's share grew rapidly from eight to thirteen per cent. Because of existing agreements between I.G. and American firms, this did not constitute a threat to U.S. interests in this area.(116) Central and southern Europe remained the most important markets in this region, although south east Europe's share grew fastest.(117) German military expansion, however, created new frontiers in Europe and economic forces no longer determined the direction of trade. The economies of the occupied countries were largely integrated into the German war economy.(118)

The diminishing importance of exports also meant that between 1933 and 1937 domestic sales were more important for I.G.'s product range, with the exception of dyestuffs and pharmaceuticals. By 1938 only pharmaceuticals retained a larger export quota, whereas before 1933 only nitrogen and chemicals possessed a larger domestic market. This meant that the German chemical industry effectively withdrew from world markets as Germany attempted to achieve economic self-sufficiency. New products related to this concept, such as rubber, plastics, metals, benzine and staple rayon increased their share of total sales from 26 per cent (1938) to 29 per cent (1943), and reflected the increasing predominance of the domestic market (table 8.1). However I.G.'s foreign relations remained friendly, even after the beginning of German expansion in 1938. In 1937 there had been a far-reaching exchange of information in the field of plastics between I.G. and du Pont (119), and a further agreement in 1939 over the european marketing of nylon between the two firms.(120) Even after the outbreak of war, relations remained friendly.(121) A similar relationship existed with British and French firms. In 1938, I.C.I. and I.G. planned to construct a common dyesuffs plant in Manchester at Trafford Park, a project which was only stopped by the declaration of war.(122) Indeed all international cartels continued to be observed until the outbreak of hostilities. In terms of international competition, therefore, I.G. was not primarily interested in war and military expansion. Moreover this expansion paradoxically seemed to threaten I.G.'s position through the integration of new competitors within the 'German' economy. Initially I.G. had no intention of suppressing foreign capital interests within the new economic order established in occupied Europe. However in a number of cases, driven by ambition and excessive zeal to eliminate competition, the company participated in the forcible integration of occupied countries into the German war economy. In 1941 I.G. obtained a controlling interest in a joint company (Francolor), set up between itself and all French dyestuff producers.(123) This was a direct result of the German occupation of France. Similarly in 1941, within the context of the attempt by the German Air Ministry to produce light metals with Norwegian water-power, I.G. was able to considerably strengthen its position in the Norsk Hydro Kvaelstoff AS at the direct expense of existing French stockholder interest. Other examples could be added.(124)

Inevitably the company became increasingly entangled in Nazi policy. Like most German firms, it not only used forced foreign labour in its workforce, but also prisoners from concentration camps. Labour had been scarce in Germany since 1937/8, when full employment was reached. Further economic growth overtaxed the German labour supply, particularly after the outbreak of the war, when millions of workers were conscripted. The demand for labour continued to grow and increasingly both forced and voluntary foreign labour, prisoners of war and concentration camp inmates were used to maintain the war economy.(125) In 1933 I.G. had about 66,000 employees, but by 1939 the workforce had grown to 137,000. At the beginning of 1940 nearly eleven per cent of the work-force was conscripted into the armed forces, while production and the construction of new plant continued to expand. By the end of 1944 total employment in I.G. had increased to 239,000, but the firm had lost 44,000 men to the armed services. The deficiency was overcome by using 63,000 foreign workers, 9,483 prisoners of war and about 7,000 prisoners from concentration camps, who constituted about one-third of the total work force.(126) This was a terrible consequence of I.G.'s integration into the war economy. The years from 1933 to 1943 were therefore a time of immense growth and technological development, but I.G. had to pay a high price for its growing entanglement in the Third Reich. After Germany's defeat the company was dissolved and some of its leading managers were arraigned before American military tribunals.

V

THE END OF I.G.

Despite their fundamental position in the German war economy, I.G. plants did not become a special target for strategic bombing. Only hydrogenation plants were heavily attacked and only the Leunawerke suffered considerable damage. The other large works mainly remained intact. War damage by early 1945 had led to a 45 per cent reduction in capacity at Ludwigshafen/Oppau, 16 per cent at Leverkusen and 2 per cent at Hoechst. The entire company retained 90 per cent of its capacity intact, and only 15 per cent, by value, was actually destroyed.(127) Although I.G. survived the war without severe physical damage, it did not survive the end of the Reich. One of the Allies' most important war aims was to finally destroy Germany's ability to wage war. Considering I.G.'s key position, the company was marked out for dissolution. The first step was the seizure of all company property and assets and the taking over of control by the four occupying powers.(128)

However, the emergent Cold War hindered the development of a common occupation policy and led to the physical division of Germany. The Western zones were integrated into the Western economic, political and military spheres, and the Soviet Occupation zone became part of the communist block. I.G. plant in the Soviet zone became public property, so that ultimately 54 per cent of the company was lost.(129) The integration of the remaining three zones into the Western sphere of influence, dominated by the United States, meant that the original intention to destroy the German economy was never implemented. The United States in particular intended to strengthen the German economy and prevent any development of socialism. However the dissolution of I.G. continued. Not the destruction of potential war capacity, but de-cartelisation and the reduction of excessive economic concentration was now the explicit reason for the final dissolution of the company. After lengthy and tough negotiations between the new West German government, the Allied High Commission, and the occupied I.G. works, a satisfactory solution was eventually reached in 1952. The I.G. Farbenindustrie was dissolved and in its place three new companies emerged; the Badische Anilin- und Soda-Fabrik AG, the Hoechst AG and Bayer AG.

VI

CONCLUSION

The development of the modern chemical industry in Germany, and not least the growth of I.G. Farben, is often regarded as a special feature of German industrialisation and Germany's industrial structure. This is only correct, however, in relation to the early stage of modern organic synthesis, especially in the fields of dyestuffs and drugs, and within the period from the 1870s to the 1920s. In general, there were no significant differences between the major industrialised countries, in terms of the per capita value of chemical production at the beginning of the twentieth century. All major industrialised countries now have a modern diversified chemical industry and the scientific basis of production is broadly the same in Germany, Britain, France and the United States. Moreover, the structure of the chemical industry, in terms of the predominance of only a few big companies and the existence of far-reaching marketing agreements, is very similar in the leading industrial nations. The history of I.G., apart from the sphere of technological development, was characterised by two processes; first, by the increasing equality of its competitors in Western capitalist markets and secondly, by Germany's political and social development during this period. This can broadly be characterised as an attempt to gain an independent role as a *Weltmacht* (world power). It resulted from a misjudgement of Germany's abilities, and the failure of German society to resolve the social conflicts generated by military defeat in 1918 and by the economic crises of the inter-war period.

The history of I.G. during this period, especially when viewed in relation to other great chemical companies such as du Pont, Allied Chemical and Dye, Imperial Chemical Industries, Kuhlmann, the Swiss enterprises or Solvay, represented a typical development pattern for a modern chemical enterprise. The difference between I.G. and the other chemical firms lay not in economic or managerial structures, nor in the pattern of technological development, nor in its relations with the state. Indeed on both a national and an international basis the historical development of I.G. was not atypical. There was a widespread employment of managers from the great chemical enterprises in the semi-public bureaucracy of the war economy between 1914 and 1918, a common search for governmental support through tariff protection, subsidies, and export promotion, and a concerted attempt across the board to improve the educational and technical quality of the labour force. In modern industrial states, national economic policy is invariably, at least in part, an instrument of sectional economic interests. The influence of I.G. on the German government during this period was certainly no more intensive than the comparative influence of du Pont and I.C.I. on the American and British governments respectively. Because it is the duty of the modern Interventionsstaat (interventionist state) to secure prosperity and social welfare, it must inevitably support certain industrial interests. The Gemeinwohl, or common good, is an abstract term which encompasses in modern industrial nations, full employment, social security, economic growth and technological progress. Its achievement substantially depends on the development of modern, advanced sectors in the economy. Therefore close connections between national economic policy and the growth and prosperity of private enterprise are only to be expected. The nature of this connection depends more on general political and social circumstances, than on the interests of single corporations, industrial sectors or the requirements of technological change.

Until the 1920s I.G. was able to maintain its technological advantage, symbolised by the high-pressure catalytic synthesis of ammonia and methylene in 1924. On the basis of a much stronger financial position, however, the American companies in particular rapidly caught up with I.G. The first commercial production of synthetic rubber and synthetic fibre by du Pont, at the beginning and end of the 1930s respectively, demonstrated that the earlier supremacy of German organic chemistry had finally passed away. Both the technological and general economic development of I.G. in the second half of the 1920s was dominated by the great effort to find a workable process for the high pressure hydrogenation of fuel from lignite and later from coal. This turned out to be a fateful mistake. Not only did it lead to immense losses which required compensation, but it also encouraged a dangerous tendency towards protectionism and autarchy. Even if the marketing problems for the expensive hydrogenised fuel could have been solved by agreement with the oil industry, this new technology could only have been profitably exploited with steady political support. But this was not a reason for I.G. to support the Nazi party, for the Republican governments from Bruening to von Papen were also able and willing to give I.G. the desired tariff protection; nor was the slogan of support for national labour a special idea of the Nazis. Following the lead of I.G., I.C.I. was also closely engaged in fuel hydrogenation and the British government did not hesitate to provide necessary support. During the 1930s a hydrogenation mania, caused to a large extent by the proliferation of autarchic policies following the Great Depression and the subsequent re-armament boom, led to the foundation of hydrogenation plants all over the industrialised world.

The decisive difference between I.G.'s activities in this area and hydrogenation projects in other countries did not lie in the cooperation between the state and private enterprise, but in the nature and character of the Nazi regime. No other government, perhaps with the exception of Japan, supported industrial hydrogenation as a means of developing an aggressive militaristic policy. As is well known, Nazi policy was not simply a continuation of the German attempt to become a Weltmacht by defeating its economic and military rivals; nor an attempt to take revenge for the defeat of 1918, although this may have been the objective of the traditional elites in Germany during the early period of Nazi rule. The Nazi regime acted in a terroristic and criminal manner against individuals, social groups and nations, although its intentions were originally hidden behind a veneer of nationalism and ideology. The German bourgeoisie may well have sought a means of overcoming economic troubles and social conflicts in a strong nationalist dictatorship, which might also have been able to restore Germany to a great power status and limit the influence of trade unions and mass democracy; instead they got a regime with its own criminal energy, which was to determine the economic rationale of its industrial supporters. This was what was peculiar about Germany and it inevitably left its mark on the pattern of industrial development. Of course, the Nazi regime could not have waged war or embarked on military expansion without the collaboration of German industry, especially the chemical industry and its greatest enterprise, I.G. Farben. But there is a great difference between supporting re-armament and government efforts to gain military strength, and launching risky uncalculable attacks on neighbouring nations, killing civilians on ideological pretexts and plundering occupied countries.

It is misleading to view German industrial development during this period as a necessary base for political activity. Neither particular technologies, nor the attitude to applied science, nor the attempt to conquer world markets were unique to German industrialisation and the German chemical industry. Like I.G., du Pont, I.C.I., Kuhlmann and other chemical firms tried to 'penetrate' the markets of both industrialised and less developed countries, and in relation to the earlier dominance of the German dye industry this process could only weaken the international position of I.G. The decline of I.G.'s share of world trade demonstrated the effect of this process, which could only be tolerated because total sales were growing at the same time. I.G. even had certain disadvantages, as a multinational enterprise, compared with its western competitors, as a result of Germany's defeat in the First World War. The strategy of I.G., mainly defensive and status quo oriented, was based on cartels and agreements with its major competitors. But this meant at the same time an implicit confirmation of the relative supremacy of I.G. and therefore the other major chemical companies were unwilling to accede to all I.G.'s demands. However, at the end of the Great Depression, world-wide cartels did secure again the dominant position of I.G. in many branches of the world market, even if this position was not as favourable as it had been in 1914. Until 1933, I.G. generally was in a defensive position, while the other major chemical companies were expanding and undermining I.G.'s position in a number of areas.

Between the onset of Nazi rule and 1945 I.G. withdrew from its traditional export-orientation and concentrated on indigenous autarchy programmes and war preparation. The technological developments associated with various aspects of autarchy also held out the promise of significant and substantial profits under normal economic conditions. Moreover as the Nazi regime assumed some of the risks and costs of research and development, I.G.'s involvement in the Nazi economy is understandable solely on economic grounds. The entanglement in the crimes of Nazi Germany was therefore not the result of the criminal disposition of the I.G. management, but a consequence of the inability of such a capitalist enterprise to act on anything other than economic criteria.

By looking merely at the structure and development of industrial and business concerns one will not find an adequate explanation for national specialisation. The sectoral pattern of national industrialisation, given similar economic conditions, was often identical. The particular and unique form of national development, on a sectoral and enterprise basis, is the result of social, historical and political events. Indeed these factors must also be taken into account in industrial and business histories in order to facilitate a complete and comprehensive analysis of the issues involved. This paper therefore can only provide a preliminary sketch of the history of I.G. and of the German chemical industry as a whole. But it has hopefully served to highlight the importance of the historic interplay between economic forces operating at the level of the individual firm, and broader political and social factors which inevitably impinged substantially on the development of I.G. during the period from 1904 to 1945.

NOTES

1. United Nations, Yearbook of International Trade Statistics, (New York, 1981).

2. In 1979 the BASF, the Hoechst AG and the Bayer AG were the three largest chemical enterprises in the world, measured by sales.

3. F.Ter Meer, *Die I.G. Farbenindustrie AG. Ihre Entstehung, Entwicklung und Bedeutung*, (Duesseldorf, 1953), pp.26-27. H.Tammen, *Die I.G. Farbenindustrie AG (1925-1933). Ein Chemiekonzern in der Weimarer Republik*, (Berlin, 1978), pp.9-20.

4. Bayer-Archiv (BA), 4A9,4A5.

5. G.Plumpe, 'Staat, Industrie und technischer Fortschritt. Die Kautschuksynthese in Deutschland 1906-1944/45', *Geschichte und Gesellschaft*, vol.4, (1983), pp.564-597.

6. L.F.Haber, *The Chemical Industry 1900-1930. International Growth and Technological Change*, (Clarendon Press, Oxford, 1971), pp.108-134.

7. BA, 126/6.

8. R.Lachmann-Mosse, *Die Stickstoffindustrie und ihre internationale Kartellierung*, (Zurich, 1940), pp.1-27. E.Galeano, *Die offenen Adern Lateinamerikas*, (Wuppertal, 1973), pp.160-164. G.W.Stocking and M.W.Watkins, *Cartels in Action. Case Studies in International Business Diplomacy*, (New York, 1946), pp.118-170.

9. BA, I.G.Sitzung vom 21.August 1919 in Frankfurt am Main.

10. BA, Akten zum 1.Weltkrieg, Hoechst AG Archiv (HA), Akten zum 1.Weltkrieg. For a general survey see G.Hardach, *Der Erste Weltkrieg*, (Muenchen, 1973), pp.63-82: G.D.Feldman, *Army, Industry and Labor in Germany 1914-1918*, (Princeton, 1966), passim. These new processes allowed the production of sulphur from gypsum, phosphorous from German ores, and the synthesis of ammonia from water, coal and air.

11. Haber, *Chemical Industry*, chapters 7 and 8. W.J.Reader, *Imperial Chemical Industries*, 2 vols, (Oxford University Press, London, New York, Toronto, 1970), vol.1, parts IV and V.

12. Reader, *I.C.I.*, vol.1, pp. 501-502. W.S.Dutton, *Du Pont. One Hundred and Forty Years*, (New York, 1951), pp.246-257, 286-294. Stocking and Watkins, *Cartels*, p.382. The published profits of the Nobel Trust rose from £318,000 (1913), to £1.7 million (1919).

13. Ausschuss zur Untersuchung der Erzeugungs-und Absatzbedingungen der deutschen Wirtschaft, III.Unterausschuss, *Die Chemische Industrie, (Chemie-Enquete)*, (Berlin, 1930), pp.9-15. Unterausschuss I, 5.Arbeitsgruppe, *Der deutsche Aussenhandel unter der Einwirkung weltwirtschaftlicher Strukturwandlungen, (Aussenhandels-Enquete)* (Berlin, 1932), pp.196-208. Reader, *I.C.I.*, vol.2, p.187 (British Dyestuffs).

14. BA, 4A4 Duisberg Denkschrift, April 1915, I.G.-Vertrag vom 18.8.1916. The merger created a supreme council (*Gemeinschaftsrat*), which was empowered to make fundamental decisions affecting the industry, a sales committee (*Kaufmaennischer Ausschuss*) for coordinating sales, and a credit commission to control investments.

15. Peace Treaty of Versailles, Article 263.

16. BA, Duisberg Briefe. On 15 March, 1920 he wrote, '... that our workers in Wiesdorf, Opladen and the other towns of the Landkreis Solingen, proclaimed a Soviet Republic and trouble followed. The English did not like that and came with guns, occupied the town hall and took away the Soviets and imprisoned the rowdies'.

17. K.Holderman, Im Banne der Chemie. Carl Bosch-Leben und Werk. (1953), pp.166-173.

18. BA, I.G.Sitzungen, Kommission zur Begutachtung der Stickstoffwerke Leuna in der I.G., Baden-Baden 9.10.1919, I.G.-Sitzung 10.10.1919 in Baden-Baden. HA Zentral -Archiv der I.G.(ZA) 220; Holdermann, Carl Bosch, pp.171-172. A common subsidiary was founded to run these plants (the Ammoniakwerke Merseburg GmbH), in order to prevent the possibility of partial nationalisation, as the Leuna-werke had been substantially financed by the German government.

19. BA, Umsaetze der I.G. 1924.

20. HA/ZA, 178/1 Tea Bericht v.4.12.1926; HA/ZA, 21, Fabrikations-Kommission.

21. BA, 4C2 Agreement vom 2.10.1925; BA 4B1; Tammen, I.G. Farben, pp.15-18; Holdermann, Carl Bosch, pp.197-200. The majority of the supreme council refused Duisberg's proposal of a holding company and followed Bosch's suggestion. Given the costs associated with such a merger, a rationalisation of the dyestuff section alone would not have been a sufficient cause of amalgamation.

22. Ter Meer, I.G.Farben, pp.29-34; Tammen, I.G.Farben, pp.21-28; W.Fischer, 'Dezentralisation oder Zentralisation-kollegiale oder autoritaere Fuehrung? Die Auseinandersetzung um die Leitungsstruktur bei der Entstehung des I.G.Farben Konzerns', in N.Horn and J.Kocka (eds.) Recht und Entwicklung der Grossunternehmen im 19.u.20.Jahrhundert, (Goettingen, 1979), pp.478-488; Nuernberger Prozess der USA gegen Carl Krauch und andere (NP VI), Document (Doc.) NI-5186; H.Pohl, 'On the History of Organisation and Management in Large German Enterprises Since the Nineteenth Century', in W.Engels and H.Pohl, (eds.), German Yearbook of Business History, (Berlin, New York, 1982), pp.111-121. The BASF formed a BG Oberrhein, the FFB a BG Niederrhein, the FWH a BG Mittelrhein/Maingau (including Cassella Kalle and parts of Griesheim), and AGFA, with the remaining parts of Griesheim, formed the BG Mitteldeutschland, divided by 1929 into a BG Berlin and a BG Mitteldeutschland.

23. NP VI Doc.NI-5184. Initially Bosch also led the BG Oberrhein.

24. NP VI Doc.NI-5184.

25. HA/ZA, 44 Teko; BA, 13/2 Kommissionen der I.G. (1931).

26. NP VI Doc.NI-5184, Doc.NI-5187, Doc.NI-6120; HA/ZA, 43, 43b; BA, 13/2 I.G.Kommissionen. These sub-committees were composed of experts from individual I.G. works and facilitated an exchange of experience and information. They also enabled central management to monitor the supply of qualified personnel.

27. NP VI Doc.NI-5187; HA/ZA, 117; HA/ZA 106 Arbeitsausschuss, 6.4.1933. The KA was installed again in 1937. Among the other important committees were bodies which represented the different commercial activities of the company: a dyestuffs committee, a committee for inorganics, intermediates, analytical methods, pharmaceuticals, solvents, plastics, artificial silk etc.

28. M.Weber, Wirtschaft und Gesellschaft, 5th edn., (Tuebingen, 1972), pp.551-555; J.Kocka, 'Entrepreneurs and Managers in German Industrialization', in P.Mathias and M.M.Postan (eds.), The Cambridge Economic History of Europe, (Cambridge University Press, London, 1978), vol.VII/I, pp.574-578.

29. BA, Autographen Sammlung, Carl Duisberg to W.V.Rath, 19.8.1929.

30. HA/ZA, Tea Protokoll, 15.8.1929; HA/ZA, 106, 28.Arbeitsausschuss-Sitzung 16.8.1929; NP VI Doc.NI-5184. The three new branches consisted of (1) nitrogen and hydrogenation (2) dyestuffs, inorganics, intermediates, chemicals and pharmaceuticals, and (3) photo-chemistry and artificial silk.

31. NP VI Doc.NI-5184; BA, 13/11 Carl Bosch to Haefliger, 10.3.1933; HA/ZA, 106, Arbeitsausschuss, 25.2.1931.

32. HA/ZA, 1065.

33. Reichsgesetzblatt 1934, Teil I, No.7, 23.1.1934.

34. NP VI Doc.NI-6120, Doc.NI-5184.

35. K.Borchardt, 'Wachstum und Wechsellagen 1914-1918', in H.Aubin and W.Zorn (eds.) Handbuch der Deutschen Wirtschafts-und Sozialgeschichte, (2 vols., Stuttgart, 1978), vol.2, pp.703-706.

36. BA, Loehr Akten.

37. BA, Umsaetze der I.G.Firmen; Ter Meer-Akten; NP VI, Grundlegendes Material der Verteidigung ueber die I.G.Farben, 2.4.1948.

38. I.Svennilson, Growth and Stagnation in the European Economy, (Geneva, 1954), p.162.

39. Aussenhandels-Enquête, vol.2, pp.169-199. Although the world's chemical exports did not stagnate, they grew at a slower rate than total exports.

40. Grundlegendes Material, p.38.

41. BA, Friedensmassnahmen, I.G.Auslandsinteressen vor dem 1.Weltkrieg. In 1913 the export quota had stood at approximately 65 per cent.

42. For the position in 1913, see BA, I.G.Auslandsinteressen vor dem 1.Weltkrieg; for the years 1926 to 1938, Grundlegendes Material, pp.40-45; for 1941, BA, I.G.Umsaetze.

43. BA, I.G.Auslandsinteressen vor dem 1.Weltkrieg.

44. Grundlegendes Material, pp.40-45. Within Europe, western countries (Switzerland, the Netherlands, Belgium and Luxembourg) had the greatest market share of 24 per cent (1929); southern European markets (Italy, Spain, Portugal and Greece) and central Europe (Russia, Poland, the Baltic States and Finland) had roughly similar shares of 22 per cent and 18 per cent respectively. Markets in south-eastern Europe (Romania, Bulgaria and Yugoslavia) were expanding rapidly, with their share having risen from one per cent (1913) to six per cent (1929). Scandinavian exports (Sweden, Norway and Denmark) retained their pre-war share of nine per cent.

45. For the position in 1913, see BA, I.G.Auslandsinteressen vor dem 1.Weltkrieg; for the years 1926 to 1937, see Grundlegendes Material, pp.32-38.

46. Stocking and Watkins, <u>Cartels</u>, pp.418-423.

47. HA/ZA, 310. A letter from Sir Alfred Mond to Carl Bosch from 11 November, 1927 expressed this position as follows, 'Quite apart', Sir Alfred wrote, 'from the economic results, (of the proposed exchange of hydrogenation technology in return for general self-restraint and cooperation) I cannot doom a staff of energetic and able scientists to a life of sterility and stagnation'. The proposed agreement would have had precisely this effect. I.G. was only intent on restoring the status quo and the earlier superiority of the German chemical industry.

48. Reader, <u>I.C.I.</u>, vol.1, pp.406-413. Brunner, Mond & Co. was to become the most important component of I.C.I.

49. BA, 10/3 I.G.Aufsichtsrats-Sitzung, 13.8.1926; HA/ZA, 183,1025,180; Tea-Korrespondenz (DAG), 30.12.1930.

50. HA/ZA, 306.

51. BA, 'Dreier-Kartell-vertrag', 26.4.1929; see Aussenhandels-Enquete, p. 203, Table 111, for the export position of Switzerland. Haber, <u>Chemical Industry</u>, pp.307-309. The Swiss I.G. consisted of the Chemische Industrie in Basel (CIBA), the Chemische Fabrik vormals Sandoz, and J.R. Geigy AG.

52. BA, 'Vertrag zwischen dem Kontinentalen Farbstoffkartell und der I.C.I. vom 26.2.1932'; Reader, <u>I.C.I.</u>, vol.2, pp.187-195.

53. Stocking and Watkins, <u>Cartels</u>, p.484.

54. BA, Kartellvertrag vom 26.2.1932. Swiss I.G. obtained 19.2 per cent, C.M.C. 8.0 per cent and I.C.I. 7.1 per cent of the cartel's exports.

55. Stocking and Watkins, <u>Cartels</u>, p.126, Table 10. This amounted to an annual growth rate of nearly 20 per cent.

56. BA, 186 D 1 Uebersicht ueber die Stickstoffindustrie der Welt.

57. Lachmann-Mosse, Stickstoffindustrie, pp.71-90.

58. French stockholders held 64 per cent of the NH capital until 1941; NP VI Doc. NI-8449, NI-2712; HA/ZA, 810, Vertrag zwischen der I.G. und der NH vom 18.10.1927 und 12.11.1927. The takeover of NH's export business was initiated by the I.G. dominated Deutsches Stickstoff Syndikat GmbH.

59. For further details on the Deutsch-English-Norwegische Gruppe (DEN), see Reader, I.C.I. vol.2, pp.145-157; Economic Division Decartelization Branch. I.G.Farben Control Office, U.S.Zone, Activities of I.G.Farbenindustrie AG in the Nitrogen Industry, (1946), pp.51-54.

60. I.G.Farben Control Office, Activities, pp.55-63, (CIA-Agreement); Lachmann-Mosse, Stickstoffindustrie, pp.102-120; Stocking and Watkins, Cartels, pp.144-147. The European cartel was known as the Convention Internationale de l'industrie de l'Azote (CIA). This mainly reserved exports to the DEN and guaranteed other producers certain shares in their own national markets.

61. HA/ZA, 80 Stickstoffbesprechungen; I.G.Farben Control Office, Activities, pp.55-62. Lachmann-Mosse, Stickstoffindustrie, p.113.

62. Lachmann-Mosse, Stickstoffindustrie, pp.120-123; I.G.Farben Control Office, Activities, pp.64-68. American banks and corporations were heavily involved in the Chilean saltpetre export trade.

63. Lachmann-Mosse, Stickstoffindustrie, pp.79,81, 123,14. There was an increase in the relative share of the United Kingdom, Norway and Japan.

64. F.A.Howard, Buna Rubber. The Birth of an Industry. (New York, 1974), pp.249-251 for the Division of Fields Agreement, pp.252-260 for the JASCO-Agreement; J.Borkin, Die unheilige Allianz der I.G.Farben, (New York, Frankfurt-am-Main, 1979, originally published as Crime and Punishment of the I.G.Farben, New York, 1978), pp.53-54; Ter Meer, I.G.Farben, pp.64-67; Tammen, I.G.Farben, pp.54-58. I.G. wanted the support of a major oil company in the marketing of its hydrogenation products, and Standard Oil was itself interested in the hydrogenation technology.

65. HA/ZA, 105 Sitzung Sparte II 23.2.33; HA/ZA, 181 Tea Korrespondenz.

66. HA/ZA, 107 Arbeitsausschuss-Sitzung 9.1.1932; Gosweiler's statement about the I.G. and the USA is obviously not true, see K.Gosweiler, Grossbanken, Industriemonopole, Staat 1914-1932, (Berlin, 1975), pp.332-340.

67. BA, 9A1 Das USA Geschaeft der I.G., Mai 1939, pp.9-12.

68. BA, 12/13 Abteilungsleiter-Besprechung, 12.7.1934 Vortrag ueber USA; BA, 9A1, USA-Geschaeft, pp.1-5; Stocking and Watkins, Cartels, p.394.

69. BA, 9A1 pp.5-9.

70. BA, 9A1 pp.3-15; BA, Beteiligungen der I.G., Juli 1930, p.4.

71. See BA, 9A1 pp.13-15 for the Internationale Gesellschaft fuer Chemische Unternehmungen, Basel (I.G.Chemie). I.G. was empowered to take over all the assets of I.G.Chemie at any time at their original value.

72. NP VI Doc. NI-5768; Borkin, Allianz, pp.161-175, but Borkin's statement (p.165) that the I.G. owned the I.G.Chemie is wrong. In 1983 the I.G.Farben AG i.L. undertook litigation to regain the I.G.Chemie's assets, especially the shares of the American I.G., see Blick durch die Wirtschaft, Frankfurt-am-Main 1983, Nos.39,41.

73. BA, I.G.Beteiligungen p.3; 15.f2, Bilanzpruefungskommission DAG/DNB. It is important to note that the Oesterreichische Nobel AG was a complete subsidiary of DNB, which, together with I.C.I. also owned the Nobel Bickford, Bratislava. DNB was also involved with the Carbidwerke Deutsch Matre, the Bosnische Elekrizitaets AG, Jajce with its subsidiary Elektrometallurgische Fabrik Toell, Meran.

74. BA, I.G.Beteiligungen; ACNA = Acienda Colori Nazionali Affini.

75. BA, I.G.Beteiligungen.

76. BA, I.G.Beteiligungen 1930/39.

77. HA/ZA, 1025. The Sprengstoffkonzern (explosives concern) contained DAG, the Rheinisch-Westfaelische Sprengstoff AG, Wolff- Walsrode and Celluloid- Eilenburg. It also produced plastics, fuses, ammunition, gunpowder and cellulose products. I.G. exercised total control by means of contractual pooling agreements.

78. A.Marcus, Die grossen Chemiekonzerne, (Berlin, 1931), pp.45-54.

79. HA/ZA, 1025.

80. See BA, 12/4 for the purchase of lignite deposits during the war, Vorstand der FFB, 28.11.1916, 5.12.1916, 7.8.1917: for coal-policy during the first half of the 1920s, see BA, Gemeinschaftsrat-Sitzungen; for the period after 1926 see the published I.G.Geschaeftsberichte. The steel division of Rheinische Stahlwerke was amalgamated with the Vereinigte Stahlwerke AG.

81. BA, Loehr Akten, BA 15F2 Bilanzpruefungskommission. The I.G. was the third largest owner of lignite deposits in Germany.

82. Tammen, I.G.Farben, pp.65-66.

83. BA, Loehr Akten. Earlier lists unfortunately do not exist.

84. Marcus, Chemiekonzerne.

85. HA/ZA, 106 Arbeitsausschuss-Sitzung, 12.4.1930. I.G. held one-third of the preference shares of the Deutsche

Gold-und Silber-Scheideanstalt (DEGUSSA), 15 per cent of the Solvay shares and approximately 5 per cent of the Kali Chemie shares. I.G. also cooperated with Theodor Goldschmidt AG in the production of hydrocarbon products, in conjunction with Ruhrchemie.

86. Borkin, Allianz, p.56.

87. HA/ZA, 43 Tea, 20.6.1929; ZA 106, Arbeitsausschuss-Sitzung 21.6.1929.

88. BA, Personlastatistik der I.G. (Buero Bertrams); Investment (HA/ZA, 426,518,521,524,637); research, (HA/ZA, 436, BA, 4B 14.3.10); cost of staff, (NP VI Grundlegendes Material, p.29).

89. Veroeffentlichte I.G.Bilanzen.; Ter Meer, I.G.Farben, p.78; BA Verwaltungsrat-Protokolle 1932; HA/ZA, 1018-1022.

90. BA, Ter Meer Akten, I.G.Umsaetze nach Sparten; BA, Loehr Akten; Tammen, I.G.Farben, pp.112-139.

91. HA/ZA, 1018.

92. HA/ZA, 1022.

93. HA/ZA, 1018-1022.

94. NP VI Grundlegendes Material, pp.32-38.

95. Dutton, Du Pont, pp.324-331.

96. Dutton, Du Pont, pp.356-362; Meyer-Larsen, Chemiefasern, pp.46-48; F.Endress, 'Die kuenstlichen Fasern', in K.Winnacker and E.Weingaertner (eds.) Chemische Technologie (5 vols. Hanser, Muenchen, 1950), vol.3, pp.708-710.

97. NP VI Grundlegendes Material, pp.32-38. I.G.'s export quota fell from 55 per cent between 1926 and 1929, to 52 per cent between 1930 and 1933.

98. HA/ZA, 107 Arbeitsausschuss-Sitzung, 15.4.1932.

99. Even the worst scenario from this point of view was not particularly serious. None of the leading managers of the I.G., in contrast to their contemporaries in heavy industry, supported the NSDAP before 30 January, 1933. E.Czichon, Wer verhalf Hitler zur Macht, (Koeln, 1967) passim; H.A.Turner jr., Faschismus und Kapitalismus in Deutschland, (Goettingen, 1972), pp.20-22, W.Ruge, 'Monopolbourgoisie, faschistische Massenbasis und NS Programmatik in Deutschland vor 1933', in D.Eichholtz, K.Gosweiler and W.Ruge (eds.) 'Faschismus in Deutschland', (Koeln, 1980), pp.67-70.

100. NP VI Exhibit Schmitz No.23, Affidavit Warmbold, pp.23-35. Warmbold had been Economics Minister in the cabinets of Bruening, von Papen and Schleicher.

101. W.Fischer, Deutsche Wirtschaftspolitik 1918-1945, (Opladen, 1968), pp.60-63; W.Sauer, Die Mobilmachung der Gewalt, (Frankfurt a.M., Berlin, Wien, 1974), pp.140-165.

102. R.Erbe, Die nationalsozialistische Wirtschaftspolitik 1933-1939 im Lichte der neueren Theorie, (Zuerich, 1958), pp.24-28, 34-37.

103. Fischer, <u>Wirtschaftspolitik</u>, pp.71-75. The New Plan was not intended to stabilize Germany's balance of payments.

104. NP VI Exhibit Schmitz No.6, Affidavit H.Bucher, pp.28-29. Carl Bosch, who remained as chairman of the supervisory board until his death in 1940, was aware of his company's role, and clearly unhappy about it.

105. HA/ZA, 85. See the first conferences of the <u>Sparte</u> I (Division I) at the beginning of the Third Reich. This related to the mandatory price cut for nitrogen fertilisers, the forced cartelisation of the nitrogen producers and the forced combination of lignite producers in a new company (the Braunkohlenbenzin AG.) to produce oil from lignite. In 1934 the I.G. was very surprised that it had to pay for the development of lignite hydrogenation on the basis of a state directive, HA/ZA, 106 Arbeitsausschuss-Sitzung, 9.10.1934.

106. W.Birkenfeld, <u>Der synthetische Treibstoff 1933-1945</u>, (Goettingen, Berlin, 1964) passim; NP VI Doc., NI-881 Benzine Contract, 14.12.1933.

107. Plumpe, 'Kautschuksynthese'. This involved initially the army's economic office (Wehrwirtschaftsstab), and was later enforced by the Ministry of Economics and the <u>Wirtschaftsbeauftragter des Fuehrers</u> (The Fuehrer's Commissioner for Economics).

108. D.Petzina, <u>Autarkiepolitik im Dritten Reich</u>, (Stuttgart, 1968), pp.117-119.

109. NP VI Doc.NI-5821; Affidavit Speer, pp.1-12; Doc.NI-8833, pp.1-4; Krauch-Doc. No.67, pp.69-70; Krauch-Doc.No.63, pp.48-62; Doc.NI-9945, pp.1-3; Petzina, <u>Autarkiepolitik</u>, pp.117-119.

110. D.Eichholtz, <u>Geschichte der deutschen Kriegswirtschaft</u>, Bd.1, (Berlin, 1971), p.9; L.Zumpe, <u>Wirtschaft und Staat in Deutschland 1933-1945</u>, (Berlin, 1980), pp.208-214, 226-235; J.Radkau, 'Deutsche Industrie und Politik von der nationalsozialistischen Machtergreifung bis zur Gegenwart', in G.W.F.Hallgarten and J.Radkau (eds.), <u>Deutsche Industrie und Politik von Bismarck bis Adenauer</u>, (Reinbeck, 1981), pp.259-263.

111. D.Eichholtz, 'Faschismus und Oekonomie', in Eichholtz, Gosweiler, Ruge, <u>Faschismus</u>, p.116.

112. BA, Loehr Akten.

113. BA, Loehr Akten.

114. BA, Loehr Akten. Among the modern plastics were polyvinyl-chloride, which accounted for 36 per cent of production in 1943, and polyvinyl-acetate, which constituted 22 per cent of production.

115. HA/ZA, 426 Kreditnachweise 1930-1945.

116. After a short period of competition in the 1920s, the connections between I.G. and du Pont in South America were excellent, and after the beginning of the war du Pont sold I.G. products as its agent. Moreover I cannot see that South

America was an American domain, where competition between European and United States enterprises was necessarily a violation of American interests, as J.Radkau implies, see Radkau, 'Von der Machtergreifung', pp.333-338.

117. This shift to South-East Europe was not only a consequence of German trade policy, but also a result of international inter-industry agreements, which mostly accepted this area as a sphere of German influence.

118. A.S.Milward, Der Zweite Weltkrieg. Krieg, Wirtschaft und Gesellschaft, (Muenchen, 1977), pp.134-153.

119. HA/ZA, 183 Tea-Korrespondenz, 16.9.1937.

120. BA, Agreement between du Pont and I.G.Farben of the 23rd day of May 1939.

121. BA, Korrespondenz Bayer, The Dow Chemical Company to I.G.Leverkusen, 6.9.1939. The former welcomed German expansion into south-eastern Europe.

122. HA/ZA, 105 Tea Sparte II, 27.1.1938, 14.9.1939.

123. An amalgamation between I.G. and the French dyestuffs firms had been intended since 1927, but was not realised until 1941, when France was occupied by German forces. Borkin, Allianz, pp.91-104; NP VI Doc. NI-6348, NI-8079; 24.I.G.Vorstandssitzung, 5.2.1941 p.3.

124. NP VI Doc. NI-2712, 6762, 8034, 8079, 8087, 8088, 8089, 8145, 8146, 8449. In relation to Norsk Hydro, Germany now had a majority shareholding of 51 per cent, whereas French participation was reduced from 64 to 36 per cent.

125. For the development of German labour supply during the Third Reich, see The US Strategic Bombing Survey, The Effects of Strategic Bombing on the German War Economy, Overall Economic Division, October 31, 1945, pp.29-39; T.Mason, Sozialpolitik im Dritten Reich, 2nd edn. (Opladen, 1978), pp.215-229.

126. Borkin, Allianz, pp.105-118; BA, I.G.Personalstatistik, NP VI Doc. NI-11411-A.

127. BA, Loehr Akten, see also US Strategic Bombing Survey, Effects p.85.

128. K.Hirsch, (ed.) Deutschlandplaene, (Muenchen, 1967), pp.188-221.

129. BA, Loehr Akten.

Table 8.1[37] : I.G. sales: the proportional share of products, 1913-1943 (in percent)

Product	1913	1924	1926	1929	1932	1938	1943
Dyestuffs	63	39	34	28	36	22	11
Chemicals	28	19	11	16	15	21	25
Pharmaceuticals	6	4	5	5	11	8	9
Photographical products	3	4	4	7	8	7	6
Nitrogen-products	-	33	43	34	21	16	8
Synthetic Rubber/Plastics	-	-	-	-	-	2	13
Metals	-	-	1	1	1	7	8
Staple Rayon/Artificial Silk	-	-	-	4	4	9	7
Gasoline	-	-	-	1	3	8	11
Other	1	1	3	3	1	2	2
Total in million RM	566	951	1027	1469	874	1648	3119

Table 8.2[42] : The regional distribution of I.G. export sales, 1913-1941 (in per cent).

	1913	1926	1929	1932	1938	1941
USA/U.K./France	43	14	16	15	13	5
Europe	33	38	41	46	48	74
Asia	22	33	26	28	23	4
Latin America	1	12	6	8	13	5
Other*	1	3	11	3	3	12
Total exports in million RM	350	576	782	473	471	461

*Including non-divisible products.

Table 8.3[45] : The proportional composition of I.G. exports, 1913-1937 (in per cent).

Product	1913	1926-1932	1933-1937
Dyestuffs	79	45	51
Chemicals	12	12	15
Pharmaceuticals	6	9	15
Nitrogen products	-	22	9
Photographical products	3	6	8
Other	-	6	2

Table 8.4[76] : Companies (with capital of more than 1 million R.M.) in which I.G. was involved (1931).

Name of Company	Field	Capital Mill.RM	I.G.Share Per cent	I.G.Capital Mill.Rm.
	I. > 75 per cent share			
Aceta GmbH, Berlin	Artificial silk	2,0	100	2,0
AG fuer Stickstoffduenger,Knapsack	Calcium-carbide fertiliser	8,0	100	8,0
Ammoniakwerke Merseburg GmbH	Nitrogen, gasoline, methylalcohol etc.	135,0	100	135,0
Behringwerke AG, Marburg	Pharmaceuticals	1,8	96,46	1,74
Leo. Cassella GmbH	Leasing their own plants	60,88	81,27	49,48
Deutsch-Koloniale Gerb-und Farbstoff GmbH, Karlsruhe	Tanning agents	1,2	91,35	1,10
Duisburger Kupferhuette	Pyrites, metallurgy	6,0	90,52	5,43
Elektrochemische Werke Frankfurt	Electro-chemistry	1,2	100	1,2
Fabrik Elektrischer Zuender	Fuses	3,0	94,0	2,82
Kalle	Cellulose, Ozalid	6,0	99,33	5,96
R. Wedekind & Co. GmbH, Uerdingen	Chromates	1,5	100	1,5
Wolff & Co. KG a.A., Walsrode	Explosives	2,5	75	1,88
Wuelfing Dahl & Co. AG, Wuppertal	Chemicals	1,0	100	1,0

Name of Company	Field	Capital Mill.RM	I.G.Share Per cent	I.G. Capital Mill.RM
	II. 50-75 per cent Share			
Carbonit AG, Koeln	Wire-ropes	1,5	52,9	0,79
Chemische Werke Lothringen, Gerthe	Nitrogen, Chemicals	6,0	50,0	3,00
Deutsche Celluloid Eilenburg	Cellulose	5,0	54,28	2,71
Dominit Werke AG, Koeln	Explosives	3,0	51,0	1,53
Hoelkenseide GmbH, Wuppertal	Artificial silk	3,0	50,0	1,50
Rheinische Gummi und Celluloid-Fabrik, Mannheim	Rubber, Plastics	4,0	59,7	2,39
Titangesellschaft GmbH, Leverkusen	Titanium	3,0	50	1,5
Dr. Alexander Wacker GmbH, Muenchen	Electro-chemistry	7,5	50	3,75
Westdeutsche Sprengstoff AG, Koeln	Explosives	2,0	50	1,0
	III. Minority Interests			
AG fuer Lithopone, Triebes	Lithopones	1,29	46,19	0,6
Deutsche Solvay Werke GmbH, Bernburg	Alkalis	75,0	25	18,75
Dynamit AG, Koeln (DAG)	Explosives, cellulose, artificial silk	37,625	27,77	10,45
Ford Motor Co., Berlin	Motor cars	15,00	15	2,25
Rheinisch-Westfaelische Sprengstoff AG	Explosives etc.	14,16	46	6,51

Table 8.4 contd.

Name of Company	Field	Capital Mill.RM	I.G.Share Per cent	I.G.Capital Mill.RM
	IV. Coal and Lignite-Mines/Deposits			
Cons. Braunkohlengesellschaft Caroline, Halle a.d.S.	Lignite	2,4	100	2,4
Deutsche Grube Bitterfeld, Halle a.d.S.	Lignite	2,5	100	2.5
Gewerkschaft Auguste Victoria, Huels	Coal, coke, tar	18,55	91	20,38
Gewerkschaft Elise II, Halle a.d.S.	Lignite, electricity	5,0	100	5,0
Gewerkschaft Garsdorf, Leverkusen	Lignite-deposit	1,8	100	1,8
Grube Auguste, Bitterfeld, Halle a.d.S.	Lignite	2,4	100	2,4
A. Riebeck'sche Montanwerke AG, Halle a.d.S.	Chemicals, but mainlylignite	50,0	56,51	28,26
Rheinische Stahlwerke AG, Essen	Coal, coke	150,0	44,71	67,07
Zuckerfabrik Koerbisdorf	Lignite	2,7	90,86	2,45

Table 8.5[84] : The twelve largest German chemical companies c.1929.

Name of Company	Capital Mill.RM	Sales Mill.RM	Employees
I.G.Farbenindustrie AG	1.100	1.469	c.110.000
Oberschlesische Kokswerke und Chemische Fabriken AG	90,3	250	25.220
Schering-Kahlbaum AG	30	62	2.910
Ruettgerswerke AG	80	52	650
Deutsche Solvay-Werke AG*	75	n.a.	5.821
Kali Chemie AG*	35	31	4.146
Deutsche Gold und Silber-Scheideanstalt*	35,6	n.a.	2.097
Th. Goldschmidt AG, Essen*	18,3	40	712
Chemische Fabrik Heyden, Radebeul	14,3	n.a.	2.045
AG fuer Chemische Produkte (Scheidemantel), Berlin	10,0	35	2.900
J.R. Riedel-de Haen AG, Berlin	10,0	n.a.	1.775
Saccharinfabrik AG, Magdeburg	10,6	11,6	645

* indicates : connections with the I.G.

Table 8.6[88]: Investment and staff in I.G., 1927-1942.

Year	Investment Mill.RM	New Capacity	Repairs per cent	Research per cent	Staff* 1.000	Staff Costs Mill.RM
1927	463	54	13	33	94	301
1928	461	54	17	29	108	353
1929	397	44	21	35	114	377
1930	299	24	44	32	88	321
1931	199	20	45	35	77	258
1932	129	16	51	33	65	215
1933	164	23	51	26	71	229
1934	270	40	43	17	85	253
1935	331	42	42	16	96	274
1936	451	46	38	16	102	324
1937	603	50	36	14	116	379
1938	727	53	34	13	128	448
1939	729	51	35	14	137	488
1940	755	48	38	14	136	513
1941	856	55	33	12	152	556
1942	1.074	60	30	10	160	610

*Since 1930 annual average.

Total 8.7[94] : I.G. sales during the depression (average rate of change, 1929-1933, in per cent).

	Total	Domestic	Exports
Division I	-17,7		
Nitrogen fertiliser	-19,2	-14,9	-25,9
Technical nitrogen	-20,8	-	-
Gasoline	+12,3	-	-
Division II	- 6,0		
Dyestuffs	- 4,3	- 1,4	- 5,2
Chemicals	- 8,4	- 8,4	- 8,5
Pharmaceuticals	+ 0,5	- 0,5	+ 3,8
Division III	- 6,6		
Artificial silk	- 6,5	-	-
Photographical products	- 8,3	- 6,0	-10,3
Total	- 9,5	- 7,2	-10,4

Table 8.8[112] : I.G. investment priorities, 1933-1944, ranked by value.

Field	Total Investment (mill.RM)	Share per cent
Synthetic rubber	789	19
Hydrogenation	786	19
Inorganics	514	12
Coal and lignite	355	8
Organics	345	8
Metals	318	8
Solvents	219	5
Plastics	215	5
Nitrogen	205	5
Staple rayon/synthetic fibres	132	3
Artificial silk	110	3
Photographical products	81	2
Dyestuffs	56	1
Pharmaceuticals	50	1
Explosives	21	1
Total	4209	100

Table 8.9[113] : Output of selected products from 1933 until 1943 (in tons).

Product	1933	1939	1943
Aluminium	2,200	24,700	40,300
Magnesium	1,300	16,600	27,400
Nitrobenzol	3,100	6,400	16,100
Formaldehyde	5,000	32,000	120,600
Synthetic rubber	-	22,400	118,700
Synthetic resins	1,000	18,200	28,100
Synthetic tanning agents	4,400	17,400	49,000
Plastics	200	13,600	52,600
Pharmaceuticals	1,400	2,600	4,400
Dyestuffs	41,100	49,800	28,600

Chapter Nine

GERMANY AND THE INTERNATIONAL ECONOMY : THE ROLE OF THE GERMAN INFLATION IN OVERCOMING THE 1920/1 UNITED STATES AND WORLD DEPRESSION

Carl-L.Holtfrerich

I

The three standard studies on the economic aspects of the German inflation after the First World War - the books by Frank D.Graham (1930), Costantino Bresciani-Turroni (1931) and by K.Laursen and J.Pedersen (1964) (1) - all offer discussions of the international causes of inflationary developments, in particular the role of the reparations issue, but they have neglected to deal with the effects of Germany's post-war inflationary boom abroad. This is all the more surprising, since Germany's economic situation and development, which in 1919 had reflected the general trend among the belligerent powers from war-time to peace-time production, contrasted markedly with developments abroad in late 1920 and in 1921. Other big industrial countries, among them the United States, suffered severely from the world economic crisis, while production, output and employment in Germany not only remained high, but even grew during those years.

In the literature there has been some treatment of the contemporary complaints by foreign producers that German goods enjoyed an unfair competitive advantage internationally due to an inflation-induced exchange depreciation.(2) The effect of the inflationary boom on the German demand for foreign imports, however, and thus on stimulating economic activity abroad has not been considered. Whether the post-war German inflation tended to dampen or to stimulate economic activity abroad should show up in trade balance statistics. The theoretical side of the issue has been the subject of the famous debate between Keynes and Ohlin on the transfer problem in the 1920s.(3) It addressed the question as to whether a country's balance of trade would depend more on relative prices (terms of trade) or on relative real income growth (economic activity) at home and abroad. In more modern terminology, the traditional Keynesian price elasticities' view of the balance of payments was discussed against the post-Keynesian income absorption approach represented by Ohlin. If relative prices mainly determined the state of the balance of payments, Germany's depreciating exchange rate during the inflation period should have created a favourable balance of trade. If, however, relative real income growth at home and abroad dominated the development of the balance of trade, then Germany's inflationary boom should have led to German trade deficits, especially during the international depression of 1920/1. Germany's rising import demand would then have exerted stimulating effects on economic activity abroad and could have been a crucial factor in overcoming the depression in 1921 in Germany's main trading partner countries. Table 9.1 shows that Germany had a trade deficit between 1920 and 1922, and a surplus for 1923, when indigenous production activity slowed down on account of the Ruhr occupation and the collapse of the mark. This evidence supports the validity of the real income approach as against the price elasticities' approach to the balance of payments.

Let me present a few figures to describe the development into and out of the economic depression in the United States in 1920/1.(4) The year 1919 and the first half of 1920 showed a booming economy in America. The US wholesale price index peaked in May 1920 at a level 25 per cent above that of the previous year.(5) In the first quarter of 1920 the output of manufacturing industries had risen nine per cent above the equivalent previous year period.(6) The average unemployment rate rose from 1.4 per cent in 1919 to 5.2 per cent in 1920. This, however, was mainly a result of a reduction in military employment by 1.2 million persons, while civilian employment increased by about that number.(7)

Since November 1919 the Federal Reserve Board had launched a restrictive monetary policy to fight the inflationary tendencies.(8) The Treasury had given up its resistance to such a policy, after it had managed to balance the federal budget. The rise in the discount rate by a full one and one-quarter percentage points in January/February 1920 'was the sharpest single rise in the entire history of the (Federal Reserve) System, before or since.'(9) The consequences of monetary action on prices and real economic activity were soon evident. As Friedman and Schwartz noted:

> From their peak in May, wholesale prices declined moderately for a couple of months, and then collapsed. By June 1921, they had fallen to 56 per cent of their level in May 1920. More than three-quarters of the decline took place in the six months from August 1920 to February 1921. This is, by all odds, the sharpest price decline in the period covered by our money series, either before or since that date and perhaps also in the whole history of the United States.(10)

The depression of real economic activity was similarly severe: from 1920 to 1921 industrial production fell by 20 per cent, employment was reduced by 2.1 million persons and the unemployment rate rose to an average of almost twelve per cent for 1921. The reduction of real economic activity was much faster than during the world economic crisis after 1929. 'The result is that although this contraction was relatively brief - the National Bureau dates the trough in July 1921 - it ranks as one of the severest on record'.(11)

After July 1921, however, recovery set in and gathered momentum so fast that by the end of 1922 full employment was reached and maintained throughout 1923.(12) During this period the unemployment rate averaged only 2.4 per cent. The output of manufacturing industry, which had dropped from an index value (1967 = 100) of 15 in 1919 and 1920 to 12 in 1921, had already recovered to 15 in 1922 and reached 18 in 1923.(13) In contrast to the great depression after 1929, the slump in 1920/1 not only bottomed out faster, but recovery ran its course much more quickly, especially in the United States.

II

If one looks for an explanation of this phenomenon in a world-wide context, taking into account recent experience with international economic recessions since the 1970s, one is tempted to advance the working hypothesis that, while the world-wide parallelism in contraction policies after 1929 was a major factor in reinforcing the depression, the continuing boom in one important industrial country, namely Germany, in 1921 (14) was an important factor in shortening and overcoming the early post-war depression. Continuing deficit spending by the Weimar Government mitigated the depressive effects of the world slump of 1920/1 on German business activity and allowed German industrial production to grow by slightly over 20 per cent in 1921, after a record growth rate of 46 per cent in 1920.(15) The unemployment rate of organised workers dropped from 3.8 per cent in 1920 to 2.8 per cent in 1921.(16) The situation was not quite as favourable in the first half of 1921 when the world depression reached its peak; but compared to what happened abroad, the German economy was booming.

Continuing economic growth in Germany must have had spreading effects abroad via import demand. Germany offered to foreign exporters a continuously expanding market throughout the depression. In 1921 German imports rose by 45.7 per cent measured in 1913 prices (table 9.1) and by 36.2 per cent according to tonnage.(17) Three-quarters of German imports consisted of raw materials and foodstuffs with a low value-weight-ratio (see table 9.2). The world's most important exporter of such items at that time was the United States, with about half of its exports in the period between 1919 and 1923 consisting of raw materials and foodstuffs (tables 9.3 and 9.4).(18)

The overall export performance of the United States during this period reflects the extent of the depression: exports in 1919 amounted to $7.8 billion, in 1920 to $8.1 billion, and fell by 45 per cent to $4.4 billion in 1921.(19) Approximately two-thirds of the United States export decline in 1921 was due to the collapse of prices, and about one-third to a fall in export volume.(20) In contrast to the overall export trend, American exports to Germany reflected the booming German situation: while the low figure of $92 million in 1919 was still a result of the war-related interruption of trade, US-German exports reached $311 million in 1920 and rose to $372 million in 1921.(21) Since prices fell - the unit value of American raw material and food exports fell by 45 per cent and 42 per cent respectively from 1920 to 1921 (22) - these figures represent more than a doubling in export volume from 1920 to 1921. The rapidly increasing significance of the German market for American exports is reflected by the German share in total American exports, which rose from 1.2 per cent (1919) to 3.8 per cent (1920) and to 8.3 per cent during the crisis year of 1921.(23) For particular primary commodities, the share of the German market in total American exports in 1921 became overwhelming: Germany bought slightly over 30 per cent of American copper and meat exports, and 22 per cent and 13 per cent respectively of total United States cotton (24) and wheat and wheat flour exports.(25) Between 1920 and 1921 American exports to Germany by volume had risen by approximately 300 per cent for wheat, 150 per cent for copper, 100 per cent for cotton and 60 per cent for meat.(26) Germany's exports to the United States remained low in 1920/1 amounting to only $89 and $80 million respectively.(27) Therefore, the increase in American exports to Germany directly contributed to a net increase in macroeconomic demand within the American economy.(28)

As annual data tend to mask the actual dimensions of the boom and the depression, and particularly their turning points, let me focus also on monthly or quarterly developments. Data on total American exports of all merchandise, to Europe, Great Britain and to Germany are contained in table 9.5. The decline in total exports is rapid in the first half of 1921, with an interruption during the summer months up until October. The low point is finally reached in the first quarter of 1922, with an export value of $860 million compared to $2,188 million in the first quarter of 1920 before the onset of the depression. United States exports to continental Europe and to Great Britain run approximately parallel to the overall export performance. United States exports to Germany, however, deviate strongly from the general trend. In the first quarter of 1921, in comparison with the equivalent period in the previous year, total American exports decreased by 30.0 per cent, while

United States exports to Germany grew by 220 per cent. The corresponding figures for the second, third and fourth quarter of 1921 reveal a fall in total exports of 51.1 per cent, 44.6 per cent and 56.6 per cent respectively, and a concomitant rise in exports to Germany of 10.2 per cent, 65.8 per cent and 42.7 per cent. In the first quarter of 1922 both sets of export figures reveal a fall of 43.8 per cent and 31.5 per cent respectively. One can clearly see that during the critical months of the depression, namely the second and third quarter of 1921, Germany increasingly purchased American goods and commodities, while other foreign customers were curtailing their demand. It was only months after the turning point of the depression had been reached in July 1921 and recovery had begun, that American exports to Germany showed negative growth rates over the figures for the previous year. In part, however, these reflect increased American exports to Germany in the early phases of the depression.

This picture is reinforced by looking at the development of United States cotton exports (table 9.6). Raw cotton was the single most important item in total American exports. In 1920 its share value had been 13.8 per cent, and in 1921 it was 11.9 per cent.(29) In Germany cotton was the single most important item in total imports in 1921, with a share value of 7.0 per cent; 80.3 per cent of total German cotton imports were of American origin (table 9.2). By examining this one item, it is possible to analyse export volume rather than export value, which inevitably reflects changes in price as well as volume. We can see in table 9.6 that when cotton prices had fallen in the second half of 1920 (table 9.7), Germany increased its cotton purchases in the United States considerably. In the last quarter of 1919 it had purchased only 4.5 per cent of total American cotton exports, while Great Britain had taken up 54.2 per cent. In the first half of 1920 the respective shares were 7.4 per cent and 44.1 per cent. In the third quarter of 1920 United States cotton exports reached their lowest quarterly level of all years considered. In the last quarter of 1920, when export sales were picking up, the British share had fallen to 31.7 per cent, while Germany's share had increased to 17.3 per cent. German purchases, however, became even more important during the height of the crisis year 1921. Export volumes of American cotton to Germany increased by 96.5 per cent in 1921 in comparison with the previous year, while exports to Great Britain fell by 33 per cent. In the first quarter of 1921 Britain's share of total American cotton exports had fallen to 23.0 per cent, while Germany's share reached 24.2 per cent. For the first time the German market had become more important than Britain for American cotton exporters. In the second quarter Britain's share reached 30.9 per cent, and Germany's 22.1 per cent. In the third quarter, at the height of the depression, the British share fell to a record low of 14.5 per cent, while American cotton exports to Germany rose to a record high of 200.2 million pounds, by volume, equivalent to a share of 32.6 per cent in total United States cotton exports. In the fourth quarter Germany's import volume rose again to 205.8 million pounds. But since Britain had now resumed buying larger quantities, total American exports had increased even further, and Germany's share had fallen to 18.5 per cent, in comparison with Britain's 32.6 per cent. In the first quarter of 1922 the situation was again reversed, with Britain absorbing only 23.8 per cent, while Germany's share increased to 26.1 per cent. When recovery gained momentum during the rest of the year, however, Britain re-established itself as the dominant market and absorbed 29.1 per cent of total American raw cotton exports in 1922, as a whole in comparison with 20.8 per cent for Germany.

In order to be able to estimate the extent of the demand stimulus generated by Germany's continuing boom, in relation to total economic American activity, one has to make certain predictions about United States exports to Germany, on the assumption that Germany had followed the same deflationary policies as the Anglo-Saxon or Scandinavian countries. Since Germany's economic size and structure resembled that of Britain (30), one can assume that American exports to Germany would have followed the same trend as United States exports to Britain in 1921, had Germany followed a deflationary path. American exports to Britain fell by 50 per cent in 1921 (table 9.5), so that a deflationary Germany in 1921 would only have purchased $155 million rather than an actual $372 million of American exports. The difference of nearly $220 million represents - under the given assumption - the direct contribution of the German inflation to the stimulation of demand in the American economy during the crisis year of 1921. This represents a little over 0.3 per cent of United States Gross National Product ($69.4 million dollars in 1921).(31) In addition, indirect effects via third countries must have played a role, but their assessment would necessitate a complicated matrix of world trade, which is beyond the scope of this paper.

Were increased American exports to Germany a sizeable contribution to checking the 1921 depression? This question can only be answered in a comparative context. For instance, the first emergency budget of the German Federal Republic designed to fight the 1967 recession provided for deficit spending amounting to 0.5 per cent of West Germany's GNP.(32) Equally during the economic summit in July 1978 the big industrial countries of the Western world agreed on a programme to stabilise the world economic situation by fiscal stimuli amounting to a total of one per cent of annual GNP, which would achieve this objective, however, only over a number of years.(33) Thus we can see that the direct contribution of the German inflation to overcoming the depression in the United States in 1921 matches approximately the relative size of modern demand stimuli programmes.

III

If again we take a step down from the macroeconomic level and take into account the structural elements of the depression in 1921, the role of the growing German import demand for stimulating activity in American and world markets shows up even more clearly. If we follow the earlier assumption that Germany's imports of American cotton in 1921 had fallen to the same extent as Britain's imports or by 33 per cent (table 9.5), and that the German authorities had instituted policies in line with international deflationary tendencies, then the import volume of cotton would have been 252 million instead of 739 million pounds. The difference of 487 million pounds can be regarded as the contribution of the German inflation to the stimulation of demand for American cotton. Since total United States cotton production in 1921 amounted to 3,972 million pounds, by volume (34), the inflation-induced German demand for American cotton can be calculated at 12.3 per cent of total American cotton production. Assuming a low price elasticity of demand, which is typical for raw materials and agricultural products, of approximately one-third, a decrease in American raw cotton exports to Germany similar to that which occurred in the British case in 1921, would have additionally deflated prices on the United States cotton market by 37 per cent. In view of the fact that American cotton export prices in January 1921 were already more than 50 per cent below their 1920 level, this would have had serious consequences for American agriculture and further aggravated the contemporary economic depression. As we can see in table 9.7, cotton export prices bottomed in July 1921 and recovered thereafter. The turning point was reached precisely during the third quarter of 1921, when the British market collapsed, but the booming German market absorbed significantly increased quantities and captured a record share in total United States cotton exports.

Besides raw cotton, many of the other major American import goods to Germany, such as grain, meat, tobacco, copper and mineral oil (table 9.2), were also important items in total United States exports. Due to the volume of US sales, America dominated world markets for most of these products. For primary commodities in general, price elasticities of demand and supply in the short run tend to be relatively inelastic. This means that small shifts in demand tend to have big effects on prices. Germany's demand for primary commodities, not small in itself on a world scale, could therefore exert a disproportionate influence on prices for raw materials and foodstuffs in the United States and in other world markets.

Over-production of agricultural products and raw materials in the 1920s is the main pillar in the structuralists' explanation of the world economic depression after 1929.(35) Surplus production as evidenced in stock-piling and falling prices for primary commodities had troubled the world economy and especially primary producers since 1925. Such a situation contained the danger of initiating deflationary spirals: primary producers, particularly farmers, react to the relative weakening of their position by keeping their purchases of industrial goods below the level necessary for full employment, industry cuts back on investment, banks find many debtors in difficulty and withhold or withdraw credit, and finally savers lose confidence in banks and withdraw funds. Charles Kindleberger in his book on the great depression argued against a purely monetarist explanation of the second half of the 1920s:

> The rise in agricultural stocks and the slippage of prices after 1925 make it clear, however, that there were structural factors at work. The abundance of credit up to the middle of 1928 helped to paper over the structural cracks while excluding the monetary explanation to that stage. The world might have evaded the consequences of raw-material overproduction had it escaped monetary deflation. Surpluses and deflation provided the fateful mixture.(36)

W.Arthur Lewis also explained the duration of the post-1929 crisis from the vantage point of primary commodity prices:

> The principal cause seems to have been the surprisingly rapid fall of agricultural and other raw material prices, which checked confidence in recovery, and persuaded businessmen to 'wait and see' rather than to make new investments.(37)

From 1929 to 1932 none of the big industrial countries stimulated demand and kept industrial output growing, as Germany had done in 1921. With the risk of some slight exaggeration, one can therefore argue that the American and world depression of 1921 might well have reached the dimensions of the later crisis of 1929-33, had not the German government stimulated economic activity *à tout prix*. An inflationary economic policy therefore allowed Germany to play the unintended role of a 'locomotive' for the world economy.

NOTES

1. Frank D.Graham, Exchange, Prices, and Production in Hyper-Inflation: Germany, 1920-1923, (New York, 1930, reprinted 1967). Costantino Bresciani-Turroni, The Economics of Inflation. A Study of Currency Depreciation in Post-War Germany, (London. 1937, 3rd edition 1968), first published in Italian, 1931. Karsten Laursen and Jorgen Pedersen, The German Inflation 1918-1923, (Amsterdam, 1964).

2. See the US government publication, US Tariff Commission, Depreciated Exchange and International Trade, (Washington D.C., 1922), especially pp.16-19. Friedrich Hesse, Die deutsche Wirtschaftslage von 1914 bis 1923. Krieg, Geldblaehe und Wechsellagen, (Jena, 1938), pp.397-398.

3. John M.Keynes, 'The German Transfer Problem', The Economic Journal, vol.34, (1929), pp.1-7. Bertil Ohlin, 'The Reparation Problem: A Discussion', The Economic Journal, vol.34, (1929), pp.172-179. Both articles are reprinted in: Readings in the Theory of International Trade, (London, 1950, 6th edition 1970), pp.161-169, 170-178.

4. There is a lot of specific information available in the League of Nations, Economic Fluctuations in the United States and the United Kingdom 1918-1922, (Geneva, 1942). Arthur F.Burns and Wesley C.Mitchell, Measuring Business Cycles, (New York, 1946). R.A.Gordon, 'Cyclical Experience in the Interwar Period: The Investment Boom of the Twenties', in Universities National Bureau Committee, Conference on Business Cycles, (New York, 1951), pp.163-215. John D.Pilgrim, 'The Upper Turning Point of 1920: A Reappraisal', Explorations in Economic History, vol.II (1973/74) pp.271-298. Hal B.Lary, The United States in the World Economy, (Washington D.C., 1943).

5. The International Conference of Economic Statistics, International Abstracts of Economic Statistics 1919-1930. (London, 1934), p.210.

6. Ibid., p.213.

7. Historical Statistics of the United States, Colonial Times to 1970, Bicentennial Edition, (Washington D.C., 1975), Part 1, p.126,135.

8. For the following see especially Elmus R.Wicker, Federal Reserve Monetary Policy 1917-1933, (New York, 1966), pp. 37-45. Milton Friedman and Anna J.Schwartz, A Monetary History of the United States 1867-1960, (Princeton, 1963, 1971 edn., pp.221-239.

9. Friedman and Schwartz, Monetary History, p.230.

10. Ibid., pp.231-232.

11. Ibid., p.232.

12. Historical Statistics, part 1, p.135.

13. Ibid., part 2, p.667.

14. In 1921/2 Germany again attained its pre-war share in the total industrial production of Western Europe, namely

about 22 per cent. Its share in world industrial production which had been 15.7 per cent before the First World War, had dropped to between eleven and twelve per cent in the 1920s. League of Nations, Industrialisation and Foreign Trade. (Geneva, 1945), p.13.

15. Figures are calculated from Rolf Wagenfuhr, Die Industriewirtschaft. Entwicklungstendenzen der deutschen und internationalen Industrieproduktion 1860 bis 1932. (Vierteljahreshefte zur Konjunkturforschung. Sonderheft 31, Berlin, 1933), p.28.

16. Hesse, Wirtschaftslage, pp.480-481.

17. 'Der Auswaertige Handel Deutschlands in den Jahren 1920,1921 und 1922 verglichen mit dem Jahre 1913 nach Warengruppen, Warengattungen und Laendern', Statistik des Deutschen Reichs, Band 310, (1924), p.I.2 (Einleitung). As in table 9.1 'special trade' represents imports for domestic consumption, and exports of domestic merchandise.

18. Historical Statistics, Part 2, p.889. Detailed annual data in, Department of Commerce, Bureau of the Census, Foreign Commerce and Navigation of the United States, (Washington D.C., annually).

19. Historical Statistics, Part 2, p.889.

20. Ibid., p.891.

21. Ibid., p.903.

22. Ibid., p.892. For export price developments of specific goods of importance in US-German trade see table 9.6.

23. Historical Statistics, Part 2, p.903. See also Statistik des Deutschen Reichs, Band 310, (1924), 'Der Auswaertige Handel Deutschlands..., p.1,17.

24. With 739 million pounds, Germany in 1921 absorbed not much less in quantity of American raw cotton than Great Britain with 834 million pounds; see table 9.5. This observation was also made by J.W.F.Thelwall and C.J.Kavanagh, Report on the Economic and Financial Conditions in Germany to March 1922, (London, 1922), p.37.

25. Calculated from US-exports by countries and products in, Department of Commerce, Bureau of Foreign and Domestic Commerce, Trade of the United States with the World 1920-1921, Part 2: Exports, (Washington D.C., 1923), pp.33-38, and data on total US-exports by product in Historical Statistics, Part 2, p.898.

26. These rates are calculated from US statistics in: Department of Commerce. Bureau of Foreign and Domestic Commerce, Trade of the United States, pp.33-34. German import statistics show different growth rates, but the general trend is the same; see table 9.4.

27. Historical Statistics, Part 2, p.906.

28. The theoretical aspects of this issue have been elaborated by Fritz Machlup, International Trade and the National Income Multiplier, (Philadelphia, 1950). In this

paper I do not deal with the question of how the excess of US-exports to Germany was financed, since I have dealt with that aspect elsewhere, see Carl-Ludwig Holtfrerich, 'Amerikanischer Kapitalexport und Wiederaufbau der deutschen Wirtschaft 1919-23 im Vergleich zu 1924-29', Vierteljahrschrift fuer Sozial-und Wirtschaftsgeschichte, Band 64, (1977), pp.497-529. Of course, inflationary demand creation in one country can spread to foreign countries only if additional imports can be financed either by means of additional exports, unilateral transfers into the inflationary country, out of stocks of foreign exchange or gold, or through capital imports. In the German case, it was financed mainly by short-term capital imports.

29. Calculated from Historical Statistics, Part 2, pp.898,903.

30. Before the First World War, Great Britain had a little more than 40 million inhabitants while Germany in its post-war territory a little under 60 million. 43 per cent of Germany's national product was generated by industry and construction; in Great Britain 38 per cent. In 1913 Germany exported 19.3 per cent of its net national product, while Britain exported 19.3 per cent of its GNP. Source: Brian R.Mitchell, European Historical Statistics 1750-1970, (London, 1978 edn.), pp.4,8,304,307,411,416,428,433.

31. Historical Statistics, Part 1, p.224.

32. Calculated from data in: Sachverstaendigenrat zur Begutachtung der gesamtwirtschaftlichen Entwicklung, Jahresgutachten, 1967/68 and 1968/69, (Stuttgart, 1967 and 1968).

33. Bonner Wirtschaftsgipfel. Treffen der Staats- und Regierungschefs am 16. und 17.7.1978, in Deutsche Bundesbank, Auszuege aus Presseartikeln, No.56, 1978.

34. Historical Statistics, Part 1, p.517.

35. Charles P.Kindleberger, The World in Depression 1929-1939, (London, 1973), pp.83-86 and 104-107. See also Peter Temin, Did Monetary Forces Cause the Great Depression? (New York, 1976), p.172.

36. Kindleberger, World in Depression, p.107.

37. W.Arthur Lewis, Economic Survey 1919-1939, (New York, 1969 edn.), p.56.

Table 9.1 : German foreign trade (special trade calculated in 1913 unit values*), in million Goldmarks.

	Imports	Exports
1913	11.206,1	10.198,6
1920	3.947,2	3.724,0
1921	5.750,7	2.988,4+
1922	6.309,8	6.206,7
1923	4.820,5	5.352,7

+ Only May to December.

* Special trade refers to goods for actual consumption and for further manufacturing after having cleared customs and to exports of domestic merchandise.

Source: 'Der Auswaertige Handel Deutschlands in den Jahren 1920, 1921 und 1922 verglichen mit dem Jahre 1913 nach Warengruppen, Warengattungen und Laendern'. _Statistik des Deutschen Reiches_, Bd. 310, Heft 1, (Berlin, 1924), p.4 (Einleitung).

Table 9.2 : The share of individual commodities in total German imports in 1921 (special trade calculated in 1913 unit values), and the proportion of products of US origin.

	Share of total German imports (1) (per cent)	Proportion imported from the USA (2) (per cent)
Rye	0.8	82.0
Wheat	6.5	72.5
Maize	3.6	27.0
Lard	2.8	92.3
Bacon	1.0	96.0
Pork	1.0	65.8
Beef	0.6	38.1
Cotton	7.0	80.3
Copper	2.8	84.6
Mineral Oil	1.2	73.2
Raw Tobacco	3.1	8.8
Iron Ore	1.8	0.008
Sheep's Wool	3.2	0.004
Raw Cocoa	2.3	0.004
Furs and Skins	5.2	7.5
Oleaginous Fruit	4.3	2.9
Unvulcanised Rubber	2.4	1.0
Total	49.6	

1. Calculated according to volume, on the basis of 1913 unit values for the individual commodities in relation to total German imports in 1913 unit values.

2. Calculated according to volume.

Source: Statistik des Deutschen Reichs, Band 310 (1924), 'Der Auswaertige Handel Deutschlands...', Heft 1, passim, Heft 2, p.VII.8 et seq.

Table 9.3 : The share of US exports to total US production for individual commodities (c.1920-3).

	Share (per cent)
Raw Tobacco	45.6
Copper	39.3
Raw Cotton	32.0
Wheat	21.1
Port	17.5

Source: Harvard Bureau of Economic Research, cited in <u>Statistik des Deutschen Reichs</u>, Bd. 310 (1924), 'Der <u>Auswaertige Handel Deutschlands</u>..., p. VII.3.

Table 9.4 : German imports of individual foodstuffs and raw materials (total, and from the US) in 1,000 tons.

	Wheat		Maize		Rye		Lard		Bacon	
	From US	Total	From US	Total	From US	Total	From US	Total	From US	Total
1913	1.005	2.546	172	919	20	353	101	107	1,0	1,6
1920	393	591	73	409	343	404	114	123	73	82
1921	1.655	2.281	505	1.871	308	376	135	146	47	49
1922	722	1.393	891	1.085	485	540	57	65	25	26

	Pork		Beef		Raw Tobacco		Cotton	
	From US	Total	From US	Total	From US	Total	From US	Total
1913	0,1	21,1	0,8	32,4	7,3	81	369	478
1920	34,3	40,3	49,9	92,9	10,4	84	102	139
1921	34,1	51,8	11,8	31,0	9,5	108	253	315
1922	10,8	18,5	6,9	29,6	7,2	76	202	252

	Copper		Mineral Oil		Furs and Skins		Oleaginous Fruit	
	From US	Total	From US	Total	From US	Total	From US	Total
1913	197	225	685	1.123	7,3	280	13,9	174,7
1920	50	60	318	311	2,1	61	22,2	207,7
1921	90	107	319	436	10,3	137	7,9	272,7
1922	108	128	454	622	3,7	141	5,5	357,8

Source: <u>Statistik des Deutschen Reichs</u>, Bd. 310, (1924), 'Der Auswaertige Handel Deutschlands...,' p.I.5 et seq., VII.8 et seq.

Table 9.5 : US exports of goods of indigenous and foreign origin (1919-1923) in million dollars (total, to Europe, U.K. and to Germany).

	1919			1920			1921		
	Total	Europe (U.K.)	Germany	Total	Europe (U.K.)	Germany	Total	Europe (U.K.)	Germany
January	623	370 (176)	-	722	458 (214)	14,6	655	326 (111)	48,9
February	585	374 (166)	-	646	384 (169)	18,6	489	242 (93)	39,6
March	603	387 (132)	-	820	465 (221)	20,9	387	199 (78)	30,5
April	715	501 (191)	-	684	364 (134)	23,5	340	175 (84)	19,2
May	604	389 (173)	0,06	746	383 (152)	20,8	330	177 (80)	20,5
June	928	655 (298)	8,8	631	297 (120)	19,7	337	178 (64)	30,8
July	569	404 (206)	2,4	651	341 (129)	28,0	325	183 (71)	36,3
August	646	417 (205)	11,7	579	293 (119)	19,4	367	206 (85)	38,3
September	595	360 (153)	8,8	605	313 (142)	19,8	325	177 (59)	36,8
October	632	407 (165)	20,7	752	423 (161)	32,4	343	196 (85)	26,2
November	740	492 (220)	23,0	677	357 (125)	35,1	294	153 (61)	24,3
December	681	432 (192)	17,3	721	389 (139)	58,4	296	155 (69)	21,7

	1922			1923		
	Total	Europe (U.K.)	Germany	Total	Europe (U.K.)	Germany
January	279	140 (65)	23,7	335	190 (84)	26,1
February	251	129 (53)	22,1	307	159 (71)	24,4
March	330	180 (73)	35,7	341	165 (64)	25,0
April	318	182 (72)	31,0	325	156 (58)	26,3
May	308	167 (74)	26,1	316	138 (48)	23,0
June	335	186 (75)	28,2	320	140 (55)	19,0
July	301	159 (62)	20,3	302	127 (45)	24,9
August	302	155 (55)	26,3	311	137 (53)	23,3
September	313	165 (71)	21,7	381	202 (90)	31,5
October	371	206 (84)	29,0	399	214 (89)	32,8
November	380	216 (90)	27,4	401	218 (102)	28,1
December	344	187 (80)	24,7	427	246 (123)	32,4

Source : Department of Commerce. Bureau of the Census, *Monthly Summary of Foreign Commerce of the United States.*

Table 9.6 : US exports of indigenous cotton in million lbs and dollars, 1919-1923 (total, to U.K. and to Germany).

	Total		To U.K.		To Germany	
	Lb	Dollars	Lb	Dollars	Lb	Dollars
1919						
January	341,0	110,3	138,8	45,5	-	-
February	233,6	73,6	93,3	29,5	-	-
March	259,3	78,8	73,4	22,2	-	-
April	211,1	61,8	102,0	29,9	-	-
May	228,3	67,3	104,4	31,0	-	-
June	321,8	101,4	171,7	54,4	-	-
July	270,7	90,0	160,9	54,4	-	-
August	242,6	81,3	121,5	41,6	10,8	3,3
September	119,1	39,7	43,3	14,5	13,8	4,3
October	181,3	60,7	97,9	33,5	16,9	5,6
November	478,5	181,3	273,0	104,6	20,4	7,1
December	450,9	180,6	231,3	94,2	16,0	6,1
1920						
January	478,0	195,0	249,2	104,1	10,0	3,4
February	329,0	136,0	168,2	71,8	16,0	5,6
March	406,7	171,9	194,8	85,1	27,9	10,4
April	277,7	117,5	83,2	36,3	35,3	14,1
May	186,1	77,5	62,2	26,7	21,3	8,4
June	122,9	50,1	36,9	16,3	21,9	7,9
July	107,4	44,2	30,8	13,2	12,9	4,7
August	74,7	28,1	22,3	9,0	22,9	7,7
September	119,1	41,4	54,9	19,8	21,9	6,9
October	305,8	91,3	109,4	33,2	40,7	11,6
November	357,7	91,9	124,9	33,3	62,1	14,4
December	413,9	92,4	107,0	40,9	83,1	15,6

1921						
January	315,1	60,9	83,3	17,7	69,3	10,5
February	256,8	44,3	60,3	10,5	61,3	8,8
March	195,0	27,1	32,7	4,9	55,3	6,7
April	165,7	20,5	50,6	6,5	44,6	4,8
May	248,2	30,6	82,0	10,3	49,5	5,9
June	251,5	30,5	73,3	9,0	52,7	6,2
July	271,5	31,8	39,9	4,9	96,6	11,0
August	74,8	28,0	22,3	9,0	22,9	7,7
September	267,3	43,2	27,0	4,1	80,7	12,7
October	452,0	91,0	166,8	34,9	76,0	14,2
November	333,6	64,3	86,5	17,7	73,5	12,5
December	327,3	61,8	109,4	21,4	56,3	9,9
1922						
January	243,1	45,2	67,1	12,8	55,9	9,1
February	173,3	31,1	32,5	6,2	43,0	6,9
March	235,8	43,3	55,7	10,5	71,2	12,5
April	306,8	55,9	107,9	19,8	76,9	13,3
May	240,5	45,9	95,4	18,6	57,9	10,4
June	252,8	52,5	79,7	16,7	52,7	10,4
July	190,0	42,5	47,4	10,7	32,1	6,8
August	217,3	25,9	29,2	3,7	54,5	6,3
September	191,8	42,7	77,0	17,3	32,6	7,1
October	418,4	93,9	122,4	27,8	73,1	16,4
November	446,1	109,4	136,5	33,5	67,3	16,6
December	315,1	79,7	89,0	22,7	54,3	13,7
1923						
January	245,2	65,3	80,2	21,8	38,8	10,3
February	186,9	48,1	54,5	15,5	31,3	8,7
March	165,6	52,2	33,5	9,9	28,8	8,3
April	133,9	39,7	5,0	1,4	39,2	11,5
May	83,1	23,0	5,5	1,5	20,9	5,7
June	111,0	31,1	17,0	4,5	25,7	7,2
July	87,6	24,2	6,2	1,6	41,7	11,4
August	140,0	31,2	33,5	7,5	28,7	6,3
September	363,1	99,4	128,2	34,8	68,5	18,6
October	405,9	116,9	109,0	31,2	79,2	22,7
November	400,9	126,6	145,8	45,7	57,7	18,2
December	436,1	148,7	203,7	70,2	56,2	17,9

Source: Department of Commerce. Bureau of the Census: Monthly Summary of Foreign Commerce of the United States.

Table 9.7 : US export prices of indigenous goods in dollars (monthly average). 1919-1923.

	Wheat (bushel)	Copper (lb.)	Cotton (lb.)	Fresh Beef (lb.)	Bacon (lb.)	Crude Oil (gallon)
1919						
January	2,47	0,245	0,324	0,24	0,282	0,07
February	2,40	0,25	0,315	0,234	0,274	0,064
March	2,35	0,224	0,304	0,251	0,277	0,06
April	2,35	0,17	0,293	0,243	0,295	0,048
May	2,48	0,17	0,295	0,213	0,312	0,053
June	2,10	0,181	0,315	0,236	0,341	0,056
July	2,40	0,198	0,332	0,231	0,356	0,06
August	2,43	0,223	0,335	0,232	0,358	0,095
September	2,40	0,22	0,333	0,22	0,35	0,061
October	2,42	0,217	0,331	0,213	0,333	0,053
November	2,37	0,22	0,379	0,247	0,307	0,055
December	2,42	0,213	0,40	0,198	0,29	0,064
1920						
January	2,43	0,206	0,408	0,208	0,277	0,055
February	2,43	0,204	0,413	0,209	0,268	0,064
March	2,39	0,197	0,423	0,198	0,266	0,051
April	2,55	0,197	0,423	0,206	0,248	0,095
May	2,80	0,196	0,417	0,20	0,227	0,091
June	2,92	0,198	0,453	0,17	0,221	0,103
July	2,96	0,198	0,411	0,19	0,221	0,102
August	2,90	0,20	0,375	0,18	0,212	0,10
September	2,90	0,197	0,348	0,164	0,217	0,09
October	2,77	0,195	0,30	0,147	0,218	0,087
November	2,60	0,193	0,255	0,155	0,225	0,086
December	2,37	0,167	0,223	0,137	0,222	0,103

1921						
January	2,13	0,142	0,193	0,19	0,188	0,088
February	2,00	0,137	0,172	0,171	0,152	0,079
March	1,92	0,136	0,139	0,17	0,14	0,076
April	1,67	0,131	0,124	0,175	0,126	0,067
May	1,60	0,133	0,123	0,173	0,115	0,058
June	1,56	0,133	0,121	0,20	0,112	0,058
July	1,50	0,132	0,113	0,127	0,127	0,042
August	1,40	0,126	0,119	0,128	0,124	0,035
September	1,34	0,124	0,162	0,124	0,122	0,036
October	1,30	0,126	0,201	0,127	0,114	0,035
November	1,18	0,132	0,193	0,138	0,11	0,043
December	1,21	0,136	0,189	0,133	0,106	0,042
1922						
January	1,21	0,139	0,186	0,149	0,106	0,039
February	1,25	0,137	0,18	0,137	0,111	0,046
March	1,36	0,131	0,184	0,153	0,122	0,049
April	1,37	0,13	0,182	0,144	0,119	0,045
May	1,39	0,131	0,191	0,148	0,122	0,054
June	1,30	0,126	0,207	0,161	0,123	0,052
July	1,31	0,138	0,224	0,178	0,122	0,048
August	1,26	0,139	0,223	0,157	0,122	0,043
September	1,17	0,14	0,223	0,136	0,12	0,030
October	1,18	0,14	0,225	0,12	0,125	0,04
November	1,23	0,14	0,245	0,145	0,123	0,04
December	1,24	0,148	0,253	0,156	0,122	0,034
1923						
January	1,28	0,146	0,266	0,14	0,12	0,032
February	1,27	0,152	0,279	0,166	0,121	0,037
March	1,30	0,168	0,293	0,161	0,125	0,033
April	1,35	0,172	0,297	0,17	0,125	0,037
May	1,24	0,170	0,276	0,161	0,121	0,035
June	1,24	0,159	0,28	0,157	0,121	0,033
July	1,18	0,156	0,276	0,135	0,119	0,039
August	1,09	0,140	0,250	0,142	0,119	0,032
September	1,12	0,147	0,274	0,145	0,126	0,03
October	1,11	0,141	0,288	0,174	0,133	0,03
November	1,10	0,138	0,315	0,161	0,14	0,027
December	1,12	0,137	0,341	0,164	0,138	0,027

Source : Department of Commerce. Bureau of the Census: Monthly Summary of Foreign Commerce of the United States.

Chapter Ten

OCCUPATION POLICY AND POST-WAR RECONSTRUCTION : BRITISH MANPOWER POLICY IN THE RUHR COAL-MINES, 1945-1947, AND WEST GERMAN ECONOMIC RECOVERY (1)

Mark Roseman

I

It is no exaggeration to say that replenishing the labour force of the Ruhr collieries after 1945 was the single most important prerequisite of West German economic recovery. In mining, as in many other industries, the death and disablement of miners called up for military service had left large gaps in the workforce. In the Ruhr pits, the post-war labour shortage was exacerbated by the mining industry's long-standing failure to recruit apprentices and juvenile labour. As a result, the end of the war saw a mining workforce that was depleted by 50 per cent and in which many of the workers remaining were destined to leave the pits over the next few years due to old age or ill health.(2) The recruitment and productive deployment of new labour was the key to reviving coal production after the war and amongst contemporaries there was no doubt that the revival of coal production was in turn the *sine qua non* of West German economic recovery.(3)

It was British policy that determined whether West Germany got its coal because the great coal fields of the Ruhr lay in British hands, whilst the other traditional German coal fields in Silesia and the Saar were no longer available for West German use. British actions in Ruhr mining were to play a very significant role in West German recovery and constituted a major aspect of British economic policy during the occupation period.

At first sight British policy towards the Ruhr mines seems paradoxical. On the one hand the Allies had already agreed before the end of the war that German coal production should be maximised, at least in the short-term. Whereas virtually nothing about Germany's long-term economic future had been decided upon by the Allies, and the economic plans of the British and Americans were either punitive, nebulous or contradictory, here was agreement and a clear cut priority. The needs of the liberated countries of Western Europe, France, the Low Countries and Scandinavia made immediate resumption of German coal production imperative, even before it was recognised that the maintenance of any sort of economic activity in occupied Germany would necessitate mining as much coal as the pits would yield.(4) However increasing coal output was above all a question of labour. Not only was the workforce depleted by about 50 per cent, but disruption and absenteeism in the first months after the war resulted in over one-third of the available workforce not reporting for work. The message was obvious. One of the first priorities of the British authorities must be to build up the depleted colliery workforce in order to increase production in the mines.(5)

Yet the fact of the matter is that effective measures to achieve just this began only towards the end of 1946. The first large-scale effective programme to channel labour to the mines was inaugurated only in January 1947 and even then it ran on promises and a prayer until late spring 1947, when there was an increased supply of foodstuffs and consumer goods, which alone could attract an adequate flow of labour into the mines. The rest of this essay is devoted to explaining this paradox and to examining the British role in German reconstruction.

II

From the start there was clear recognition on the part of the British agency which ran the mines, the North German Coal Control (NGCC), that well over 100,000 men would have to be found to bring production up to pre-war levels.(6) For the first few months of its operation the NGCC was reasonably successful. By November absenteeism had dropped from 36 to 17 per cent and 35,000 miners who had been prisoners of war in the British zone were back in the pits. As a result of these measures monthly production between April and October 1945 rose from 268,000 to 3,607,000 tons. By way of comparison, the equivalent figure in 1938 was over ten and a half million tons. However these early successes soon turned to disaster. From October, production rose much more slowly until January 1946, then fell, regaining the January levels only in July, falling again in September and not consistently passing the January 1946 level until during 1947. This is all the more surprising given the priority which was accorded to coal production and the urgency with which the Ruhr coal was needed.(7)

The failure was in large part due to British manpower policy. Until October 1945, when things began to go wrong, the majority of the men brought back to the mines had been Ruhr miners happy or, at least, not too unwilling to return to their former employment. Neither the administrative efficiency nor the coherence of the British recruitment policy had so far been put to the test. Once the supply of former miners began to dry up, the British were indeed faced with a problem. Despite the depressed economy few workers were coming onto the labour market. This was because money had lost much of its value, so that the normal relationship between wages and production did not apply. There was thus no pressure on the employers to streamline the workforce and many big industrial companies were 'hoarding' their workers in the hope of being able to resume production in the foreseeable future. Complicated administrative machinery would be required to sort out those employed in essential work from those who could with advantage be transferred to the mines. Of those workers who actually did come onto the labour market, only about one-third were fit for heavy labour. As a result there was no obvious source of new labour for the mines.(8) Further, the combination of war-time evacuations, the destruction of much of the housing in the cities and official direction of the flow of refugees and expellees to rural areas with intact housing rather than to urban areas where vital employment was available, meant that much of the usable labour was not where it was most needed, being instead employed on the land.(9) The greatest obstacle to successful recruitment was that there was very little incentive for men to turn to the mines for work. Anyone with any sense stayed on the land where there was most chance of finding a house that was not destroyed and of obtaining food. Mining work, unattractive at the best of times, appeared to offer very little at the end of 1945.

The British response to this situation was to set the administrative wheels in motion to direct, i.e., coerce, 'green labour' to the mines. By March 1946, 99 per cent of recruitment to the mines was achieved by directions to work.(10) Unemployed men who registered with labour exchanges were given a medical examination and if fit sent off to the mines; discharged prisoners of war were checked for suitability for mine work; German labour officials and British Military Police carried out spot checks on street and cinema queues to flush out likely labour and a series of labour supply directives established the overriding manpower priority of hardcoal mining.(11) Although a huge amount of administrative time and energy was expended on this approach, the policy was disastrous. The influx of new men lowered the general level of productivity without noticeably raising output. Moreover directed labour did not stay in the mines, often fled in the first week of employment and frequently absconded with the work clothing that was so hard to replace. Up to March 1946 labour exchanges had sent 60,000 workers to the mines, but by the end of that month only 18,000 of them were still in the pits. Between January and the end of September 1946 almost 50,000 men were dragged unwillingly to the pits; yet over that same period the number of workers underground increased by less than 10,000. Productivity fell because of the inexperience of the new men and because the unwilling conscripts further lowered the general level of morale in the mines, thereby reducing the output of the experienced men as well. In turn the low level of productivity made it necessary to recruit more men to achieve production targets.(12) The situation was serious, not just for the mining industry, but for the recovery of the German and European economy. The British found themselves having to choose between neglecting the urgent supply needs of their European allies, or attempting to satisfy their demands by depriving the British zone of indigenous coal supplies and thereby risking a catastrophe.(13)

Why was the coercive policy such a failure? In part it was because of worsening conditions in the Ruhr which are outlined below. However, even if conditions for the Ruhr miner had remained static, it is doubtful whether the direction of labour would have been any more successful. At the best of times compulsory direction of labour is a make-shift measure, unlikely to enhance workforce productivity. It can work only if the measures are generally regarded as legitimate or if a police state exists to enforce them. In war-time Germany and Britain, conscription to the mines had enjoyed some success due to a combination of both factors. By contrast the British measures in post-war Germany were neither generally accepted, nor supported by an administrative and military apparatus sufficiently extensive to ensure that the directions were not evaded.

General acceptance was lacking because the British were after all a foreign occupying power and it was not obvious that they were acting in the German national interest. Most informed Germans who thought about the problem felt that the transfer of more resources to Germany or to the Ruhr, for instance through the payment of a more realistic price for German coal exports, would obviate the need for compulsory directions.(14) Even those senior officials, like Robert Lehr, President of the Rhine Province until the creation of North-Rhine Westphalia (NRW), who were prepared to support the British measures found it expedient, after testing public opinion, to withdraw their support.(15)

Opposition to the British policy sabotaged its success in a number of ways. Undoubtedly the negative attitude of the German authorities transmitted itself to the recruits and encouraged them to resist the orders. On a number of occasions protests by the German labour authorities about the quality of the accommodation offered led to the suspension of labour transports to the Ruhr. The doctors of the miners' Health and Old Age Association, the _Knappschaft_, who had to give each new recruit a medical examination, were more concerned with the possible future burden on the _Knappschaft's_ resources occasioned by accepting large numbers of medically sub-standard recruits, than with the production goals of the British. According to British evidence they were overzealous in rejecting potential recruits.(16) Again, the colliery managers, as far as they dared, showed themselves more concerned with preserving discipline and the long-term productivity of the workforce, than with supporting the British recruiting drive. They continually attempted to sack unruly new recruits, although they must have been aware that they were providing grounds for other unwilling recruits to behave badly in the hope of being sent home, thereby undermining the whole coercive approach. Again and again, the Ruhr Coal Controllers had to warn the mine managers that they could not simply dismiss men when they wanted to.(17) In addition, the German authorities could not be relied upon to carry out the checks and controls which were supposed to identify likely recruits within the general population and to locate recalcitrants and deserters. It is difficult to quantify the effects of these various elements of resistance to the British recruitment drive, but the contrast with war-time conditions, when medical, safety and training standards had been sacrificed in the Ruhr mines without demur, and when the Fremdarbeiterpolitik (foreign labour policy) of the Nazis had been generally accepted, could not have been more marked.(18)

Theoretically the British could have compensated for the lack of indigenous support by the use of force. Yet British soldiers, though effective enough at street-corner checks, proved unable to enforce a thorough screening of the population for recruits and deserters. One operation at the end of 1945 which was supposed to produce 50,000 new miners by screening prisoners of war prior to their release, produced just 384 bright new recruits for the mines. One reason for this was money: on financial grounds alone the British could not engage enough troups or police to screen the population effectively.(19) Furthermore, in contrast to the French, the British did not believe in a massive military and military-police presence. Whenever the French demanded a tougher policy towards the mines and the posting of more officials to each pit, the British argued that such a military presence would only be counter-productive. As Morgan of the Labour Supplies Branch argued: '...we have to consider facts, we have to see how far we can drive the human machine'.(20) The French argued that the best way to deal with deserters was to be very strict with the first offenders, but Morgan could not agree: 'I am afraid they will go into other zones.... You cannot go beyond a certain point. You cannot use the human machine beyond a certain point'.(21) This approach was not peculiar to the authorities concerned with the coal industry. It was one of the fundamental characteristics of the entire British occupation policy. The British were reckoning on a lengthy period of occupation which, in their view, called for indirect rule, both for financial reasons and because they did not want to be confronted with the type of civil resistance which the French had faced during the Ruhr occupation of 1923.(22)

At the same time as the British were initiating their disastrous policy of labour direction there was a general deterioration in the living and working conditions of the Ruhr miner. This was the other major factor undermining British attempts to increase production. It made recruitment even more difficult than it would otherwise have been and further depressed the morale and productivity of the experienced miners. The miner's financial position had worsened. Wage levels, which had dropped badly relative to other important industrial groups in the Ruhr during the 1930s, suffered an absolute drop when the Goering decree of 1939 was repealed soon after the capitulation. During the war the State had helped the industry by funding a major part of the contributions to the miners' pension scheme. The British did not continue this support and, as a result, pensions were heavily cut; one type of pension, the *Bergmannssold* being eliminated altogether. These cuts also affected working miners, since miners with reduced working capacity received a pension on top of their wages and all miners over 50 who had paid the requisite contributions customarily received the *Bergmannssold*, as a fixed payment on top of their wages, even when employed.(23) By far the most important deterioration was the cut in miners' rations. As from March 1946, because of the general food crisis, miners received only 2,864 calories per day, instead of the 3,400 formerly allocated. This had an immediate psychological effect, as evinced by the drop in productivity after the cuts had been announced, but before they had been introduced. Married miners were additionally affected since they naturally tended to share their scanty supplementary allowances with the rest of the family who were on meagre civilian rations. According to British nutritional calculations, even single miners on the full ration allocation were receiving little more than half the calories necessary to do very heavy work. Small wonder that the productivity of the experienced hewers averaged only 70 per cent of the equivalent 1938 figure.(24)

III

If increasing coal production had not been such a clear cut priority, one might be tempted to accept these factors as an adequate explanation for the delayed recovery of the coal industry. But it really is mysterious that the British allowed the miners to be affected by a general food cut. It is even more mysterious that the British became involved in extensive compulsory direction of labour when such a policy surely offended against their own cardinal tenet of avoiding open and direct coercion of the indigenous population. Yet the British persisted in directions on a mass scale until towards the end of 1946. Indeed they made serious preparations for the introduction of a system of universal conscription for the mines, which, like a military call-up, would have affected every male of a certain age-group.(25)

It is necessary first of all to ask why they resorted to directions initially. In the very short-term it was the logical thing to do because the demand for coal was so pressing. The Potter/Hyndley mission to North West Europe reported in June 1945 that unless major coal exports from Germany were forthcoming, a coal famine would result in Europe 'destroying all semblance of law and order'.(26) The British did not have much time to experiment with other measures which might have made labour directions unnecessary, such as the provision of increased rations to attract enough new miners on a voluntary basis or necessary capital investment to increase German labour productivity in this critical sector. In the short-term everything stood in favour of the simple, direct expedient of sending men down the mines. Nevertheless the British could easily have employed a double strategy of coercing labour and at the same time enhancing the attractiveness of work in the mines. Yet they did not.

Why were there no attempts to transfer to the Ruhr those resources, particularly increased food and consumer goods, which would have ensured a plentiful supply of voluntary and well-motivated labour? It was characteristic of British economic policy towards Germany at the end of the war that the negative goals, the dismantling of munitions and weapons production, strict production limits on other industries and so forth, were well defined, whilst the positive facets of policy, such as establishing which branches were to be encouraged to expand in the long-term and how quickly their recovery was to be promoted, remained vague.(27) Formulation of a clear reconstruction programme had been inhibited by the desire to protect British industry from future German competition. As late as the beginning of 1945, for example, there were still vague fears amongst the British Economic and Industrial Planning Staff that German coal mining might in the future compete with the British coal industry, and it was therefore 'unthinkable that the circumstances which may preserve the German coal industry intact to meet a vital short-term European coal deficiency should be allowed to give that industry any undue initial advantage when normal supply conditions again prevail'.(28) As a result, there was no initial willingness to spend money on the miners or to put the industry on a secure long-term footing. Even when it became apparent soon after the war that there would be a major fuel shortage in Europe for many years to come and even after the authorities within the Ruhr had realised that satisfying the coal industry's labour requirements would be a long-term task, there was still no attempt to introduce viable alternatives to a coercive labour recruitment policy or to transfer necessary resources to the Ruhr. There was no overall policy framework, or long-term economic reconstruction strategy for Germany that might have encouraged the British to respond to the international coal shortage with a plan for rebuilding the German mining industry.

The British remained committed to a policy of indirect rule on the assumption that harsh coercive policies were not enforceable and would jeopardise that element of minimal consensus between rulers and subjects which was necessary for an effective administration of their occupation zone. The animosity to the Germans which characterised French occupation policy was largely absent in the British case. Despite this, British economic policy in Germany was essentially negative: constructive initiatives were ill-defined or circumscribed by Britain's own economic interests, and economic policy in general was imbued with a clear hostility towards the German people. There was a general feeling that the Germans had made their bed and now they could jolly well lie in it. Such an attitude, however justified, was not conducive to finding an effective solution to the mining industry's labour problems and encouraged the further implementation of coercive measures.(29) Given this climate of opinion it is perhaps not surprising that initially the British opted for a compulsory direction of labour without at the same time offering major inducements to work in the mines. Taken in conjunction with Britain's own financial problems at home, it was clear that Britain was not going to make resources available out of her own pocket to help the Ruhr get on to its feet again.

Inevitably, the Military Government agency directly responsible for the coal industry, the North German Coal Control, realised fairly quickly that a different manpower policy was needed. It could not fail to recognise that the regeneration and rejuvenation of the mining workforce required major, long-term improvements in the miners' status and their relative and absolute material position. As early as September 1945 the NGCC was arguing for special incentives for the miners. At a meeting with the French, NGCC representatives concurred wholeheartedly with the French opinion that more food should be available for the miners, but regretted that this did not lie within the competence of the coal authorities. When the Deputy Controller General of the NGCC was asked in February 1946 what effect a small reduction in the miners' ration would probably have, he predicted accurately the disastrous consequences which did in fact ensue in March of that year. Yet his views went unheeded and the directions continued.(30) This persistence in a clearly disastrous policy is difficult to explain. Even if the British were not prepared to invest money in Ruhr mining themselves, they still had the option of using German resources for this purpose. Indeed the mining industry received sizeable subsidies from the German zonal budget to cover operating losses. Supplying the miners with adequate food and consumer goods could have been achieved either by allowing the Germans to earn enough foreign currency to buy the necessary supplies on the international market or by diverting the scanty German stocks in the British zone to the miners. Both options could have been introduced at little financial cost to the British government.

The most obvious way for the Germans to earn additional foreign currency in order to make essential purchases and raise internal levels of consumption was by exporting coal. Indeed, by the end of 1947, the three Western zones had exported 25 million tons of coal, primarily to France, the Low Countries and Scandinavia. As German experts continually pointed out to the British, had the Germans actually received the market price of 25 to 30 dollars per ton, or had they been allowed to use the coal to produced finished goods for export at market prices, there would have been no difficulty in boosting the calorific value of the miners' ration, and thence the level of coal production.(31) In 1945 the British did indeed try to raise the price of German coal. The problem was that coal prices had been made a matter for quadripartite decision, and after the war America and France, who were both consumers of Ruhr coal, refused to countenance an increase. A unilateral increase by the British authorities would have had grave international consequences.(32) The obvious response for the British to this situation should have been to reduce the underpriced coal exports from the British zone. The coal exports went largely to other countries and scarcely benefitted the British economy. In fact they actually cost Britain large amounts of money. If the zone had been properly recompensed for its coal, it could itself have afforded to pay for the large-scale food imports into Germany, which constituted a severe burden on British finances.(33)

British policy can almost be explained in one word: France. In 1945 and early 1946 the British were far from seeing the Americans as their principal allies; they were still pursuing the traditional policy of a balance of power in Europe designed to limit any future German threat. Cheap exports from Germany were the means to cement a European alliance and France was undoubtedly the most important destination for these exports. Clear confirmation of the intimate connection between Britain's coal export policy and her attitude towards France came in May 1946 at a conference between British experts and the German Zonal Advisory Council to discuss ways of improving German coal production. The Germans called for a moratorium on coal exports to allow them to produce finished goods that could be exported at a more realistic price. Over lunch the Deputy Chief of Staff, Major General Bishop, confided to Robert Lehr, Oberpraesident of the North-Rhine Province that a cessation of exports to France would not be in the British interest, because France might interpret a moratorium as an unfriendly act, particularly as elections were pending in France. No more indigenous coal could be spared to finance the reconstruction of German industry.(34)

There was still one option open to the British. They could have used German stocks of food and consumer goods to give the miners preferential treatment along the lines continually urged by the French. A rigorous transfer of the meagre German resources to the Ruhr might well have ensured a flow of manpower to the mines, but this was just the type of ruthless occupation policy that the British were not prepared to undertake. So strong was their fear of public unrest that, while the food situation in the zone remained critical, the British refused to countenance giving extra rations to the miners even when these were offered by other countries and would therefore not have been provided at the expense of the indigenous consumer.(35) This was why in March 1946 the miners had had to suffer a ration cut like everyone else. When, in July, the British re-established the miners' pre-March rations, they were so nervous about the move that it was not made public; as a result, the impact on recruitment was very limited.(36)

IV

The British were caught in a dilemma. They were unwilling and unable to enforce the direction of labour rigorously or squeeze productivity gains from the miners by police measures and martial law. They were equally unwilling to transfer resources into the mining sector at a short-term cost either to themselves, the French, or the German people, although such a policy would have helped to improve voluntary labour recruitment and to raise productivity. The basic problem was that the plan to reconstruct the coal industry was out of step with the rest of British policy. If the British had been pursuing a general policy aimed at the reconstruction of German industry, these problems would not have arisen. In the first place, from very early on, there would have been official recognition at the highest level of the need to find a non-coercive method of labour recruitment. Secondly the German public, recognising the efforts being made to rebuild the economy, would have been far more willing to accept a short-term transfer of resources to the miners. Conversely, if

British occupation policy had been more consistently punitive and coercive, if from the start they had been able and willing to post large numbers of soldiers at each mine to control desertions and punish the slackers, the British might well have been successful in extracting more coal from the mines, at least in the short-term. Shoot the first offenders, the French had advised, and the situation will soon settle down. But this was not the British approach.

The failure of the British to increase coal production retarded recovery in Germany and the liberated countries alike. It also put the British authorities in the Ruhr in a very embarassing situation. Not only was it clear that their production programme was foundering, but they themselves were called upon by their superiors in London to implement a policy in which they did not believe. By the spring of 1946, everyone from the Deputy Military Governor downwards knew that more resources should be made available to the coal mining industry in the Ruhr. In August 1946, General Robertson himself said to the Zonal Advisory Council that there was overall agreement on the need to employ voluntary and well-motivated labour in the mining sector, and a recognition that coercive recruitment policies would not provide in the long-term an adequate labour supply.(37) Yet just a couple of months later, with the labour shortage in the mines growing increasingly desparate, and with no support from London for a more positive policy, the Control Commission felt compelled to ask the Zonal Advisory Council whether it would accept the introduction of universal conscription for the mines.(38)

The British lost prestige not only because of the contradictory and ineffectual nature of their policy, but also because it was so blatantly undemocratic. As Konrad Adenauer pointed out, Britain, with its democratic tradition, could afford to introduce the Bevan boys, but Germany needed a taste of freedom.(39) The goal of democratisation seemed to have been forgotten. A report prepared in September 1945 by the Manpower Division on the question of compulsory directions for the mines concluded cheerily that 'Management interviewed were reasonably confident of success in the light of their war experience and in spite of the reluctant attitude of the recruits'.(40) It comes as something of a surprise to see how readily this and other reports speak of reintroducing the German 'machinery' i.e. the Nazi apparatus for controlling labour, and of compelling youngsters to work in the mines against their will. There would appear to have been an overt willingness to adopt the strategy of German war-time mine management and to squeeze production out of undernourished and poorly housed slave-labour. Of course all the occupying powers recognised the need to direct labour as a short-term measure; Control Council Directive number three explicitly empowered them to do just that. It is nevertheless striking, particularly in contrast with the American manpower administration, that the desirability of establishing a free labour market as quickly as possible was only rarely discussed in the relevant British administrative circles. Perhaps because Britain had been more thoroughly immersed in the climate of total war for a longer period, the British in Germany found it harder than the Americans to restore the normal freedoms of democratic life.

V

Change was inevitable. In the summer and autumn of 1946 far-reaching changes in Britain's general foreign and occupation policy were taking place. It is very likely that British difficulties in increasing coal production in the Ruhr were influential in bringing about changes not only in British, but also in American policy.(41) Whatever the facts of the case, the implications for coal production were extremely important. Britain moved away from the idea of a close alliance with France towards a pact with the United States. This made it easier to contemplate lowering the level of coal exports. America increasingly recognised that European economic recovery depended on German industrial reconstruction and that this, in turn, would necessitate the provision of additional aid. The thought of giving the Ruhr financial support thereby became more acceptable. Within a general context of promoting German reconstruction the British also had fewer qualms about temporarily concentrating rations and consumer goods on the Ruhr. Even so it is remarkable how long the British took to overcome their reluctance to give the Ruhr miners a privileged status or to supply adequate outside assistance. The introduction of a points system in January 1947, whereby all miners earned points which enabled them to obtain scarce consumer goods and foodstuffs, proved to be the key to tapping the hidden labour reserves in the British zone and increasing coal production. Even now the scheme almost collapsed because the necessary goods were not at first made available; the first shipments of textiles, for instance, did not arrive until April and in general the scheme depended on meagre German reserves and not on increased imports. This was certainly not the way the scheme had been originally conceived on the German side, nor how it was usually presented to the public by British propaganda.(42)

The impression should not be given that the role of the British Military Government in this aspect of German economic recovery was wholly negative. Important preparatory work, carried out during this period, made a swift expansion of output possible in the course of 1947. Moreover once the self-imposed obstacles to a successful manpower policy in the mines had been removed, the British, in cooperation with the

United States, made an important contribution to German industrial recovery. Perhaps the most important aspect of the measures implemented by the Military Government was the degree to which scarce German goods were concentrated on the Ruhr. Miners and their families constituted only one-thirtieth of the population of the British zone, yet they received, for example, one-fifth of all allocated textiles in 1947/8.(43) Such prioritisation was necessary to overcome the labour bottleneck, yet a German goverment would probably not have dared to have risked such a policy.(44) Things being as they were, the German economic authorities were able to say that the points system was introduced at Allied request and supplemented by allied stocks. Until the introduction of the points system, the German planning authorities had tended to spread the scarce stocks of coal, other materials and industrial and consumer goods as evenly as possible. With the incentive schemes for miners and the subsequent special programmes implemented in relation to transport and other fields, the British and Americans effectively introduced a new principle of concentration on key sectors. There is no doubt that this unpalatable but effective prioritisation was of major importance for German economic recovery. Even assuming that a German government, left to its own devices, would have been daring enough to have assumed responsibility for such measures, the full burden of having to introduce dirigistic policies accompanied by internal distributional conflicts might well have been an insuperable test for a fledgling German democracy. Sparing the Germans this burden was probably one of the most important British contributions to West German economic reconstruction.

NOTES

1. The material for this piece was gained during research work for my PhD 'New Miners in the Ruhr 1945-1958'. I am indebted to the German Academic Exchange Service, the Leverhulme Trust and the German Historical Institute, London, for enabling me to carry out the field-work in Germany. The paper was originally presented at an international symposium on German Post-War Economic Recovery held at the Centre for Interdisciplinary German Studies, University of Liverpool. I am also very grateful to my mother, for civilising the first draft of this article.

2. In 1938 the Ruhr mines had employed 228,813 workers underground. In April 1945 the figure was just 127,525, see _Zahlen der Kohlenwirtschaft_, (Essen, 1946). Heft 1.

3. On the importance attributed to coal, see Werner Abelshauser, _Wirtschaft in Westdeutschland 1945-1948, Rekonstruktion und Wachstumsbedingungen in der amerikanischen und britischen Zone_, (Stuttgart, 1975), p.139.

4. The goal of a short-term maximisation of coal production was clearly established by the autumn of 1944, see Economics and Industrial Planning Staff. The German Coal Industry. Report of the working party (September 1944), in Public Records Office, London (PRO), FO 942:178. The U.S./U.K. Potter/Hyndley mission in June 1945 emphasised the overriding importance of supplying coal to North West Europe, see report by the Potter/Hyndley Mission to North West Europe, June 1945, PRO, FO 942:179. The Potsdam Agreement called for an immediate increase in the level of coal production.

5. On absenteeism, see Manpower Division, Control Commission of Germany, British Element (CCGBE). Report on Labour, Housing and Working Conditions in the Ruhr, Luebeck 25.9.1945, PRO, FO 1005:345.

6. NGCC Monthly Report No.2, September 1945, PRO, FO 1005:345.

7. The figures on absenteeism are taken from the Manpower Division report referred to above (note 5) and the NGCC Monthly Progress Reports 2-4, PRO, FO 1005:345. Monthly production figures are to be found in _Zahlen der Kohlenwirtschaft_ (ZdK) (Essen, 1946), Heft 1, and subsequent volumes for the following years. On the British operation to release former miners from prisoner of war camps, Operation 'Coalscuttle', see EIPS 97/47, PRO, FO 942:183 and EIPS 97/64, PRO, FO 942:180.

8. Exact labour market figures are not available for 1945, but in 1947 when a similar labour market situation still prevailed, unemployment stood at 274,000 for the British zone or just three per cent of the employed workforce, despite the fact that industrial production in the same geographical area was barely more than one-third of the 1936 level. For these figures and an analysis of the fitness of labour for heavy work, see the report by the Zentralamt fuer Arbeit (ZAA) in the Federal Archive Koblenz (BAK), Z40:308 and the figures in Abelshauser, _Wirtschaft_, p.36.

9. See the above-mentioned report by Manpower Division CCGBE.

10. See the article by August Niehues, 'Ruhrbergbau und Arbeitsvermittlung', _Arbeitsblatt fuer die britische Zone_, vol.1, no.3 (1947), pp.88-90.

11. On the screening procedures, see Manpower Division, CCGBE. Technical Report, fortnight ending 29.12.1945 in PRO, FO 1005:1822 and the 'Minutes of the Committee to investigate coal production, 1946. Visit of Russian, French and U.S. experts to the Ruhr. Minutes of meeting held on Tuesday August 6th 1947', especially the interview with August Halbfell, PRO, FO 1005:1947. For labour supply directives, see PRO, FO 1005:1824.

12. The enormous expenditure of administrative effort is detailed in 'Sechs Jahre Aussenstelle Bergbau des

Landesarbeitsamtes NRW', unpublished Ms.(1952), p.4, which was kindly lent to me by Herr Nasskrendt of the Regional Labour Exchange in North Rhine-Westphalia. The drop in productivity is described in the 'Brief for Chancellor of Duchy of Lancaster. Prepared by Economic Sub-commission CCGBE. Part I Hard Coal Production British Occupied Zone of Germany' 8.4.46, note 13, in PRO, FO 942:183. The figures of labour losses are taken from 'Minutes of the Committee to investigate coal production...' referred to above and from figures in the Papers of the Regional Office of Mines in Dortmund (OBAD), I8010/723/47.

13. The pressure on the British to give Germany even less coal than it was already receiving is clear in the communications between Eaton Griffiths of the European Coal Organisation (ECO) and the Control Office, see 'Eaton Griffiths ECO to BERCOMB for Econ. Coal, Berlin', in PRO, FO 942:183. See also the discussions which took place under the auspices of the Control Office in 'Informal discussions on German coal problems', EIPS 1/7/4/26A, PRO, FO 943:183.

14. For the importance of the export question on miners' morale in general, see Ullrich Borsdorf. 'Speck oder Sozialisierung. Produktionskampagnen im Ruhrbergbau 1945-1947', in Hans Mommsen and Ullrich Borsdorf (eds.), <u>Glueck auf Kameraden! Die Bergarbeiter und ihre Organisationen in Deutschland</u>, (Koeln, 1979), pp.345-366. At a higher level, limiting coal exports and making more available for the reconstruction of the coal industry itself was advocated by the German Economic Advisory Council for the British zone (<u>Deutscher Wirtschaftsrat</u>), see 'Oberbergamt Dortmund. Verfuegung zu 1147/46, Vermerk 9.8.1946', in OBAD I8000/1147/46.

15. Lehr's willingness to accept compulsory directions, especially if they were to be extended to <u>'eine Art Ehrendienstpflicht'</u> for all fit young men, was expressed at a conference with the British authorities in May 1946, see 'Oberpraesident der Nordrhein-Provinz, Notizen von der Konferenz im britischen HQ in Luebbecke am 9.5.1946, Duesseldorf, 13.5.1946', in the State Archive of NRW, Duesseldorf, (HStaD), NW 53:272. This suggestion was readily taken up by the British and presented to the highest German body in the zone, the Zonal Advisory Commission (ZAC). After initially sounding out the trade unions, Lehr and the ZAC then effectively withdrew the suggestion. See 'ZAC/P(46) 93' in the German Parlamentsarchiv, Bonn, (PA), File 1:203.

16. Two examples of protest from labour administration officials can be found in 'Praesident des Landesarbeitsamtes Hannover an Militaerregierung Hannover, 22.2.46', in OBAD I8000/1147/46, and in the remarks of Dr.Hewegen, in OBAD I6301/927/46. Manpower Division complained that the labour exchanges were not taking the orders to place youngsters in

the mines seriously; see the Manpower Division Report in PRO, FO 1005:1819. On the quality control carried out by the Regional Labour Exchange, see 'Gespraech zwischen Hentrich und Ullrich, November 1945', in OBAD I6300/1289/45 and the comments by Labour Minister Halbfell in 'Niederschrift ueber die 13. Sitzung des Koordinierungsausschusses 12.6.1947', HStaD, NW 73:135. On the medical standards of the Knappschaft, see the 'Minutes of the Committee to investigate coal production...'

17. A general assessment by American observers was that it was to be expected that 'under existing price and subsidy policies, the board of managers should keep production at the lowest possible level consistent with its members continuing in office', see 'Special Intelligence Report. Some German views of the political, economic and sociological aspects of Ruhr mining, by L.E. de Neufville, Dep. Director of Intelligence, 19.6.1948', in the United States Military Government (OMGUS) records which I saw on microfiche in the Westphalian Industrial Archives, Dortmund, (WWA), File S15, OMGUS BICO BISEC 11/104 - 1/39. The friction that had existed between German managers and British authorities emerges in 'Ritchie, Ruhr Coal District 1 417HQ CCG(BE), Hamborn, an Concordia Bergbau AG, 21.11.1947', in WWA F26:783. The conflicts over disciplinary measures can be followed in more detail in 'P.D.Kennet, 1.RCD, an Concordia, 17.1.1946', in WWA F26:379; 'HQ 1.RCD an Betriebsdirektor Concordia, 5.6.1946' and 'HQ 1.RCD an Betriebsdirektoren, 5.6.1946', both in WWA F26:380; '1.RCD an Generaldirektoren, 5.9.1946' and '1.RCD an Generaldirektoren, 9.9.1946', in WWA F26:782; '1.RCD an alle Bergwerksgesellschaften, 26.8.47', in WWA F26:783.

18. It was the Labour Minister of NRW, Halbfell, who revealed that the German officials had not been effective in carrying out the checks, see 'Minutes of the Committee to investigate coal production...', op.cit. On the treatment of the Zwangsarbeiter (forced labour), see Christian Streit, Keine Kameraden. Die Wehrmacht und die sowjetischen Kriegsgefangenen 1941-1945, (Stuttgart, 1978), pp.268-288.

19. On the ill-fated operation, 'Operation Clobber', see Rundschreiben 161 of the German Mines Supplies Organisation (GMSO), 7.12.45, in WWA F35:3495; 'Manpower Division Fortnightly Technical Reports for fortnight ending 29th December 1945' and ditto for fortnight ending 12th January 1946, in PRO, FO 1005:1822; '6 Jahre Aussenstelle Bergbau...', op.cit., p.3. On the general importance of financial constraints on British policy towards the miners, see 'Meeting at Norfolk House 22nd June', in PRO, FO 943:183.

20. Remarks contained in the 'Report of the Working Party on Manpower, Housing and Related Subjects' which can be found in the 'Minutes of the Committee to investigate coal production'.

21. Ibid.

22. In the quadripartite Experts Committee, the British opposed French calls for direct Military Government control of mining operations with explicit reference to the Ruhr struggle of 1923, see 'Brief on special points arising from Coal Experts' report for use in Foreign Sec's discussion with the French', (October 1946), in PRO, FO 943:185, Doc.103. This was not just a tactical measure for use against the French. In May 1947 the Deputy Controller General of the NGCC reported his anxieties about the general situation in the Ruhr thus: 'It was most essential to correct this attitude (the miners' hostility, MR) at the earliest possible moment; otherwise we might be faced with a situation much the same as that which arose in 1923', contained in 'Informal Meeting with Mr. H.E.Collins... at Norfolk House, 6.5.1947', PRO, FO 943:186.

23. For the material losses, see Klaus Wisotzky, Der Ruhrbergbau im Dritten Reich, (Duesseldorf, 1983), p.146, 244 et seq., and Werner Mielert, 'Die verschenkte Kontrolle. Bestimmungsgruende der britschen Kohlepolitik im Ruhrbergbau 1945-1947', in Dietmar Petzina and Walter Euchner (eds.). Wirtschaftspolitik im britischen Besatzungsgebiet 1945-1949, (Duesseldorf, 1984), pp.105-120, here pp.112-113.

24. The effect of the fall in rations is detailed in 'The Coal Industry in the British Zone, April 1947', in PRO, FO 943:186. The psychological impact emerged during the visit of the coal experts to the Ruhr. See the notes of the fifth meeting, in 'Minutes of the Committee to investigate coal production...', op.cit. In some areas in the Ruhr, calories dropped to as low as 900 a day for civilians. See the ZAA report, in BAK Z40:308, which also contained the British nutritional calculations. The productivity of the hewers is my calculation based on figures in Abelshauser, Wirtschaft, p.140.

25. The preparations for introducing the scheme can be found in Labour Supply Branch (Manpower Division) Directive 17, 19.9.1946, in PRO, FO 1005:1824 and in ZAC/P(46) 93, in PA 1:203.

26. The papers of and the response to the Potter/Hyndley mission can be found in PRO, FO 942:179 and in WWA S15 OMGUS AG 45-46 103 1.

27. On the lack of a reconstruction strategy on the part of the British, see Falk Pingel, 'Ein Konzept geht verlustig. Britische Wirtschaftsplanung im Rahmen der Besatzungspolitik', a paper delivered at the conference 'Wirtschaftspolitik, Bewirtschaftsungssystem und soziale Verhaeltnisse im britischen Besatzungsgebiet 1945 bis 1948/9', Lennestadt/Sauerland, F.R.G. 25/26.6.1983, a modified version of which was subsequently published under the title 'Der aufhaltsame Aufschwung', in Petzina and Euchner (eds.), Wirtschaftspolitik, pp.41-64. At a higher level, Alan Milward

has also concluded that 'es in der britischen Deutschlandpolitik wenig Voraussicht gab', in ibid, pp.25-40, here p.37.

28. 'EIPS: The German Coal Industry. Report of the Working Party, September 1944', in PRO, FO 942:178.

29. The point about the general attitude of the powers that be was confirmed by Mr. H.E.Collins, former Deputy Controller of the NGCC in an interview 29.6.1984. The influence of this attitude on, for example, the tone of labour supply directives can be seen from 'Manpower Division to HQ Military Government., Hannover, Westfalen etc, 14.5.1946. Subject: recruitment of juveniles for mining', in PRO, FO 943:190.

30. The NGCC's 'Interim Report on the General and Financial Situation of the Ruhr Mining Industry', cited in Astrid Foellmer Edling, 'Die Politik des Industrieverbands Bergbau im Ruhrgebiet 1945-1948...', unpublished Hausarbeit, University of Bochum, 1977, pp.6-7, argued the case for special incentives. The meeting with the French is documented in 'Conversations with Parisot', PRO, FO 942:183. Mr.H.E.Collins supplied the information about his response of February 1946 in an interview.

31. On the coal price and Germany's losses in foreign currency, see Werner Abelshauser, <u>Wirtschaftsgeschichte der Bundesrepublik Deutschland 1945-1980</u>, (Frankfurt, 1983), p.31.

32. Information about the British attempt was supplied by Mr.H.E.Collins in an interview.

33. Pingel, 'Aufschwung', makes the good point that, by deliberately deciding to export underpriced coal, the British in a way opted for the costly food shortages: 'Die aussenpolitischen Praeferenzen der Londoner Regierung waren mit dafuer verantwortlich, dass diese Kosten (from importing food, MR) so hoch waren', p.9.

34. The conference and Major Bishop's confidential remarks are documented in 'Oberpraesident der Nordrhein-Provinz, Notizen von der Konferenz im britischen HQ in Luebecke am 9.5.1946, Duesseldorf 13.5.1946', in HStaD NW 53:272. Another sign of the British desire to placate France in the coal question was the coal conference in Essen between 12th and 14th April 1946, organised to give the French a chance to air their grievances about the situation in the Ruhr. See PRO, FO 942:183.

35. The evidence for this can be found in 'Record of a conversation between Mr.Blaisdell, Mr.Galbraith of the State Department and Mr.Mark Turner (11th June 1946)', in PRO, FO 943:183.

36. The decision not to announce the increase is documented in 'Council of Foreign Ministers. Conversations between British, French and American experts about German coal. First Meeting, 4th July 1946', in PRO, FO 943:183. The rations increase still made sense as far as productivity was concerned, of course.

37. General Robertson's address to the Zonal Advisory Council's sixth Meeting, 14.8.1946, can be found in W.Vogel, Vorgeschichte der BRD 1945-1949. Band 1, September 1945 - December 1946, (Muenchen, 1976), p.676.

38. The compulsory service scheme was put to the ZAC in October, see ZAC/P(46) 93, in PA 1:203.

39. Documented in 'Interview with Konrad Adenauer', Coal Production Committee (COPROD) paper P(46)18, in PRO, FO 1005:379.

40. Manpower Division CCGBE. Report on Labour, Housing and Working Conditions in the Ruhr, Luebeck 25.9.1945, in PRO, FO 1005:1819.

41. John Gimbel, for example, stresses the role of the German coal problem in shifting American policy from its initial punitive stance to the Marshall Plan, see John Gimbel, Amerikanische Besatzungspolitik in Deutschland 1945-1949, (Frankfurt, 1971), p.200.

42. With the introduction of the points system, the labour situation in the Ruhr was transformed overnight. Within weeks of the critical labour shortage in the collieries other industries in the Ruhr were complaining about labour losses to the pits, see 'Simpson to H.E.Collins, 4.3.1947', in PRO, FO 943:185 and the figures in the monthly reports of the Central Office of Mines, in OBAD I8010 Bd. 2,3,4 and 5. On the delicacy of the negotiations prior to the introduction of the points system, see 'Versorgungszentrale des deutschen Kohlenbergbaus an Oberbergamt Dortmund, 2.12.1946' and ditto 3.12.1946, in I8000/2624/46. On the almost accidental way in which the scheme finally came into force and the burden on German supplies, see 'Wirtschaftsminister NRW an Vorstand des IVB, 13.2.1947', in OBAD I8000/542/47 and 'Bericht der Arbeitsgruppe Kohle ueber die Taetigkeit seit Anfang Dezember 1946, Duesseldorf 14.1.1947', in OBAD I8000/294/47.

43. 'Miners Points Scheme, Extract from BIBM(47)3 of 3rd March 1947', in PRO, FO 943:185.

44. This is difficult to establish with certainty. Werner Abelshauser rightly points out that Victor Agartz of the German Economics Advisory Board indicated his readiness, if need be, 'die benoetigten Lebensmittel auf Kosten der allgemeinen Bevoelkerung der britischen Zone bereitzustellen', in Werner Abelshauser, Der Ruhrkohlenbergbau seit 1945, Wiederaufbau, Krise, Anpassung, (Muenchen, 1984), pp.37-8. On the other hand Agartz, as an economic advisor to the British Military Government, was not confronted with the political pressures that would have faced an independent government. Those German officials, such as the Oberpraesidenten of the provinces, who were less exclusively concerned with economic matters and more exposed to public opinion were much more hostile to the idea of concentrating resources on the miners. At a conference held under the auspices of the Zonal Advisory

Council in May 1946, at which Deissmann voiced Agartz's view that the miners should get more rations no matter what the cost, the Oberpraesidenten of North-Rhine and Westphalia both stated categorically that the normal consumer could not be called on to make any further sacrifices for the provision of an increased ration for the miners. See 'Conference held at Main HQ CCG on 10th May 1946 on the subject of "Methods of increasing the coal output in the British Zone" (Luebbecke)', in HStaD NW 53:272.

CONTRIBUTORS

W.R.Lee is currently Senior Lecturer in Economic History at the University of Liverpool, Director of the Institute for European Population Studies, and Assistant Director of the Centre for Interdisciplinary German Studies. He is the author of *Population Growth, Economic Development and Social Change in Bavaria, 1750-1850* (New York, 1977), editor of *European Demography and Economic Growth* (London, 1979), and co-editor of *The German Family : Essays on the Social History of the Family in Nineteenth-and Twentieth-Century Germany* (London, 1981), and *The German Peasantry. Conflict and Community in Rural Society from the Eighteenth to the Twentieth-Centuries* (London, 1986). He is also the author of numerous articles on the demographic, economic and social history of Modern Germany.

Rainer Fremdling studied economics and economic history at Muenster, and gained his *Habilitation* in 1983. Since 1981 he has been assistant professor at the Institute of Economic and Social History at the Free University of Berlin. He is now Professor of Economic History at the University of Groeningen, Holland. His major publications include *Eisenbahnen und deutsches Wirtschaftswachstum, 1840-1879* (Dortmund, 1975), and *Technologischer Wandel und internationaler Handel* (Berlin,1986) He has edited, or co-edited three important publications; *Industrialisierung und Raum, Studien zur regionalen Differenzierung im Deutschland des 19. Jahrhunderts* (Stuttgart, 1979), *Productivity in the Economies of Europe* (Stuttgart, 1983), and *Staat, Region und Industrialisierung* (Ostfildern, 1984).

Rolf H.Dumke obtained his doctorate at the University of Wisconsin, Madison in 1976 ('The Political Economy of German Economic Unification : Tariffs, Trade and Politics in the Zollverein Era'). More recently he has been *Wissenschaftlicher Assistent* at the University of Muenster

(Institut fuer Wirtschafts-und Sozialgeschichte). He has published widely on the Zollverein and contributed a number of seminal papers to edited volumes, including 'Die wirtschaftlichen Folgen des Zollvereins', in W.Abelshauser and D.Petzina (eds.). Deutsche Wirtschaftsgeschichte im Industriezeitalter (Duesseldorf, 1981). He is one of the foremost proponents of cliometrics in West Germany.

Wilfried Feldenkirchen studied economics and history and gained his 'Habilitation'in 1980 at the University of Bonn, for which he also won the Maier-Leibnitz Prize. He is currently head of the Auslandsamt of the University of Bonn, with research interests in the economic and business history of the nineteenth-and twentieth-centuries. In addition to a large number of articles on German economic, business and banking history, his main publication is Die Eisen und Stahlindustrie des Ruhrgebiets 1879-1914 (Wiesbaden, 1982). He is at present writing up a major publication on German agrarian policy after 1945.

Richard Tilly received his Ph.D. from the University of Wisconsin. He is at present at the Institut fuer Wirtschafts-und Sozialgeschichte, Westfaelische Wilhelms-Universitaet, Muenster. He is one of the foremost writers on German economic history with a particular expertise in banking and business history. His main publications include Financial Institutions and Industrialization in the Rhineland, 1815-1870 (Madison, 1966), Kapital Staat und sozialer Protest in der deutschen Industrialisierung (Goettingen, 1980) and as editor (with Rainer Fremdling), Industrialisierung und Raum. Studien zur regionalen Differenzierung im Deutschland des 19. Jahrhunderts (Stuttgart, 1979) and (with T.Pierenkemper), Historische Arbeitsmarktforschung (Goettingen, 1982).

Jochen Krengel completed his doctoral thesis at the Free University, Berlin (Institute for Economic and Social History). His main publication is Die deutsche Roheisenindustrie , 1871-1913. Eine quantitativ -historische Untersuchung (Berlin, 1983). He has also published a number of articles and contributed papers to edited volumes, including 'Zur Berechnung von Wachstumswirkungen konjunkturell bedingter Nach frageschwankungen nachgelagerter, Industrien auf die Produktionsentwicklung der deutschen Ruheissenindustrie, 1871-1912', in W.H.Schroeder and R.Spree (eds.). Historische Konjunkturforschung (Stuttgart, 1981). He is now working in the world of banking and finance.

Hermann Schaefer after studying in Frankfurt. a.M., Bonn and Freiburg, is at present Director of the Haus der Geschichte in Bonn. He has worked extensively on regional economic policy during the First World War (Regionale Wirtschaftspolitik in der Kriegswirtschaft. Staat, Industrie und Verbaende waehrend des Ersten Weltkrieges in Baden. Stuttgart, 1983) and has jointly edited, with Hugo Ott, Wirtschafts- Ploetz Die Wirtschaftsgeschichte zum Nachschlagen (Freiburg, 1984). In addition he has published a number of important articles on German Economic and Social History, dealing with such topics as unemployment, trade-unions, Italian migrant workers, and workers' culture.

Gottfried Plumpe having been a Wissenschaftlicher Assistent at the University of Marburg (1977-1983), is at present a Hochschule Assistent at the University of Bielefeld. His major publications include, Die wuerttembergische Eisenindustrie im 19. Jahrhundert (Stuttgart, 1982), and a number of articles on technological change in various sectors of the German economy in the nineteenth-and twentieth-centuries. His present research interest is mainly centered on German industrial development since 1900, particularly in relation to the chemical industry.

Carl- Ludwig Holtfrerich studied Economics and law at Muenster and Paris, and gained his Habilitation at the Free University of Berlin, Department of Economics. Since 1983 he has been Professor of Economics and American Economic History at the Free University. His major publications include Quantitative Wirtschaftsgeschichte des Ruhrkohlenbergbaus im 19. Jahrhundert. Eine Fuehrungssektoranalyse (Dortmund, 1973), Die deutsche Inflation 1914-1923 (Berlin and New York, 1980) and Alternative zu Bruenings Wirtschaftspolitik in der Weltwirtschaftskrise (Wiesbaden, 1982).

Mark Roseman is at present a lecturer in the Department of Modern Languages, University of Aston in Birmingham. He has recently completed his doctoral thesis 'New Miners in the Ruhr 1945-1958', and is continuing to extend his research into different aspects of German post-war history. He has published a number of articles and recently contributed a chapter to W.R.Lee and E.Rosenhaft (eds.), The State and Social Change in Germany 1880-1960 (Berg, 1989), forthcoming.

Name Index

Adenauer, Konrad 296

Balassa, B 80
Berding, H 84, 89, 97
Biersack, H.L. 89
Bishop, Major-General 296
Bismarck 83
Blackbourne, D. 1,10
Bockenforde, E.-W. 94
Bodman, von 213
Boehme, H. 1, 83, 116
Borchard, K. 89
Borchardt, K. 99
Borries, B. von 84
Bosch, Carl 224, 227, 228, 2
244
Bowring, J. 47
Bresciani-Turroni, C. 265
Bruening, Heinrich 237, 244

Cairncross, A. 149
Clapham, J.H. 1, 82
Cline, W.R. 81, 86, 87
Cooper, C.A. 79
Cooper, R.N. 80

Daebritz, W. 119
Davis, L.E. 92
Denison, J. 81
Dieterici, C.F.W. 82
Dufraisse, R. 96
Duisberg, Carl 217, 221, 223, 224
Dumke, R.H. 3, 10, 11, 12, 25 47, 77, 82, 85, 306

Eddie, S. 99
Edison, Thomas A. 200, 201
Eïstert, E. 13, 116, 117
Eley, G. 1, 10
Engels, F. 83

Feldenkirchen, W. 13-14, 116, 307
Fischer, W. 75, 81
Fremdling, R. 3, 9, 10, 47, 117, 307

Gerschenkron, A. 2, 8, 12, 14
Goering, H. 238, 239, 291
Gottlieb, M. 150, 163, 164
Graham,F.D. 265

Hahn, H-W. 87, 97
Henderson, Otto 10, 84
Henning, F.W. 161
Hilferding, R. 116
Hitler, A. 237
Hoffmann, W.G. 15, 82, 118, 150, 190
Hohorst, G. 85
Holtfrerich, C-L. 15, 20-21, 25, 265, 308
Huber, E.R. 83,
Hunscha, K. 164
Hyde, C.K. 48

Jacobi, H.W.L. 55
Johnson, H.G. 79-80

Keynes, J.M. 185, 265
Kindleberger, C. 272
Kirchain, G. 85, 86
Kirdoff, Emil 133
Kitchen, M. 1, 9, 10
Kocka, J. 3
Kondratieff, 19
Krauch, Karl 5, 238, 239
Krauss,M.B. 80
Krengel, J. 15-16, 25, 185, 307
Krueger, H. 83
Kuehne, L. 87
Kutz, M. 84

Landes, D. 15, 98
Laursen, K. 265
Lee, W.R. 1, 306
Lehr, Robert 289, 295
Lewis, W.A. 272
List, F. 48, 82, 84, 89
Loreth, H. 87
Luetge, F. 82

Massell, B.F. 79
McCloskey, D.N. 186, 188
Meade, J. 77
Megerle, K. 87
Mevissen, Gustav 121
Miller, Oskar von 215
Milward, A. 83, 99
Morgan (Labour Supplies Branch) 290
Mottek, H. 82

Neuburger, H. 116
Niethammer, L. 18
North, D.C. 92

Oechelhauser, W. 54
Ohlin, B. 265
Ohnishi, T. 85, 89
Oncken, H. 83
Oppenheim, Abraham 121
Oppenheim, Saloman 120

Papen, Franz von 237, 244
Pedersen, J. 265
Plumpe, G. 3, 4, 220, 308
Pohl, M. 117
Pollard, S. 47, 82, 99

Rathenau, Emil 202, 203, 204, 205
Reich, E. 161
Reisser, Paul 201
Ringel, J. 13
Robertson, General 296
Roseman, M. 3, 24, 25, 286, 308
Rostow, W.W. 82, 119
Rueschemeyer, D. 97

Saul, S.B. 83
Schacht, H. 237
Schaefer, H. 3, 7, 25, 200, 307
Schleicher, Kurt von 237
Schmitz, Herman 227, 228, 237
Schmoller, G. 48, 82, 99
Schremmer, E. 99
Schumpeter, J.A. 200
Schwartz, J.A. 267
Sheehan, J.J. 1
Siemens, Werner 128
Sombart, W. 116
Spree, R. 19
Stokes, H. 116
Streseman, G. 237
Svennilson, I. 229

Taylor, A.J.P. 95
Teuteberg, H.-J. 172
Thieriot, J.H. 86, 90
Thomas, B. 148
Tilly, R.H. 1, 3, 14, 18-19, 25, 82, 99, 116, 117, 118, 148, 207
Treitschke, H. von 82, 91

Viebahn, G. von 86
Viner, J. 77-78

Waltershausen, A. Sartorius von 82
Warmbold,237
Wellenreuther, T. 172
Wischermann, C. 161, 172
Wysocki, J. 83

Subject Index

acetone 222
age at marriage, median 159
AGFA-Ansco 233
agrarian depression 160
air ministry 238, 241
Aktiengesellschaft fuer Anilin Fabrikation, Berlin 220
Allgemeine Elektrizitaets Gesellschaft 128, 134, 203, 206, 207, 209, 217, 213
Allied Chemical and Dye Co. 243
Allied
 Control Commission 296
 Control Council 296
 Control Office 220
 High Commission 242
 occupation policy 22, 286-305
Allies
 war aims 223
Alps 209
Aluminium Aktiengesellschaft, Neuhausen 204
Aluminium Company of America 232
American I.G. Chemical Corporation 233
ammonia
 plants 231
 synthesis 221, 222, 244
Ansco Corporation 233
Arbeitsausschuss 225
arc-lights 206
Arnsberg 55
Asia 230, 240
aspirin business 233
Atlantic Union 77
Austria 89, 94, 234
autarchy 237, 244
auto-financing 123
 see also self-financing

Baar area 208
backward linkages 15, 16
 of pig-iron industry 186, 192
Baden 7, 11, 82, 204,207
 cotton industry 87
 electrical power 201-209
 electricity policy 211
 electricity supply areas 208
 municipal reform 212
 negotiations with Swiss Cantons 205
 private enterprise 220
 railway companies 212
 Second Chamber 211
Badenwerk A.G. 213
Badische Anilin-und Soda-Fabrik A.G. 220, 221, 222, 224, 243
Badische Kraftlieferungsgesellschaft, Freiburg 208
balance of trade
 German 21
Bank fuer Handel und Industrie (Darmstaedter Bank) 116, 120, 121
banking
 and economic growth 116-146
 and electrical engineering 204

backwardness in 119
in Berlin 227
Basel 208, 233
Baugenossenschaften 17
Bavaria 7, 8, 11, 85
electrical power 213-214
electricity policy 213
industrialisation 215
railway interests 215
railway network 214
Wuerttemberg customs union 11
Bayer A.G., Leverkusen 220, 243
Belgium 8, 10, 12, 49, 50, 54, 231
capital 122
iron and steel production 185
iron ore imports 188
pig-iron 53, 55
Benzine 240
Bergmann-Elekrizitaets-Werke 144
Bergmannssold 291
Berlin 17, 89, 161, 167, 227
banks 121
block station 202
construction industry 163
dwellings stock 150
first Edison system 201
housing rents 168
urban migrants 159
Berliner gemeinnuetzige Baugesellschaft 17
Berliner Handelsgesellschaft 116, 120, 126, 134
Betriebsfuehrer 228
Betriebsgemeinschaft 225
Bevan boys 296
Beznau on Aare
power station 209
Bizonia 23
Black Forest 201, 206, 212
Bleialf 121
block unit
in Berlin 202
Bochumer Verein 126
bourgeoisie 3, 10, 83, 92, 245
Breisgau 208, 213
Brown, Bovery Company 206, 207, 209
Brunner, Mond and Co. 230, 232, 234
Brunswick 91
Brussels 122
building
costs 163, 167
cycle 149
business cycles 19
butadiene 229

Canada 233
capital
fixed and working in textile industry 12
foreign 14
imports 218
international finance 235
cartels 117, 129, 133, 185, 230, 235, 241, 246: see also output cartels
cellophane 235
cellulose 238
Central American Common Market 81, 86, 87
chemical industry 14, 25, 123, 129
concentration 135
diversification in 229
family-owned firms 128
German overseas subsidiaries 221
heavy chemical trade 222
importance in war 238
in America 220
Chemische Fabrik Griesheim-Elektron 220, 221, 222
Chemische Fabriken vormals Weiler-ter Meer 220, 223

Chile
saltpetre deposits 222
saltpetre exports 231, 232
China 230
cholera 17
cliometrics 15, 25
coal mining
employment in 188
hewers 291
hydrogenation 244
in Wuerttemberg 208
industry 15, 23, 188
coal tar 234
coffee 88
coke blast furnace 48
coke smelting 119
Cold War 23, 242
Cologne 54, 161
banks in 14, 118
small-scale housing 19
colonial goods 85
commercial crises 87, 88
Commerz-und Disconto-Bank 116
Compagnie Nationale de Matières Colorantes et Manufactures de Produits Chimique du Nord Reunis 231, 243, 245
Companies Act (1884) 126
concentration camp prisoners 242, 242
Congress of Vienna 98, 94, 98
Constance, lake 208
constitutionalism 11
construction industry 16, 163 187
Continental system 8
copper
US exports 168
Costa Rica 81
cotton industry 47
export prices 271
South German 86
US cotton exports 268,270
weaving 86
see also Baden, Prussia, Saxony and Wuerttemberg
credit institutions
urban 18
Crédit Mobilier 120
Crystal Palace 48
currency reform 22
Customs Union (see also Zollverein)
Austro-Hungarian 86
Bavaria-Wuerttemberg 91
Prussia-Hesse 91
Czechoslovakia 234

Darmstadt 206
de-cartelisation 242
Degussa, sodium factory 204
Deichmann and Co. 127
demand stimuli 21
depression
great (1874-94) 19
international (1920-32) 21, 227, 228, 235, 245, 267
world (1920-21) 21
Detillieux Frères and Cie 121
Deutsche Bank 14, 116, 131, 135
Deutsche Edisongesellschaft 202, 206
Deutsche-Hollaendischer Aktieverein 221
Disconto-Gesellschaft 116, 120, 121, 127 134
dismantling 292
Division of Field Agreement 232
Dortmund 127, 150
Dortmunder Union 126
Dowlais iron works 51
Dreibund 221, 234
Dreierverband 221
Dresdner Bank 116, 134
Duesseldorf 161
Duesseldorfer Roehren- und Eisenwalzwerke AG 134
Duisburg 150

Duncker, mayor of Berlin 206
Du Pont 222, 223, 230, 231, 234, 237, 241, 243, 244, 245
dyestuffs 220, 221, 222, 224, 229, 230, 233, 235, 236, 240, 243
  cartel 242
Dynamit Aktiengesellschaft 230
Dynamit Nobel Bratislava 234

East Elbian provinces 160
economic summit 270
education
  role of the state in 3
  technical institutes 9
Eisen-und Stahlwerk Hoesch 128
Elberfeld 206
electrical engineering industry 14, 201, 211
electricity
  current storage 210
  electrical power 200-219
  industry 6, 7, 25
  policy 211
  polyphase alternate current 203
  pool system 209
  private enterprise in supply 214
  state development models 214
electro-chemical industry 215
electro-technical industry 129, 134, 135
Elektrochemische Werke Bitterfeld 204
El Salvador 81
emigration 160
employment
  sectoral data 188
  multiplier 190
England 8, 12
  english capital 117
  iron exports 48
  occupation policies 22
entrepreneurs 4, 6, 7, 20
Essener Credit-Anstalt 129
Europe
  Economic Community 77, 78, 80, 98
  economic recovery 297
exchange rate 266
explosives 222, 234, 238
export led growth 12

Fabrication Nacional de Colorantes y Explosivos 234
Farbwerke Hoechst 220, 221
Federal Reserve Board 267
fertiliser sales 23
filament lamp 201
fire insurance returns 167
First World War 19, 20,116, 128, 133, 134, 171,185, 200, 207, 208, 209,210, 214, 215, 221, 222,233, 234, 237, 246, 265
foreign labour 241
foreign trade 55
  Anglo-German 82
  German 85
  taxation of 87
Four Year Plan 5, 238
France 8, 49, 50, 240,243, 286, 290, 294, 296
  Franco-German dye cartel 231
  french capital 122
  chemical industry 229
  German chemical plants in 221
  growth rate 81
  IG exports to 230
  IG nitrogen agreement224
  iron ore exports to 188
  occupation policies 8
  war with 123
Francolor 241
Frankfurt-am-Main 51, 150 203, 206, 227
  urban migrants to 159

free trade 91
Freiburg 208
Fremdarbeiterpolitik 290
Fuehrer principle 228

gasoline 229, 236
  hydrogenation 224
Gelsenkirchener Bergwerks AG 127, 133, 134
General Aniline Co. 231, 233
General Association of German Banks and Bankers 21
German Air Force 238
German Federal Republic 270
German Zonal Advisory Council 294, 296
Glasgow 149
glycols 232
Godalming 200
Grasselli Chemical Co. 233
Great Britain (see also England) 52, 119, 243, 268
  Anglo-French relations 24
  Economic and Industrial Planning Staff 292
  economic policy to Germany 292
  Empire 5, 233
  entrepreneurial performance 200
  entry into EEC 80
  export statistics 49
  first industrial nation 200
  IG exports to 230
  iron and steel industry 186
  manpower policy 286-305
  manufacturing techniques 9
  military Government 297-8
  occupation zone 26
  pig iron 53
  planning of steel industry 23
  share of US exports 269-70
  zonal economic policy 23
Great Depression 19
Green labour 288
Grenzach 204
Grossbanken 116
Gruenderperiode 119, 123
Gruendungskrise (1871-3) 127
Guatemala 81
Gutehoffnungshuette 128

Haber-Bosch process 222
Hamburg 17, 18, 51, 89, 158
  construction industry 163
  demographic variables 162
  empty dwellings 164
  housing legislation 19
  housing question 17
  housing rents 168
  income estimates 160
  net migration to 157-8
  public power station 202
  stock of dwellings 150
Hanover 91, 161
Hanse towns 91
Harpener Bergbau AG 120, 127
heavy industry 117, 119, 123, 126, 129, 135, 192, 235
  concentration in 14
  in Rhineland-Westphalia 134
  output agreements 127
  price cartels 127
Heimat 25
Hermannshuette 120
Herstatt banking house 118, 122
Hesse 11
  Hessian states 85, 97
  industrialisation in 87
  tariff revenues 89
Hesse-Darmstadt 89
historical school of economics 169
Hoechst AG 243
Hoerder Bergwerks-und Huettenverein 126, 127
Hohenzollern legend 83
holding companies 134
Holland 53
  capital investment 122

growth rate 81
Honduras 81
household demand hypothesis 149
Housing
cottage ideal 18
industry 18
prices 157
question 17, 168
reform movement 18
rents 168
urban 2, 17
Hueck, banking house 122
Hungary 234
hydrogenation process 5, 232, 242

IG Chemie 233
IG Farben 4, 220-264
administrative committee 227
capital 223
divisions 228
employees 223
exports 230
French nitrogen agreement 224
impact of depression 236
investment policy 227
overseas plants 233
rationalisation 224
research investment 236
sales 229
social commission 228
trade in explosives 234
Imperial Chemical Industry 5, 231, 243, 244, 245
Imperial Statistical Office 185
import substitution 10, 12, 52, 222
indanthrene 229
India 49
British 230
inflation 20
German 265-285
insurance companies 163
Interessengemeinschaft 221, 233
Interessengemeinschaft Wuerttembergischer Elektrizitaetswerke 209
intermediate goods 48
international trade theory 11
Interventionsstaat 224
investor's expectations hypothesis 149
Ipari Robbanoyag 234
Ireland
irish capital 122
iron and steel industry 15, 16
British planning 23
puddling and rolling process 48, 50
share capital 131
Thomas production method 126
iron ore 15
employment in mines 188
mines 187
Italy 234
growth rate 81
IG connections in 234
IG exports to 230
investments by Bochumer Verein 126

Jacobinism 95
Japan 230, 232
hydrogenation in 245
Japanese-Chinese war 240
Joint American Study Company 232
Joint stock companies 122, 123, 128, 133, 135
law 225

Kaiserreich 17, 19, 169, 171, 172

Kalle and Co. AG 221
Kanderthal 208
Karlsruhe 209
Kaufmaennische Ausschuss 227
Kleinwohnungen 170
Koeln-Muesener-Bergwerks-Aktiegesellschaft 120
Koelner Bergwerks-Verein 120
Koelnische Baumwollspinnerei- und Weberei 120
Koelnische Maschinenbau AG 120
Koeniggraetz, battle of 83
Knappschaft 289
Kreditbanken 12-14
Krupp 126, 128

labour
  conscription 292
  control apparatus 296
  exchanges 288
  productivity by sector 192
Lahr-Wolfach line 208
land
  policy, urban 18
  prices 164
Landesgeschichte 25
Latin America 230, 231, 233, 240
Laufenburg power station 208, 209, 213
Lauffen 203
law
  company law reform 228
  legal framework 8
  Organisation of National Work 228
  Trade Regulation Law 6
leading sectors 15
Leopold Cassella and Co. 220
Leuna-Werke 224, 242
Level-of-Industry Plan 22
Leverkusen 242
light industry 117
linen 47
  industry 86
limestone 187
liquidity, first degree 133
Liverpool 56, 99
Loentsch power station 209
London, pioneer steam station 200
long swings 148-9
  see also urban development
Lorrach 204
Low Countries 286, 294
Ludwigshafen/Oppau 242
Luebeck 206

machine construction industry 10, 14, 187
magnesium 232, 235
managers, in chemical industry 243
Manchester, Trafford Park 241
Mannheim 206, 209
manpower division 296
Markgraeflerland 208
marriage market 159
Maschinenbau AG Humboldt 126
meat
  US exports 268
mechanical engineering 123, 128, 129
Mecklenburg 91
mergers 133
  role of banks in 134
metal-working industries 9
methylalcohol 235
  synthesis 224, 229
Middle German Commercial Union 91
Mietskasernen 18
migration 18, 150, 158
  effects on housing investment 158
  net in Hamburg 158
  overseas 158
  push and pull factors 160
  urban-bound 148
monarchic constitutionalism 89
Montecatini Co. 234
Morgenthau Plan 22

mortgage
Bank Law (1899) 171
banks 157
Muelhausen, power station 208, 213
Munich 95, 150
municipal authorities 7, 206
reform act in Baden 212
Murg
power plant 213
river 212

Napoleonic Wars 8, 89, 94
National Aniline and Chemical Corporation 231
Nationalbank fuer Deutschland 116
National Bureau (US) 267
Nazi
Fremdarbeiterpolitik 290
labour control apparatus 296
Law on the Organisation of National Work 228
military expansion 245
State and IG 237-43
Neckar 207
water supply 201
Neckarwerke AG Esslingen 210
New Plan (1934) 237
Nicaragua 81
nickel 235
nitrogen 222, 235
cartel 232
fertilisers 229, 231
international trade 231
plants 224
products 229
sales 236
synthetic 231
Nobel Dynamite Trust Co. 222, 223
Norsk Hydro Kvaelstoff AG 231, 232, 233, 241
North German Coal Control 287, 293
North-Rhine Westphalia 289
Norway 231
nylon 241

Oberdirektion des Wasser-und Strassenbaus 212
Oberschlesische Kokswerke und Chemische Fabriken AG 234
Oberschwaebische Elektizitaetswerke 207
Odenwald 207, 208
Oldenburg 91
oppanol 229
Oppenheim bank 118, 120, 122
output agreements, in heavy industry 127
overdraft credit 131, 133
Ozalid Co. 233

Paris 122
electrical engineering fair 201
stock exchange 121
pharmaceuticals 220, 222, 229, 230, 236, 240
Phoenix Co. 121, 122
photographics 235, 236
pig-iron industry 9, 16, 25
import substitution 15
imports from Belgium 10
induced employment effect 188
macro-economic growth 185-199
value added multiplier 191
plastics 235, 236, 240, 241
Plenipotentiary for Special Questions (see also Krauch, Karl) 238
poison gas 222
points system 298
political elites 17

population growth, urban 158
portfolio diversification 14
Potter/Hyndley mission 292
power stations 235
Preussische Bank 122
price cartels, in heavy industry 127
price elasticities 265
Prima Societate Romana de Explozivi 234
prisoners of war 241, 242, 287, 290
profits, distributed and retained 132
proto-industrial production 87
Prussia 52, 85, 88
- capital market 118, 122
- Commercial Union 47
- cotton industry 87
- economic policy 9
- Housing Bill (1904) 19
- industrial policy 83
- joint-stock company foundation 118
- mining law (1851) 119
- Prussian-Hessian tariffs 86
- railways 52
- residential construction 150
- tariff of 1818 9, 90, 91
- technological advantage 9
- urban growth 158

public loans
- interest rate 118

Quebec Agreement 23

Raffke (money-grubbers) 20
railways
- construction 15, 49, 51, 52
- employment on 188
- leading sector 119
- social savings 15
- state interests in Bavaria 215
- state-owned companies in Baden 212
- state-owned network in Bavaria 214

rations 291, 295
Ravensburg 207
rayon 222, 238, 240
rearmament 5, 237, 245
reconstruction programme 292
refugees 288
Reichsbank
- discount rate policy 20

Rheinfelden 203, 205, 208
- power station 203, 208, 209, 213

Rheinisch-Westfaelische Sprengstoff AG 234
Rheinische Stahlwerke 234
Rhine
- province 289
- Upper Rhine 203, 205, 208, 209, 211
- water supply 201

Rhineland 48, 54
- heavy industry 134
- iron masters 55
- puddling and rolling mills 54

Riebeck'sche Montanwerke 234
rolling mills 49, 51, 54
rubber 236, 238, 239, 240
- synthesis 232, 238, 244

Ruhr 53
- anthracite 201
- British control of 23
- coal controllers 290
- coal industry 15, 23, 119
- coal-mining companies 121, 129
- coal shipments from 223
- discovery of blackband 119
- French occupation of 266, 291
- heavy industry 120
- manpower in coal mines 286-305
- mines 2, 24

pig-iron production 187
steel industry 14, 119
urban development 18
Russia 49
German chemical subsidiaries 221
see also Soviet Union

Saar-Lorraine
anthracite 201
coal fields 286
pig-iron production 187
savings
banks 163
level of 118
Saxony 6, 11, 85, 86, 92
cotton industry 87
Scandinavia 270, 286, 294
Schaaffhausen'sche Bankverein 116, 118, 120, 126, 127
Schieber (racketeers) 20
Schuckert Company 205
Schleswig-Holstein 161
Scotland
pig iron 55
Second World War 4, 21, 224, 231
self-financing 13, 132
see also auto-financing
Siegerland 55
Siemens 7, 200, 209
and Halske 202, 207
Siemens-Schuckert, fusion with Bergmann 134
Silesia 286
silk 47
artificial 229, 236
Social market economy 22
Social Question 168
social reformers 169-70
social savings,
in railway development 15
Sociedad Electroquimica de Flix 234
Societa Chimica Lombarda 234
Solvay 243
solvents 235
Sonderweg 1, 3, 24
Soviet Union 23, 24
occupation zone 242
see also Russia
Spain 234
investments by Bochumer Verein 126
Sparta plan 23
Sprengstoffkonzern 234
Standard Oil 232
State 3
administrators 4
bureaucracies 10, 11
electrical power development 200-219
monopoly capitalism 239
multiplicity of forms 7
patent policy 4
railways development 6
tariff policy 3
steam-engine manufacturing 9
Steel Works Association 131
Stein, banking house 118
Sterling Incorporation 233
Stickstoffabrik Ruse 234
Stinnes trust 234
Stockach 208
stock exchange
Berlin 227
Paris 121
stockholders 225
Stockungsspanne (slack phase) 123
Studiengesellschaft (research company) 201
Stuttgart 201, 205, 206, 210
electrical lighting 202
sugar 88
sulphuric acid
contact process 221
supervisory board
IG 239
representation of banks on 126, 129, 134

Sweden
  charcoal iron 51
Switzerland 89, 204
  cantons 205
  Swiss IG 231, 233
  villages 208
syndicates 235

take-off 7, 19
  in Baden 215
tariff policy
  Bavarian Zollordnung (1765) 8
  Prussian tariff (1818) 9
  see also Zollverein
tariffs
  administration 87
  protection 5, 243
Tauber region 207, 208
Technischer Ausschuss (Tea) 227
technology
  development 243
  in chemical industry 229
  in iron industry 9, 47-76
  transfer 50
Tettnang 207
textile industry 123, 128, 129
  fixed and working capital 12
  in south-west Germany 121
  in Wiesenthal 208
textiles
  allocation to miners 298
  shipments 297
Third Reich 4, 238
  autarchy 6
  command economy 4
  economic policy 4
Third World markets 6
Thuringian states 85
tobacco 88
trade
  balance of 265
  long-term growth
  terms of 265
trade unions 245
Triberg 206

Ueberlandzentralen 207, 214
Ueberlingen 208
unbalanced growth theory 15
unemployment 267
  male 283
unified power system 209
Union Carbide and Carbon Chemical Corporation 232
Union of German Merchants and Manufacturers 89
United Kingdom 231, 240
  German chemical subsidiaries 221
  see also Great Britain
United States of America 50, 52, 200, 242, 243, 294, 297, 298
  chemical industry 220, 229
  exports 268
  German chemical subsidiaries 221
  gross national product 270
  IG exports to 230
  interests in Latin America 240
  military tribunals 242
  occupation policies 22
  post-war situation 21
  world economic crisis 266
Upper Silesia
  pig-iron production 187
urban development
  housing 18-19
  long swings in 3, 142-76
urbanisation 16, 17
  in the Ruhr 18
  population pull factors 18

vacant dwellings 163
value added
  induced 191
  multiplier 191
  net (1870-1913) 123
  sectoral, pig-iron industry 186

Verbundsystem (unified power system) 210
Verein fuer Socialpolitik 133
Vereinigte Praesident 121
Versailles, peace treaty 223
Verwaltungsrat 225, 228
Vulcan AG 122
vulcanisation-accelerators 229

Walchensee, power station 214
Wangen 207
Weimar
  constitution 20
  deficit spending 267
  period 213
  republic 237
Weiss group 233
Weltmacht
  German ambitions 243, 245
Westdeutsche Sprengstoff AG 234
West Germany 22
  economic recovery 286-305
  government 242
  gross national product 270
  see also German Federal Republic
Westphalia 48
  heavy industry 134
  iron masters 55
wheat
  US exports 268
Wiesental 204, 208
Winthrop Chemical Company 233
Wolff and Company 234
wool
  woollen thread 47
working-class
  housing construction programme 170
  living conditions 168
  politicisation 169
  radicalisation 17
Wuchermiete (rent gauging) 169

Wuerttemberg 7, 11, 85, 107
  coal 208
  cotton industry 87
  electrical power 209-211
  electricity policy 211
  electricity pool system 209
  king of 202
Wyhlen 204

Yugoslavia 234

Zollverein 2, 10-12, 47-8
  bar-iron duty 61
  economic integration 77-115
  fiscal gains 94
  'optimal jurisdiction' 92-93
  protective tariff (1844) 10
  tariff policy 53, 55
  transaction costs 93
  see also Customs Union